ORTHODOX CHRISTIANITY

Volume I:

The History and Canonical Structure of the Orthodox Church

METROPOLITAN HILARION ALFEYEV

ORTHODOX CHRISTIANITY

Volume I:
The History
and Canonical
Structure of the
Orthodox
Church

WITH A FOREWORD BY
His Holiness Alexei II
Patriarch of Moscow and All Russia

Translated from the Russian by Basil Bush

ST VLADIMIR'S SEMINARY PRESS
YONKERS, NEW YORK 10707

Library of Congress Cataloging-in-Publication Data

Ilarion, Hieromonk.

   [Pravoslavie. English]

Orthodox Christianity / Metropolitan Hilarion Alfeyev.

   p.   cm.

Includes bibliographical references.

ISBN 978-0-88141-878-1

   1. Russkaia pravoslavnaia tserkov'–History.   2. Orthodox Eastern Church–Russia
(Federation)–History.   3. Russkaia pravoslavnaia tserkov'–Doctrines.   4. Orthodox
Eastern Church–Russia (Federation)–Doctrines.   5. Russkaia pravoslavnaia tserkov'.
6. Orthodox Eastern Church–Russia (Federation).   I. Title.

   BX485.I4313 2011

   281.9'47–dc22

2011002385

Pravoslavie
Tom 1: Istoriia, kanonicheskoe ustroistvo i verouchenie
Pravoslavnoi Tserkvi
originally published by Sretensky Monastery, 2008

ST VLADIMIR'S SEMINARY PRESS

575 Scarsdale Rd., Yonkers, NY 10707
1-800-204-2665
www.svspress.com

ISBN 978-0-88141-878-1

PRINTED IN THE UNITED STATES OF AMERICA

Table of Contents

Foreword

Beloved Brothers and Sisters in the Lord,

In writing these introductory words to this book by Bishop Hilarion of Vienna and Austria, I would like to note the timeliness of its appearance. Such an all-encompassing study of the history, teaching, and liturgical services of the Orthodox Church is long overdue. I am convinced that the publication of this first volume will inspire lively interest among readers both in Russia and abroad.

Orthodoxy is one of the few religious confessions whose membership is growing rather than declining. After many decades of persecution, a major revival of spiritual life is underway in Russia and other countries of the former Soviet Union, and it brings us joy that the number of parishes, monasteries, and theological schools is significantly increasing.

The Orthodox Church in Russia now occupies a fitting place in the life of the people and exerts a powerful and positive influence on many areas of society. Millions of people have found a spiritual home in the Church. The Church helps people to find a moral bearing; for centuries it has defended those values on which the stability and spiritual health of the nation, the family, and the individual are based.

Today, churches are accessible to all, religious literature is published in abundance, icons and reproductions of them are sold everywhere, services are broadcast on television, sermons of clergymen and bishops can be heard on the radio, and church music is available on compact discs.

Nevertheless, Orthodoxy remains a mystery for many people—both in our homeland and abroad. What does the Orthodox Church teach? What is its history, and how does it relate to the modern world? What are the foundations of Orthodox theology? What rules regulate the celebration of the liturgical services in Orthodox churches? What is the meaning of icons? What principles lie at the foundation of church art?

This book seeks to provide answers to these and many other questions. It examines not only the history and contemporary life of the Orthodox

Church, but also Orthodoxy as such: as a theological and ethical system, as a way of life and thinking.

The author of this book is not acquainted with the wealth of the theological and liturgical tradition of the Orthodox Church by hearsay. After receiving a broad education, Bishop Hilarion has authored numerous works on theology and church history, translated works from ancient languages, and composed liturgical music. His many years of service to the mother church, his rich creative activity, and his broad perspective enable him to present the tradition of the Orthodox Church in all its diversity.

I would like to express my hope for the success of this book not only in Russian but also in other languages. I would also like to wish its author God's help in his further archpastoral and theological work for the good of the Orthodox Church and the people of God. Finally, I pray that the reader will have a profound and meaningful encounter with the Orthodox Church, which is the "Church of the living God, the pillar and bulwark of the truth" (1 Tim 3.15).

+Alexei
Patriarch of Moscow and All Russia
August 7, 2007

Preface

THIS IS THE FIRST volume of a detailed and systematic exposition of the history, canonical structure, doctrine, moral and social teaching, liturgical services, and spiritual life of the Orthodox Church.

The basic idea of this work is to present Orthodox Christianity as an integrated theological and liturgical system—a world view. In this system all elements are interconnected: theology is based on liturgical experience, and the basic characteristics of church art—including icons, singing, and architecture—are shaped by theology and the liturgy. Theology and the services, in their turn, influence the ascetic practice and the personal piety of each Christian. They shape the moral and social teaching of the Church as well as its relation to other Christian confessions, non-Christian religions, and the secular world.

Orthodoxy is traditional and even conservative (we use this term in a positive sense, to emphasize Orthodoxy's reverence to church tradition). The contemporary life of the Orthodox Church is based on its historical experience. Orthodoxy is historic in its very essence: it is deeply rooted in history, which is why it is impossible to understand the uniqueness of the Orthodox Church—its dogmatic teaching and canonical structure, its liturgical system and social doctrine—outside of a historical context. Thus, the reference to history, to the sources, will be one of the organizing principles of this book.

This book covers a wide range of themes relating to the history and contemporary life of the Orthodox Church. It contains many quotations from works of the church fathers, liturgical and historical sources, and works of contemporary theologians. Nevertheless, we do not claim to give an exhaustive account of the subjects discussed: this book is neither an encyclopedia, a dictionary, nor a reference work. It is rather an attempt to understand Orthodoxy in all its diversity, in its historical and contemporary existence—an understanding through the prism of the author's personal perception.

A special feature of this book is that it strives to provide a sufficiently detailed wealth of material. It is addressed to readers who are already acquainted with the basics of Orthodoxy and who desire to deepen their knowledge and, above all, to systematize it.

The first two parts of this first volume present a brief account of the historical path of the Orthodox Church through almost twenty centuries. During the first ten centuries after Christ's nativity, the Christians of the east and west shared a common history; however, after the "Great Schism" of the eleventh century, the eastern and western Churches went different ways.

Numerous studies of the history of the Orthodox Church have already appeared. There is also an extensive literature devoted to particular historical periods of the Orthodox Church, personalities, the history of dogmatic movements and theological disputes, monasticism, and the liturgical services. The history of the Russian Orthodox Church has been given broad treatment in the works of Russian and foreign scholars. It is difficult to add anything fundamentally new to this corpus, if one is presenting not a study on a particular aspect but a general account, as is the case with the present work.

Nevertheless, without a historical background it is impossible to write a book about Orthodoxy. Thus, before speaking about the Orthodox Church today, it is necessary to underscore some key moments in its history and mention some of its most significant persons.

The second part of this volume is heavily weighted with an emphasis on the history of the Russian Church and culture. This by no means indicates that the author underestimates other local Orthodox traditions. This emphasis is due to the fact that the author belongs to the Russian Church and that the volume was originally intended for a Russian readership. A suggestion was made by the author to the editors of the English edition that some of these materials should be omitted. The editors, however, decided to keep these sections, since the book, in their opinion, would suffer a loss of continuity had they attempted to cut them. Moreover, they felt that these sections would serve as a "case study," as it were, of how Orthodoxy can infuse the literature, art, and philosophy of an entire culture

The third part of the present volume examines the canonical structure of the Orthodox Church. This brief historical overview describes the emergence and development of diocesan structures, metropolias, and patriarchates in the Christian east. It then discusses the contemporary structure of world Orthodoxy as well as the principle of "canonical territory," which forms the basis of inter-Orthodox relations.

Subsequent volumes will cover the doctrine of the Orthodox Church, beginning with an examination of the sources of Orthodox teaching, including the Old and New Testaments, the decrees of the ecumenical and local councils, the writings of the fathers and teachers of the Church, and works of liturgical poetry. Further sections will expound the Orthodox teaching on God, creation, and man. Additionally, separate chapters will be devoted to Orthodox christology, ecclesiology, and eschatology. We will then go on to examine the services, sacraments, and rituals of the Orthodox Church, its ascetic and mystical teaching, as well as church art, including architecture, iconography, and liturgical singing. The moral and social teaching of the Orthodox Church as well as its relations with other Christian confessions, other religions, and the secular world, will also be discussed.

PART ONE

HISTORY: THE FIRST MILLENNIUM

I

Early Christianity

CHRIST – THE FOUNDER OF THE CHURCH

A<small>T THE FOUNDATION</small> of Christian history stands the unique and enigmatic person of Jesus Christ, a man who called himself the Son of God. Conflict over his person and teaching began during his lifetime and has continued for almost twenty centuries. Some acknowledge him as the incarnate God, others as a prophet who was undeservedly exalted by his disciples, still others as an outstanding teacher of morality. Some even maintain that he never existed. Jesus did not leave behind any writings or any visible proof of his presence on earth. What remained was a group of disciples, whom he called the Church.

Christ Pantocrator (Hagia Sophia, Constantinople, 13th c.)

The Church is synonymous with Christianity: one cannot be a Christian without being a member of the Church. "There is no Christianity without the Church," writes the hieromartyr Hilarion (Troitsky).[1] Archpriest Georges Florovsky noted that "Christianity *is* the Church."[2] Christianity has never existed without the Church or outside the Church. Following Christ has always meant joining the community of his disciples, and becoming a Christian has always meant becoming a member of the body of Christ:

> Christianity was from the very beginning a corporate reality, a community. To be a Christian meant belonging to this community. No one could be

---

[1]Hilarion (Troitsky), *Works* (Moscow, 2004), 2.192.
[2]Georges Florovsky, "My Father's Home," in *Selected Theological Articles* (Moscow, 2000), 10. Italics are the author's.

The Savior
(Andrei Rublev, 15th c.)

a Christian by himself, as a separate individual, but only together with "the brethren," only in conjunction with them. *Unus Christianus, nullus Christianus* (one Christian is not a Christian). Personal convictions and even one's way of life do not yet make one a Christian. Christian existence assumes inclusion and implies membership in the community.[3]

Christianity can be reduced neither to moral teaching, nor to theology, nor to church canons, nor to liturgical services. It is also not the sum of these parts. Christianity is the personal revelation of the *theanthropos* (God-man), Christ, through his Church:

The Church preserves and imparts its teaching and the "divine dogmas"; it proposes the "rule of faith," the order and statutes of piety. But the Church is something immeasurably greater. Christianity is *not only the teaching on salvation but salvation itself*, accomplished once and for all by the *theanthropos* . . . In the Orthodox consciousness Christ is first and foremost the Savior, and not only a "good teacher" or a prophet. He is above all King and High Priest, "the king of peace and the savior of our souls." And salvation consists not so much in the good news of the heavenly kingdom as in the theanthropic person of the Lord himself and in his deeds, in his "saving passion" and "life-giving cross," in his death and resurrection.[4]

The Church is the keeper of Christ's teaching and the continuer of his saving mission. It is the site of Christ's living presence, the receptacle of his grace. But it is not so much the Church that saves people through Christ's grace as it is Christ who saves people through the Church. Through the Church, Christ continues his saving work, which, having being accomplished once in the past, does not cease to be accomplished in the present. He did not grant his body and blood to his disciples only once, but ever nourishes the faithful in the sacrament of the eucharist. Not just once did he save

[3]Florovsky, "The Church: Its Nature and Mission," *Selected Theological Articles*, 188.
[4]Florovsky, "My Father's Home," 10–11. Italics are the author's.

humanity by his suffering on the cross, death, and resurrection—he always saves. And the Church perceives the events of Christ's life not as facts of the past, but as acts of enduring significance that have no end in time.

For this very reason the word "today" is frequently used in the services dedicated to events from Christ's life: "today Christ is born in Bethlehem of the Virgin"[5]; "today the Lord of creation stands before Pilate"[6]; "today salvation has come to the world, let us sing to him who has risen from the grave."[7] These are not just examples of church rhetoric: the Church is the "today" that lasts eternally, the never-ending revelation of Jesus Christ as God and Savior. The life, sufferings, death, and resurrection of Christ are experienced here and now in the Church: again and again it experiences these stages of the divine economy. Through the Church Christians are introduced not only to Christ's teaching, and not only to his grace, but also to his life, death, and resurrection. The economy of salvation accomplished by Christ becomes a reality for the believer, and events from Christ's life become facts in the personal spiritual biography of the Christian, who personally experiences Christ and gets to know him in the Church.

Orthodox Christians read the New Testament with reverence, as a collection of books that recount the life and teachings of Christ, his founding of the Church, and the first years of its historical existence. But they do not regard the Church founded by Christ two thousand years ago as something fundamentally different from the Church they belong to today. Christ reveals himself to the faithful through today's Church with the same fulness he once revealed himself to his disciples: his presence has not grown weaker, his grace has not been depleted, and his saving power has not run dry or been diminished.

The canon of the New Testament contains four gospels—those according to Matthew, Mark, Luke, and John. In the field of biblical studies, the first three are called the "synoptic" gospels because there is much that is similar among them, because they contain texts that are identical in places, because they follow the same chronological sequence, and because they essentially describe the same events. The fourth gospel, however, is unique: it was written, as it were, as an addition to the first three and directs the reader's

[5]Matins of the Nativity of Christ, stichera at Praises.
[6]Vespers of Good Friday, stichera at "Lord, I have cried."
[7]Sunday Matins, troparion after the Great Doxology, tones 1, 3, 5, 7.

John dictating his gospel to Prochoros (miniature)

attention not so much to Christ's miracles and parables as to the theological significance of his life and teaching.

Still, there are some differences between the evangelists. For example, Matthew speaks of the healing of two possessed men (Mt 8.28–34), while the parallel accounts by Mark and Luke recount the healing of only one. The narratives of the four evangelists about the myrrhbearing women at the empty tomb after Christ's resurrection differ in their details. However, these and other differences can be explained by the fact that the same events were recounted by different people, and that some of them were eyewitnesses of the events while others wrote about them based on the words of others. Furthermore, the narratives were composed many years after the events described. The presence of small differences only enhances the credibility of the gospel stories, attesting to the fact that there was no collusion among their authors. In other words, there are no substantive differences between the evangelists.

The word "church" is mentioned in the gospels only once, but this reference is of key significance for the development of the Christian teaching on the Church. The Gospel according to Matthew relates how Jesus, traveling through the lands of Caesarea Philippi, asked his disciples: "Who do men say that the Son of man is?" The disciples answered: "Some say John the Baptist, others say Elijah, and others Jeremiah or one of the prophets." Jesus asked: "But who do you say that I am?" Peter replied: "You are the Christ, the Son of the living God." Jesus then said to him: "Blessed are you, Simon Bar-Jona! For flesh and blood has not revealed this to you, but my Father who is in heaven. And I tell you, you are Peter, and on this rock I will build my church, and the powers of death shall not prevail against it" (Mt 16.13–18).

This passage underwent different interpretations in the Christian churches of the east and west. The west emphasized the role of Peter as leader of the apostles and Christ's vicar on earth, who passed on his primacy to the bishops of Rome. In the east, a widely held interpretation maintained that the Church is based on the faith in the divinity of Jesus Christ that was confessed by Peter.[8] In one of his epistles, St Peter himself affirms that the cornerstone of the Church is Christ (1 Pet 2.4).

THE APOSTOLIC COMMUNITY

The community of Christ's disciples was the original Church, in which the believers received the divine revelation from the mouth of the incarnate Word of God. Their discipleship in faith consisted in assimilating this experience. They called Jesus "teacher" and "Lord," and Christ accepted this as something appropriate: "You call me Teacher and Lord; and you are right, for so I am" (Jn 13.13). Christ defined the task of his disciples first and foremost as the imitation of him. After washing their feet during the last supper, he said to them: "If I then, your Lord and Teacher, have washed your feet, you also ought to wash one another's feet. For I have given you an example, that you also should do as I have done to you" (Jn 13.14–15). Conscious of his dignity as a teacher, Christ said: "A disciple is not above his teacher, nor a servant above his master; it is enough for the disciple to be like his teacher, and the servant like his master" (Mt 10.24–25). At the same time, he emphasized that his disciples were not servants or slaves of their teacher but rather friends and initiates in God's mysteries: "No longer do I call you servants, for the servant does not know what his master is doing; but I have called you friends, for all that I have heard from my Father I have made known to you" (Jn 15.15).

Christ's attitude toward his disciples differed from that toward the people as a whole. He taught the people in parables and, not being able to tell them everything that he could say to his disciples, he even hid some things from them. By contrast, he revealed the great and hidden mysteries of the kingdom of heaven to his disciples:

> Then the disciples came and said to him, "Why do you speak to them in parables?" And he answered them, "To you it has been given to know the secrets of the kingdom of heaven, but to them it has not been given. For to him who has will more be given, and he will have abundance; but from him who has not, even what he has will be taken away. This is why I speak

---

[8]Cf. John Chrysostom *Homilies on the Gospel according to Matthew* 44.2: "On this rock, that is, on this confession of faith, I will build my Church."

to them in parables, because seeing they do not see, and hearing they do not hear, nor do they understand . . . But blessed are your eyes, for they see, and your ears, for they hear. Truly, I say to you, many prophets and righteous men longed to see what you see, and did not see it, and to hear what you hear, and did not hear it. (Mt 13.10–17)

Christ's disciples were the Church that Jesus Christ gathered at the last supper and to which he gave his body and blood in the form of bread and wine. This event, described by three evangelists and the apostle Paul (Mt 26.26–29; Mk 14.22–25; Lk 22.19–20; 1 Cor 11.23–25), marked the beginning of the Church as a eucharistic community. After the resurrection of Christ the apostles, in fulfilment of the Savior's commandment, gathered on the first day of each week—which they named "the Lord's day"—in order to celebrate the eucharist.

At the last supper, Christ gave to the disciples a commandment that was to form the foundation of the moral teaching of the Christian Church: "A new commandment I give to you, that you love one another; even as I have loved you, that you also love one another. By this all men will know that you are my disciples, if you have love for one another" (Jn 13.34–35). This commandment is further developed with particular urgency in the epistles of the apostle and evangelist John the Theologian, who in Orthodox tradition is called "the apostle of love":

For this is the message which you have heard from the beginning, that we should love one another . . . We know that we have passed out of death into life, because we love the brethren. He who does not love abides in death . . . By this we know love, that he laid down his life for us; and we ought to lay down our lives for the brethren . . . Little children, let us not love in word or speech but in deed and in truth . . . And this is his commandment, that we should believe in the name of his Son Jesus Christ and love one another, just as he has commanded us . . . He who does not love does not know God; for God is love. (1 Jn 3.11–23; 4.8)

Jesus Christ taught the apostles so that they could transmit his gospel to succeeding generations. However, the central theme of the apostles' preaching was not Christ's moral or spiritual teaching, but the good news about his death and resurrection. The resurrection of Christ gave Christianity the uniqueness and novelty that enabled Christians to call their faith the "new covenant," by analogy with the "old covenant," which God had concluded with the people of Israel. The fundamental importance of the fact of Christ's resurrection was so obvious for the early Christians that they realized that their faith would be vain and deceitful had Christ not risen from the dead:

> If Christ has not been raised, then our preaching is in vain and your faith is in vain. We are even found to be misrepresenting God, because we testified of God that he raised Christ, whom he did not raise . . . If Christ has not been raised, your faith is futile and you are still in your sins . . . But in fact Christ has been raised from the dead, the first fruits of those who have fallen asleep. (1 Cor 15.14–20)

These words essentially mean that if Christ did not rise from the dead, he would have been just one of the many prophets and teachers that have appeared over the course of history. If Christ did not rise from the dead, he would have only repeated that which others had said before him. Even if he had been a messenger and a son of God, but did not rise from the dead, he could not have been the Savior, and you would be "still in your sins." But Christ did rise from the dead, having become the first fruits of the departed, that is, having conquered death and opened up to people the way to salvation.

Christ's resurrection is the central fact of the gospel and a key moment in the history of the Church. However, this was not acknowledged immediately or by everyone. Christ's resurrection occurred just as unnoticed as his nativity: nobody saw him leaving the tomb. And from the first days after the resurrection many people, even those who had been Christ's closest disciples, even those who had known and loved him, doubted his resurrection. The gospel does not hide this fact, instead relating the following about how the disciples met the risen Christ: "And when they saw him they worshiped him; but some doubted" (Mt. 28.17). God did not wish to have the resurrection of his Son be a miracle occurring before the eyes of all humanity. Instead, he allowed it to happen in such a way that faith in the resurrection requires of each person, even the apostles, an internal spiritual effort and the overcoming of hesitation and doubts.

When the apostles announced to Thomas, one of the disciples, that they had seen the risen Lord, he answered: "Unless I see in his hands the print of the nails, and place my finger in the mark of the nails, and place my hand in his side, I will not believe" (Jn 20.25). These words reflect the skeptical reasoning of man, which requires logical, tangible proofs. But here there are no such proofs and there cannot be such proofs since the Christian faith transcends the limits of reason; it is super-rational. In Christianity it is not possible to logically prove anything—neither the existence of God, nor Christ's resurrection, nor other truths, which can only be accepted or rejected by faith.

"No one has ever seen God." These words were not uttered by an atheist but by one of Christ's closest disciples: the apostle John the Theologian (Jn 1.18). Despite all the attempts to prove God's existence, no single religion has been able to produce convincing proof, and Christianity is no exception. But it also never looked for it, just as it did not look for proof of Christ's resurrection. Nevertheless, in spite of the Christian faith's seeming absence of proof, millions of people have come, still come, and will come to Christ; they have believed, they believe, and they will believe in the resurrected Christ; they have accepted, they accept, and they will accept God's existence, because they have met the risen Christ in their lives and recognized him as God. For such people additional proof is unnecessary.

This is what occurred with the two disciples of Christ who met the risen Jesus on the road to Emmaus. At first they did not recognize him in the traveler who approached them, because Christ's external appearance had changed after the resurrection. The Lord conversed with them during the entire course of their journey and entered with them into the house. The disciples recognized him only when he broke the bread, whereupon he immediately vanished. And then they said to each other: "Did not our hearts burn within us while he talked to us on the road?" (Lk 24.32). They then spoke with joy to the other disciples about their encounter with the risen Teacher.

It was not their physical eyes that helped the disciples recognize the risen God when he was next to them, but the spiritual eyes of the soul. But the very moment they recognized him he became invisible, because physical vision is not necessary when the heart is set ablaze by faith. This is what happened, and still happens, to Christians who have not seen God but have come to believe in him because their hearts burn with love for him. Christ spoke about such people when he said to Thomas: "Blessed are those who have not seen and yet believe" (Jn 20.29). They are blessed since they looked not for logical proofs but for that fire God ignites in peoples' hearts. And Christians believe in Christ's resurrection not because someone convinced them of this, and not because they read about it in the gospel, but because they themselves have come to know the risen Christ through inner experience.

Over the centuries man's skeptical reason repeatedly claimed: "Unless I see I will not believe." And Christianity answered: "Believe, even though you do not see." Through its teaching on the resurrection, Christianity threw down the gauntlet to the world, which demanded the logical substantiation of faith. It defied human reason, which was inclined to doubt even the existence of God, and especially the idea that a person, even if he were the Son of God, could die and rise again. But it is precisely on the faith in the resurrection—a faith confirmed not by tangible proofs but by the inner experience of millions of people—that the life of the Church has been founded and continues to this very day.

After the resurrection, Christ entrusted his disciples with the mission to evangelize and teach: "Go therefore and make disciples of all nations, baptizing them in the name of the Father and of the Son and of the Holy Spirit, teaching them to observe all that I have commanded you" (Mt 28.19–20). However, during the first weeks after Christ's resurrection the disciples still did not understand what he had taught them, continuing to hope instead that he was the king of Israel who would restore the lost political might of the Jewish people. They had heard Christ's parables and witnessed his many miracles; they had been with him during his last days, witnessed him suffering and dying on the cross, and seen him after his resurrection. But even after the resurrection they still continued to ask: "Lord, will you at this time restore the kingdom to Israel?" (Acts 1.6). Their thoughts were still limited to the Judaic state, about whose fate they were sincerely concerned.

In order to fulfil the apostolic mission, they needed the assistance of the Holy Spirit, who, according to the promise given by the Savior, would teach them everything (Jn 14.26). The descent of the Holy Spirit on the disciples occurred on Pentecost. This event, described in the Acts of the Apostles, turned the disciples of Christ—simple fishermen from Galilee, unlearned and uneducated—into daring preachers of the gospel. The descent of the Holy Spirit dispelled any last doubts the disciples might have had about Christ's resurrection, any remaining hesitation about the correctness and necessity of the mission entrusted to them by the Lord. When the Holy Spirit descended on the Savior's disciples, when they spoke in foreign tongues, when they felt new strength and new possibilities within themselves, they began to understand their truly ecumenical calling, which consisted in teaching "all the nations" (Mt 28.19) and preaching the gospel "to the whole creation" (Mk 16.15).

By Pentecost, the number of Christ's disciples had reached several dozen (Christian tradition speaks of the twelve apostles closest to the Savior as well as seventy other apostles), while the total number of people who believed in Christ was apparently several hundred or perhaps even several thousand. In any event, this group was very insignificant in number. The Church still had a long road ahead of it before it became truly ecumenical or "catholic."

The rapidity with which the new faith began to spread is striking. At first the apostles, like Christ himself, preached among the Jews—in the Jerusalem temple, in synagogues, and in private houses (Acts 5.21; 5.42; 13.14). However, several years after the resurrection of the Savior, the apostles began to preach beyond the boundaries of Judea, spreading the faith throughout the entire Roman empire and even beyond its limits. Moreover, they evangelized not only among the Jews but also among the pagans. And if their mission among the Jews met to a certain extent with failure, their preaching among the pagans opened up a boundless field for missionary activity in which they sowed the seeds of the word of God; and these seeds rapidly began to bear fruit.

The decision to begin preaching among the pagans was taken by the Church on the initiative of the apostle Peter (Acts 11.2–18), who was also the first to insist on abolishing circumcision as a condition for joining the Church (Acts 15.7–11).

However, it was not Peter but Paul who "worked harder than any" (1 Cor 15.10) for the enlightenment of the pagans; he later went down in the history of the Church as the "apostle of the nations." Paul was not among Christ's disciples during the Savior's earthly life, and after his resurrection he actively persecuted the Church. But Paul's conversion, described in the Acts of the Apostles (9.1–9), was no less significant for the Church than Pentecost. Paul went from being a persecutor of the Church to its zealous defender and preacher. He undertook four missionary journeys and sealed his missionary labors with a martyr's death in Rome. The Orthodox Church glorifies him, together with Peter, as one of two "leaders" of the apostles.

*The apostles Peter and Paul
(Palatine chapel, Palermo, 12th c.)*

St Paul's epistles make up a significant part of the New Testament. Paul's significance for the subsequent development of the Christian Church was so great that he was frequently compared to Christ himself. John Chrysostom even stated that Christ was able to say more to people through Paul than he could during his ministry on earth.[9]

The apostle Paul was the founder of Orthodox ecclesiology—the doctrine on the Church. He defines the Church as "the body of Christ" (Col 1:24) whose head is Christ himself (Eph 4.15), as a living organism in which each member has his own function, calling, and service. The unity of the members of Christ's body is sealed by the unity of the eucharist—the common table at which bread and wine are transformed into the body and blood of Christ by the prayers of the Church. During Paul's times the eucharist (from the Greek *eucharistia*, "thanksgiving") was more a meal than a liturgical service. However, this meal was accompanied by readings from scripture, a sermon, the singing of psalms, and then by the recital of the eucharistic prayers, which were improvised. As a rule, the eucharistic gathering began after sunset and continued until dawn. These gatherings are described in Paul's epistles and in the Acts of the Apostles. With time the eucharist acquired the features of a liturgical service, and the eucharistic prayers were written down. Despite the changes in the form of the eucharistic gathering, it has remained essentially the same from Paul's times to the present. The essence of the eucharist was expressed in the following words of the apostle:

> The cup of blessing which we bless, is it not a participation in the blood of Christ? The bread which we break, is it not a participation in the body of Christ? Because there is one bread, we who are many are one body, for we all partake of the one bread. (1 Cor 10.16–17)

The theme of love dominates the moral teaching of Paul, just as it did in Christ's teaching. "Let all that you do be done in love," exhorts the apostle (1 Cor 16.14). According to Paul, no trials or tribulations can separate the believer from the love of God:

> Who shall separate us from the love of Christ? Shall tribulation, or distress, or persecution, or famine, or nakedness, or peril, or sword? As it is written, "For thy sake we are being killed all the day long; we are regarded

[9]John Chrysostom *Homilies on the Epistle to the Romans* 32.3.

as sheep to be slaughtered" [Ps 43.23]. No, in all these things we are more than conquerors through him who loved us. For I am sure that neither death, nor life, nor angels, nor principalities, nor things present, nor things to come, nor powers, nor height, nor depth, nor anything else in all creation, will be able to separate us from the love of God in Christ Jesus our Lord. (Rom 8.35–39)

Paul's teaching is profoundly christocentric. He does not separate himself or his life from the person and life of Christ: "I have been crucified with Christ; it is no longer I who live, but Christ who lives in me" (Gal 2.19–20); "For to me to live is Christ, and to die is gain" (Phil 1.21); "I bear on my body the marks of Jesus" (Gal 6.17). According to Paul, faith in the resurrection of Christ is the foundation of the apostles' preaching. At the same time Paul admits that the message of the crucified and risen Christ is a challenge for both Jewish and Hellenistic consciousness:

For the word of the cross is folly to those who are perishing, but to us who are being saved it is the power of God . . . Where is the wise man? Where is the scribe? Where is the debater of this age? Has not God made foolish the wisdom of the world? For since, in the wisdom of God, the world did not know God through wisdom, it pleased God through the folly of what we preach to save those who believe. For Jews demand signs and Greeks seek wisdom, but we preach Christ crucified, a stumbling block to Jews and folly to Gentiles, but to those who are called, both Jews and Greeks, Christ the power of God and the wisdom of God. (1 Cor 1.18–24)

The truth of these words of the "apostle of the nations" was confirmed in the second and third centuries, when the Christian faith began to spread rapidly while at the same time encountering open resistance from both Jews and pagans.

THE AGE OF MARTYRDOM

During the first three centuries of its existence, the Christian Church found itself in a state of conflict with the surrounding world. The challenge it presented to the Judaic tradition was the reason for the sharp opposition between Christianity and Judaism. This opposition began already during

Christ's earthly life: his main opponents were the spiritual leaders of the Jewish people—the high priests, Pharisees, and Sadducees, who could not forgive him his seemingly disdainful attitude toward Judaic traditions. They obtained his death sentence from the Roman prefect Pontius Pilate, and they began the systematic persecution of his disciples after his resurrection.

The Acts of the Apostles mentions a "a great persecution against the church in Jerusalem," which scattered Christians throughout Judea and Samaria (Acts 8.1). One of the victims of this persecution was Stephen, one of the seven men whom the apostolic community selected to "serve tables" (Acts 6.2). After being arrested, Stephen appeared before the high priests and, in a long accusatory speech, presented the entire history of the people of Israel. He concluded his accusation with the words: "You stiff-necked people, uncircumcised in heart and ears, you always resist the Holy Spirit. As your fathers did, so do you. Which of the prophets did not your fathers persecute? And they killed those who announced beforehand the coming of the Righteous One, whom you have now betrayed and murdered, you who received the law as delivered by angels and did not keep it" (Acts 7.51–53). In response to this speech, which became the first written work of anti-Jewish polemics, the Jews took Stephen out of the city and stoned him to death.

James, the brother of the Lord

Another martyr who suffered at the hands of the Jews was James, son of Zebedee and brother of John, whom Herod killed with the sword (Acts 12.1–2). Also murdered by the Jews was James, the brother of the Lord, who according to church tradition was the first bishop of Jerusalem. He was thrown from the roof of the Jerusalem temple.[10] The Jewish persecutions of the Christians ended with the seizure and devastation of Jerusalem in the year A.D. 70 by the army of the Roman general Titus, who subsequently became emperor. The polemics between Christianity and Judaism were continued in the second century by Irenaeus of Lyons and Justin the Philosopher, in the third century by Origen, and in the fourth century by Aphrahat the Persian and John Chrysostom.

---

[10]The Orthodox Church distinguishes between James the brother of the Lord (presumably Joseph's son from his first marriage) and first bishop of Jerusalem, and James the son of Zebedee, as well as James the son of Alphaeus.

Persecution of the Christians by the pagans began in A.D. 64, when a substantial part of Rome was destroyed by fire and Emperor Nero, in order to divert suspicion of arson from himself, accused Christians and Jews of having been its perpetrators. The Roman historian Tacitus has preserved the following account of this:

> Therefore, in order to get rid of the report, Nero fastened the guilt and inflicted the most exquisite tortures on a class hated for their abominations, called Christians by the populace. Christus, from whom this name had its origin, suffered the supreme penalty during the reign of Tiberius at the hands of one of our procurators, Pontius Pilatus, and a most mischievous superstition, thus checked for the moment, again broke out not only in Judea, the first source of the evil, but even in Rome, where all things hideous and shameful from every part of the world find their center and become popular. Accordingly, an arrest was first made of all who pleaded guilty; then, upon their information, an immense multitude was convicted, not so much of the crime of setting fire to the city, as of hatred against mankind. Mockery of every sort was added to their deaths. Covered with the skins of beasts, they were torn by dogs and perished, or were nailed to crosses, or were doomed to the flames and burnt, to serve as nightly illumination when daylight had expired. Nero offered his gardens for the spectacle, and was exhibiting a show in the circus, while he mingled with the people in the dress of a charioteer or stood aloft on a car. Hence, even for criminals who deserved extreme and exemplary punishment, there arose a feeling of compassion; for it was not, as it seemed, for the public good, but to satisfy one man's cruelty, that they were being destroyed.[11]

For the Christian Church, the words of the Roman historian are an important witness of the early years of its existence and the beginning of the age of persecution. It is of particular value because it was recorded by a person who was not only not a member of the Church but hostile toward it.

Other important testimonies from the same era are the acts of the martyrs—the minutes of interrogations of Christians sentenced to death, recorded on the order of their tormentors. An example of these is the record of the trial of St Cyprian of Carthage (†258), compiled by the office of the procon-

[11]Tacitus *Annals* 15.44.

sul of Africa. Other historical sources are the accounts of Christians who had witnessed the sufferings of martyrs. Among these are *The Martyrdom of St Polycarp of Smyrna* (†156), *The Martyrdom of St Justin the Philosopher* (†c. 165), and *The Martyrdom of Ss Perpetua and Felicitas* (†202).

A special kind of witness is found in the epistles of St Ignatius the God-bearer, bishop of Antioch (†c. 107), who was martyred during the persecution of Emperor Trajan (98–117). In 106 Trajan ordered his citizens to make offerings to the pagan gods on the occasion of his victory over the Scythians. Ignatius refused to do so and was sentenced to death. After receiving his sentence, Ignatius was placed in shackles and, accompanied by soldiers, sent off to Rome, where he was to be torn to pieces in public by lions. The journey took the bishop through different cities, to the Christians of which he addressed his epistles. These epistles are striking testimony of the bishop's spiritual heroism and firmness in the face of his approaching death. In his epistle written in Smyrna and delivered by the Christians of Ephesus, Ignatius asks the Christians of Rome not to petition for the cancellation or softening of his punishment:

> I write to the churches and emphasize to them all that I shall willingly die for God, unless you hinder me. I ask of you not to show unseasonable good will toward me. Let me become food for the wild beasts, through whose action I will be granted to attain to God. I am the wheat of God, and let me be ground by the teeth of the wild beasts, that I may be found the pure bread of Christ. Rather entice the wild beasts, that they may become my tomb and may leave nothing of my body . . . Entreat Christ for me, that by these instruments I may be found a sacrifice to God . . . From Syria to Rome I fight with beasts, by land and sea, by night and day, being bound to ten leopards, or rather a band of soldiers, who, even when they receive benefits, show themselves all the worse. But I am rather instructed by their injuries to act as a disciple of Christ; yet am I not thereby justified. May I enjoy the wild beasts that are prepared for me; and I pray that they will be eager to rush upon me, which I will also entice to devour me speedily . . . And let no one, of things visible or invisible, envy me that I should attain to Jesus Christ. Let fire and the cross, the crowds of wild beasts, the tearings, breakings, and dislocations of bones, the cutting off of members, the shatterings of the whole body, and all the

The martyrs Sergius and Bacchus

dreadful torments of the devil come upon me: only let me attain to Jesus Christ. All the pleasures of the world and all the kingdoms of this earth shall profit me nothing. It is better for me to die on behalf of Jesus Christ than to reign over all the ends of the earth . . . It is him that I seek, who died for us. It is him that I desire, who rose again for our sake . . . Let me obtain the pure light; and when I have departed from here, I shall indeed be a man of God. Permit me to be an imitator of the passion of my God.[12]

The persecutions by the Roman authorities in the first three centuries of the Church were irregular: they began, subsided, and were then renewed. In the second century Emperor Trajan banned all secret societies that had laws differing from those of the state. Naturally, Christians came under this ban. During his reign Christians were not singled out, but if the judicial authorities charged someone with belonging to the Christian Church, they sentenced him to death. During the reign of Marcus Aurelius (161–180), one of the most educated Roman emperors, Christians were hunted down, and a system of tortures was introduced to force them to renounce their faith. Christians were banished from their homes, whipped, beaten with stones, tied to horse tails and dragged on the ground, and thrown into prisons; their bodies were left unburied. Emperor Decius (249–251) decided to eliminate Christianity; however, his rule was too brief to realize his purpose. Emperor Diocletian (284–305) issued several edicts calling for, among other things, the destruction of Christian churches, depriving Christians of property and civil liberties, subjecting them to torture during court hearings, the imprisonment of all clergy, and requiring Christians to offer sacrifices to the pagan gods.

Early Christian literature has preserved numerous testimonies of the heroism of martyrs in the face of trials and persecutions. But there were also cases where Christians apostasized and renounced Christ. During the persecution unleashed by Decius this acquired mass proportions, as attested to by Dionysius of Alexandria: "Fear struck them, and many of the more influential

---

[12]Ignatius *Epistle to the Romans* 4–6.

Christians gave in immediately, some giving way to fear, others, as civil servants, to the requirements of their positions, still others drawn along with the crowd. Some were pale and trembling, as if it were not they who were making sacrifices to the idols but they themselves who were being brought to sacrifice; and therefore the crowd mocked them."[13] And Cyprian of Carthage wrote: "They did not wait to be interrogated and to ascend the Capitol under arrest in order to deny Christ . . . Of their own accord they rushed into the Forum . . . to cap the crime, even infants, placed in their parents' hands or lead that way, lost now as small children what they had acquired in baptism right at the first moment after their birth."[14]

During the first three centuries persecutions arose for different reasons. First of all, there was a wall of mutual nonacceptance. The pagans' hatred toward the Christians—reflected in the excerpt from Tacitus' *Annals* above, as well as in the writings of Suetonius, Pliny, Celsus, and other Roman authors—reflected the widespread view of Christianity as a secret, superstitious sect that was harmful to society. The fact that the eucharistic gatherings were closed to outsiders contributed to the spread of allegations of Christians practicing "abominations" and even cannibalism at these meetings. The failure of Christians to bring sacrifice to the gods was viewed as "atheism" and their refusal to worship the emperor as defiance of the religious and social order of the empire.

The age of martyrdom, which ended in the Roman empire in 313,[15] profoundly shaped the history of the Christian Church. The veneration of martyrs that emerged at this time continues even today. In the Orthodox Church, the Divine Liturgy is still celebrated on an altar containing a particle of the relics of a martyr or saint, or on an *antimension*—a special cloth into which such a particle has been sewn. This accords with the ancient Christian practice of celebrating the eucharist on the tombs of martyrs.

Tertullian (c. 150–c. 220) once wrote that "the blood of the martyrs is the seed of Christianity."[16] This pithy phrase of the third-century Roman church writer emphasizes that persecution does not weaken but, on the contrary,

---

[13]Eusebius *Ecclesiastical History* 6.42.11, cited in Alexander Schmemann, *The Historical Road of Eastern Orthodoxy* (Crestwood, NY: SVS Press, 1977), 57.

[14]*On the Lapsed* 8, 9, in Allen Brent, trans., *On the Church: Select Treatises* (Crestwood, NY: SVS Press, 2006), 111, 112.

[15]Beyond the boundaries of the empire, Christians were fiercely persecuted during the fourth and fifth centuries, particularly in Persia.

[16]*Apology* 50.13.

strengthens the Church, fostering the spiritual unity of the faithful. The truth of these words was confirmed each time persecution of the Church flared up—even up to the twentieth century, which became a new age of martyrdom and unprecedented spiritual heroism in the history of the Orthodox Church.

EARLY CHRISTIAN LITERATURE

The preaching of Paul and the other apostles marked the beginning of a complex and painful process of understanding the religion revealed by God as a path to salvation not limited to the Jewish ethnic tradition. For a long time, the good news of the incarnate, crucified, and risen God remained "foolishness" for the Hellenistic world, which still had to mature for its Pentecost and find its own approach to the mystery of the incarnation. Born into a different cultural heritage, the Hellenistic consciousness required another pedagogical approach from the apostles and their successors: the apostolic fathers and church teachers of the first three centuries. Their experience shows how difficult it was to convey the truths of revelation and the experience of the life in Christ to the classical world.

The first three centuries saw the appearance and development of Christian literature and Christian theology. This period also saw the emergence of the first heresies to challenge the Christian Church.

The most ancient and authoritative works of Christian literature are those that became part of the New Testament. They were all written in Greek no later than the end of the first century. The currently recognized canon of the New Testament includes the gospels according to Matthew, Mark, Luke, and John; the Acts of the Apostles; the epistle of James; two epistles of Peter; three epistles of John; the epistle of Jude; fourteen epistles of the apostle Paul; and the Book of Revelation. The canon of the New Testament in its present form was established only at the end of the fourth century. Canon 47 of the Council of Carthage (397) lists the following books: "The gospels—four books; the Acts of the Apostles—one book; the epistles of Paul—thirteen; his epistle to the Hebrews—one; Peter—two epistles; John the apostle—three; James—one; Jude—one; the Apocalypse of John."

Along with the canonical texts the ancient Church also knew many works called *apocrypha* (from the Greek *apokryo,* "to hide"). Among these were the gospels of Thomas, Philip, Peter, Nicodemus, and the Protoevangelium of James. Among the apocryphal writings that enjoyed broad acceptance during the first centuries of Christianity were works that were very different both in their provenance and content. Their fate in the Christian Church varied: some apocryphal gospels, particularly those of heretical origin, were condemned by the Church and withdrawn from use. And despite the fact that they did not form part of the New Testament canon, those apocrypha whose content did not contradict church teaching were preserved in tradition in an indirect way: many of the ideas expressed in them found their way into liturgical texts and hagiographical literature. Among the apocrypha that influenced the development of Christian liturgy were the Protoevangelium of James, which speaks about the birth, childhood, and youth of the Most Holy Virgin Mary, and the Gospel of Nicodemus, which relates Christ's descent into hell. Both works do not contain ideas foreign to Christianity, are comprised of biblical material, and fill lacunae in the New Testament.

The next stage in the development of early Christian literature is represented by the works of the apostolic fathers, who lived in the second century. A number of them, such as Papias of Hierapolis, personally knew some of Christ's apostles, while others, such as Ignatius of Antioch, were successors of bishops consecrated by the apostles. Ignatius' epistles, already mentioned, have not only spiritual and moral but also theological significance: they contain a well-developed teaching on the unity of the Church and the three levels of the church hierarchy, consisting of the bishop, presbyters, and deacons. The works of the apostolic fathers also include two epistles of St Clement of Rome (the authenticity of the second epistle is disputed), the Epistle of St Polycarp of Smyrna, *The Shepherd of Hermas*, the Epistle of Barnabus, and *The Teaching of the Twelve Apostles* (*Didache*).

An important Christian writer of the second century was St Irenaeus of Lyons (†c. 200), who devoted much effort to combating the gnostic heresies. Gnosticism was a totality of religious movements that developed in parallel with Christianity but departed profoundly from it in doctrinal matters. The gnostic systems of Valentinus, Basilides, and Marcion differed considerably from one another; however, the combination of elements of Christianity and elements of eastern religions, occultism, magic, and astrology was common to all of them. Most gnostic systems were characterized by the idea of two coequal forces in the universe: the force of good and the force of evil. Valentinus contrasted the good God, who appeared in Christ and rules the spiritual world, with the evil god of the Old Testament, whose authority encompasses the material world. The gnostic systems did not view man as a being endowed with free will, but rather as a toy in the hands of good or evil forces.

The person of Christ did not occupy a central place in any of the gnostic systems. Only certain elements of his spiritual and moral teaching were integrated into their phantasmagoric philosophy. Not satisfied with the gospels used in the Church, they created their own, alternative versions. One of these was the Gospel of Judas, which was mentioned by Irenaeus of Lyons and has been preserved in a Coptic translation. For a long time this gnostic gospel was considered lost, but its text was published in 2006. In this work Judas is depicted as a particularly close disciple of Jesus, to whom the Lord reveals the "mysteries of the kingdom." Judas betrays Jesus, as it were, at the latter's behest.

St Irenaeus contrasts Christian theological teaching, based on the New Testament and holy tradition, with "false gnosis." He advances faithfulness to church tradition as a fundamental criterion of doctrinal truth:

> it is not necessary to seek the truth, which can be easily obtained from the Church, among others. For the apostles, like a rich man depositing his money in a bank, placed in her hands all things pertaining to the truth, so that every person who wishes can draw from her the water of life. For she is the entrance to life; all others are thieves and robbers. For this reason we are bound to avoid the latter, choose the things pertaining to the Church with the utmost diligence, and lay hold of the tradition of the truth. For how do things stand? Suppose there arises a dispute over some important question. Should we not have recourse to the most ancient churches with which the apostles were in constant contact, and learn from them what is certain and clear in regard to the question at hand? What if the apostles themselves had not left us any writings? Would it not be necessary in that case to follow the tradition that they handed down to those to whom they entrusted the churches?[17]

The age of persecutions gave birth to a new genre of Christian literature—apologetics. Among the authors of second-century apologetic works were Athenagoras of Athens, St Theophilus of Antioch, Minutius Felix, St Justin the Philosopher, and Tatian the Assyrian. A significant part of the *Apology* of

---

[17] *Against Heresies* 3.4.1.

Tertullian is devoted to defending Christians against accusations of not respecting the emperor. Addressing the Roman authorities, Tertullian emphasized the loyalty of the Christians to the earthly ruler: "The emperor is more ours than yours, for our God has appointed him. Therefore, having this propriety in him, I do more than you for his welfare, not only because I ask it of Him who can give it, or because I ask it as one who deserves to obtain it, but also because while placing the majesty of Caesar lower than that of God, I commend him to God, to whom alone I make him inferior."[18] In these passages Tertullian is guided by a tradition that goes back to the apostles Peter and Paul, who admonished Christians to be obedient to all human authorities (Rom 13.1; Titus 3.1), honor the earthly king (1 Pet 2.13–17), and pray for him (1 Tim 2.1–3).

An important work of third-century apologetic literature is the anonymous *Epistle to Diognetus*, which describes the lifestyle of Christians during the age of persecutions:

For the Christians are distinguished from other people neither by country, nor by language, nor by the customs they observe. They do not inhabit cities of their own, or employ a peculiar form of speech, or lead a life in any way different from that of others . . . But, while inhabiting both Greek and barbarian cities, as the lot of each of them has determined, and following the customs of the natives concerning clothing, food, and everything else, they display to us their wonderful and truly striking way of life. They dwell in their own homeland, but only as sojourners. As citizens, they take part in all aspects of life, and yet endure all things as if they were foreigners. Every foreign land is to them as their native country, and every land of their birth as a land of strangers. They marry, as everyone else does; they beget children, but do not destroy their offspring. They have a common table, but not a common bed. They are in the flesh, but do not live after the flesh. They live on earth, but are citizens of heaven. They obey the prescribed laws, and at the same time surpass the laws by their lives. They love all men, but are persecuted by all. They are unknown, but condemned; they are put to death, and restored to life. They are poor, yet make many rich; they experience lack in all things, and yet abound in all. They are dishonored, and yet in their very

---

[18] *Apology* 33.

dishonor are glorified. They are slandered, and yet are justified; they are reviled, and bless. They are insulted, and repay the insult with honor. They do good, yet are punished as evildoers. When punished, they rejoice as if quickened into life. They are assailed by the Jews as foreigners and persecuted by the Greeks; yet those who hate them are unable to give any reason for their hatred.

In one word—what the soul is to the body, Christians are to the world . . . The soul is imprisoned in the body, yet preserves that body; and Christians are confined in the world as in a prison, and yet they are the preservers of the world.[19]

The Christian writers of the second and third centuries made considerable efforts to compare Christianity with the Hellenistic tradition. The works of Justin the Philosopher and Clement of Alexandria (150–c. 215) in particular are devoted to this theme. Clement attached great importance to the study of Greek philosophy and believed that the Christian faith should not be opposed to philosophy. He wrote that "philosophy does not turn people away from the faith"; on the contrary, "we are protected by it as by a solid stronghold, and acquire in it an ally with whom we also strengthen our faith."[20] According to Clement, "although there is only one way to the truth, different streams flow into it, forming a river that flows into eternity."[21] One of these streams is ancient Greek philosophy, which is a "preparatory teaching that clears and levels the path to Christ."[22] Philosophy was given to the Greeks as a divine gift, as an "incarnate image [icon] of truth."[23] It was the same *paidagogos* to Christ (Gal 3.23–24) for the Greeks that the Old Testament was for the Jews.[24] Clement uses the word "philosophy" in a broad sense: for him it did not mean the teaching of Plato, Epicurus, or Aristotle, but "the best that each of these schools teaches about justice and pious knowledge."[25]

The most significant church writer in the Christian east of the third century was Origen (c. 185–c. 254). For many years he headed the catechetical school in Alexandria and then in Caesarea, gaining renown as an outstanding

[19] *Epistle to Diognetus* 5–6.
[20] *Stromata* 1.2.
[21] *Stromata* 1.5.
[22] *Stromata* 1.5.
[23] *Stromata* 1.2.
[24] *Stromata* 1.5.
[25] *Stromata* 1.7.

teacher. One of Origen's students was St Gregory Thaumaturgus, who composed an *Oration and Panegyric Addressed to Origen*. According to Gregory, his teacher devoted considerable attention to the study of ancient philosophy and literature, and his students studied the systems of the Greek philosophers. At the same time, this inquiry into Greek philosophy was viewed only as a preparation for the basic course of studies, which consisted in the reading and interpretation of scripture. Gregory's panegyric also contains interesting facts about Origen's pedagogical method. His basic concern was to inculcate in his students a taste for independent reflection on the material they studied. Origen understood perfectly well that his task was not to impart a certain sum of knowledge, but to teach his students to independently answer questions that might arise during the study process. Like another great pedagogue—Socrates—Origen did not provide his students with ready answers, preferring to convince each of them with arguments of his own. Gregory testifies to the profound influence that Origen's personality exerted on him:

> He also wounded me by the sting of friendship, which is not easily withstood, sharp and most effective, by the sting of a kind and affectionate disposition toward me, which was reflected in the very tone of his voice when he addressed me and conversed with me . . . Like a spark that fell into my soul, love was kindled and set on fire—my love for both the Holy Word, who is most worthy of our love and who in his ineffable beauty is more attractive than anything else, and for this man, his friend and herald.[26]

Some contemporary scholars call Origen the founder of Christian theology.[27] Origen wrote many exegetical, theological, apologetic, and ascetic works. His corpus of exegetical writings includes commentaries on almost all books of the Old and New Testaments. His *Against Celsus* is an expanded apology of Christianity, written in response to accusations by pagans, and his treatise *On First Principles*, one of his early works, represents the first attempt at a systematic exposition of Christian dogma. Finally, his *On Prayer* is one of the earliest works of ascetic literature and contains valuable information on the practice of prayer in the third-century Church.

In *On First Principles* (preserved in its entirety only in an edited Latin translation), Origen presents Christian dogma as it was preserved from the time

---

[26] *Oration and Panegyric Addressed to Origen* 81–83.
[27] John Meyendorff, *An Introduction to Patristic Theology* (Klin, 2001), 103.

of the apostles, adding his own commentary on the apostolic tradition. According to him there is one God, who created all things and who brought them from nonexistence into existence. This God, in accordance with the predictions of the prophets, sent the Lord Jesus Christ in order to call to himself first Israel, and then the pagans. This God, the righteous and good Father of our Lord Jesus Christ, gave the law, the prophets, and the gospel. He is also the God of the apostles and of the Old and New Testaments. Jesus Christ, according to church tradition, was born of the Father before all creation. He served the Father during the creation of the world, and "in the last times," having humbled himself, he became incarnate and was made man, remaining that which he was before, that is, God. He took on a body similar to ours, the only difference being that his was born of the Virgin and the Holy Spirit. Jesus Christ was born and truly suffered, and underwent not an illusory but a real death. He truly rose from the dead, spent time with his disciples after the resurrection, and ascended into heaven. The Holy Spirit is equal in honor with the Father and the Son. In this connection Origen writes: "It is not clear here if the Holy Spirit was born or not, and if he should be considered Son."[28] This statement testifies to the insufficient elaboration of pneumatological dogma during his time.

According to Origen, church tradition teaches of posthumous recompense as consisting in either the inheritance of eternal life and bliss or eternal fire and torment. It also affirms the universal resurrection of the dead, when the human body will rise in glory. The reasonable soul possesses freedom of choice and must struggle to the end against the devil and his angels. The fact that people have a free will means that they are not forced to do good or evil.[29]

As for the good angels, Origen writes that they "serve God for the salvation of people. However, the questions of when they were created, what they are like, or how they exist, are not answered with sufficient clarity."[30] Concerning the devil and his angels, "very many are of the opinion that this devil was formerly an angel, and after apostasizing, convinced many other angels to turn away from God with him."[31] Furthermore, church tradition asserts that the world was created and began to exist from a particular point in time; however,

[28] *On First Principles* 1.Pref.4.
[29] *On First Principles* 1.Pref.5.
[30] *On First Principles* 1.Pref.10.
[31] *On First Principles* 1.Pref.6.

"what was before this world or what will be after it remains unknown to many, because church doctrine does not speak clearly about this."[32]

Finally, Origen notes that scripture has not only a literal meaning, "but also another sense that is hidden from most people, since that which is described here serves as a prefiguration of certain sacraments and an image of divine things." The spiritual meaning of scripture "is known not by all, but only by those who are given the grace of the Holy Spirit in the word of wisdom and knowledge."[33] This latter statement points to the allegorical method of interpreting scripture. This method, widespread in the Alexandrian tradition, was based on the idea of the existence of two levels in scripture—the literal and spiritual—and on the necessity of perceiving an allegorical, symbolic meaning in each word. By using this approach, which might seem useless and meaningless to people today[34] but which was in keeping with the cultural tradition of educated Greeks of his time, Origen interpreted many books of scripture.

The theological formulations in Origen's works are, as a rule, rather cautious: if church tradition offers no unambiguous answer to a particular dogmatic question he either leaves it unanswered, citing its insufficient elaboration, or proposes his own interpretation, emphasizing that it is his personal opinion. At the same time, in *On First Principles* he expresses ideas that were rejected and condemned by subsequent church tradition. For example, in this treatise Origen holds that the souls of reasonable creatures initially abided in the contemplation of God; however, as a result of the fall of man, they grew cold and were sent into human bodies. (Origen derives the word *psyche,* "soul," from the verb *psychroō,* "to cool something.") Through spiritual and moral purification, and thanks to the incarnation of the Son of God, souls can be restored to their previous state. This restoration (*apokatastasis*) will encompass all reasonable beings, including people, the devil, and demons. At the same time it will not be final, since the freedom of reasonable creatures entails the possibility of a new fall and return to the body,[35] and therefore the necessity of another incarnation. The idea of an infinite cycle of reincarnation that this theory implies contradicts the Christian teaching on the unity of soul and body and on the uniqueness of Christ's redemptory act, which could take place only once.

[32] *On First Principles* 1.Pref.7.
[33] *On First Principles* 1.Pref.9.
[34] Meyendorff, *Introduction,* 110.
[35] Ibid., 120.

Origen's personality and writings exerted enormous influence on later church writers, and in many respects determined the further development of Christian thought. His allegorical method of interpreting the Old Testament was widely used later in Christian tradition. Among Origen's admirers in the fourth century were Ss Basil the Great and Gregory the Theologian, who compiled an anthology of Origen's works entitled *The Philokalia*, as well as St Gregory of Nyssa, who adopted his theological method and many of his dogmatic views.

At the same time, debates over certain aspects of Origen's teaching began already during his lifetime and continued after his death. At the end the third century St Methodius of Olympus disputed Origen's teaching on the preexistence of souls and the nature of resurrected bodies. In the fourth century St Epiphanius of Cyprus polemicized against Origen in the east, while Blessed Jerome did the same in the west. In the year 400, a council in Alexandria condemned Origenism. Nevertheless, Origen's writings continued to exert influence in monastic circles in Egypt and Palestine, where debates over various aspects of his teaching continued until the middle of the sixth century. Finally, the Church officially condemned Origenism at the Council of Constantinople of 543 and at the Fifth Ecumenical Council of 553. The following teachings from the works of Origen or his followers were singled out for condemnation: the notion that human souls preexisted in the world of ideas but then fell away from divine contemplation and were sent into bodies for punishment; the belief that the soul of Jesus Christ preexisted and was united with God the Word before the incarnation from the Virgin, while his body was first formed in the womb of the Virgin and only after that united with God the Word; the teaching that God the Word likened himself to the entire celestial hierarchy by becoming a cherubim for the cherubim and a seraphim for the seraphim; the idea that the bodies of people will rise again in a spherical form; the view that the sky, sun, moon, stars, and spaces higher than the waters are animated; the belief that Christ will be crucified in the age to come for the sake of the demons as well as for people; the idea that God's might is limited in space and that he created only as many things as he could encompass; and the teaching that the punishment of the demons and the impious is only temporary and will end after a certain time, that is, that there will be a restoration (*apokatastasis*) of the demons and the wicked. A substantial part of Origen's work was lost after the Fifth Ecumenical Council, and some of his writings have survived only in Latin translation.

In addition to defending the faith against external enemies, the Christian writers of the second and third centuries were forced to react to heresies inside the Church itself. The most significant heresies of this period, besides the gnosticism we already mentioned, were Montanism, Sabellianism, and Manichaeism.

Montanism emerged in the middle of the second century after the pagan priest Montanus converted to Christianity. However, he did not join the Church, preferring instead to found his own sect, whose followers recognized him as the Paraclete (the Holy Spirit). Dogmatically, Montanism did not seem to differ from Christianity. Nevertheless, the founder's desire to pass off his sect as a new revelation equal in importance to the New Testament, to place his works and those of his followers on the same footing as scripture, as well as the sect's extreme moral rigorism and eschatological expectations (the Montanists believed that Christ's second coming would occur soon, in the Phrygian village of Pepuza, which they called the "New Jerusalem"), all evoked sharp protest from the Church. Their teaching was condemned by the First Ecumenical Council.

The Sabellians, who took their name from the Roman priest Sabellius, taught that the Father, Son, and Holy Spirit are three designations of one and the same divine person, whom Sabellius called the "son-father." In the Old Testament this person revealed himself as the Father, in the New Testament as the Son, and in the Church after Christ's ascension as the Spirit. Although Sabellius was excommunicated by Pope Callistus, his teaching continued to find adherents until the second half of the fourth century.

Manichaeism arose in the middle of the third century in Seleucia-Ctesiphon, capital of the Persian Sassanid empire. Its founder was Mani (†c. 270), who claimed to be the envoy of God. The teaching of Mani was based on the dualistic notion of an eternal struggle between God and the devil so characteristic of gnosticism. Mani attributed the creation of the material world, including plants and animals, to the devil. However, humanity is called to be liberated from the bonds of matter and return to the kingdom of light. The heralds of the light and divine revelation were Buddha, Zoroaster, and Jesus Christ. And Mani was the Paraclete whom Jesus promised to send in order to prepare the final victory of the light. Manichaeans preached an extreme asceticism whose purpose was liberation from the fetters of matter, prescribed abstention from meat and alcohol, and held marriage and childbearing in contempt. They created a hierarchy similar to that of the Church, with its own esoteric cult in which only the initiated were allowed to participate.

Manichaeism proved to be the longest lived of the heretical movements that emerged during the age of persecutions. After the death of Mani, his teaching spread beyond the borders of Persia and into the African provinces of the Roman empire. In the fourth century Manichaeism captured the attention of Augustine, who subsequently became a Christian bishop and teacher of the Church. Manichaeism continued to exist in different forms in Byzantium and the west until the eleventh and twelfth centuries, when it evolved into new heretical groups. Groups of Manichaeans remained in the east outside the Byzantine empire until the thirteenth century.

2

The Age of the Ecumenical Councils

TRINITARIAN CONTROVERSIES

THE PERIOD FROM the fourth to the eighth centuries is characterized by the rapid spread of Christianity in the east and west, its transformation into a major world religion, the flowering of Christian theology, the emergence and development of the monastic movement, and the flourishing of church art. At the same time, it was marked by bitter struggles against heresies and numerous church schisms.

This new period of church history began in 313, when Emperor Constantine issued the Edict of Milan, which gave Christians the same rights as members of other religions. For Constantine the recognition of Christianity was more of a political move: he apparently saw in Christianity a spiritual and moral force capable of uniting the population of the empire. Thanks to him, over the next two decades Christianity became a privileged religion. However, Constantine himself was baptized only on his deathbed in 337. To the end of his life he maintained the title "supreme priest" (*pontifex maximus*), which had been traditional from pagan times and which was reconceptualized by Christians as indicating the divine election of the emperor and his role as defender and patron of the Christian Church on earth.

The significance of the Edict of Milan in the history of Christianity cannot be overemphasized. For the first time after nearly three hundred years of persecution, Christians were granted the right to legally exist and openly profess their faith. If earlier they had been outcasts of society, they could now participate in public life and occupy government posts. The Church now had the right to acquire real estate, build churches, and conduct charitable and educational activities. The Church's status had changed so radically that out of gratitude it decided to preserve the memory of Constantine forever, proclaiming him a saint equal to the apostles.

Immediately after the legalization of Christianity, the Church was shaken by new divisions and heresies. The Donatist schism arose in the African Church after some of the Christians refused to recognize the election of Caecilianus as bishop of Carthage. In his place the bishops of Numidia consecrated Donatus, the head of the group of dissatisfied Christians. The teaching of the Donatists was characterized by extreme rigorism: for example, they considered it inadmissible to accept the repentance of those who had renounced the faith during persecution, and made the validity of sacraments dependent on the moral state of the clergyman administering them. Donatism was condemned at church councils in Rome (313) and Arles (314); nevertheless, Donatists appealed the decisions to Emperor Constantine. In 316 the emperor summoned them to court, and again their teaching was condemned. When they refused to accept the decision of the ecclesiastical and secular authorities, Constantine ordered the confiscation of their churches and property and had their leaders exiled. This was the first case of open interference by the emperor in a church dispute. Despite the repressive measures, which were employed periodically throughout the fourth century and in the first quarter of the fifth century, Donatism continued to exist until the seventh century.

At the beginning of the fourth century in Alexandria the Arian heresy arose. Arius (256–336) was a presbyter who taught that only God the Father is eternal and unoriginate, and that the Son was born in time and is not coeternal with the Father. He emphasized that "there was a time when the Son did not exist," attempting to prove that the Son is one of God's creations, completely different from the Father, and not like him in essence. Arius' teaching was condemned at a church council in Alexandria around 320; nevertheless, his heresy began to spread beyond Alexandria and soon reached Constantinople. In 325 Emperor Constantine convened the First Ecumenical Council in Nicaea, in which 318 bishops took part. The importance of this council lies not only in the fact that it was the first such representative meeting of bishops after the age of persecutions, but above all in the fact that it formulated the faith in the Holy Trinity in terms that have been preserved in the Christian Church ever since. The Symbol of Faith of the Council of Nicaea, which begins with the words "I believe in one God" and contains an exposition of Orthodox triadology, became the classical expression of the faith of the Church.

Arianism did not cease after the Council of Nicaea. On the contrary, the second and third quarters of the fourth century witnessed its continued propagation and the persecution of its opponents, particularly its main adversary St Athanasius, bishop of Alexandria (c. 296–373). This confessor of "consubstantiality" was deposed four times and forced to live in exile, where he wrote works against the Arian heresy. The Arians were supported by civil authorities through Emperor Constantine, who had joined their camp during the last years of his life, by his successor Constantius, and by Valens, who ruled over the eastern half of the Roman empire.

In third quarter of the fourth century the main exponent of the revived Arianism was Eunomius, the bishop of Cyzicus (†398), who spoke about "unbegottenness" as the primary, essential characteristic of the Father, and about the "otherness" of the Son, who is not unbegotten and therefore has no part in the Godhead. The Son, according to Eunomius, did not emerge from the essence of the Father but was created by him: the Son is the "work and creation" of the Father, created *ex nihilo*. The three "Great Cappadocians"—Basil the Great, Gregory the Theologian, and Gregory of Nyssa—wrote refutations of this heresy. Following Athanasius of Alexandria and the Nicene fathers, they insisted on the consubstantiality and equality of the Father, Son, and Holy Spirit. One of the accomplishments of the great Cappadocians was the elaboration of terminology that clearly formulated the notions of unity and difference in the Trinity. They chose the term "hypostasis" to designate the existence of the trinitarian persons and "essence" to denote ontological community. The Father, Son, and Holy Spirit are three hypostases, equal and consubstantial with each other—that is, having one and the same divine essence.

The second and final condemnation of Arianism occurred at the Second Ecumenical Council. However, before examining this event, another heresy should be mentioned, namely that of Apollinarius of Laodicea, which was condemned at the Council of Alexandria in 362. Apollinarius followed the Nicene Council as regards the divinity of the Son. However, he believed that the Son's human nature could not be perfect since two perfect natures—one immutable (divine) and another mutable (human)—could not be united in one person. On the basis of the classical division of human nature into the mind, soul, and body, Apollinarius asserted that Christ did not have a human mind; in its place was the divine Logos. The teaching of Apollinarius foreshadowed the christological disputes of the fifth century.

The attempts to revive paganism by Emperor Julian the Apostate (331/332–363) should also be noted here. Brought up in the Christian faith, baptized in his youth, and even ordained a reader, Julian secretly sympathized with paganism. After acceding to the throne in 361, he brought his hidden sympathies into the open and aimed to restore paganism as the dominant religion. Unleashing open and mass persecutions of the Church similar to those of the pre-Constantine era was not part of his plan, since the Christian Church had become too strong, numerous, and influential for an open struggle. Instead, Julian chose a more surreptitious tactic. In the summer of 362 he issued an edict on teachers, whose purpose was to ban Christians from teaching in universities and schools. The edict was intended to deal a blow to the Christian intelligentsia, which was still rather small in number. It is difficult to ascertain how Julian's policies would have developed thereafter, since his short reign came to an end when he perished during a military campaign against the Persians.

Julian's rule represented paganism's last stand in the history of the Roman empire. During the reign of Valens, who was a protector of Arianism, paganism once again faded into the background, and Emperor Theodosius the Great (347–395) delivered a decisive blow after outlawing it in 380 and making Christianity obligatory for his subjects. In 381 Theodosius convened the Second Ecumenical Council in Constantinople, which condemned Arianism once again, along with a number of other heresies, including Montanism, Apollinarianism, and Sabellianism.

Also condemned were the *pneumatomachoi* or Macedonians (from Macedonius, bishop of Constantinople), who taught that the Holy Spirit is not equal to the Father and the Son and is not God. During the period preceding the council, the teaching on the Holy Spirit was a bone of contention not only between Arians and the defenders of the Nicene faith, but also among the latter. Basil the Great cautiously avoided calling the Holy Spirit God, for which he was reproached by Gregory the Theologian. Gregory zealously defended the divinity of the Holy Spirit at the Second Ecumenical Council and thereafter. The fathers of the council substantially expanded the Nicene Creed, having replaced the laconic "and in the Holy Spirit" with: "And in the Holy Spirit, the Lord, the Giver of Life, who proceeds from the Father; who with the Father and the Son together is worshiped and glorified; who spoke by the prophets." However, in these words there is no explicit assertion that the Holy Spirit is God. After rejecting the heresy of the *pneumatomachoi* and recognizing the Spirit as equal to the Father and Son, the council fathers decided not to introduce an affirmation of the divinity of the Holy Spirit into the creed. This understanding became generally accepted in Orthodox triadology after the Second Ecumenical Council.

CHRISTOLOGICAL CONTROVERSIES

The fifth century witnessed intense christological disputes provoked by the heresy of Nestorius. Nestorius relied on the christological doctrine of Theodore of Mopsuestia (c. 350–428), who introduced a radical separation of the divine and human natures in Jesus Christ. Theodore taught, among other things, that God the Word "assumed" the man Jesus; that the unoriginate Word of God "took up abode" in the man Jesus, who was born of the Virgin; that the Word lived in Christ as in a temple; that it took on human nature as if it were clothing; and that the man Jesus, through his feat of redemption and death on the cross, was united with the Word and assumed divine dignity. In essence, Theodore spoke of God the Word and the man Jesus as two subjects, whose union in the one person of the incarnate Son of God is not so much ontological or essential as it is conditional, that is, existing in our perception: in worshiping Christ, we unite the two natures and confess not "two sons," but one Christ–God and man.

It was this particular teaching that formed the basis of the christological doctrine of Nestorius, who was enthroned as archbishop of Constantinople in 428. Soon after his episcopal consecration Nestorius began in his sermons to dispute the term Theotokos, which by that time had gained widespread acceptance. According to him, Mary had given birth not to God but only to a person, with whom the Word of God, who was born of the Father before all ages, united himself. The person of Jesus, born of Mary, was only the abode of God and the instrument of our salvation. This person, through the working of the Holy Spirit, became Christ, the anointed one, and the Word of God remained with him in a special kind of moral or relative union. Nestorius suggested replacing the term Theotokos with Christotokos. St Cyril of Alexandria came out against this teaching. In his polemics against Nestorianism, he insisted on the hypostatic unity of God the Word: the unoriginate Word is the very same person as Jesus, who was born of the Virgin. Because of this, one cannot speak of the Word and Jesus as two different subjects.

Cyril's christology was confirmed by the Third Ecumenical Council, which was convoked in Ephesus in 431. The council was an arena of stormy debates and took place without the participation of a group of bishops from Antioch who, arriving at the council after a considerable delay, refused to support its condemnation of Nestorius. In 433 the Antiochian bishops were reconciled with Cyril of Alexandria, and a dogmatic formula was signed that represents a theological summary of the Council of Ephesus. This formula speaks of Jesus Christ as "perfect God and perfect man," who "was born before the ages of the Father according to his divinity, and in the last days for us and our salvation of the Virgin Mary according to his humanity." In this text the Virgin Mary is called the Theotokos, on the basis of the "unconfused union" of two natures in Jesus Christ.

Condemned by the Council of Ephesus, Nestorius was exiled to Egypt, where he died. However, his teaching—or more precisely, the christological doctrine of Theodore of Mopsuestia—gained acceptance beyond the limits of the Byzantine empire, namely in the Sassanid empire of Persia, where a major Christian church refused to recognize the decrees of the council. This church, which was called the Church of the East, was subsequently called the "Nestorian" Church, although Nestorius was not its founder and had no direct relation to it. The Church of the East continues to exist today: its official name is the Assyrian Church of the East, and it counts around 400,000 adherents.

Toward the middle of the fifth century a new christological heresy called monophysitism emerged. Its originator was the Constantinople archimandrite Eutychius or Eutyches, who taught that Christ's human nature was completely absorbed by his divine nature. In 448 this teaching was condemned at a council in Constantinople headed by Flavian, archbishop of Constantinople. However, Eutychius enjoyed the support of the Alexandrian archbishop Dioscorus, who had another council convened—this time in Ephesus in 449. The Ephesus council of 449, convoked by Emperor Theodosius II (401–450) as an ecumenical council, restored Eutychius to the priesthood and justified his doctrine. A leading role at this council was played by Dioscorus of Alexandria, and his enemies, including Flavian of Constantinople, were deposed. The council's acts were approved by the emperor, which seemed to indicate a complete victory for Dioscorus. However, the legates of the Roman pope who were present at the council sided with Flavian, and after returning to Rome they reported the council's justification of Eutychius to Pope Leo.

A council was convened in Rome and the decisions of the Ephesus council were declared invalid.

In 451 a new council, which entered history as the Fourth Ecumenical Council, was gathered in Chalcedon. It recognized the Ephesus council of 449 as a "robber council" and, following the council of Rome, revoked all its decisions. Moreover, it confirmed the condemnation of Eutychius and deposed Dioscorus. The Council of Chalcedon, in which 630 bishops took part, adopted a dogmatic definition that states:

> Following the saintly fathers, we all with one voice teach the confession of one and the same Son, our Lord Jesus Christ, perfect in divinity and perfect in humanity, truly God and truly man, with a soul and a body; consubstantial with the Father as regards his divinity, and consubstantial with us as regards his humanity; like us in all respects except for sin; begotten before the ages from the Father as regards his divinity, and in the last days begotten for us and for our salvation from Mary, the Virgin Theotokos as regards his humanity; one and the same Christ, Son, Lord, Only-begotten, acknowledged in two natures without confusion, change, division, or separation (so that at no point was the difference between the natures taken away through the union; instead the properties of both natures are preserved, and are united into One Person and One Hypostasis); he is not parted or divided into two persons, but is one and the same Son, the Only-begotten God the Word, the Lord Jesus Christ.[1]

The expression "without confusion, change" is directed against the monophysitism of Eutychius, and "without division or separation" against Nestorianism. However, some churches saw the Chalcedonian definition as a reversion to Nestorianism and refused to accept the decisions of the council. Vigorous opposition could be observed especially on the outskirts of the Roman empire—in Egypt, Syria, and Armenia—and also beyond the empire's borders, particularly in Persia. In Egypt and Syria one could find both bishops who recognized Chalcedon and bishops who rejected it. In Alexandria its opponents were headed by Timothy Aelurus (†477), in Antioch by Peter Gnapheus (†488). The Armenian Church also did not recognize the council, officially rejecting it in 506. Thus arose the first great division in the history of Christianity, which still exists today. In the sixth century two parallel hier-

---

[1]Cited in Meyendorff, *Introduction*, 319.

archies were formed in Egypt, both headed by a "Patriarch of Alexandria and All Africa": one that recognized the Council of Chalcedon and another that rejected it. In the Greek-speaking part of Syria, Christianity was also divided into two branches, each of which was led by its own "Patriarch of Antioch and All the East." In Armenia the Church preserved its unity but retained its anti-Chalcedonian position. At present pre-Chalcedonian Christianity is represented by several churches in Armenia, Egypt, Ethiopia, Eritrea, Syria, Lebanon, India, and the diaspora. The combined number of their members is approximately fifty million.

Although the main opposition to the Council of Chalcedon was concentrated on the edges of the eastern Roman empire, attitudes toward the council in Constantinople remained ambiguous. While emperors Marcian (450–457) and Leo I (457–474) supported it, Zeno (474–475; 476–491) took a more cautious stance. In 482, in an attempt to reconcile the monophysites with the diophysites, Zeno issued the Henotikon—a general exposition of the faith that passed over Chalcedon in silence. The Henotikon was supported by Patriarch Akakius of Constantinople († 488); however, Pope Felix III demanded that he unequivocally accept the Council of Chalcedon. Not having achieved this, he deposed and excommunicated Akakius at a council in Rome in 484. Thus began the first schism between Constantinople and Rome, lasting thirty-five years. It continued during the reign of Anastasius I (491–518) and was healed in 519, during the rule of Emperor Justin I (518–527), when Patriarch John of Constantinople and legates of Pope Hormisdas together condemned all who rejected Chalcedon. In 525 Pope John I visited Constantinople, sent to the imperial capital by King Theodoric of the Ostrogoths (c. 454–526), who ruled Rome at the time.

An important role in the history of the Christian Church in the east was played by Emperor Justinian I (527–565). This outstanding ruler, who ousted the Ostrogoths from Rome in 536 and restored the political unity of the Roman empire for the last time in history, also strove to restore its religious unity. In 537 he built Hagia Sophia in Constantinople—the most majestic church of the Christian east.

In the 540s the emperor initiated a reconsideration of the Church's attitude toward several theologians whose writings continued to cause debate. In 542 he issued an edict containing ten anathemas against Origen and his adherents. This edict was examined and approved at a council in Constantinople in 543, which condemned Origen, as well as Didymus of Alexandria and Evagrius of Pontus–fourth-century writers in whose works the council perceived Origen's influence.

In 544 Justinian issued a new edict condemning Theodore of Mopsuestia, the writings of Theodoret of Cyrus (c. 393–c. 460) against Cyril of Alexandria, and the epistle of Ibas of Edessa to

Hagia Sophia

Maris the Persian (fifth century). This edict consisted of three chapters (corresponding to the three bishops condemned in them), and came to be known as the "The Three Chapters." Many perceived the three chapters as a blow to the Council of Chalcedon, as it concerned theologians who had been justified at the council. The eastern patriarchs finally signed it when they were threatened with deposition and exile. However, the emperor also thought it necessary to have the signature of Pope Vigilius (537–555), who was brought to Constantinople by force for this purpose in 547. Upon arriving in the capital, the pope at first refused to sign the imperial edict; however, he agreed to do so under pressure. In 551 Justinian issued a new edict concerning the three chapters, which the pope categorically refused to sign. Fearing for his life, Vigilius took refuge in the church of St Peter; attempts were made to arrest him there, but he resisted desperately. Finally, he was subjected to house arrest and continually pressured.

It was against this background that the Fifth Ecumenical Council was convoked in Constantinople in 553. Although Pope Vigilius refused to participate, he did send his legates. The council condemned Theodore of Mopsuestia and repeated the anathema against Origen, Didymus, and Evagrius. As for Theodoret of Cyrus and Ibas of Edessa, they were not condemned; only their works against Cyril of Alexandria and the teaching of the Third Ecumenical Council were denounced. The fathers of the council struck the name of Pope Vigilius from the diptychs, on the ground that he had changed his stance toward the three chapters several times before the council. After the council, the deposed Vigilius and his supporters were exiled. Finally, Vigilius withdrew his protest against the three chapters and recognized the decisions of the council. He was allowed to return to Rome, but died on the way. The Roman

Church did not recognize the deposition of Vigilius, but did accept the Fifth Ecumenical Council. The decisive role in this recognition was played by Pope Pelagius I (556–561), Vigilius' successor, during whose time relations between Rome and Constantinople were normalized.

The Constantinople council of 543 and the Fifth Ecumenical Council were the first councils in church history to condemn persons who had died in peace with the Church, who had not been condemned during their lifetime. It was to this that Pope Vigilius objected when he refused to sign the condemnation of Theodore of Mopsuestia, while agreeing to denounce his writings in which he detected Nestorianism. In pronouncing his verdict against Theodore and certain writings of Theodoret and Ibas, Justinian aimed to restore unity with those monophysite churches that still refused to recognize the Council of Chalcedon, considering it to be Nestorian. Justinian did not achieve this goal, as the monophysites held to their positions.

Justinian went down in the history of the Church as a pious emperor who strove to realize the ideal of "symphony" between church and state. This ideal is reflected in his Sixth Novella, which speaks of the priesthood and the empire as two of the greatest goods established by God, between which there should be unity and cooperation. The emperor saw the preservation of dogma and the unity of the Church as his mission, while the ordering of public life in a God-pleasing way was the Church's mission. In practice, however, his concern for dogmatic purity was expressed in his decisions on particular doctrinal questions and in his edicts, which the bishops had to sign. In essence it was a very crude form of state interference in the matters of the Church. This interference also continued with Justinian's successors, and in many respects determined the subsequent history of the Christian Church in the east.

Toward the end of his life, Justinian issued an edict in defense of the heretical teaching of Julian of Halicarnassus (d. after 518) on the incorruption of Christ's body. The main tenet of this teaching was that the body of God the Word did not undergo decay. In subsequent literature Julian's followers were called "aphthartodocetists" (those who believe in incorruption), since they were accused of believing that Christ's human nature was not complete and that the sufferings of the Savior on the cross were illusory. Patriarch Eutyches of Constantinople refused to sign Justinian's heretical edict and was exiled. Justinian's successor, Justin II (565–578), consigned the edict to oblivion.

A new wave of christological disputes arose during the reign of Emperor Heraclius (610–641), who went down in history as one of the most brilliant Byzantine rulers, having achieved several major military and diplomatic victories in an age when Byzantium was being threatened by Persians, Arabs, and Huns. In his religious policies he pursued the same aims as Justinian, striving to bring the monophysite population of the empire to obedience. Their markedly negative attitude toward imperial authority was aggravated as a result of constant persecutions, which made them potential allies of Byzantium's enemies and threatened the safety of the empire. A new form of compromise with the monophysites was monothelitism, whose ideological predecessor was monoenergism. Without denying the presence of two natures in Christ, the monoenergists taught that in Christ the divine action had completely absorbed the human action, whereas the monothelites spoke about the absorption of Christ's human will by his divine will. Patriarch Cyrus of Alexandria, Patriarch Sergius of Constantinople, and Pope Honorius contributed to the development of monothelite doctrine. Despite his advanced years, St Sophronius, the patriarch of Jerusalem, voiced his protest against the new heresy.[2]

Heraclius' successor Constans (641–668) actively supported the monothelites. During his reign the main opponents of monothelitism were Pope Martin in the west and the Constantinople monk Maximus the Confessor in the east. Pope Martin condemned monothelitism at the Lateran Council of 649. In his writings, Maximus elaborated the teaching that Christ had two wills—one divine and one human—as well as two actions. But in contrast to others, who held that the presence of a will necessitates a choice between good and evil, Christ's human will was always directed toward the good and was therefore in harmony with the divine will. The two wills and two actions in Christ were in a state of "interpenetration" (*perichoresis*). For their confession of the doctrine of Christ's two wills both confessors—Pope Martin and St Maximus—were subjected to repressions by Emperor Constans, who had sided with the heretics. Pope Martin was arrested and taken to Constantinople, where he was tried in 655 and banished; in the same year he died in exile in Cherson. At the same time Maximus the Confessor was condemned and exiled. In 662 Maximus was brought to the capital, condemned once again,

[2]Vladimir Lossky, *Dogmatic Theology* (Moscow, 1991), 274.

subjected to flagellation, and had his hand and tongue cut off, after which he was sent into exile, passing away soon thereafter.

However, the Sixth Ecumenical Council, convened in 680–681 during the rule of Constantine Pogonatus (654–685), condemned monothelitism and issued the following doctrinal statement: "[W]e likewise declare that in him are two natural wills and two natural operations, indivisible, inconvertible, inseparable, unconfused, according to the teaching of the holy fathers. These two natural wills do not contradict each other (God forbid!), as the impious heretics assert. His human will does not contradict or oppose, but follows, or rather, obeys his divine and omnipotent will." When the emperor placed his signature under this definition, the bishops present exclaimed: "Many years to the emperor! You have elucidated the perfection of the two natures of Christ our God! You have cast out all heretics!"[3] The victory of Orthodoxy was once again sealed by the emperor.

THE ICONOCLASTIC CONTROVERSY

The last great debate during the age of the ecumenical councils took place during the eighth and ninth centuries, when Byzantium went from being a powerful empire to a small state threatened from different sides by Arabs and barbarians. The subject of the debate was the veneration of icons, which was opposed by Emperor Leo the Isaurian (716–741). In 726 and 730 he issued edicts forbidding their veneration.[4] Pope Gregory II and Patriarch Germanus of Constantinople refused to obey the emperor, and in 727 Gregory convened a council in Rome that confirmed the veneration of icons. For refusing to sign the edict Patriarch Germanus was deposed and exiled; his place was taken by the iconoclast patriarch Anastasius (730–753). The most aggressive phase of iconoclasm was during the reign of Constantine Copronymus (741–770), who went down in history as a cruel persecutor of the venerators of icons. In 754 the emperor held a council in Constantinople at which 338 bishops signed an iconoclastic *horos*. After the council fierce persecutions were unleashed, particularly on monasticism, which, unlike the episcopate,

---

[3]M.E. Posnov, *History of the Christian Church (up to the Separation of the Churches – 1055)* (Brussels, 1964), 454.

[4]Some scholars hold that there was only one edict, in 730.

firmly upheld the veneration of icons. Many monks became confessors and martyrs.

The ideological motives for iconoclasm have not been fully understood. Perhaps it was inspired by Islam, which had grown stronger at the time and which forbade images of people, allowing only depictions of beasts and birds, as well as ornamental painting. Among the simple people there were instances where the veneration of sacred things was abused and where believers endowed icons with magical powers. Thus, icons were made godparents at baptisms, and paint scraped from icons was mixed with the wine used for the eucharist. However, iconoclasm rejected not only these abuses, but also the very idea of sacred images of God the Word, the Theotokos, and the saints. The iconoclasts explained the inadmissibility of depicting Christ by the fact that Christ was both God and man, and that only his human nature could be depicted. Iconoclasts also appealed to the Old Testament prohibition of images and the worship of idols (Ex 20.4–5).

One of the ideological opponents of iconoclasm was St John of Damascus (c. 676–c. 754), who wrote three treatises against the iconoclasts soon after the appearance of the edict of 726. In them he demonstrated that the Old Testament tradition did not allow images of God since God was invisible; but after God became visible by taking on human flesh, it is possible and indeed necessary to depict him. The veneration of icons has nothing in common with idolatry since the veneration (*proskynesis*) offered to the material image rises to the immaterial prototype, to whom adoration (*latreia*) is rendered.

John of Damascus

> Of old, God the incorporeal and formless was never depicted, but now that God has been seen in the flesh and has associated with human kind, I depict what I have seen of God. I do not venerate matter, I venerate the fashioner of matter, who became matter for my sake and accepted to dwell in matter and through matter worked my salvation, and I will not cease from reverencing matter, through which my salvation was worked.[5]

---

[5]John of Damascus *First Treatise on the Divine Images* 16, in Andrew Louth, trans., *Three Treatises on the Divine Images* (Crestwood, NY: SVS Press, 2003), 29.

The teaching of John of Damascus formed the basis of the dogmatic definition of the Seventh Ecumenical Council, held in 787 during the reign of Empress Irene (775–802). The council decreed:

> we keep unchanged all the ecclesiastical traditions handed down to us, whether in writing or verbally, one of which is the making of iconic representations, which is in keeping with the preaching of the gospel and which are used to assure us of the true, and not imagined, incarnation of God the Word . . . just like the figure of the precious and life-giving Cross, we define that the holy icons, whether in color, mosaic, or some other material, should be exhibited in the holy churches of God, on sacred vessels and liturgical vestments, on walls and furnishings, in houses and along roads, namely the icons of our Lord, God and Savior Jesus Christ, that of our Lady the Theotokos, those of the venerable angels and those of all saintly people. For the more frequently these representations are contemplated, the more often we who contemplate them remember and love their prototype, honor them with a kiss and bows of veneration, but not with real worship, which according to our faith is proper only for the divine nature. We venerate these with the veneration we accord to the figure of the precious and life-giving Cross, the book of the gospels and other holy objects, through incense and the lighting of candles, according to the ancient pious custom. For the honor paid to the image passes on to that which the image represents, and he who reveres the image reveres the person represented in it.[6]

After the Seventh Ecumenical Council, persecutions of the iconodules (those who venerated icons) were renewed during the time of Emperor Leo V the Armenian (813–820). In 815 he had Patriarch Nicephorus of Constantinople deposed and replaced with the iconoclast Theodotus Kassiteras. A council of bishops was convoked to condemn the Seventh Ecumenical Council and recognize the council of 754, which had denounced the veneration of icons. Thereafter persecutions against the iconodules became even more widespread than during the reign of Constantine Copronymus. The main opponent of the iconoclasts after Patriarch Nicephorus' deposition was an abbot of the Stoudios monastery in Constantinople, St Theodore the Studite, who held a procession with icons on Palm Sunday in 815 in which

---

[6]Cited in Leonid Ouspensky, *The Theology of the Icon in the Orthodox Church* (Paris, 1989), 102.

approximately one thousand monks took part. Theodore was exiled, and dozens of bishops and monks were banished, tortured, or executed. The persecutions continued during the rule of Emperors Michael II (820–829) and Theophilus (829–842).

The age of iconoclasm ended with the death of Emperor Theophilus. In 843 his wife Theodora ended the persecution and had the confessors of iconodulism returned from exile. The patriarchal see of Constantinople was occupied by St Methodius (†847), who had suffered during the persecutions. On the first Sunday of Great Lent, on March 11, 843, the restoration of icon veneration was solemnly proclaimed in Hagia Sophia. Since then, and even today, the Orthodox Church celebrates the Triumph of Orthodoxy on this day.

The iconoclastic controversy was not simply a debate about the decorative aspect of church life, and was not a dispute about ritual. Iconoclasm threatened the entire spiritual life of the Christian Church in the east, which had been formed over the course of seven centuries. As Leonid Ouspensky writes:

> Iconoclasm was connected with the overall increase of laxity in the Church, the dechurching of all aspects of its life. Its internal life was forcibly disrupted by the intrusion of secular authorities, churches were flooded with worldly images, and the divine services were distorted by worldly music and poetry. Therefore, in defending icons, the Church not only defended the very basis of Christian faith, namely the incarnation, but also the very sense of its existence. It fought against its own dissolution into the world.[7]

Because of this, the victory of the Church over iconoclasm was not simply a victory over a particular heresy: it was a victory for Orthodoxy as such.[8]

During the age of iconoclasm Christianity's first theological "encounter" with Islam, a new religion that had emerged in the Arabian steppes, took place. The founder of this religion, Muhammad, died in 632. However, his followers continued the military campaign begun by him and established an Arabian caliphate on territories seized from the Persians and Byzantines, which by the middle of the seventh century included Persia, Palestine, Syria, and Egypt. Byzantium had felt the military might of Islam as early as during

[7]Ibid., 111.
[8]Ibid., 113.

the reign of Emperor Heraclius; however, it was only during the age of icon-oclasm that Byzantium began to reflect on Islam as a religious phenomenon. One of the first Byzantine theologians to devote attention to Islam was St John of Damascus, who included Islam in the list of Christian heresies that he compiled:

> There is also a wandering people which to this day prevails, a forerunner of the Antichrist and shadow of the Ishmaelites. They are descended from Ishmael, who was born to Abraham of Agar, which is why they are called both Agarenes and Ishmaelites . . . They used to be idolaters and wor-shiped the morning star and Aphrodite, whom in their own language they called *Khabar*, which means "great." And so until the time of Heraclius they were great idolaters; from that time to the present a false prophet named Muhammad has appeared in their midst. Having come across the Old and New Testaments and, so it seems, having conversed with an Arian monk, this man invented his own heresy. Having won the favor of the people by his show of piety he indulges in empty talk, saying that a certain book had been sent down to him from heaven. After writing down some ridiculous fabrications in this book of his, he gave it to them as an object of veneration.[9]

In this excerpt St John probably had in mind the traditional Arab greet-ing "Allah akbar," interpreting it as worship of Aphrodite.[10] Although he par-aphrases several chapters from the Koran in what follows, his knowledge of Islam was on the whole superficial. In another writing entitled *Conversation between a Christian and a Saracen*, St John once again engages in polemics with Islam. In this work, Islam is presented as a distortion of Christianity rather than as an independent religion requiring serious study.

The Significance of the Ecumenical Councils in the History of Christianity

The significance of the age of the ecumenical councils for the Christian Church lies, first and foremost, in the fact that Orthodox doctrine was given

[9] *On Heresies* 101.
[10] Meyendorff, *Introduction*, 373.

its definitive formulation during this time. The process of establishing and developing dogma began as early as apostolic times, and in St Paul's epistles we can find all the basic elements of Christian theology, such as the doctrine on Christ as the Son of God and the teaching on the Church. This continued in the writings of the apostolic fathers and the church fathers and teachers of the second and third centuries. But it was at the ecumenical councils of the fourth century that the Orthodox teaching on the Trinity received its final form, and it was during the christological disputes from the fifth to the seventh centuries that Orthodox christology was definitively laid down. Finally, the iconoclastic controversy completed the development of Orthodox theology during the first eight centuries of the Church's existence.

Despite all the negative events that accompanied them, despite the interference of emperors and the court, despite church intrigues, and despite the mutual excommunications and schisms that sometimes followed, the ecumenical councils were moments of victory for the truth of the Church. The doctrinal definitions of the ecumenical councils began with words "it seemed good to the Holy Spirit and to us," pointing to the joint activity (synergy) of the Holy Spirit and people in the formulation of dogma. Thus, the dogmas of the ecumenical councils have always been recognized as divinely inspired and not subject to revision in the Orthodox Church. Although all seven ecumenical councils took place in the east, representatives of the western Church—namely, the legates of the Roman pontiff—participated in them, and the dogmatic decisions of the councils were approved by the Church in the west. Thus, the eastern Church made a decisive contribution to shaping the theology of the entire ecumenical Church.

Each ecumenical council was an answer to a heresy that shook the Church in a particular historical period of its existence. Because of this, it can be said that heresies became the driving force in the development of Orthodox theology. It was in response to heresies that challenged the Church, its teachings, and its spiritual life that theologians found the precise formulations that were to form the basis of Orthodox dogmatic tradition.

Orthodox canon law also took shape during the age of the ecumenical councils. In addition to dogmatic questions, each council examined disciplinary matters and issued canonical decrees. In this way was laid the foundation of the Church's canonical tradition, which has remained the same ever since. Canons have survived from the first four ecumenical councils and from the seventh council. As for the fifth and sixth councils, they did not issue canonical decrees; a special council—the so-called "Quinisext Council"—was convoked in Constantinople in 692 to deal with canonical questions. In addition to the statutes of the ecumenical councils, the canon law of the Orthodox Church includes canons of several local councils, including those whose dogmatic positions were not accepted by the Church (namely the Councils of Gangra [c. 340] and Antioch [341]).

Church-state relations were also defined during the age of the ecumenical councils. From Emperor Constantine's times, these relations were complex. Although the principle of "symphony" between church and state had been formulated already during Constantine's reign, it received its final form with Justinian and was confirmed in the *Epanagoge*, compiled at the end of the ninth century on behalf of Emperor Basil I (†886) and his sons. This document describes the emperor and patriarch as equals. According to it, the emperor must be "of the highest perfection in Orthodoxy and piety," "versed in the dogmas concerning the Holy Trinity and in the definitions concerning salvation through the incarnation of our Lord Jesus Christ." Regarding the patriarch, it states that he must speak to the emperor without fear about the truth and the protection of dogmas, and that only he "must interpret the maxims of the ancients, the definitions of the holy fathers, and the statutes of the holy councils."[11] In practice, however, this "symphony" was always dictated by the emperor, and not the patriarch, and the emperor imposed his will on the Church. This was true not only with regard to disciplinary matters but also dogma. If the emperor took the side of Orthodoxy, the bishops could sign his edicts with a clean conscience; but if the emperor was inclined to heresy, difficult times awaited the Church, and those who disagreed with the emperor's will were repressed or executed.

Unfortunately, however, throughout the history of Byzantium the bishops agreed only too frequently with the emperor, even when their consciences should have caused them to demonstrate civil disobedience. Moreover, the same bishops signed both heretical and Orthodox decisions. The number of such opportunist bishops is striking: 135 bishops took part in the "robber" council of 449, and 338 were present at the iconoclast council of 754. Many of those who had signed Orthodox doctrinal definitions at Orthodox councils also signed the heretical documents of the "robber" councils.

[11]Cited in Schmemann, *Historical Road*, 215.

The opposite was also true: those who had succumbed to pressure from heretics repented at the Orthodox councils. This opportunism of the church hierarchy, which became particularly apparent during the iconoclast controversy, caused the authority of bishops to diminish in the eyes of simple believers, and contributed to an increase in the authority of monastics. In many instances when hierarchs failed to fulfil the demands of their lofty position, it was the monks who were entrusted with the mission of protecting Orthodoxy (suffice it to recall Maximus the Confessor, John of Damascus, and Theodore the Studite).

What has been the canonical status of ecumenical councils in the history of the Church? Among the Orthodox there is a widespread opinion that the ecumenical council is the highest authority in the Church, to which local councils and the first hierarchs of local Orthodox churches are subject. Some see the difference between the western and eastern churches in the fact that the Roman pontiff is considered to be the highest authority in the west, while in the east this authority rests with the ecumenical council. This understanding does not correspond to historical reality. Ecumenical councils were never seen as the supreme authority in the Orthodox Church. For the almost three centuries before the convocation of the First Ecumenical Council, the Church had no conception of such a council. And during the twelve centuries that have elapsed since the end of the Seventh Ecumenical Council, the Orthodox Church has survived without one. The basic role of the ecumenical councils from the fourth to the seventh centuries consisted in the refutation of particular heresies that shook the Orthodox world at a given moment. One should not think that the Christian Church in the fourth through eighth centuries lived "from council to council," since ecumenical councils were held irregularly, with intervals of twenty, fifty, one hundred or more years. Whenever necessary each local church, be it in Rome, Constantinople, Antioch, Caesarea in Cappadocia, or another city, resolved–without waiting until the convocation of an ecumenical council–the problems facing them at local councils, which took decisions that became obligatory for them.

It should also be noted that the ecumenical councils were not "ecumenical" in the literal sense. The word *oikoumene* ("universe") mainly signified the Roman empire; those churches located on the outskirts of the empire or beyond its limits, such as the Armenian Church or the Church of the East, did not, as a rule, participate in the ecumenical councils. Over time these churches took a stance—positive or negative—on the ecumenical councils at their own local councils. The decisions of ecumenical councils did not become obligatory for churches until their own local councils had affirmed the former's resolutions. Thus, it was the local council of each church, and not the ecumenical council, that was the final and highest authority on fundamental dogmatic and canonical questions. It goes without saying that the views of other churches were considered, but only to the extent that they did not contradict the particular church's own position.

Thus, the notion of reception is essential to answering the question of the significance of the ecumenical councils for the Christian Church. History shows that they were not received passively or automatically by the local churches. On the contrary, it was left to the churches to decide the fate of each council, to accept or reject it, to accept it as an ecumenical or local council, to accept all of its decisions or only some. The process of reception called for an active discussion of the councils and their decisions within each local church. For this very reason the reception of some councils was a painful process, accompanied by intense disputes, popular unrest, and the interference of civil authorities. Moreover, the recognition of a council assumed not only the official promulgation of its teaching by the ecclesiastical authorities, but also its acceptance among theologians, monastics, and laymen. The totality of the church community was involved in the process of reception.

Secondary factors were often involved in this process, with national and linguistic considerations sometimes influencing the acceptance of councils by a local church. For example, not all dogmatic formulations by Greek-speaking churches were adequately translated into Latin or the national languages of some regions of the east (e.g., Coptic, Ethiopian, Syriac, Arabic, and Armenian), leading to dissent and misunderstandings that caused schisms. The process of reception was also influenced by political factors, such as national resistance to Byzantine ecclesiastical and political domination in Egypt, Armenia, and Syria from the fourth through sixth centuries. Finally, personal factors also influenced reception: in those cases where the teaching of a particular hierarch became the teaching of an ecumenical council, theologians and bishops who were his personal enemies or were dissatisfied with his activities attempted to shape popular opinion within their church, so that the decisions of the council were not accepted.

Thus, the reception of the ecumenical councils was a gradual process that required much time and was influenced by very diverse factors. The final criterion for the acceptance or rejection of an ecumenical council was not the fact of its convocation, but the consensus regarding its "acceptance," which was achieved only later, when the local churches handed down their verdict on a particular council. For example, the Nicene (First Ecumenical) Council of 325, which condemned Arianism, was not recognized unanimously by all churches of the Roman empire until the Council of Constantinople of 381 (Second Ecumenical Council). In some churches the reception of the Nicene Council took even longer. Thus, the Church of the East accepted this council only eighty-five years later, at a local council in Seleucia-Ctesiphon in 410. The Council of Ephesus of 449 displayed all the characteristics of an ecumenical council, yet the Orthodox churches rejected its decisions, and the Council of Chalcedon of 451 (Fourth Ecumenical Council) declared it a "robber council." The iconoclast council of 754 also had all the hallmarks of an ecumenical council, but was later rejected by the churches.

The role of the Roman Church in the history of the ecumenical councils has yet to be fully elucidated. All seven ecumenical councils took place in the east, and the Roman pontiffs did not take part in them personally, opting instead to send legates. Even when the pope happened to be in the city where a council was being held, he did not participate in the council sessions (as was the case with Pope Vigilius, who was in Constantinople during the convocation of the Fifth Ecumenical Council). After the council the legates informed the pope about the dogmatic decisions taken, and he confirmed them. Canonical decisions were confirmed by the pope selectively. For example, Pope Leo the Great protested against canon 28 of the Council of Chalcedon, which granted the bishop of Constantinople the same rights as those of the Roman bishop; during the council this canon was disputed by his legates. In the eyes of the western Church it was the pope's confirmation of a council's decisions that gave it legitimacy. In the eastern Church the process of reception was more complex, and papal recognition of a council was not viewed as a necessary condition for its legitimacy.

The reception of the ecumenical councils among Christians throughout the world has not been completed even today. The Assyrian Church of the East recognizes only two ecumenical councils, the "pre-Chalcedonian" churches only three. The Roman Catholic Church, unlike these, also considers the following councils to be ecumenical: the Council of Constantinople of 869–870; the Lateran Councils of 1123, 1139, 1179, and 1215; the Council of Lyons of 1245 and 1274; the Council of Vienna of 1311; the Council of Constance of 1414–1418; the Council of Basel of 1431; the Council of Ferrara-Florence of 1439; the Lateran Council of 1512–1516; the Tridentine Council of 1545–1563; and the Vatican Councils of 1869–1870 and 1962–1965–a total of twenty-two councils.

The question of one's stance on the ecumenical councils is on the agenda of contemporary inter-Christian dialogue. But for the Orthodox Church seven ecumenical councils from the fourth to the eighth centuries remain the foundation on which its theology, canonical tradition, and liturgical life are based.

Theological Literature of the Age of the Ecumenical Councils

The age of the ecumenical councils was the most productive period of theological thought in the history of the Christian Church of the east. The church fathers honored in Orthodox tradition as "universal teachers and hierarchs" lived and wrote in this time. The most authoritative theologians of this period were Athanasius the Great, Basil the Great, Gregory the Theologian, Gregory of Nyssa, Cyril of Alexandria, Theodoret of Cyrus, Maximus the Confessor, and John of Damascus. A special case is the author of the works that have been preserved under the name of Dionysius the Areopagite.

St Athanasius of Alexandria was present at the First Ecumenical Council as a deacon accompanying his bishop, Alexander of Alexandria. After Alexander's death Athanasius became his successor and occupied the see of Alexandria for almost half a century (with four interruptions). Athanasius is the author of a large number of dogmatic, ascetic, and moral writings. In his *Against the Heathen*, Athanasius criticizes Greek mythology and defends Christianity from attacks of the pagans, thus continuing a tradition begun by the apologists of the second and third centuries. In his homily *On the Incarnation*, Athanasius expounds the dogma of redemption within the context of polemics with Arianism. His *Against the Arians*, the epistle *On the Holy Spirit*, and several other epistles and homilies are characterized by their anti-Arian orientation. Athanasius also wrote several exegetical works, as well as the *Life of St Anthony*—the first work of Christian hagiography, which exerted enormous influence on all subsequent hagiographic literature. This work honored St Anthony the Great, an ascetic of the Egyptian desert and contemporary of Athanasius.

Athanasius' main contribution in the area of dogma was his refutation of the Arian heresy and formulation of Orthodox teaching on the consubstantiality of the Father, Son, and Holy Spirit. In his works he developed the teaching on redemption and the deification of man accomplished by Jesus Christ. Speaking of the incarnation of Christ, Athanasius writes:

> [The Word] assumed humanity that we might become God. He manifested himself by means of a body in order that we might perceive the mind of the unseen Father. He endured shame from men that we might inherit immortality. He himself was unhurt by this, for he is impassible and incorruptible; but by his own impassibility he kept and healed the suffering men on whose account he thus endured. In short, such and so many are the Savior's achievements that follow from his incarnation, that to try to number them is like gazing at the open sea and trying to count the waves.[12]

St Basil the Great (c. 330–379) went down in history as an untiring defender of Orthodoxy at a time when Arianism had spread throughout the entire Christian east. He received an outstanding education at the Academy in Athens, the main pagan educational institution of the eastern Roman empire. He was baptized as an adult and then became a priest. In 370 he was elected archbishop of Caesarea in Cappadocia, where he had fifty bishops under him, the majority of which had Arian sympathies. Basil was decisive in his defense of the Orthodox faith, and when the imperial prefect Modestus began to threaten him with punishment and torture, he answered:

St Basil the Great

[12]*On the Incarnation* 54, A Religious of C.S.M.V., trans. (Crestwood, NY: SVS Press, 1953), 93.

He who has nothing cannot be subject to the seizure of property, except for this hair shirt or the several books in which my entire wealth consists. I do not know of exile because I am not confined to any place, and the place where I live now is not my own; and any place where I might be taken will become my own. It would be better to say: every place is God's place, where I will be a wanderer and newcomer. And what can tortures do to me, who has no body? . . . . For me death is a blessing since it will take me to God, for whom I live and act.[13]

Struck by Basil's boldness, the prefect informed Emperor Valens of his unbending resolve. Valens, who had exiled many Orthodox bishops, decided not to have Basil replaced. Basil died at the age of forty-nine.

Among his dogmatic works is the treatise *Against Eunomius*, in which Basil refutes the idea that the quality of not being born is the essence of God. The treatise *On the Holy Spirit* contains an exposition of Orthodox pneumatology; in it Basil avoids calling the Holy Spirit God and "consubstantial" with the Father and Son, preferring the more neutral term "equal in honor." Basil was the author of a large number of exegetical writings, of which the most famous is his *Hexaemeron*, an interpretation of the account of creation from the first chapter of the book of Genesis. Basil also penned fifteen homilies on the psalms and twenty-eight homilies on dogmatic and moral themes. One of these is entitled *Address to Young Men, on the Right Use of Greek Literature*; in it Basil instructs Christian youth on the correct attitude toward secular literature. Basil's corpus of ascetic writings includes the *Moral Rules*, addressed to all Christians, as well two collections of rules for ascetics, which formed the basis of subsequent monastic rules—the *Longer Rules* and the *Shorter Rules*. Extant are more than three hundred of his letters, which were collected by his disciples and which were devoted to ascetic, moral, and practical questions. Finally, Orthodox tradition attributes to Basil the text of a liturgy that is celebrated ten times a year—on his feast day, on the eves of the Nativity of Christ and Theophany, on all Sundays of Great Lent, and on Great Thursday and Saturday.

St Gregory the Theologian was a friend of Basil the Great; both had studied at the Athens Academy. Like Basil, Gregory was baptized at approximately the age of thirty. Striving for seclusion and wishing to devote his life

---

[13]Cited by Gregory of Nazianzus *Orations* 43.49.

to literary endeavors, Gregory avoided ordination to the priesthood, but finally submitted to the will of his father, the aged bishop of Nazianzus, and assisted him in governing the Church. Basil the Great consecrated Gregory bishop of Sasima, but Gregory did not go there, remaining instead in Nazianzus and continuing his literary work. In 379 he was invited to Constantinople, where he led a group of adherents of the Nicene faith. Emperor Theodosius, who banished the Arians from Constantinople in 380, confirmed Gregory as archbishop of Constantinople. However, he was ousted from this see at the Second Ecumenical Council and ended his days in seclusion.

St Gregory the Theologian

Gregory's literary opus includes forty-five orations—sermons rewritten in a literary manner. Of these, the most well-known are his Five Theological Orations, which contain a classic exposition of the Orthodox doctrine on the Trinity. It was for this work that he received the title "Theologian," which came into use long ago in Orthodox tradition. His two homilies against Julian the Apostate, polemic in character, were written after the death of the impious emperor. The *Panegyric to Basil the Great* is among the best works of this genre; in it Gregory expresses his respect and love for his best friend, teacher, and elder brother in Christ. Several homilies were devoted to church feasts and the memory of martyrs and saints. Gregory also penned a large number of poems, most of which are of an autobiographical or didactic nature. Gregory was the first Byzantine author to collect and edit his own letters; these letters are varied in content and were addressed to different people, including bishops, civil servants, and friends.

Gregory the Theologian was the most authoritative, popular, and frequently cited author during the entire life of the Byzantine empire: on the "scale of frequency of citation" his works were second only to the Bible.[14] Many expressions and entire fragments from his festal homilies entered the liturgical texts of the Orthodox Church. The words of the Easter service, "The

[14]Cf. J. Noret, "Grégoire de Nazianze, l'auteur le plus cité, après la Bible, dans la littérature ecclesiastique byzantine," in Justin Mossay, ed., *II Symposium Nazianzenum* (Paderborn-München-Wien-Zürich, 1983), 259–66.

day of resurrection, let us be radiant, O people! Pascha, the Lord's Pascha,"
"the Feast of Feasts and the Festival of Festivals," "The day of resurrection; let
us be radiant for the festival, and let us embrace one another. Let us say,
brethren, even to those that hate us, 'Let us forgive all things by the resurrection,'" are direct quotations from Gregory's Easter sermons. The words
"Christ is born, glorify him! Christ comes from the heavens, meet him!
Christ is upon the earth, be exalted!," were borrowed from his Christmas
homily, and "We celebrate Pentecost and the coming of the Holy Spirit" is
from his homily on Pentecost.

In speaking of God, Gregory asserts that man cannot know God as he
knows himself: he can only know about God through Christ and by contemplating the visible world. God's essence is inscrutable for the human mind.
For Gregory, the knowledge of God is a path that transcends the limits of what
can be grasped by the human mind, while for Eunomius it was a movement
within the boundaries of discursive thinking. Reason can bring a person to
accept the existence of God, but it can in no way penetrate God's essence. In
expressing this idea, Gregory polemicizes not only with Eunomius, but also
with the "theologian" of Greek antiquity, Plato, citing the latter's famous
maxim, which many Christian authors had referred to before Gregory:

> "It is difficult to comprehend God, and impossible to speak of him," as
> one of the Greek theologians wrote . . .[15] But I say: it is impossible to
> speak of him, and even more impossible to comprehend him. For that
> which has been comprehended can be expressed in words—if not fully,
> then at least approximately—to those whose ears have not been damaged
> for good and whose reason has not been completely dulled. It is totally
> impossible to grasp such a reality with the mind, and this not only for
> those who wallow in laziness and are inclined to the earth, but also for
> those who are noble and love God . . . This nature cannot be contained
> and is inscrutable. I call inscrutable not the fact that God exists, but that
> which he is.[16]

God remains outside the human categories of time, place, words, and reason, and therefore cannot be expressed through the medium of human language, as Gregory emphasizes:

[15]Cf. Plato *Timaeus* 28c: "One cannot search for the Creator and cause of this universe; if we do
find him, we will not be able to speak about him to everyone else."

[16]*Orations* 28.4.

God always was, is, and will be; or rather, he always "is." For the words "was" and "will be" are taken from our temporal distinctions and from transient nature, but he who is always is, and this is how he called himself when speaking with Moses on the mountain. For he possesses total existence and unites it in himself, having neither beginning nor end. Like an ocean of essence, boundless and without limit, he transcends all notions of time and nature, and can only be outlined by the mind—and this in a very unclear and incomplete manner, and not himself but that which is around him, when one tries to piece together different ideas about him into one semblance of truth, which escapes before it is caught and slips away before it is comprehended . . . Thus, God is infinite and difficult to contemplate, and there is only one thing that is completely comprehensible about him—his infinity.[17]

At the heart of Gregory's theology lies his teaching on the Holy Trinity, whom he often calls "my Trinity," underscoring the personal, almost intimate character of his relationship with God. He speaks of the Father, Son, and Holy Spirit as a single Godhead and single Power:

First and foremost preserve the good thing that was committed to you (2 Tim 1.14), for which I live and rejoice, which I would like to have at the end of my life, by which I endure all tribulations and despise all that is pleasant, namely the confession of the Father, Son, and Holy Spirit. And now I entrust this good thing to you; with it I will immerse you in the font and raise you from it. I give it to you as your helper and defender for your entire life—the one Godhead and the one Power, which . . . does not increase and does not decrease . . . [w]hich is equal everywhere, everywhere one and the same, like one beauty and the one grandeur of the sky. It is the infinite shared nature of the three infinite ones, so that each of them seen individually is God . . . but also the three examined together are also God: the former because of their consubstantiality, the latter because there is one source of life.[18]

Another theme of Gregory's works is the salvation and deification of man accomplished by the incarnate Word. Although earlier church writers had written on deification, with Gregory it became the focal point of his entire

[17]*Orations* 38.7.
[18]*Orations* 40.41.

theological discourse. According to him, the path to deification lies in the Church and the sacraments, particularly baptism and the eucharist, as well as in love for God, good deeds, the ascetic way of life, prayer, and communion with God. The path to deification begins during a person's earthly life and is completed after death. Deification is the crowning and the summit of the knowledge of God:

> if it has been purified, [God] enlightens our mind as quickly as lightning illuminates our eyes. Perhaps he does this in order to attract others by that which can be comprehended—since that which is absolutely incomprehensible is hopelessly inaccessible, and in order to instill a sense of wonder by that which is incomprehensible, through this wonder to awaken a greater desire, through this desire to purify, and through this purification to make us godlike. When we have been brought to such a state we converse with God as we do with those dear to us, so let our words be bold! We converse with God, who has united himself with gods and is known by them—perhaps to the same extent as he knows those who have been known by him (1 Cor 13.12).[19]

Gregory the Theologian's poetic legacy is extensive and diverse. His poetry is mostly imitative, making use of ancient meters based on the alternation of short and long syllables. Among his works in this genre are a poetic narration of gospel passages, reflections on theological and moral themes, epigrams and funeral orations, as well as prayers and denunciations of enemies and offenders. Some poems are autobiographical; of these perhaps the most interesting is the one entitled "About My Life," which contains an extensive autobiography. Although pessimism predominates in his later poems, they are nevertheless permeated by deep religious feeling:

> Yesterday, worn out with anxieties, away from others
> I was in a shady grove, my soul consumed.
> For how I do so love this drug for sufferings,
> to speak in quiet, me with my own soul.
> And the breezes whispered while the birds sang,
> granting from the branches a sound slumber,
> though for a soul quite weary. While, from the trees,

---

[19] *Orations* 38.7.

deep chanting, clear-toned, lovers of the sun,
whirring locusts made the whole wood to resound.
Nearby flowed cold water by one's feet . . .
But privately, my mind in a whirlpool spinning,
I had this sort of battling round of words:
Who was I? Who am I? What shall I be? I don't know clearly.
Nor can I find one better stocked with wisdom . . .
I am. Think: what does this mean? Something of me's gone by,
something I'm now completing, another thing I'll be . . .
Now, we've heard of places free of wild beasts, as Crete was once,
and places strangers to cold wind-borne clouds;
but no one among mortals has ever made this boast, that,
unvanquished, he has left life's hateful pains.
Feebleness, poverty, birth, death, enmity, rogues,
Sea-beasts and land beasts, sufferings: all this is life.
I have known many woes and utter unhappiness,
But of good things, nothing wholly free from pain,
From the time that that bitter price got wiped on me
by the destroying taste, and the adversary's spite.[20]

St Gregory of Nyssa (c. 335–c.394) was one of the most profound and original thinkers in the history of Christianity. The younger brother of Basil the
Great, he considered himself the latter's student, and some of Gregory's
works were conceived as the continuation of Basil's unfinished works. For
example, the treatise *On the Creation of Man*, which contains an exposition of
Christian anthropology, is a sequel to Basil's *Hexaemeron*, and *Against
Eunomius* continues Basil's work of the same name.

Gregory of Nyssa was the most fruitful writer of three great Cappadocians, and his literary output is extremely broad and diverse. In addition to
the above-mentioned works, it includes the exegetical treatise *On the Life of
Moses the Lawgiver*, which interprets the book of Exodus as an allegory of
Christian mystical experience. The allegorical method, which Gregory inherited from Origen, is also employed in other exegetical works such as the *Homilies on the Song of Songs*, which interprets this biblical book as an allegory of
the spiritual marriage of the human soul and the Church with Christ, the

---

[20]*Poems* 1.2.14, "On Human Nature," in Peter Gilbert, trans., *On God and Man: The Theological
Poetry of St Gregory of Nazianzus* (Crestwood, NY: SVS Press, 2001), 132–34.

St Gregory of Nyssa

Bridegroom; the *Exact Interpretation of Ecclesiastes of Solomon*; and his homilies *On the Epigraphs of the Psalms*. Gregory also uses the allegorical method in his theory of the knowledge of God, which, according to his teaching, comprises three stages: purification from the passions (catharsis); the acquisition of "natural vision," which makes it possible to clearly see and understand the created world; and finally the knowledge of God proper, the vision of God, or communion with God face to face. An allegorical image of this path is the biblical account of Moses' ascent of Sinai: this began with the removal of his sandals, which symbolizes the liberation from all that is passionate and sinful, and concluded with his entrance into darkness, which symbolizes the renunciation of all discursive thought and immersion in the "incontemplatibility of the divine nature."[21]

As a teacher of dogmatic theology, Gregory of Nyssa held the same views as Basil the Great and Gregory the Theologian, refuting Eunomianism and defending the consubstantiality of the Father, Son, and Holy Spirit. His dogmatic writings, in addition to the treatise *Against Eunomius*, include the *Epistle to Ablabius, That There Are Not Three Gods*, two books *Against Apollinarius, On the Holy Spirit, Against the Macedonian Pneumatomachoi, On the Holy Trinity, To Eustathius*, the epistle to Simplicius *On Faith*, and the treatise *To the Greeks, on the Basis of General Concepts*. In his *Great Catechetical Homily* Gregory systematically expounds the fundamental dogmas of Christianity—the Trinity, the incarnation, and redemption—and the sacraments of the Church. The homily also contains eschatological reflections that were further developed in the treatise *On the Soul and the Resurrection*. Dogmatic questions are also examined in *Concerning Infants Who Have Died Prematurely* and *On Fate*.

Gregory of Nyssa also authored a large number of moral and ascetic writings, such as *On Virginity and Perfection, On Perfection*, and *How a Monk Should Be*. The treatise *On the Life of Macrina*, dedicated to his and Basil's sister, was written soon after her death. In the small treatise *To Armonius, on What the Name "Christian" Means*, Gregory reveals the meaning of Christianity in the following words:

[21]Cf. Meyendorff, *Introduction*, 228–33.

If one takes upon himself the name of Christ but does not practice the way of life associated with it, he falsely bears this name. Such a person is like a soulless mask with human features superimposed on a monkey. For just as Christ cannot be Christ if he is not justice, purity, the Truth, and the estrangement from all evil, so cannot he who does not demonstrate the characteristics associated with this name be a Christian. Thus, if it were necessary for someone to express the meaning of the word "Christianity" in a definition, we would say that it is the imitation of the Divine Nature.[22]

Gregory of Nyssa is well known in the history of Orthodox theological thought since he, like Origen, did not consider the torments of hell to be eternal, and allowed for the possibility of the final salvation of all, including the devil and demons. This teaching of the bishop of Nyssa should not be identified completely with Origen's version of the *apokatastasis*, which was discussed earlier.

Another outstanding church writer of the fourth century was St John Chrysostom (c. 347–407), whose literary output surpassed in quantity that of all previous Greek fathers—and possibly even Origen. Chrysostom was a brilliantly educated person, and became famous during his years of priestly service in Antioch for his sermons, for which he received the epithet "Chrysostom," or "golden mouth." In 397 he was summoned to Constantinople and elevated to the rank of archbishop. In the imperial capital his gift of teaching revealed itself fully. Chrysostom's sermons, frequently delivered while sitting in the reader's pulpit surrounded by people, attracted droves of people and were recorded by stenographers. However, the saint's popularity and the accusatory tone of his sermons provoked dissatisfaction among the episcopate and within the court, and in 403 he was deposed by a hostile council of bishops headed by Theophilus of Alexandria. Chrysostom was exiled, but was soon

St John Chrysostom

[22] *To Harmonius*, cited in Hieromonk Hilarion (Alfeyev), ed., *The Eastern Fathers and Teachers of the Church of the Fourth Century* (Moscow, 1996), 2.351.

recalled on the insistence of the people. When a silver statue of the empress was erected at the hippodrome, Chrysostom gave the famous sermon that began with the words: "Again Herodias rages, again she is confounded, again she dances, again she demands the head of John on a charger." A council was again convened, and he was exiled once more. Chrysostom died in Comana (now in the territory of Abkhazia), exhausted and forsaken by all. His last words were: "Glory be to God for all things."

A complete list of all of Chrysostom's works would require several dozen pages. Like Origen, he commented on a substantial part of the Bible; unlike Origen, however, he applied a literal, not allegorical, method of interpretation. His best-known exegetical works are the *Homilies on the Book of Genesis*, commentaries on numerous other Old Testament books, *Homilies on the Gospel according to Matthew*, *Homilies on the Gospel according to John*, and commentaries on the Acts of the Apostles and the epistles of Paul.

Among his dogmatic and polemical works are his *Against the Anomeans, on the Inscrutability of God*; *Against the Jews*; and the *Discourse against the Jews and the Heathens, that Jesus Christ is the True God*. Chrysostom's works also include many moral and ascetic homilies, sermons on church feasts and saints, panegyrics, and sermons on various occasions. Of his ascetic works, several stand out in particular: the two *Exhortations to Theodore the Fallen*, devoted to repentance and believed to have been addressed to Theodore of Mopsuestia; two treatises *On Contrition*; three epistles *To Stagirius, on Despondency*; and the book *On Virginity*. Of special interest are the *Six Homilies on the Priesthood*—along with Gregory the Theologian's third oration, it is one of the first treatises on this topic. More than two hundred letters have also been preserved. Chrysostom's name was so revered that during the Byzantine era many works actually penned by other authors were attributed to him. Finally, he is believed to have composed the liturgy that is served in the Orthodox Church daily, with the exception of weekdays during Great Lent and the ten days of the year when the Liturgy of Basil the Great is celebrated.

Chrysostom's letters to the Constantinople deaconess Olympias, written during his exile, are a testimony to his profound spiritual strength. In them the hierarch, exhausted morally and physically but unbroken in spirit, underscores the need to patiently bear sufferings and comforts Olympias, who grieved deeply over the saint's banishment:

We see that the sea stormily rises from the very bottom; some seamen sail over the surface of the water as corpses, while others have sunk to the seafloor. The ship's boards become undone, the sails are torn up, the masts are broken, the oars have dropped from the hands of the rowers. The helmsmen do not sit at the rudder but on the decks, holding their knees with their hands and sobbing all the while, crying loudly and lamenting their hopeless situation. They do not notice the sky or the sea, seeing everywhere only this profound, hopeless, and gloomy darkness that does not allow them to make out even those near them. The noisy crash of the waves is heard, and beasts of the sea rush toward the swimmers. But how long must we seek that which is unattainable? Whatever similarity I may have found to describe the present calamities, words pale in comparison with them and fall silent. And although I am aware of the entire situation I do not despair, hoping for better circumstances and remembering the Helmsman of all this, who does not prevail over storms by skill since he can stop the agitation of the sea in an instant. But if he does not do this at the very outset or immediately, it is because this is how he usually acts: he does not eliminate dangers at the beginning, but only when they have intensified and reached their final limits, and when most people have lost all hope—and then he, finally, accomplishes the wonderful and unexpected, manifesting his might and schooling in patience those exposed to dangers. Therefore, do not despair.[23]

Chrysostom went down in church history not so much as a theologian or dogmatist but an ardent preacher, a great interpreter of scripture, and a teacher of the moral and spiritual life. His sermons preserve the linguistic brilliance, vividness, freshness, beauty of thought, and moral and spiritual power that so struck his contemporaries. He was frequently compared with St Paul, whom Chrysostom himself deeply venerated—a fact testified to by his final homily from the cycle of commentaries on the Epistle to the Romans:

Who will now allow me to throw myself around Paul's body, cling to his coffin and see the remains of this body, which filled up that which was lacking in the afflictions of Christ, which bore Christ's wounds and sowed the gospel everywhere; the dust of that body in which Paul traveled through the entire world, the dust of that body through which Christ

---

[23]*Epistles to Olympias* 1.

spoke, through which a light more brilliant than any lightning shone forth, through which a voice resounded that was for the demons more terrible than any thunder . . . This voice . . . purified the universe, stopped diseases, banished vice, instilled the truth; in this voice Christ himself was present, and everywhere went about with him; and what the cherubim were, this was Paul's voice. As Christ is seated on the heavenly powers, so was he seated on Paul's tongue . . . If I could only see the dust of this mouth, through which Christ uttered great and ineffable secrets, even greater than those which he himself had proclaimed! . . . If I could only see the dust not only of Paul's mouth, but also of his heart, which can rightly be called the heart of the universe, the source of countless blessings, the beginning and element of our life! . . . His heart was Christ's heart, a tablet of the Holy Spirit and a book of grace . . . it was vouchsafed to love Christ in a way that no one else had loved.[24]

Of the theologians of the fifth century, the most important were St Cyril of Alexandria (c. 377–444) and the blessed Theodoret of Cyrus. Both authored a large number of exegetical, dogmatic, and apologetic works that have become part of the treasured legacy of Christian literature. Cyril and Theodoret represent two different schools of exegesis and christology: the Alexandrian and the Antiochian. From the times of Clement and Origen, the Alexandrian school was characterized by an allegorical interpretation of scripture, while the Antiochian was marked by its literal and moral approach. Alexandrian christology emphasized the unity of Christ's natures, while the Antiochian school underscored their difference. In both schools there were theologians who were condemned by the Church as heretics: Theodore of Mopsuestia and Nestorius among the Antiochians and Eutyches among the Alexandrians. However, both currents produced theologians who were later to be numbered among the great fathers of the Church. Preeminent among the Antiochians was John Chrysostom, and among the Alexandrians St Cyril. The victory of Alexandrian christology came at the Third Ecumenical Council, while Antiochian christology was approved by the Church at the Fourth Ecumenical Council.

However, during the period between these councils, when the struggle between the two schools was particularly intense, Cyril and Theodoret ended

---

[24]*Homily on the Epistle to the Romans* 32.3.

up on different sides of the barricades: the former came out against the heresy of Nestorius, while the latter for a long time defended Nestorius and wrote polemical works against Cyril. These works of Theodoret were condemned at the Fifth Ecumenical Council; still, all his other writings were recognized as being Orthodox, and Theodoret was canonized along with Cyril. Thus, in the consciousness of the Church, two great theologians were reconciled who could not be reconciled during their lifetimes, but who—each in his own way—defended and developed Orthodox doctrine.

A special place in the eastern Christian literature of the age of the ecumenical councils is occupied by the works attributed to Dionysius the Areopagite, which are called in the scholarly literature the Corpus Areopagiticum. Dionysius the Areopagite lived in the first century, was converted to Christianity by St Paul (Acts 17.34) and, according to tradition, was the first bishop of Athens. However, the first mention of the works attributed to him appeared in the second quarter of the sixth century, and by the middle of the sixth century these writings were widely read. Although attempts to discover the name of the real author have been repeatedly made, they have proven unsuccessful to this day. Contemporary scholarship is dominated by the view that the Corpus Areopagiticum appeared no later than the turn of the sixth century. Nevertheless, the uncertain authorship of these works does not diminish their value as an important source of Christian doctrine and as one of the most striking, profound, and significant works of Byzantine literature.

The corpus includes the following works: *On the Divine Names*, which offers a theological interpretation of the names of God; *On the Celestial Hierarchy*, containing a systematic account of Christian teaching on angels; *On the Ecclesiastical Hierarchy*, which describes the hierarchical structure of the Church and gives a mystical, allegorical interpretation of the liturgical services; and *On Mystical Theology*, which depicts the attainment of the knowledge of God as an entrance into the mystical depths of the "divine darkness." The corpus also contains ten epistles, which develop the ideas expounded in *On Mystical Theology*.

The most characteristic feature of the Areopagite's teaching is the notion of the hierarchic structure of the world and the idea that the "divine procession" (God's energies) are handed downward from God to the lower ranks of created beings. The nine ranks of the angelic hierarchy, headed by Jesus himself, flow over into the church hierarchy. This hierarchy's purpose is to bring the entire created world, including man, to a state of deification. The way to deification or the way to the knowledge of God is described in the Corpus Areopagiticum in the same way as in Gregory of Nyssa's writings, based on the biblical account of Moses' ascent of Mount Sinai. This path begins with catharsis or purification, and concludes with ecstasy, the human mind's transcending of the limits of discursive knowledge:

> For the divine Moses did not immediately hear the many-voiced trumpets, and see many lights shining pure and diverse-streaming rays, but only after purifying himself completely, since he was first bidden to cleanse himself and separate himself from those not purified. After this he left the crowd and, together with the chosen priests, attained the summit of divine ascent. But even there he did not converse with God himself and did not behold him, since he is invisible, but rather the place where he dwells. This shows, so it seems, that the most divine and highest of things contemplated and understood are only some suggestive expressions of the things subordinate to him who surpasses all things, which reveal the inconceivable presence of him who rests on the noetic summits of his most holy places. And then Moses breaks free from all that is seen and sees, and penetrates into the truly mysterious darkness of ignorance, after which he leaves behind all cognitive perception and is enwrapped in total darkness where nothing is visible, himself being wholly beyond all things, belonging neither to himself nor to anything else, uniting himself in the best sense with the inactivity that knows no knowledge and comprehending that which exceeds understanding by knowing nothing.[25]

Dionysius' teaching had an enormous impact on all aspects of church life in the east and west, including theology, liturgical services and church art. His influence can be seen in many works by St Maximus the Confessor (†662), who composed a large number of works devoted to dogmatic, moral, ascetic, and mystical themes. Among his exegetical writings are *Questions to Thallasius* and other works written as answers to difficult theological questions, such as the *Ambigua*, a collection with a Latin title that explores difficult passages in the works of Dionysius the Areopagite and Gregory the Theologian. His

---

[25] *On Mysical Theology* 1, in Hieromonk Hilarion (Alfeyev), ed., *Eastern Fathers of the Fifth Century* (Moscow, 2000), 258.

exegetical writings also include the *Commentary on Psalm 59*, the *Commentary on the Lord's Prayer*, as well as the *Scholia* on Dionysius' works, which in the Byzantine manuscript tradition has been preserved together with the Corpus Areopagiticum and mixed with commentaries by other authors (e.g., John of Scythopolis). In his many epistles, the *Dispute with Pyrrhus*, and his *Centuries on Theology and the Incarnate Dispensation of the Son of God*, Maximus deals with dogmatic questions such as the teaching on Christ's two natures, two operations and two wills. His corpus of moral and ascetic literature includes four *Centuries on Love* and a *Homily on the Ascetic Life*. Unique among his works is the *Mystagogy*, a mystical, symbolic commentary and meditation on the Church and the liturgy written in the tradition of Dionysius' *On the Ecclesiastical Hierarchy*.

A theological summary of the development of eastern Christian thought during the age of the ecumenical councils was undertaken in the writings of St John of Damascus. Among these is an extensive work entitled Fountain of Knowledge, consisting of three parts. The first is called the *Philosophical Chapters* and is basically an introduction to Aristotelian dialectics. The second part, called *Concerning Heresy*, is a compendium of all known heresies compiled on the basis of the *Panarion* of St Epiphanius of Cyprus (fifth century), with the addition of some later heresies, including, as mentioned above, Islam. The third part of the book is the best known, and is entitled *An Exact Exposition of the Orthodox Faith*—a concise exposition of Christian dogma. Of St John's other dogmatic works, the most significant are the three treatises *On the Divine Images*, which became the manifesto of the iconodules during the age of iconoclasm, as well as a number of treatises against the Jacobites, monophysites, monothelites, and Manichaeans. He also wrote several sermons on church feast days and compiled the *Sacred Parallels*, a collection of sayings of various authors on theological and moral questions. John of Damascus also went down in church history as an outstanding hymnographer: he is credited with authoring many texts that are now part of the liturgical life of the Orthodox Church.

The majority of St John's works have a compilative character since he made systematic use of the writings of others in his works. He understood his task first and foremost as collecting church tradition and putting it into order. Like Basil the Great, John understood tradition or traditions as the spiritual, theological, and liturgical legacy that is handed down orally in the Church and that, in his opinion, is no less important for church life than scripture:

> The eye-witnesses and ministers of the word not only handed down the
> law of the Church in writings, but also in certain unwritten traditions. For
> whence do we know the holy place of the skull? Whence the memorial
> of life? . . . What is the origin of threefold baptism, that is with three
> immersions? . . . Whence veneration of the cross? Are they not from
> unwritten tradition? Therefore the divine apostle says, "So then, brethren,
> stand firm and hold to the traditions which you were taught by us, either
> by word of mouth or by our letter" [2 Thess 2.15] Since many things have
> been handed down in unwritten form in the Church and preserved up to
> now.[26]

Church tradition is the criterion of faithfulness to Christ and the gospel by
which true Orthodoxy can be distinguished from heresy. For the Church, this
inner criterion is more important than any other that might be imposed from
the outside, including imperial edict. In his polemics with the state authorities, St John unequivocally states the Church's answer to the policy of interference by secular rulers in ecclesiastical affairs, which was so characteristic of
the entire age of the ecumenical councils:

> It is not for emperors to legislate for the Church . . . Political good order
> is the concern of emperors, the ecclesiastical constitution that of pastors
> and teachers . . . We submit to you, O Emperor, in the matters of this life,
> taxes, revenues, commercial dues, in which our concerns are entrusted to
> you. For the ecclesiastical constitution we have pastors who speak to us
> the word and represent the ecclesiastical ordinance. We do not remove
> the ancient boundaries, set in place by our fathers, but we hold fast to the
> traditions, as we have received them. For if we begin to remove even a
> tiny part of the structure of the Church, in a short time the whole edifice
> will be destroyed . . . I do not accept an emperor who tyrannically
> snatches at the priesthood. Have emperors received the authority to bind
> and to loose? . . . I am not persuaded that the Church should be consti-
> tuted by imperial canons, but rather by patristic traditions, both written
> and unwritten.[27]

[26] *Second Treatise on the Divine Images* 16, in Louth, trans., 72–73.
[27] *Second Treatise on the Divine Images* 12, 16, in Louth, trans., 68–69, 73.

3

The Rise of Monasticism
and Ascetic Literature

THE RISE OF MONASTICISM

THE AGE OF THE ecumenical councils was marked by the appearance and development of the monastic movement, which exerted enormous influence on all aspects of the spiritual life of the Orthodox Church. Although some trace the origin of monasticism to the communities of virgins and even the Old Testament Nazarene and Essene sects, it is obvious that the rapid spread of monasticism is connected with the end of the age of persecution during the reign of Constantine the Great and with the transformation of the Christian Church into a well-organized institution enjoying all the benefits of civilization.

In the Egyptian desert during the fourth century, there were three types of monasticism: anchoritic, cenobitic, and skete. Hermits lived alone, monks of cenobitic monasteries in large groups, and monks in sketes in small groups of two to three people (the word "skete" is taken from the desert of Scetis, where this way of life was attempted for the first time). The leader of the Egyptian recluses is traditionally considered to be St Anthony the Great (c. 251–c. 356), whose life is described in detail by Athanasius of Alexandria. Anthony was born in a Christian family. During his youth he heard in church the words of Christ: "If you would be perfect, go, sell what you possess and give to the poor, and you will have treasure in heaven; and come, follow me" (Mt 19.21). These words made such a powerful impression on the young Anthony that he gave away all his property and began to lead an ascetic way of life—first at home and then in the desert, to which he retired to spend twenty years in solitude, overcoming the temptations of the devil. When Anthony's way of life was discovered, disciples began to gather around him. According to Athanasius the Great, the desert gradually became a city:

Monasteries appeared in the mountains, and the desert was colonized by monks who had left behind their property and enrolled themselves in the citizenship in the heavens ... The monasteries in the mountains were like a tabernacle filled with divine choirs of psalmodists and those who loved reading, fasting, and prayer ... It was, as it were, a certain area filled with piety and justice, where there was neither oppressor nor oppressed, nor reproach from the tax-collector. There were a multitude of ascetics, but they all shared the same thought: to labor for virtue.[1]

Although this excerpt credits Anthony with establishing cenobitic monasteries, tradition considers St Pachomius the Great (c. 290–346), the compiler of the first monastic rule, to be the originator of this type of monasticism. The first half of the fourth century also witnessed the activities of St Hilarion the Great, the organizer of Palestinian monasticism, as well as the two great Macariuses, the Alexandrian and the Egyptian. Also during this time the protomonastic movement called the "sons of the covenant" flourished in Syria.

The spread of monasticism in Cappadocia owed much to Eustathius of Sebaste, who for many years (until 373) was a friend and teacher of Basil the Great. Eustathius belonged to a group of ascetics that had been condemned by the Council of Gangra (c. 340), and we can reconstruct the main tenets of Eustathius' teaching from the decisions of this council. Among other things, it anathematized those who condemned lawful marriage, rejected the eating of meat, refused to take communion from married priests, practiced virginity because they disdained marriage; those who, while observing the vow of virginity, extolled themselves over the married, those who fasted on Sundays, and those who shunned church gatherings or organized their own separately from the local bishop. It also anathematized women who, under the pretext of the ascetic life, left their husbands or neglected their children's upbringing. It is wholly possible that Eustathius himself did not support the extremities condemned by the Council of Gangra, and that these erroneous views were shared by only certain individuals in his group. However, since his writings have not survived, it is difficult to ascertain whether the council's anathemas were actually aimed at his teaching.

---

[1]Athanasius of Alexandria *The Life of St Anthony*, in *The Works of Our Father among the Saints Athanasius, Archbishop of Alexandria* (Sergiev Posad, 1902–1903), 3.192, 214–15.

Although Basil the Great shared many of Eustathius' ideas, the extreme individualism characteristic of the communities of ascetics condemned by the Gangra council was deeply foreign to him. Quite to the contrary, he emphasized in every way possible the "ecclesiastic" nature of the monastic movement. He strove to ensure that the emerging monasticism not be in opposition to the Church, that it not degenerate into a sect of rigorist ascetics, but that it might become an integral part of the church organism. Moreover, in Basil's *Rules* the word "monk" is not used at all, and "monasticism" is not spoken of as a separate group of people within the Church. Basil's concern was rather the church community as such, that is, the entire Church as a united community of "perfect Christians." Within this macro-community there can exist—and this was certainly the case during Basil's times—microcommunities of ascetics, virgins, and recluses. These communities became the nucleus of a spiritual revival that, according to Basil, should encompass the entire Church. To a great extent thanks to Basil's efforts, the monastic movement never—neither in his time nor subsequently—set itself in opposition to the Church, but remained inside it. Basil can also be credited with helping the ideal of monastic life penetrate into broad sections of Byzantine society, as well as with fostering the formation of "monasticism in the world": many laymen were inspired by the ascetic norms of monasticism and implemented various elements of monastic spirituality in their own practice.

After monasticism emerged in fourth-century Egypt as a way of withdrawing from the world, a rapid increase in the number of urban monasteries subsequently occurred, with monks beginning to return to the world and settling in cities. This was a kind of monastic mission in the world, which led to a gradual Christianization of the world and the penetration of the ideals of monasticism into many sections of Byzantine society. However, life in urban monasteries took on a form that was different from that in the early Egyptian desert. Although the basic principles of the cenobitic monasteries remained intact, they were no longer isolated communities but missionary and educational centers. Laymen attended the monastic services, and the monks were faced with the necessity of offering them spiritual guidance, having close and constant contact with urban life, and visiting or welcoming people. The transformation of eastern monasticism from a spontaneous movement of zealots of the spiritual life into a separate class of people within

Ruins of the Stoudios monastery

the Church was completed during the post-iconoclastic period. Since then it has played a leading role in the Orthodox Church.

The monastic movement during the age of the ecumenical councils had a mass character: in the middle of the sixth century there were seventy-six monasteries in Constantinople alone, and according to some sources there were approximately a hundred thousand monks in Byzantium at the beginning of the iconoclastic controversy.[2] The Stoudios monastery in Constantinople was one of the most famous urban monasteries of Byzantium. Founded in the middle of the fifth century, it became particularly important during the years when St Theodore the Studite (†826) was its abbot, as this period coincided with the height of the second phase of the iconoclastic controversy. Addressing the monks of his monastery, Theodore spoke of the importance of urban monasticism in comparison with the ascetic life in the desert:

> I believe that God will accept you and your good intentions if you remain
> the same even after moving from the most silent places (between the
> mountains) to noisy and populous ones (Constantinople), from the
> desert to the city . . . But I hope that you . . . will continue to live as you
> did in the desert, even while being in the city, and will preserve peace and
> tranquility of soul amidst the noise of the city. This is indeed a trial for
> you, but if you endure you will be truly worthy of admiration . . . Being
> silent in the desert and preserving tranquility in solitude do not deserve
> great praise. But it is another thing to live in the city as if you were living
> in solitude, and to abide among noisy crowds as if you were in the desert.[3]

The influence of the Stoudios monastery was great not only in Constantinople itself but also far beyond, particularly on the Holy Mountain of Athos. The monastery conducted wide-ranging educational activities and possessed a rich library and scriptorium, where an entire team of scribes

[2]Cf. Schmemann, *Historical Road*, 210.
[3]Theodore the Studite *Catecheses*, Homily 198 (*Philokalia* 4.376).

engaged in the systematic copying of books. During the iconoclastic and post-iconoclastic periods, Studite monks wrote much that later entered into the service books of the Orthodox Church and are sung to this very day.

Another important aspect of the Studite tradition was the provision of spiritual guidance for monks and laymen. This practice became extremely popular during the iconoclast controversies. The rule of Stoudios prescribed the "revelation of thoughts"—the regular confession of all monks to the abbot, who was their spiritual father. While daily revelation of thoughts already existed in early monasticism, the practice of monastics providing spiritual guidance to laymen was a characteristic of the age of iconoclasm. The same period also saw the emergence of the institution of "elders," whose tasks included hearing the confessions of laymen. Having acquired a paramount role in the spiritual guidance of laymen, the elders stretched the limits of spiritual fatherhood: unlike the early Christian spiritual mentors, who were, so to speak, only spiritual advisers, the elders controlled all aspects of their spiritual children's lives. The ideal of total obedience characteristic of monasteries was frequently applied to relations between elders and their lay spiritual children.

In order to understand the nature of eldership, which still exists in the Orthodox Church, we should take into account the historical circumstances that led to its development during the iconoclastic period. As Bishop Kallistos Ware notes, there are two forms of apostolic succession in the Church: "First there is the visible succession of the hierarchy, the unbroken series of bishops in different cities . . . Alongside this, largely hidden, existing on a 'charismatic' rather than an official level, there is secondly the apostolic succession of the spiritual fathers and mothers in each generation of the Church."[4] Both types of succession often coexist peacefully, and in many cases they are combined: for example, when bishops and priests serve as spiritual guides of the people. During the iconoclastic period, however, polarization arose between these two lines of succession. The reason for this was the dwindling authority of the "official" hierarchy in the eyes of the people due to the compromises made by many bishops with the iconoclasts. When members of the hierarchy and clergy apostasized from the tradition of venerating icons, the people turned to the monks, whom they saw as the defenders of Orthodoxy.

[4]Kallistos T. Ware, "The Spiritual Father in Saint John Climacus and Saint Symeon the New Theologian," in Irénée Hausherr, *Spiritual Direction in the Early Christian East*, trans. Anthony P. Gythiel (Kalamazoo: Cistercian Publishers, 1990), vii.

After the end of the iconoclastic controversy, monasticism was transformed into a major church institute enjoying special status in the Byzantine empire. While the attempts of the state to "tame" the church hierarchy were in many instances successful, the emperors failed to control monasticism and absorb it into the social and political structure of the empire.[5]

Monasticism's position inside the Church was described in the following way in Theodore the Studite's *Catecheses*: monks are the Church's "nerves and her support," the "salt of the earth and the light of the world," a "light for them that sit in darkness," and an "example and a declaration."[6] In essence, monasticism was able to "tame" the Christian Church in the east for many centuries. It was from among the monks that bishops were chosen during the post-iconoclastic period, monastic services gradually replaced the parish liturgical typika, monastic asceticism formed the foundation of church fasting regulations, spiritual education was concentrated in the hands of monks, and monks became the father confessors of laymen. In contrast to the Latin west, where the autonomy of monastic orders was reflected, above all, in their administrative independence from episcopal structures, Byzantine monasteries remained under the jurisdiction of the local bishop. Moreover, the bishops themselves were monks, and monastics were frequently appointed to leading positions in dioceses. This practice remains in many Orthodox churches to this day.

ASCETIC LITERATURE

Monasticism in the age of the ecumenical councils produced a rich ascetical literature, which even today enjoys enormous popularity in the Orthodox Church. Moreover, it is read not only by monks but also by laymen. The sayings of the early Egyptian fathers such as Anthony, Arsenius, Macarius, Pachomius, and Sisoes (all of whom are called "the Great") all found their way into collections entitled "paterikons," in which these sayings (*apophthegmata*) were arranged either in alphabetical order or according to subject. In addition to these collections of sayings, ascetical treatises appeared beginning

---

[5]For more on this see Florovsky, "Christianity and Civilization," in *Selected Theological Articles*, 218–27.

[6]Cited in Schmemann, *Historical Road*, 212–13.

in the fourth century written by individual authors and addressed to monks. The important monastic writers from the fourth to the ninth centuries, in addition to the aforementioned Maximus the Confessor and Theodore the Studite, were Evagrius of Pontus, Macarius of Egypt, John of the Ladder, and Isaac the Syrian.

Evagrius of Pontus (c. 346–399) was a disciple of St Gregory the Theologian, a younger contemporary of St Pachomius the Great and other "desert fathers," and a witness of the golden age of Egyptian monasticism. From Origen he adopted some erroneous views primarily in the area of christology, for which he was condemned by the Fifth Ecumenical Council. However, in his moral and ascetical teaching Evagrius was an exponent of the authentic monastic tradition, which is why many of his works were preserved after the Fifth Ecumenical Council under the names of other authors. Evagrius wrote mainly in the genre of *apophthegmata* characteristic of early Egyptian monasticism, and his sayings were bundled into groups of a hundred (called "centuries"). His most famous extant works—the *Praktikos,* the *Gnostikos,* the *Gnostic Chapters*, and the *Chapters on Prayer*—are collections of sayings. The last of these is a collection of 153 chapters (according to the number of fish caught by Christ's disciples, see Jn 21.11), preserved under the name of St Nilus of Sinai. In this treatise Evagrius outlines the fundamental characteristics of prayer in the monastic tradition:

> Prayer is a conversation of the mind with God. What state must the mind reach in order to be able to stretch out toward its Master and converse with him without any mediator?

> If Moses, who attempted to approach the burning bush, was forbidden from doing so until he removed his sandals (Ex 3.5), should not you, who desire to contemplate him who is higher than all senses and thought and become his interlocutor, remove from yourself all passionate thoughts?

> Above all pray for the gift of tears, in order to soften the callousness of your soul, and in order to obtain from him forgiveness after confessing your sins to the Lord (Ps 31.5).

> Stand diligently and pray fervently, turning away from the cares and reasoning that overcome you. For they lead to bewilderment and confuse you in order to weaken you.

Strive to have your mind deaf and dumb during prayer, and then you will be able to pray.

Prayer is the ascent of the mind to God.

He who loves God always converses with him as with a father, avoiding all passionate thoughts.

If you are a theologian, you will pray truly; and if you pray truly, you are a theologian.[7]

Other important works of monastic literature are the homilies attributed to Macarius of Egypt (fourth century). While scholars still debate their authenticity, the majority believe that they were written in the second half of the fourth century, and not in Egypt but in Syria. Some tenets of the homilies were borrowed by the Messalians, a heretical movement among monastics that became widespread in the fourth century. The Messalians, or Euchites, i.e., those who pray (from the Greek *euche,* "prayer"), believed prayer to be the one and only activity necessary for salvation and rejected scripture, the liturgical services, and the sacraments of the Church. The fact that the Messalians made use of the Macarian homilies, however, in no way undermined their authority among the Orthodox, with whom they continued to maintain their popularity during the entire Byzantine period. There are several collections of Macarius' works; of these, the best known is the second collection, which circulated during Byzantine times under the title *Spiritual Homilies.* Their central theme is the teaching on Christian perfection, which is attained through prayer and communion with God. The author of these homilies speaks of Christianity as an inner, spiritual struggle, as a way of life of the "new creation," thereby demonstrating similarities with the author of the *Epistle to Diognetus,* which was quoted earlier:

Christians have their own world and their own way of living, thinking, speaking, and acting. Those of the people of the world are different. The Christians are one thing, those who love the world are another, and the distance between them is great. For the inhabitants of the world, the children of this age, are like wheat poured into the sieve of the world, and are sifted by the restless thoughts of this world, constantly being agitated

[7]Evagrius *On Prayer* 3; 4; 5; 9; 11; 36; 55; 61.

by earthly cares, desires, and numerous material concerns. Satan tosses around such souls and sifts the entire sinful human race with a sieve, that is, by means of worldly pursuits . . . But our citizenship is in the heavens (Phil 3.20). It is through this that true Christians differ from the rest of mankind . . . Since the mind and the understanding of Christians is always occupied with thoughts of the heavenly, they contemplate the eternal goods through communion with the Holy Spirit. Since they have been born again from God, they have truly been vouchsafed in power to become God's children. Through many and protracted struggles and efforts they have achieved constancy, firmness, tranquility, and rest; their thoughts do not become scattered and are no longer disturbed by inconstant and vain thoughts. It is because of this that they are above and better than the world, because their minds and the thoughts of their souls remain in Christ's peace and the love of the Spirit . . . Therefore, Christians differ not in their exterior appearance, as many think . . . It is through the renewal of the mind, peace of thoughts, love, and the heavenly devotion to the Lord that the new creation—Christians—differ from all the people of the world.[8]

A classic of monastic literature is the *Ladder* of St John Climacus (†mid-seventh century). The book consists of thirty chapters, each of which is dedicated to the description of a particular virtue or passion. In it, the path to spiritual perfection is conceived as the gradual ascent of a ladder in which each successive rung is reached by the acquisition of a particular virtue or the liberation from a particular passion. The way of the ascetic begins with the "renunciation of the world"—the first rung of the ladder. Thus, the monastic character of the book is highlighted from the very beginning. This is followed by chapters on detachment, exile (retirement

St John Climacus

from the world), obedience, penitence, the remembrance of death, mourning, placidity and meekness, remembrance of wrongs, speaking evil of others and slander, talkativeness and silence, lying, despondency and laziness, glut-

[8]Macarius of Egypt *Spiritual Homilies* 5.1–5.

tony, chastity, avarice, poverty, insensitivity, sleep and psalmody, alertness, fear, vainglory, pride, simplicity and guilelessness, humility, discernment, stillness, prayer, and dispassion. The book's final chapter is dedicated to the union of three virtues—faith, hope, and love, which are the highest rung of the ladder:

> Faith is like a ray, hope a light, and love the sun itself. Still, they make up a single radiance and a single splendor.

> He who wishes to speak of the love of God is undertaking to speak of God himself; talking about God is sinful and dangerous for the unattentive.

> God is love (Jn 4.8), and he who wishes to define what God is in a word is blind and attempts to measure the sand in the depths of the sea.

> Love, by its nature, is a likening to God—to the extent that this is possible for humans. In its activity it is the inebriation of the soul, and its distinctive feature is that it is a fountain of faith, an abyss of longsuffering, and a sea of humility.

> If the presence of a beloved person changes all of us in a way visible to all, so that we are joyful, glad, and carefree, what change will not be wrought by the presence of the Heavenly Master, who invisibly enters the pure soul?

> The growth of the fear of God is the beginning of love, and the perfection of purity is the beginning of theology.[9]

A special place in the history of monastic literature is occupied by St Isaac the Syrian (seventh century). Unlike the other authors mentioned earlier, he lived not in the Roman but in the Persian empire, wrote not in Greek but in Syriac, and belonged not the Byzantine Church but to the Church of the East. Nevertheless, his writings were read widely in Byzantium thanks to a Greek translation made at the end of the eighth and beginning of the ninth centuries. Until recently only one collection of Isaac's works was known: the *Ascetical Homilies*. However, in the twentieth century Syriac manuscripts containing the second volume of his works were discovered and published.[10]

---

[9] *The Ladder* 30.2, 4, 6, 7, 16, 20.

[10] For more on this see Bishop Hilarion (Alfeyev), *The Spiritual World of St Isaac the Syrian*, 2d ed. (St Petersburg, 2002), 37–43.

Isaac represents a rich tradition of Syrian theological and spiritual literature that includes such writers as Jacob Aphrahat (fourth century) and St Ephraim the Syrian (c. 306–c. 373). Isaac's christology and eschatology were influenced by Theodore of Mopsuestia, although Isaac is a stranger to the extremities of Antiochian christology condemned at the Third Ecumenical Council.

St Isaac the Syrian

Throughout the centuries, Isaac the Syrian has been known in the Orthodox Church not so much for his theological views as for his ascetical and moral teaching, which are intimately connected to his understanding of God's love. Those who strive for holiness should, first and foremost, imitate God's love: that all-encompassing co-suffering love that makes no distinction between the righteous and sinners, between friends of the truth and its enemies:

> And what is the merciful heart? . . . It is the warming of the heart of man toward all creation, toward people, the birds, the animals, the demons, and all creation. When he remembers them or beholds them his eyes shed tears of a great and intense pity that encompasses the heart. And from great suffering his heart diminishes, and cannot endure, hear, or see any creature suffer harm or even small grief. Because of this, he brings forth prayers every hour with tears for the speechless creatures, the enemies of the truth, and those who do him harm, so that they might be protected and be purified; he also offers prayers with great pity for that which creeps on the earth; this pity is aroused in his heart until he has likened himself in this respect to God.[11]

Love for God should have the same spiritual power that propelled the martyrs to their death and inspired the apostles in their preaching and the desert fathers in their ascetic feats. Following St Paul, who wrote that we are "fools for Christ's sake" (1 Cor 4.10), Isaac describes divine love as a feeling that makes a person foolish and spiritually inebriates him:

[11]*Homilies* 48, in Abba Isaac the Syrian, *Ascetical Homilies* (Sergiev Posad, 1911), 206.

Love is hot by nature, and when it flares up in a person without measure, it makes the soul foolish. Because of this the heart that has felt this love cannot contain and endure it . . . It is with this spiritual inebriation that the apostles and martyrs were drunk, and they traveled the entire world, laboring and enduring insults, while others shed blood like water from limbs that were cut off. In the midst of terrible sufferings, they did not lose heart but endured valiantly, and being wise, were declared fools. Still others wandered "in deserts and mountains, in dens and caves of the earth" (Heb 11.38–39), and were the most composed and calm during times of trouble. May God grant us to attain this folly![12]

[12] *Homilies* 73, in *Ascetical Homilies*, 369–70.

4

The Baptism of the Slavic Peoples

I N THE POST-ICONOCLASTIC period the "symphony" between the ecclesiastical and worldly authorities in Byzantium reached its peak. Now the patriarch could be replaced by a simple decree of the emperor, and relatives of the emperor were often appointed to the patriarchal see. Characterizing this period of church history in Constantinople, Alexander Schmemann wrote:

> the completely arbitrary nature of state authority always remained an incurable sore in church life; still worse was the almost equally complete acceptance of this arbitrariness by the church hierarchy. It was as though, having isolated its dogmatic doctrine in an inviolable holy of holies, protected by vows and with the empire itself subjected to it, the Church no longer felt any limit to imperial authority. It was as though, having become completely Orthodox, the emperor could now do anything that suited him in the Church.[1]

In the year 847, after the death of St Methodius, Ignatius (†877), son of Emperor Michael I (811–813), was elevated to the patriarchal throne of Constantinople. Ignatius enjoyed great popularity among the monastics, and was supported by the monks of the Stoudios monastery. At that time the emperor was the underage Michael III (842–867); but the empire was actually ruled by Empress Theodora. In 856 Michael III removed Theodora from rule and took power. Patriarch Ignatius was deposed, and in his place Photius, who had occupied the post of chief imperial secretary, was elevated in 858. Photius was highly educated and one of the most brilliant patriarchs in the history of the patriarchate of Constantinople. However, the influential monastic party did not recognize the deposition of Ignatius. In 863 Roman Pope Nicholas I (†867) desposed Patriarch Photius, an act viewed in Constantinople as meddling in the internal affairs of the Constantinopolitan Church. This caused a

---

[1]Schmemann, *Historical Road*, 220–21.

new division between Rome and Constantinople, the second of its kind after the Akakian schism of the fifth century. In 867 Photius convened a council in Constantinople which, in its turn, deposed Nicholas I.

Photius was the first patriarch of Constantinople to level doctrinal accusations against the Roman Church. On the eve of the Council of 867 he sent an encyclical to the other eastern patriarchs in which he pointed out the Roman Church's doctrine of the *filioque*, that is, the teaching that the Holy Spirit proceeds from the Father and the Son. In addition to serious theological accusations, the encyclical contains numerous attacks against the Latins over certain ritual details. Fasting on Saturdays is described as a "small deviation" that can nevertheless "lead to a complete disregard for dogma." The western practice of beginning Great Lent one week later than in the east is described as a "temptation to drink milk, eat cheese, and similar acts of gluttony," which drives the Latins toward the "path of sin" and "leads them astray" from the straight, royal path.[2]

In 867 Emperor Michael III was killed, and his place was taken by Basil the Macedonian (†886). The day after he ascended the throne he deposed Photius and restored Ignatius. From 869 to 870 a council was held in Constantinople with the participation of the legates of Pope Adrian II (867–872), which confirmed the deposition of Photius and the restoration of Ignatius. The Roman Church recognized this council as the Eighth Ecumenical Council.

Nevertheless, events in Constantinople continued to unfold, and in 877, after Ignatius died, Photius was elevated a second time to the patriarchal see. In 879 another council was convened in Constantinople, which confirmed Photius' restoration. The stormy rule of Photius ended in 887, when the new emperor, Leo VI the Wise (†912), removed him from the see and appointed his sixteen-year-old brother Stephen. The Church of Constantinople subsequently canonized both Ignatius and Photius.

Relations between Constantinople and Rome worsened during the expansion of missionary activity in the Slavic lands. After the Kievan princes Askold and Dir attacked Constantinople in 860 (an event described in the *Tales of Bygone Years*), Byzantium made diplomatic efforts to normalize relations with its northern neighbors. In 861 a mission was sent to Khazaria comprised of two brothers, Constantine and Methodius, who spoke the Slavic language and translated scripture into it. In 863 the Moravian prince Rostislav

---

[2]Photius of Constantinople *Encyclicals* 5.

wrote to Michael III and Patriarch Photius asking them to send missionaries to Moravia. Once again Constantine and Methodius were chosen for the task, and they continued their translation work in the Moravian lands. Around 864 the Czech prince Borivoy and his wife Ludmila were baptized by St Methodius. But since the missionary activities of the two brothers were being carried out in lands that were in the Roman Church's sphere of influence, the brothers traveled to Rome in 868 to settle their church affairs (by this time Patriarch Photius had been deposed). They were solemnly received by Pope Adrian II in Rome. Soon after this Constantine became ill, and after taking monastic vows and receiving the name Cyril, he died in February 869.

In the middle of 869 Methodius was sent by the pope to Moravia, and at the end of the year he returned to Rome and was consecrated archbishop of Pannonia. On his way to Moravia, Methodius was taken prisoner by the Bavarians, who saw his activity as an infringement on the hierarchical rights of the archbishop of Salzburg (before Methodius was appointed to the see of Pannonia, this province was under the jurisdiction of the diocese of Salzburg). However, he was released on the insistence of Rome. In 881–882 he traveled to Constantinople, where he met with Emperor Basil I and Patriarch Photius. Methodius died in 885. After his death the mission among the Slavs of Moravia was abandoned and his disciples banished. However, this mission continued among other peoples, including the Bulgarians, Serbs, and Russians.

King Boris I of Bulgaria (852–889) was baptized in the 860s. After receiving Christianity from Byzantium, Boris attempted to create an autocephalous church in his country. Having failed to receive autocephaly from Constantinople, he asked Rome to send bishops to Bulgaria. They were dispatched, but this provoked the disapproval of Patriarch Photius, which is reflected in his encyclical. At the Constantinople Council of 869–870 the question of the ecclesiastical jurisdiction of the Bulgars was resolved in favor of Constantinople, despite the protest of the papal legates. The first Bulgarian archbishop was St Joseph, who was consecrated by Patriarch Ignatius. A major contribution to the Christianization of the Bulgarian people was made by the disciples of St Methodius: Ss Clement, Naum, and Gorazd.

In the mid-860s a Greek bishop was sent to Rus', a fact mentioned by Photius in his encyclical:

For not only did this people [the Bulgarians] exchange their former impiety for faith in Christ, but also the so-called Ros, well-known to many and exceeding all in ferocity and bloodshed, those who, having subjugated those around them and thereby becoming extremely proud, rose in arms against the very Romaian empire! But now they have also exchanged the pagan and godless beliefs which they held earlier for the pure and unfeigned religion of the Christians, having lovingly made themselves subjects and rendering hospitality, in place of the plundering and great brazenness shown to us recently. And their passionate striving and zeal for the faith has been so ignited . . . that they have accepted a bishop and shepherd, and take part in Christian rituals with great diligence and zeal.[3]

It is still not clear how long the first episcopal see existed in Rus'. The fruits of the "first baptism of Rus'" described by Photius were evidently destroyed during the times of Prince Oleg (†after 911). However, when a treaty between Byzantium and Rus' was concluded during the reign of Prince Igor (†c. 945) in 944, there were Christians among Russian merchants and the prince's militia, and there was a "cathedral" of the Prophet Elias in Kiev.[4] In the middle of the tenth century Prince Igor's widow, Princess Olga (c. 945–c. 960), became a Christian in Constantinople during the reign of Emperor Constantine VII Porphyrogenitus (†959). Like the Bulgarian King Boris almost a century earlier, Olga sent a request for bishops and priests not to Constantinople but to Rome. In 961 the German bishop Adalbert arrived in Kiev, but his mission was unsuccessful. It is possible that German missionaries spent time in Kiev during the reign of Yaropolk (972–978).[5]

In 987 a rebellion occurred in Byzantium, caused by two military commanders—Vardas Phokas and Vardas Skliros—who hoped to divide the empire among themselves after seizing power. Emperor Basil II (976–1025) did not have the means to crush the rebellion, and sent a delegation to Prince Vladimir of Kiev requesting assistance. Vladimir agreed on the condition that he receive the hand of the emperor's sister, Anna. In 988 six thousand Russ-

[3]Photius of Constantinople *Encyclicals* 35.

[4]*Tales of Bygone Years*, year 6452 (944), in V.P. Adrianova-Perets, ed., *Tales of Bygone Years (Povest' Vremennykh Let)*, trans. D.S. Likhachev and B.A. Romanov (Moscow and Leningrad, 1950).

[5]A.V. Nazarenko, "The Russian Church from the Tenth to the First Third of the Fifteenth Century," in *Orthodox Encyclopedia* (Moscow, 1997), 39.

ian troops set out for Byzantium and helped Basil II subdue the rebellion the year after. But because the emperor delayed sending Anna to Rus', Vladimir seized Cherson, where Anna was then sent to marry him.

There are two accounts of Prince Vladimir's baptism. According to the first, this took place in 989 or 990 in Korsun immediately before the marriage ceremony; according to the second, this was in 987 or 988 during the signing of the treaty with Basil II. The Russian Orthodox Church officially dates the baptism of Rus' to 988. After the prince and his armed force were baptized, mass baptisms of the population and the destruction of pagan shrines took place in Kiev and other cities of Rus'.

For Prince Vladimir, the baptism of Rus' was undoubtedly motivated by political considerations: first, it promised an alliance with Byzantium; and second, the wise prince saw that Christianity was a spiritual force that could help him unite the Russian people. At the same time, becoming a Christian was an act of courage for the prince, since he exposed himself to risks by breaking with the religion of his ancestors. Moreover, accepting Christianity was an act of personal piety for Vladimir since it required him to change his way of life and reject polygamy and other pagan customs. The Russian Church highly valued the prince's moral efforts and canonized him with the appellation "equal-to-the-apostles."

The *Tales of Bygone Years* contains a vivid account of how Vladimir, during the years preceding his baptism, met with Muslims from Bulgaria, German Christians, Khazar Jews, as well as a certain Greek philosopher. He rejected Islam since it required circumcision and forbade the eating of pork and the consumption of alcohol. "For Rus' drinking is a joy, and we cannot live without it," the prince said to the Muslims. To the Germans, who claimed that observing fasts was not necessary, Vladimir said: "Go back to where you came from, for our fathers did not accept this." The Khazar Jews told Vladimir that their homeland was in Jerusalem, but that God had punished them for their sins, given their land over to Christians, and dispersed them throughout different countries. Having heard this Vladimir said: "How can you teach others when you yourselves have been forsaken by God and dispersed? If God loved you and your law, you would not be scattered in foreign lands. Or do you wish the same to happen to us?"[6]

---

[6] *Tales of Bygone Years*, year 6494 (986), 258.

Of all the preachers Vladimir liked only the Greek philosopher, but the boyars and elders advised him to dispatch a delegation to different lands before making a final decision:

> Their words pleased the prince and all the people. And they chose glorious and intelligent men, ten in number, and said to them: "Go first to the Bulgarians and test their faith." They set off, and after arriving, saw their vile deeds and worship in the mosque, and returned to their land. And Vladimir said to them: "Go now to the Germans, examine everything, and from there go to the Greek lands." They came to the Germans, saw their church service, and then arrived in Constantinople and appeared before the emperor. The emperor asked them why they had come, whereupon the delegation told him everything. Having heard their story, the emperor rejoiced and honored them greatly that day. The next day he sent a message to the patriarch saying: "The Russians have arrived to test our faith. Prepare the church and clergy, and don your episcopal vestments so that they may behold the glory of our God!" Having heard this, the patriarch ordered that the clergy be gathered and celebrated the festal service as usual; the censers were lighted and the choirs sang. And he went with the Russians into the church, and they were led to the best place, and he showed them the beauty of the church, the singing and hierarchical service, the presence of the deacons, and spoke to them about serving his God. They were delighted and surprised, and praised the service. And the emperors Basil and Constantine called for them and said: "Go back to your land," and bid them farewell with great gifts and honor."[7]

According to the *Tales of Bygone Years*, after the delegation returned to Kiev Vladimir convened the boyars and addressed the delegation: "Speak before the *druzhina*." The delegates told Vladimir and the boyars:

> We went to the Bulgarians, saw how they prayed in church, that is, in the mosque, and how they stood there without belts. After making a prostration, they sit down and look back and forth like madmen, and there is no joy among them—only sorrow and a great stench. Their law is not good. Then we went to the Germans and saw the festal service in their churches, but didn't see any beauty. And then we came to the Greek lands, and were

[7] *Tales of Bygone Years*, year 6495 (987), 273.

taken to the place where they serve their God, and we didn't know if we were on heaven or on earth, for there is no such sight or beauty on this earth, and we do not know how to describe it to you. We only know that God is there with his people, and that their services are better than in all the other lands; we cannot forget this beauty. And just as no person will accept bitterness after having tasted sweetness, so can we no longer remain pagans.

The boyars then said: "If the Greek law had been bad, your grandmother Olga would not have accepted it, and she was the wisest of all people." Vladimir then asked: "Where shall we be baptized?" They answered: "Wherever you like."[8]

Whatever the authenticity of this story, it is obvious that at this time Rus' was a "tasty morsel" for missionaries from foreign countries. And while the story of the missions of the Jews and Muslims seems hardly probable, the account of the mission of the German bishops is thoroughly credible. It is also an undisputed fact that in the second half of the ninth century and in the tenth century, all Slavic lands, including Moravia, Pannonia, Bulgaria, Serbia, and Rus', witnessed parallel missions of the Byzantine and Latin churches, which conducted their activities not so much in the spirit of cooperation as in the spirit of rivalry.

[8] *Tales of Bygone Years*, year 6495 (987), 273–74.

5

Summary of the First Millennium

T HE FIRST MILLENNIUM was marked by the spread of Christianity, which was transformed from the faith of a small group of Christ's followers into the religion with the largest number of believers on the planet, with millions of adherents in Europe and Asia. In the fourth century Christianity became the state religion of the Roman empire and was preached far beyond its borders. The expansion of the sphere of Christian influence continued until the rise of Islam in the seventh century. After this the spread of Christianity in lands conquered by Arabs came to a halt, but continued in eastern Europe, among the Slavic peoples, as well as in Asia, where Christian missionaries reached China and India.

During the first millennium the canonical structure of the Christian Church took shape. The main ecclesiastical center of the west was Rome, and in the east there were four patriarchates, the most important being that of Constantinople. The unity of the Church in the east and west, despite all the increasing differences, was preserved at the end of the first millennium. Nevertheless, Christendom was already clearly divided into the spheres of interest of the western and eastern churches, and the alienation between the two churches became more evident with each year.

The first millennium witnessed a flowering of Christian holiness. Among the saints of this era were apostles, martyrs, confessors, hierarchs, monks, righteous princes, and fools for Christ's sake. The Church accorded a particularly profound veneration to the apostles, of whom Peter and Paul were singled out as "Leaders of the Apostles." From the first centuries the Church also venerated with particular fervor the martyrs, who gave their lives for Christ: they were venerated as saints immediately after their deaths, churches were built at the places of their martyrdom, and their remains were venerated as holy relics. Those witnesses to the faith who had suffered for Christ but did not die from torture were called confessors. Saints who were bishops were called holy hierarchs, and those monks and ascetics who had led a God-pleasing life were venerated as monastic saints. Among the saints were many people who had occupied important places in society, including emperors, kings, and righteous princes, whom the Church canonized for their personal piety or for the services they had rendered to the Church. A special place in the history of Christian holiness is occupied by the fools for Christ's sake, that is, those who voluntarily assumed a semblance of insanity in order to conceal their gift of clairvoyance, prophecy, and miracleworking.

The first millennium saw the emergence and development of a fully developed Christian doctrine. The works of the church fathers and definitions of the ecumenical and local councils formulated the teaching that has remained unchanged in the Orthodox Church to this day. The theology of the church fathers is the foundation on which the unity of world Christianity, which was lost in the second millennium, can be restored.

Christian moral and ascetic teaching, developed in the works of the ascetic writers of the east and west, was also elaborated during the first millennium. Enormous influence on the development of Christian asceticism was exerted by monasticism, which by the end of the first millennium had gained a leading role in the eastern Church.

During this time the Christian liturgy was also shaped and developed. Beginning with the eucharistic gatherings, which were improvised and spontaneous, in the second and third centuries the Christian liturgy became a highly developed ritual with its own liturgical texts. Christian liturgical ceremony was significantly enriched in the Constantinian and post-Constantinian era, after the Church had left the catacombs. In the eighth through tenth centuries the development of the services was considerably influenced by monastic hymnographers, including St Andrew of Crete (seventh–eighth century), John of Damascus (eighth century), Cosmas of Mayuma (eighth century), Theodore and Joseph the Studites (eighth–ninth century), Theophan the Branded (ninth century), and Joseph the Hymnographer (ninth century).[1] These authors, like many others whose works entered the liturgical books but whose names have not been preserved for posterity, were not only "professional" poets and hymnographers, but also outstanding theologians who were able to clothe the riches of Orthodox dogmatics in poetic forms.

[1] For more on Byzantine hymnographers see Archimandrite Kallistos Ware, "The Meaning of the Great Fast," in *The Lenten Triodion*, trans. Mother Mary and Kallistos Ware (London: Faber and Faber, 1977), 40–43.

They enriched the services with numerous texts that form the basis of the daily, weekly, and annual cycle of services in the Orthodox Church. At the same time, the eucharistic liturgy has continued to occupy a preeminent position in liturgical life, around which all other services—matins, vespers, nocturnes, compline, and the third, sixth, and ninth hours—are centered.

The annual cycle of church feasts also emerged during the first millennium. Since the beginning of the Church's existence, the main feast was, and still is, the Resurrection of Christ, also called "Pascha," in remembrance of the Jewish feast that coincided with Christ's crucifixion and resurrection. The second most important church feast is Christ's Nativity, which until the fourth century was called Theophany. After the fourth century the feast of Theophany came to be identified with the remembrance of Christ's baptism in the Jordan, and started to be celebrated separately from the feast of the Nativity. In addition to feasts dedicated to various events from Christ's life, those devoted to the Theotokos—such as the Nativity of the Theotokos, the Meeting of Our Lord in the Temple, the Annunciation, and the Dormition—also appeared in the first millennium. Due to the constant increase in the number of saints, many days of the church calendar were dedicated to their memory. By the end of this period the Church commemorated saints on each day of the year.

During the first thousand years the annual cycle of both one-day and longer fasts also took shape. The number of fasting days gradually grew, mainly due to the influence of the monastic tradition. In the fourth century Christians were required to observe fasts on Wednesdays and Fridays throughout the year, as well as the forty-day Great Lent before Easter.[2] By the end of the millennium three other fasting periods had been added: before the Nativity of Christ, the feast of Ss Peter and Paul, and the Dormition of the Theotokos. The length of these fasts was different for monks and laymen. Thus, in the tenth century St Symeon the Studite required that monks observe "three forty-day fasts" during the year.[3] On the other hand, the synod of the Church of Constantinople under Patriarch Nicholas III (1081–1111) decreed that the length of the Nativity, Dormition, and Apostles' fasts for laymen be limited to one week.[4] Thereafter monastic rules governing longer fasts were applied to laymen as well.

[2]Cf. Apostolic Canon 69.
[3]Symeon the Studite *Ascetic Homilies* 22.
[4]Cf. *The Canons of the Orthodox Church with Commentaries by Nikodim, Bishop of Dalmatia and Istria* (Moscow, 2001), 1.150.

The first millennium also saw the energetic development of Christian architecture and fine arts. Beginning in the fourth century, churches started to be built in every populated area where there were Christians, particularly in large cities. The size of these churches depended to a large extent on the political significance of the city in which they were located. The main church of a city with an episcopal see was decorated with special care. Originally, churches took the form of a basilica (a long rectangular building); later they were built in the form of a cross. In the east Christian churches, particularly after the iconoclastic controversy, were decorated abundantly with icons, frescoes, and mosaics, while in the west statues of martyrs and saints were also used.

The first millennium also witnessed the emergence of the basic principles of church singing. In the ancient Church the services were comprised of a dialogue between the celebrant (bishop or priest) and the people, who responded to his prayers and exclamations, and the entire congregation took part in singing. But in the post-Constantinian age choirs gradually began to replace the congregation in this role, and the services became a musical act with elements of choreography (censing, solemn entrances and exits, group prostrations). During this millennium church singing was monophonic, and was not accompanied by any musical instruments.

PART TWO

HISTORY: THE SECOND MILLENNIUM

6

Late Byzantium

THE GREAT SCHISM

THE BEGINNING of the second millennium of Christian history was marked by a further deepening of the rift between Constantinople and Rome, which sadly led to the well-known events of 1054. The differences between the east and the west had accumulated over the centuries and involved political, cultural, ecclesiological, theological, and ritual factors.

The political differences between the east and the west were rooted in the radically distinct relationships between church and state in Constantinople and Rome. In the post-Constantinian era, the Constantinople patriarchs were totally dependent on the Byzantine emperor. They also helped shape the "symphony" that, although formally granting them equal rights with the emperors, in reality placed them in a subordinate position. The Roman pontiffs, on the other hand, preserved their independence from the Byzantine emperors and did not submit to imperial edicts if they did not deem it necessary. Moreover, if they disagreed with imperial decisions, they spoke out openly against them. Political antagonism between the Roman popes and the Byzantine emperors intensified considerably in 732, when the iconoclast emperor Leo III the Isaurian wrested the dioceses of southern Italy from the pope, placing them under the jurisdiction of the patriarch of Constantinople—a decision that was met with indignation in the west. In 756 the Papal States came into being, after the Frankish king Pepin the Short (714–768) presented land in the territory of the former exarchate of Ravenna (in northern Italy) to Pope Stephen II. After this, the pope possessed not only spiritual but also secular authority. In 800 Pope Leo III crowned the Frankish king Charlemagne emperor of the Holy Roman Empire, thereby making a final break with the Byzantine emperor, who bore an analogous title.

The cultural alienation between the east and west was caused to a considerable degree by the fact that Greek was spoken in the eastern Roman empire while Latin was used in the west. In the middle of the fifth century few in the west could speak Greek, while Latin was not understood in Byzantium beginning in the seventh century. In the east Plato and Aristotle were read, in the west Cicero and Seneca. The main theological authorities of the eastern Church were the fathers of the age of the ecumenical councils, such as Gregory the Theologian, Basil the Great, John Chrysostom, and Cyril of Alexandria, whereas in the west the blessed Augustine (who was hardly known in the east) was the most widely read. For the barbarians who had converted to Christianity, his theological system was more easily understandable than the subtle speculation of the Greek fathers. The contemporary Greek theologian Christos Yannaras wrote:

> The preference for Augustine was unquestionably the result of a political choice. When the military and political genius of Charlemagne unified the autonomous barbarous principalities and feudal possessions into one authority in the ninth century, the appearance of a second empire within the boundaries of the *oikoumene* known at the time became a political necessity for the west. However, in accordance with the standards of state government at the time, the new empire required a new cultural foundation (analogous to the *pax romana*), which would be based first and foremost on the religion of the empire (*religio imperii*). A pure westerner in his education and character, Augustine revealed to Charlemagne's educated court a variety of Christian teaching that could be used to dissociate the religion, culture, and politics of the "empire of the Germanic tribes" from the only imperial structure existing at the time: the Hellenized Roman empire of New Rome or Constantinople. The cultural autonomy of the new west was based on an Augustinian understanding of Christianity and a politically founded, aggressive anti-Hellenism.[1]

The ecclesiological differences between Rome and Constantinople were caused by the gradual development throughout the period of the ecumenical councils of the doctrine of the bishop of Rome as the head of the ecumenical Church—the successor of Peter, who had received the keys of the kingdom of heaven. At the same time, the primacy of the bishop of Constan-

[1]Christos Yannaras, "The Church in Post-Communist Europe," *Tserkov' i Vremya* 3.28 (2004): 92.

tinople was consolidated in the east, and from the end of the sixth century he bore the title "Ecumenical Patriarch." However, the patriarch of Constantinople was never perceived in the east as the head of the ecumenical Church: he was only the second in rank after the Roman bishop and the first in honor among the eastern patriarchs. In the west, however, the pope began to be seen as the head of the ecumenical Church, with jurisdiction throughout the entire world. These were completely different ecclesiological models, and they will be examined in more detail in the section on the canonical structure of the Orthodox Church

The doctrine of papal primacy was repeatedly advanced in the east by papal legates, without encountering any serious objections from eastern theologians until Patriarch Photius. Thus, when the epistle of Pope Leo was read aloud at the Fourth Ecumenical Council, the eastern bishops unanimously proclaimed: "It is Peter who speaks through Leo's mouth!" Moreover, there were many instances where eastern bishops and theologians who did not find support in Constantinople turned to the pope for protection, seeing him as the supreme arbiter. John Chrysostom sought protection from Pope Innocent I after being unjustly deposed; Cyril of Alexandria appealed to Pope Celestine I during his dispute with Nestorius; Maximus the Confessor looked for aid from Pope Martin I in his struggle against the monothelites; and Theodore the Studite appealed to Pope Leo III during the iconoclastic controversy. Calling the Roman pontiff the "most divine head of all heads," Theodore wrote:

> Since Christ our God has granted to the great Peter, in addition to the keys to the kingdom of heaven, the dignity of being the first among pastors, it is necessary to report to Peter or his successor everything new that has been introduced in the catholic Church by those deviating from the truth. Thus, having learned to do this from our ancient holy fathers, we too, the most humble and lowly of all, in view of the innovation introduced to our Church, consider it our duty . . . to report this to the Angel of your supreme beatitude in our humble letter.[2]

St Maximus the Confessor is equally clear regarding the privileges of the Roman see:

---

[2]Theodore the Studite *Epistles* 33, to Leo, pope of Rome.

He is only wasting words who thinks that he must convince or lure such people as myself, instead of satisfying and entreating the blessed pope of the most holy catholic Church of Rome, i.e., the Apostolic Throne, which is from the incarnate Son of God himself and which, in accordance with the holy canons and the definitions of faith, received from all the holy councils universal and supreme dominion, authority, and the power over all of God's churches throughout the world to bind and loose.[3]

All the ends of the world . . . unswervingly gaze at the holiest Church of the Romans as the sun of eternal light, and at its confession and faith, taking from it the brilliant splendor of the patristic and holy dogmas . . . For from the very beginning, since the incarnate God the Word descended to us, Christian churches everywhere have viewed the Roman Church, the greatest among them, as a common stronghold and foundation, as being—according to the Savior's promise—forever invincible against the gates of hell, as possessing the keys to the Orthodox faith.[4]

The popes saw in such letters a confirmation of the understanding of their authority that would become firmly established in the west. Eastern Christians wrote to the popes primarily when the Orthodox faith needed to be defended against heretics. When Maximus the Confessor wrote the lines just quoted, all four eastern patriarchates—Constantinople, Alexandria, Antioch, and Jerusalem—supported the monothelite heresy, whereas Rome remained Orthodox. According to Maximus, the Roman Church is catholic and apostolic as long as it confesses the Orthodox faith.[5] When the iconoclasts were triumphant in Constantinople during the lifetime of Theodore the Studite, Rome rejected the iconoclast heresy; Byzantine iconodules therefore appealed to the pope as the keeper of the true faith.

The main point of theological contention between the churches of the east and west was the Latin teaching on the procession of the Holy Spirit from the Father and the Son. This doctrine, based on the trinitarian views of the blessed Augustine and other Latin fathers, led to a change in the wording of the Nicene-Constantinopolitan Creed: instead of "who proceeds from the Father," the phrase "who proceeds from the Father and the Son [filioque]" was

---

[3] Theological and Polemical Works 12.
[4] Theological and Polemical Works 11.
[5] See Jean-Claude Larchet, St Maximus the Confessor: Mediator between the East and West (Moscow, 2004), 181–82.

introduced in the west. The expression "who proceeds from the Father" is based on the words of Christ himself (Jn 15.26) and therefore possesses indisputable authority, whereas the addition "and the Son" has no basis either in scripture or in the tradition of the early Christian Church. Indeed, it was first inserted into the creed at councils in Toledo in the sixth and seventh centuries, supposedly as a defense against Arianism. From Spain the *filioque* spread to France and Germany, where it was affirmed at the Council of Frankfurt in 794. The court theologians of Charlemagne even began to reproach the Byzantines because they recited the Symbol of Faith without this addition. For some time Rome resisted the introduction of changes to the creed. In 808 Pope Leo III wrote to Charlemagne that, while the *filioque* was acceptable from a theological standpoint, its insertion into the creed was undesirable. Leo placed tablets with the Symbol of Faith without the *filioque* in St Peter's Cathedral. Nevertheless, by the beginning of the eleventh century the reading of the creed with the addition "and the Son" had also become Roman practice.[6]

The first to focus attention on the *filioque* in the east was St Maximus the Confessor, who demonstrated that when the Latins spoke about the procession of the Holy Spirit from the Father and the Son, they had in mind the same thing as the Greeks: namely, the procession from the Father through the Son.[7]

While Maximus took a conciliatory stance, Patriarch Photius was more rigid. He wrote the following about the Latins:

They have attempted–O, the intrigues of the enemy!–to distort the most sacred and holy Symbol of Faith, indestructibly affirmed by all the councils and ecumenical decisions, with erroneous theorizing and [falsely] ascribed words, in their excessive impudence contriving the innovation that the Holy Spirit proceeds not only from the Father, but also from the Son. Has anyone ever heard the impious utter such words? What insidious snake belched this out into their hearts? Who can endure Christians introducing two sources to the Holy Trinity: the Father as the origin of the Son and Spirit, and another, the Son, also as the origin of the Spirit? In so doing they destroy the notion of one source through bitheism, and

[6]Bishop Kallistos Ware of Diokleia, *The Orthodox Church* (Harmondsworth, 1967), 58–59.
[7]PG 91.133d–136a.

tear Christian theology into pieces, of which remains something that is no better than Greek mythology, and treat with contempt the dignity of the super-essential and life-giving Trinity.[8]

Ritual differences between the east and west existed during the entire history of Christianity. The liturgical rubrics of the Roman Church differed from those of the eastern churches in an entire array of details, particularly those mentioned in Patriarch Photius' encyclical. However, it was only after Photius' time that they began to attract serious attention. In the middle of the eleventh century, the main liturgical problem in debates between the east and the west was the Latin use of unleavened bread in the eucharist (the Byzantines used leavened bread). The Byzantines saw in this seemingly trifling detail a reflection of serious theological differences in the understanding of the essence of Christ's body, which is given to the faithful in the eucharist: if leavened bread symbolizes the consubstantiality of Christ's body with ours, then unleavened bread is a symbol for the difference between Christ's body and ours. The Greeks viewed the use of unleavened bread as an attack on the very heart of eastern Christian theology: the teaching on deification, which was little known in the west.[9]

Polemics over this issue preceded the dispute of 1054. The direct cause of this conflict was a decree by Patriarch Michael Cerularius of Constantinople (1043–1058) to close Latin rite churches and monasteries in Constantinople where the eucharist was celebrated using unleavened bread. Issued in 1052, this order was in retaliation for oppression in the Byzantine provinces of Italy, where the Normans, collaborating with the popes, forced the Greeks to accept the Latin rite. In 1053 Cerularius entrusted Archbishop Leo of Ochrid, and in 1054 the Studite monk Nicetas Stethatos, with the task of developing theological arguments against the liturgical use of unleavened bread. These writings were then read in Rome, causing Pope Leo IX (1049–1054) to dispatch legates to Constantinople.

Although the legates—Cardinal Humbert, Cardinal-Deacon Friedrich (the future Pope Stephen IX), and Archbishop Peter of Amalfi—were formally sent to Emperor Constantine IX Monomachus (1042–1055), they also met with the

[8]Photius of Constantinople *Encyclicals* 9 (PG 102.725d–728a).

[9]For more on this see M.A. Busygin, "The Dogmatic Content of the Polemics over Unleavened Bread," in *Patrology, Philosophy, Hermeneutics: Works of the Higher School of Religion and Philosophy* 1 (St Petersburg, 1992), 20–27.

patriarch, whom they treated with extreme contempt. Soon after their arrival the legates, together with the emperor, visited the Stoudios monastery, where a debate with Nicetas Stethatos on unleavened bread took place. In response to Nicetas' work, which had become known to the legates prior to their arrival in Constantinople, Cardinal Humbert wrote a treatise entitled *Against the Greek Slander*. In this work, Humbert hurled insults at Nicetas instead of offering substantive answers to his theological arguments. For example: "You are more foolish than a donkey . . . your place is not in the Stoudios monastery but in a circus or a brothel . . . you have vomited forth so much that you are no better than filthy and rabid dogs in your distortion of divine doctrine."[10] One can assume that the debate at Stoudios took place in the same vein. At the end of the dispute Nicetas acknowledged defeat and recanted his treatise, which was immediately burned in the monastery courtyard.

The papal legates insisted on holding negotiations with the patriarch; the patriarch, however, offended by the legates' disrespectful behavior during their first meeting, stubbornly refused. Having lost all patience, on July 15, 1054 the legates entered Hagia Sophia—which was filled with worshipers— went into the altar and, interrupting the service, leveled accusations against Patriarch Michael. They then placed on the altar a bull, written in Latin, that declared the excommunication of the patriarch and his adherents and listed ten charges of heresy, one being the "omission" of the *filioque* from the Symbol of Faith. After this the legates left the cathedral, shaking the dust from their feet and proclaiming: "God sees and judges." The patriarch, speechless from what had transpired, at first refused to accept the bull, but then had it translated into Greek. When its content became known to the people, it provoked unrest so intense that the legates had to leave Constantinople in haste. On July 20, Michael Cerularius convened a council of twenty bishops, at which he excommunicated the pope and his legates.

Thus occurred the great schism, which divided Christendom into two parts and has yet to be healed. Formally it was a break between the local churches of Rome and Constantinople; however, the patriarch of Constantinople was subsequently supported by the other eastern patriarchates and the younger churches that had entered into Byzantium's sphere of influence, including the Russian Church. Over time the Church of the west came to be called the "Catholic" Church, that of the east the "Orthodox," although both

[10] *Epistle to Marinus.*

designations originally referred to the united ecumenical Church both in the east and the west.

Soon after, Michael Cerularius sent a letter to Patriarch Peter of Antioch. In it he enumerated all the points on which he believed the Latins had deviated from the right faith and lapsed into "Judaism":

They do the following according to Jewish practice: The use of unleavened bread is in itself an error; so is the fact that they eat things strangled, that they shave, that they observe Saturdays, that they eat unclean things, that their monks eat meat and pig fat and the entire skin up to the meat, that they eat cheese during the first week of the fasts and meatfare week, that they eat meat on Wednesdays, cheese and eggs on Fridays, and on Saturdays fast the entire day. In addition to these violations, they have introduced an addition to the holy Symbol, based on malicious and dangerous reasoning, which runs thus: "in the Holy Spirit, the Lord, the Giver of Life, who proceeds from the Father and the Son." And at the beginning of the divine sacrament they pronounce: "One is holy, one is Lord, Jesus Christ, to the glory of God the Father through the Holy Spirit." Moreover, they forbid the marriage of priests; in other words, they do not allow those with wives to the priestly rank, instead ordaining celibate men. And cousins are allowed to marry each other. And during communion at the liturgy, one of the celebrants kisses the others while eating unleavened bread. And the bishops wear rings on their hands, since they have supposedly taken their Church as wife, and—so it is said—wear engagement rings. And heading out into battle, they besmirch their hands with blood, inciting souls against themselves and being themselves incited. As some have assured us, when performing holy baptism they baptize through one immersion, calling on the name of the Father, Son, and Holy Spirit, filling the mouth of the baptized with salt . . . And they do not venerate the relics of the saints, and some of them, even the holy icons. And they have not canonized, alongside the other saints, our holy and great fathers, teachers, and hierarchs, namely Gregory the Theologian, Basil the Great, and the divine Chrysostom, and even completely reject their teaching. Instead they have added some others, who can hardly be joined to the choirs of the saints—even partly.[11]

[11]Michael Cerularius *Epistles* 3.12–14.

The majority of these faults of the Latins are purely ritual in nature and do not relate to the essence of the faith (the wearing of rings by bishops, the shaving of beards, fasting on Saturdays, the eating of meat by monks), while others reflect practices of church life in the west (celibacy of the clergy), and still others are due to cultural peculiarities of the Latin west (scanty knowledge of the Greek fathers). Only one serious dogmatic difference between the east and west is mentioned: the teaching on the *filioque*, but it is mentioned in passing, along with other liturgical trifles. In this epistle Cerularius makes no mention of the main reason for the division: namely, papal primacy.

In another letter to Peter of Antioch, Cerularius mentions that "from the times of the holy Sixth Ecumenical Council, the commemoration of the name of the pope in the sacred diptychs of our holy churches ceased because Vigilius, who was pope at the time, did not answer this council and did not anathematize Theodoret's writings against the right faith and the twelve chapters of St Cyril, as well as the epistle of Ibas. And since then the pope has been cut off from our most holy and catholic Church."[12] Two points should be mentioned in this connection. First, what was meant here was not the sixth but the Fifth Ecumenical Council. Second, after the Roman Church acknowledged the Fifth Ecumenical Council, the pope's name was restored to the diptychs of the eastern churches.

The Crusades and the Union of Lyons

At first the schism of 1054 seemed to be only one of the numerous misunderstandings that occurred from time to time in relations between churches. Although attempts at reconciliation were subsequently undertaken, it soon became clear that the division was much deeper and more tragic than expected. The entire Orthodox east was rapidly drawn into anti-Latin polemics, which was not always conducted with theological professionalism. For example, St Theodosius of the Kiev Caves wrote the following to Izyaslav Yaroslavich, grand prince of Kiev, "on the faith of the Varangians":

> Do not go over to the Latin faith or practice their customs; avoid their communion and all their teaching, and shun their habits . . . for they

[12]Michael Cerularius *Epistles* 4.2.

believe wrongly and live impurely: they eat dogs and cats and drink their urine. They eat lions, wild horses, and donkeys, that which has been strangled, carrion, bear meat, beaver meat, and the tails of beavers. And they eat meat during fasting days . . . And they fast on Saturdays and, having fasted in the evening, eat milk and eggs. And when they sin, they do not ask God for forgiveness but their priests, who forgive them in exchange for gifts. Their priests do not enter into lawful marriage but beget children with slaves, and continue to serve unhindered; and their bishops have concubines and go to war. And they venerate the host outside the liturgy. They do not kiss icons or the relics of saints. And they kiss the cross after drawing it on the ground, whereupon they stand up and trample on it with their feet. They place corpses with their feet to the west . . . They are baptized through one immersion, we through three; when we are baptized we are anointed with myrrh and oil; they, however, pour salt into the mouth of the one being baptized. While doing this, they do not give the person the name of a saint but the name that happens to be uttered by the parents. And they say that the Holy Spirit proceeds from the Father and the Son. There are many other evil deeds that they do, and their faith is full of depravity and ruin, and they do things that even the Jews do not.[13]

Commenting on this text, whose authenticity is disputed by a number of scholars, Metropolitan Makary (Bulgakov) notes: "Among the accusations leveled against the Latins in the letter, there are some that might relate to certain individuals but by no means to the entire Roman Church, and some that are not entirely accurate."[14] In reality, the letter of Theodosius of the Kiev Caves is nothing other than a paraphrase of the letter of Michael Cerularius to Patriarch Peter of Antioch, with the addition of several anecdotal details. Just as during the times of Patriarch Photius, no distinction is made between the Roman Church's serious dogmatic deviations from ancient church tradition, such as the *filioque*, and various ritual trifles through which Latin practice differed from that of the east. The addition of anecdotal information on how the Latins ate strangled things and drank urine was calculated to create the image of an enemy and to discredit and demonize the "Varangian" faith.

[13]Cited in Metropolitan Makary (Bulgakov), *History of the Russian Church* (Moscow, 1994–1996), 2.551.

[14]Ibid., 191.

An image of the enemy was also created in the west. In the second half of the eleventh century, the idea of undertaking a crusade to the east in order to liberate the ancient Christian holy sites seized by the Arabs and Turks was conceived. The First Crusade began very successfully: in 1098 the crusaders ousted the Turks from Antioch, and in 1099 from Jerusalem. However, the crusaders did not take into account that Christians with their own churches and patriarchs continued to live in the liberated lands. Instead, they banished the lawful eastern patriarchs from their sees and appointed Latin bishops in their stead. The creation of an "alternative" hierarchy in territories that had belonged to the eastern patriarchates since ancient times demonstrated that a final break between the east and the west had taken place, and that in the west the eastern churches were no longer recognized as churches. In 1204, when Constantinople was seized and barbarously pillaged during the Fourth Crusade, the Latins also assigned their own patriarch to the see of Constantinople. The Latin patriarchates of Antioch and Constantinople ceased to exist after the expulsion of the crusaders from the east at the end of the thirteenth century. But although the Latin patriarchate of Jerusalem was abolished in 1291, it was reestablished by the Catholic Church in 1847 and still exists today.

The sack of Constantinople by the crusaders on April 13, 1204 was one of the most tragic events not only in the history of Byzantium, but also in the history of Orthodox-Catholic relations. Christian holy sites and sanctuaries were mercilessly destroyed and desecrated by the Latins. The Byzantine historian Nicetas Choniates, who was an eyewitness of the events, describes this in the following words: "Alas, the venerable icons have been shamelessly thrown down! The relics of martyrs who suffered for Christ have been scattered throughout unclean places! One could see—though just hearing of it is horrifying enough—how the divine body and blood of Christ was being thrown to the ground and spilled. Plundering the precious vessels that held these, the Latins smashed some of them and hid the jewels that had embellished them in their bosom, while others were taken to be used at their tables."[15]

According to Nicetas, the crusaders "committed iniquity against the people of Christ: they refused to accord anyone the least amount of condescen-

---

[15]Nicetas Choniates, *History, Beginning with the Reign of John Comnenos* (St Petersburg, 1860–1862), 2.321.

sion, instead depriving them of all their money, property, housing, and clothing, leaving absolutely nothing to those who had possessed something . . .
These are the zealots who had borne the cross on their shoulders and swore
many times before it and the Word of God to traverse Christian lands without bloodshed . . . and to arm themselves against the Saracens and stain their
swords with the blood of the pillagers of Jerusalem!"[16] The testimony of this
Byzantine historian is confirmed by analogous reports by the crusaders themselves, who wrote of the innumerable treasures, gold, silver, church vessels,
and precious gems they had plundered, and of the fact that Latin priests who
had arrived with them also took part in pillaging the city.[17]

The Fourth Lateran Council, convened by Pope Innocent III (1198–1216)
in 1215, approved of the seizure of Constantinople by the crusaders. The council confirmed the powers of the Latin patriarch of Constantinople and
declared Constantinople the second episcopal see of the Christian world,
which had rejoined the "mother church." It allowed for the temporary use of
the Byzantine rite, and permitted Greek bishops to continue to serve in areas
where the overwhelming majority of the population was Greek, provided
they swear an oath of loyalty to the pope. The council also decided that Latin
bishops should be appointed to territories where Greeks and Latins lived
together, as well as to vacant sees in the east.

From the thirteenth to the fifteenth centuries, papal policy on the eastern
churches was determined by the conviction that the Catholic Church was the
only true Church, and that salvation was impossible outside it. This idea is
present in all the documents of the Roman *magisterium* of this period, including papal epistles and encyclicals, such as the letter of Pope Honorius III
(1216–1227) to the "kings of Rus'" of January 17, 1227. The aim of this letter was
to secure the possibility for Latin missionaries to act unhindered in the territory of Livonia and Estonia, although the pope desired to see all of Rus'
under his spiritual authority:

[16]Ibid., 324–25.
[17]Geoffroy de Villehardouin, *On the Conquest of Constantinople*, cited in Metropolitan Kirill of
Smolensk and Kaliningrad, "From Tragic Divisions to the Search for Unity: The East and West at the
Threshold of the Millennium," in *Proceedings of the International Scholarly-Practical Conference "Orthodox
Byzantium and the Latin West" (On the Occasion of the 950-year Anniversary of the Division of Churches and
the 800-year Anniversary of the Taking of Constantinople by the Crusaders), Moscow, May 26–27, 2004*
(Moscow, 2005), 10.

Wishing to attend soundly to the salvific teaching, you are ready to completely repudiate all the errors you have committed, as mentioned earlier, due to a lack of missionaries, for which the Lord became angry with you and has exposed you to many tribulations. A more terrible misfortune will befall you if you do not depart from the path of error and enter on the path of truth. For the longer you persist in error, the more terrible the misfortunes will be that await you. Thus, even if the Lord does not grow angry every day, the sword of his retribution still hangs over those who despise baptism. Therefore, desiring to receive an answer from you whether you wish to receive a legate of the Roman Church, in order to understand through his sound teaching the truth of the catholic faith, without which nobody is saved, we urgently ask, exhort, and entreat all of you to inform us of your wish in this respect through letters and trustworthy envoys. For the time being, however, while maintaining a lasting peace with the Christians of Livonia and Estonia, do not hinder the spread of the Christian faith and thereby incur the indignation of the divine apostolic see, which can easily exact retribution should it so desire. It would be better for you instead to be deemed worthy of mercy and love from both—through the complete forgiveness that is the Lord's, and show true obedience and preserve the divine rituals.[18]

Rome's policy of union, which caused immeasurable suffering to Orthodox Christians, emerged at the end of the thirteenth century. The first ecclesiastical union between Rome and Constantinople was concluded on the initiative of Byzantine emperor Michael VIII Palaeologos (†1282). In 1259 he was declared emperor in Nicaea, and in 1261 he liberated Constantinople from the crusaders. In order to consolidate his power, Michael VIII blinded the underaged John Lascaris, the lawful successor to the throne; for this he was excommunicated by Patriarch Arsenios (1255–1259, 1261–1267). Michael then ordered that a council be convened, which deposed Arsenios and appointed Germanos III patriarch (1267). However, due to popular support for Arsenios, Germanos was unable to remain in his position for long. In 1266 Joseph, spiritual father of the emperor, became patriarch (1266–1275, 1282–1283) and rescinded the excommunication.

---

[18]Cited in V.I. Matuzova and E.L. Nazarova, *The Crusaders and Rus'* (Moscow, 2002), 219–20.

However, conflict soon arose between the patriarch and emperor over the latter's desire to enter into union with Rome. For several years Michael corresponded with several Roman pontiffs on this subject, considering a union to be a political necessity for consolidating his power and hindering a new crusade. Answering one of the emperor's letters, Pope Gregory X invited him to send a delegation to a council in Lyons and stated that a union of churches would hinge upon the acceptance of the *filioque* and papal primacy by the eastern bishops. After Patriarch Joseph rejected such a union, a delegation headed by the former patriarch Germanos was sent to Lyons. At the Council of Lyons of 1274, the delegates from Constantinople signed an act of union with Rome on the conditions suggested by the pope. The council ended with the singing of the creed with the *filioque*.

The majority of the Greek hierarchy, led by Patriarch Joseph, did not recognize the union, and the emperor appointed John XII Vekkos (1275–1282), a supporter of the union, to the see of Constantinople. Thereafter began a persecution of the union's opponents, who were exiled, imprisoned, deprived of their property, and tortured. Nevertheless opposition to the union could not be crushed, and when Michael Palaeologos died, he was not even accorded a church burial. According to the historian Nicephoros Gregoras, several people brought the emperor's body from the palace at night and buried it as an apostate. Andronicos II Palaeologos (1283–1328), Michael's son, rejected the union and held a council in Constantinople in 1283 that condemned the Latin teaching on the procession of the Holy Spirit from the Father and the Son. Patriarch John Vekkos abdicated the see and retired to a monastery, and churches where uniate services had been held were reconsecrated.

The Union of Lyons entered the history of the Orthodox Church as one of the most shameful incidents in Orthodox-Catholic relations. In the Roman Catholic Church, however, it is recognized as an ecumenical council. At the same time, the Roman Catholic Church has recently acknowledged its guilt for the distress caused to the Orthodox. In June 2004, Pope John Paul II asked for forgiveness from Patriarch Bartholomew I for the sack of Constantinople by the crusaders. Earlier, in 1965, Pope Paul VI and Patriarch Athenagoras lifted the mutual excommunications that were imposed in 1054 by Cardinal Humbert and Patriarch Michael Cerularius. Both of these events testify to the desire to move beyond the dark pages in the history of Orthodox-Catholic relations and make a new beginning.

This will is further attested to by the fact that official representatives of the Catholic and Orthodox churches signed a document in Balamand in 1993 condemning Uniatism as a practice contradicting the traditions of both churches.[19] The document states that past attempts to restore unity between the eastern and western churches through such unions only exacerbated existing divisions.[20]

The Union of Lyons and all the subsequent unions that will be examined later proved that the forceful imposition of Latin dogmas and rituals on the Orthodox cannot restore the unity of the Church. One contemporary historian writes: "Such attempts at union were, in fact, especially responsible for reinforcing separation; the question of the unity of the churches was long confused by falsehood and calculations and poisoned by nonecclesiastical and base motives. The Church recognizes only unity and therefore cannot recognize any 'union.' The latter implies a lack of confidence in unity, a denial of the unifying fire of grace which makes all that is 'natural'—all historical insults, limitations, gulfs, and misunderstandings—nonexistent, and can overcome them by force of the divine power."[21]

LATE BYZANTINE CHURCH LITERATURE: HESYCHASM AND THE PALAMITE CONTROVERSY

The period between the tenth and the mid-fifteenth centuries witnessed the gradual decline of the eastern Roman empire and of the political significance of the Byzantine emperor. For the Christian Church in the east, it was a time of difficult trials, brought on by the crusades and the advance of the Seljuk Turks, who were now approaching the very heart of the empire—Constantinople. Part of the territories where eastern Christians lived were in the hands of Arabs. At the same time, the reigns of the Macedonian (867–1057), Comnenos (1057–1204), and Palaeologos dynasties (1251–1453) were marked by a number of "rebirths" in literature, science, and art, respectively called the Macedonian, Comnenian, and Palaeologan renaissances. These flowerings also

---

[19]"Uniatism, Method of Union of the Past, and the Present Search for Full Communion," para. 2 (Balamand, 1993), in *Unity: The International Mixed Theological Commission* (Paris, 1995), 141.

[20]Ibid., para. 9, 145.

[21]Schmemann, *Historical Road*, 254.

*St Symeon the New Theologian
(contemporary Greek icon)*

occurred in the Church, which continued to enjoy an intense liturgical, theological, ascetic, and mystical life, despite the strained circumstances.

A major Byzantine writer and mystic who flourished at end of the tenth and beginning of the eleventh centuries was St Symeon the New Theologian (†c. 1022). The abbot of one of Constantinople's monasteries, Symeon exerted great influence on the capital's aristocracy and had numerous disciples. His fiery sermons stimulated spiritual renewal not only among monastics but also the laity. Symeon's corpus of writings includes 3 *Homilies on Theology*, which expound the teaching on the Holy Trinity, 15 *Moral Homilies*, 34 *Catechetical Homilies*, 225 *Theological, Gnostic and Practical Chapters*, and 2 *Prayers of Thanksgiving*. The leitmotif of all these works, in which theological, ascetic, and mystical themes are intertwined, is the contemplation of the divine light and the spiritual union of the person with God. Among his works are also the 58 *Hymns of Divine Love*, a collection of prayers, philosophical and theological treatises, and descriptions of mystical experience written in poetic form—a work unique in world literature.

Symeon's mystical ardor and moral radicalism aroused criticism among certain official representatives of the church hierarchy, leading to his banishment from Constantinople by a church synod. Among other things, he held that salvation is impossible without exalted mystical gifts and the contemplation of the divine light. Symeon was extremely open about his own visions of this divine light:

> What is this unforeseen wonder that is happening even now?
> Does God now wish to be seen by sinners also,
> He Who long ago ascended on high, and has taken his seat on a throne
> in his Father's heaven, and remains hidden? . . .
> I shudder to consider these very things, and how shall I write them in
>   words?
> What sort of hand shall conduct the service, what sort of pen shall
>   write?

What sort of word shall recount, what nature of tongue shall speak out?
What sort of lips shall say the things seen happening in me,
things being accomplished throughout the day?
Furthermore, in both night itself and in darkness itself,
I see Christ frightfully opening the heavens for me, (Acts 7.56)
himself stooping to look and to be seen by me
at the same time with the Father and the Spirit, the thrice holy light,
a light that is one in three and three in one.
By all means they are the light, and the one light is the three
which also enlightens my soul more than the sun,
and illuminates my darkened mind . . .
and the things which cannot be known I have somewhat understood,
and now from afar I look upon the beautiful invisible things,
I am violently struck down with astonishment by the
     unapproachableness
of the light, the unbearableness of the glory, oppressed by trembling . . .
And so I was troubled by the wonder, and trembling greatly;
I was beyond myself, the whole of me fainted, entirely at a loss,
not bearing the unendurable I turned away from the glory,
and during the night I ran away from my perceptions here,
and I was sheltered by my thoughts and concealed among them.[22]

Being an outstanding teacher of the moral life, Symeon wrote many works admonishing monastics and laymen on moral, ascetical, and spiritual questions. In his poem "Who is a Monk, and What is his Work?" Symeon outlines the ideal of the monastic life:

The monk is one who is not mixed with the world
and always converses with God alone,
seeing he is seen, loving he is loved,
and he becomes a light mysteriously shining.
Being glorified he seems all the more a beggar,
and belonging he is like a stranger.
Oh marvel that is in every way strange and inexpressible!
On account of boundless riches I am a poor man,

---

[22]Hymn ii, in Daniel K. Griggs, trans., *Divine Eros: Hymns of St Symeon the New Theologian* (Crestwood, NY: SVS Press, 2010), 64–67.

and possessing much I seem to have nothing.
And I say that I thirst through an abundance of waters,
and I ask who shall give to me what I have in abundance,
and where shall I find what I see each day?
And how shall I grasp what is both within me
and outside the world, for it is entirely unseen?
If anyone has ears to hear, let them hear (Mt 11.15)
and truly understand the words of an illiterate![23]

Symeon's uniqueness is due not only to the autobiographical nature of his writings, so uncharacteristic of the eastern fathers, and not only to the originality of their content, but also to the unusual form in which he clothed his ideas. He was a church poet, writing not liturgical texts but free poetry, and using not the ancient meters characteristic of the studied poetry of his age but the syllabic-tonic rhythms of folk poetry. This made his poems accessible not only to the learned but also to the simple folk. All of his poetic works were permeated by profound religious feeling:

How are You both a fire gushing forth,
and also a sprinkling water,
how do You both inflame and sweeten,
how do You make mortality disappear?

How do You turn humans into gods,
how do You make darkness light,
how do You raise up from hell,
how do You prevent mortals from perishing?

How do You drag darkness to the light,
how do You seize the night,
how do You illuminate my heart,
how do You entirely transform me?

How do You become one with human beings,
how do You make them children of God,
how do you make them burn with desire for You,
how do You wound without a sword?

[23]Hymn 3, ibid., 48–49.

> How do You endure, how do You tolerate,
> how do You not immediately render what is due,
> how is it that You Who dwell beyond everyone
> see the duties of all?
>
> How, though You are far from us,
> do You look down on the practice of each?
> Give patient endurance to your servants,
> so that afflictions do not bury them![24]

Symeon's teaching also influenced the development of monastic life on Mount Athos—which is confirmed by the large number of manuscripts of his works in Athonite monasteries. In the tenth and eleventh centuries, the peninsula of Athos in northern Greece was densely populated by monks: according to certain hagiographical sources, around three thousand men of different nationalities led monastic lives during this period. For more than a thousand years Athos has been a confederation of men's monasteries united by one typikon; women are strictly forbidden from visiting the Holy Mountain. This rule began to crystalize during the lifetime of St Athanasius of Athos (c. 925/30–c. 1000), the founder of the Great Lavra that bears his name. In the tenth and eleventh centuries were founded the monasteries of Vatopedi, Iviron, the Amalfitan, Xiropotamou, Zographou, St Panteleimon, St Xenophont, Esphigmenou, Karakalou, Konstamonitou, Simonopetra, and Chilandar. Other monasteries as well as sketes and monastic cells appeared later. Athos was noted for its international character: from the tenth century Iviron was populated by Georgians; the Amalfitan monastery by monastics from southern Italy; from the eleventh century the monastery of Xilourgou was owned by Russians, who later received the monastery of St Panteleimon in the twelfth century; and from the end of the twelfth century Serbs inhabited the Chilandar monastery and the Bulgarians Zographou.

In the thirteenth century Athos was the epicenter of a monastic movement that scholars would later call hesychasm. Hesychasm (from the Greek *hesychia,* "silence") usually denotes a movement that engulfed broad circles of Byzantine monasticism from the thirteenth through the fourteenth centuries and is reflected in the writings of the Athonite monks Nicephoros the Hesychast, Gregory the Sinaite, Gregory Palamas, and a number of other ascetic

---

[24]Hymn 6, ibid., 55–56.

writers. Among other things, this school is characterized by its interest in the contemplation of the divine light, on which Symeon the New Theologian wrote, as well as in the psychosomatic technique used for the Jesus prayer.

The practice of the Jesus prayer, or the continuous uttering of "Lord Jesus Christ, Son of God, have mercy on me" (or, in the shorter forms, "Lord Jesus Christ, have mercy on me," "Son of God, have mercy on me," and "Lord, have mercy"), had been known in monastic circles since the eighth century. During the age of hesychasm, however, the practice of this prayer began to be accompanied by certain physical techniques, which were described in detail for the first time in a treatise entitled *Method of Sacred Prayer and Vigilance*, which is attributed to Symeon the New Theologian but was probably penned by a different author.[25] The essence of the psychosomatic method for the Jesus prayer described in the treatise lies in the following:

> Sit down in a quiet cell, alone in a corner, and try to do that which I will tell you. Close the door of your mind and raise your mind above everything vain and temporary. Then, placing your beard on your breast and directing your sensual eye with your entire mind toward the middle of your abdomen, that is, the navel, control the breathing of your nose so as not to breath frequently, and with your mind gaze into your depths in order to find the place of the heart, where all the powers of the soul are usually found. At first you will find only darkness and an impenetrable wall; but if you constantly continue these endeavors day and night, you will discover—O miracle!—unceasing joy! For as soon as the mind finds the place of the heart, it immediately beholds that which it never knew of before. Within the heart it will see air and itself, everything that is bright and filled with discernment. Thereafter, by calling on Jesus Christ, it will drive out and destroy thoughts at their very appearance, before they can fully take shape. From this time onward the mind, recalling the hatred of the demons, seeks and destroys the noetic enemies with natural anger. With God's help you will learn the rest, watching over the mind and keeping Jesus in your heart.[26]

---

[25]For more on this see Hegumen Hilarion (Alfeyev), *St Symeon the New Theologian and Orthodox Tradition*, 2d ed. (St Petersburg, 2001), 44–46.

[26]*Method of Sacred Prayer and Vigiliance*, in *The Path to Holy Silence* (Moscow, 1999), 23–24.

In the second quarter of the fourteenth century, this prayer technique and the hesychast teaching as a whole were the subject of debates in Byzantium. The main participants in these debates were Barlaam of Calabria (1290–1348) and St Gregory Palamas (1296–1359). Barlaam, who came from the Greek Uniate community in southern Italy, carved out a brilliant career as a philosopher and scholar at the imperial court after arriving in Constantinople in the early 1330s. On behalf of the emperor he conducted negotiations with papal legates on the reunification of the churches. During these talks, Barlaam

St Gregory Palamas

wrote several treatises against the Latin teaching on the *filioque* in which he held that neither the Greeks nor the Latins could assert the correctness of their teaching since God is totally unknowable, and since reasoning about him cannot be based on sensual experience. This standpoint did not satisfy Pope Benedict XII (1334–1342), to whom Barlaam's treatises were presented. For the pope dogmatic relativism was unacceptable, and he demanded that the Orthodox recognize the *filioque* as a necessary condition for concluding a union.

On the Orthodox side, Barlaam's writings evoked negative reactions from Athonite monastics headed by Gregory Palamas, who was a monk of the Great Lavra at the time. The correspondence between Gregory Palamas and Barlaam, which began with the question of the limits of the knowledge of God, soon turned into a debate over the essence of "noetic activity," the psychosomatic technique for the Jesus prayer, and the contemplation of the divine light. Barlaam mocked the psychosomatic method, calling its monastic practitioners *omphalopsychoi*, or "those having their souls in their navel"—as if they believed that the human soul is located in this part of the human body. Barlaam considered the hesychast experience of contemplating the divine light to be a sensual and demonic phenomenon. In order to counter these accusations, which were leveled in both correspondence and in personal meetings with Barlaam, Gregory Palamas wrote the *Triads in Defense of the Holy Hesychasts*.

In this work Gregory first and foremost defends the monastic practice of the Jesus prayer, asserting that prayer is not only a mental but also a bodily act, that it is not only an Evagrian "ascent of the mind to God"[27] but also an act involving the entire person: the mind, heart, soul, body, eyes, and breathing. According to Gregory, the soul is a "single power with many capabilities; it makes use of the body, which receives life from it, as a tool." The bodily organ in which the human mind is localized is the heart, and it is here that the mind should be focused.[28] If the mind remains outside the body during prayer, as the opponents of hesychasm recommended,[29] it will never be able to achieve attention, and concentration and will remain distracted. The mind descends into the heart through the breath and along with it:

> Since even the concentrated mind is constantly distracted among those who have just begun the battle, necessitating that they refocus it, it slips away from the inexperienced, who do not yet know that there is nothing more difficult to control and fleeting than their own mind. Because of this, some recommend that those living in spiritual sobriety carefully observe their inhalation and exhalation and withhold their breath a little. In doing so, they withhold, as it were, the mind, until they learn to focus it thoroughly, "wrapped up in single-mindedness,"[30] after attaining, with God's help, the higher levels, when the mind ceases to wander and mingle with other thoughts. This comes naturally when one focuses attention: whenever one reflects on something attentively, particularly when people with a relaxed body and mind do so, the breath goes in and comes out peacefully. By resting spiritually and limiting the actions of the body as much as possible, the hesychasts stopped all the comparative, enumerative, and various other cognitive activity of the spiritual powers, all sensory perception and all voluntary bodily action in general, limiting all semi-voluntary actions, such as breathing, to the extent they could.[31]

Another issue on which Palamas came out decisively against Barlaam is the question of the knowledge of God. Addressing Barlaam's contention that God is completely unknowable, Gregory Palamas theologically substantiated the eastern Christian understanding of God as being simultaneously

[27]Evagrius *On Prayer* 36.
[28]Gregory Palamas *Triads* 1.2.3, in St Gregory Palamas, *Triads in Defense of the Holy Hesychasts*, trans. V. Venyaminov (Moscow, 1995), 43–44.
[29]*Triads* 1.2.6, ibid., 46.
[30]Dionysius the Areopagite *On the Divine Names* 4.9.
[31]*Triads* 1.2.7, Venyaminov, trans., 47–48.

unknowable and knowable, transcendent and immanent, unnamed and named, inexpressible and expressible, with whom one can both not have communion and have communion. One way of explaining this paradox in the eastern Christian tradition is the notion of the divine "energies," which are distinct from the divine essence. While God's essence is invisible, his energies can be seen; while his essence is unnameable, his energies can be named; and while God's essence is ineffable, his energies can by grasped by the mind.

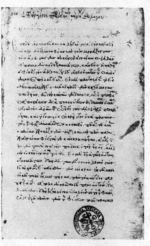

*Manuscript with writings of
St Gregory the Sinaite*

Finally, the third issue in the polemics between Barlaam and Palamas was the doctrine on the nature of the divine light contemplated by the hesychasts during prayer. According to Palamas, this light is not the essence of God, which is invisible and unattainable. At the same time, the divine light is not a material phenomenon or a created light, which are of a different nature than God's essence. The divine light contemplated by the hesychasts is an uncreated energy of God, coeternal with him and indivisible from him.

The arguments given by Palamas did not satisfy Barlaam, and he demanded that the emperor convene a council to resolve the questions raised during the debate. This council took place in Hagia Sophia on June 10, 1341; there Barlaam acknowledged defeat, and on the same day fled Byzantium for Avignon, to Pope Clement VI (1342–1352), who appointed him bishop of the city of Gerace in the kingdom of Naples. The appointment was made through the influence of Francesco Petrarca, to whom Barlaam had taught Greek.[32] However, the controversy did not cease, and in the decade thereafter Akindynos, a former disciple of Palamas, as well as the court historian Nicephoros Gregoras, came out against Palamas. But the Constantinople councils of 1347 and 1351, convoked by Emperor John IV Cantacuzenos (1341–1355), confirmed Palamas' teaching for the second and third times. From 1347 until his death Gregory Palamas was archbishop of Thessalonica, and his disciples Isidore I (1347–1350), Kallistos I (1350–1354, 1355–1363), and Philotheos Kokkinos (1354–1355, 1364–1376) were elevated to the patriarchal throne of Con-

[32]Venyaminov, "An Overview of the Life and Thought of St Gregory Palamas," in ibid., 356.

stantinople. In 1368, nine years after his repose, Gregory Palamas was solemnly canonized by Patriarch Philotheos Kokkinos, and a decision was made to commemorate him each year on the second Sunday of Great Lent.

Gregory Palamas was also involved in an interesting episode in the history of relations between Christianity and Islam. By that time, Christians and Muslims had already lived side by side in many lands for centuries, and the initial, harshly negative attitude toward Islam among the Orthodox had softened to a certain extent. Typical in this respect are the acts of the Council of Constantinople of 1180, convened by Emperor Manuel Comnenos (1143–1180). The council examined the anathema contained in the Greek Book of Needs against the "God of Muhammad, of whom Muhammad says that he is God *olosfyros*,[33] that he does not give birth or was born, and that no one is like him." This anathema, formulated in the council's decision, troubled those who wished to convert from Islam to Orthodoxy. The council took the decision to remove this anathema against the "God of Muhammad" from the service book and retain only the anathema against Muhammad.

Polemics between Gregory Palamas and Muslims took place in 1354–1355, while he was being held captive by the Turks. Spending more than a year in captivity, Palamas spoke with the highest-ranking persons of the Turkish state, including Prince Izmail, the grandson of Grand Emir Orkhan. He wrote in detail about these conversations in his *Letter to My Church*, addressed to the flock of Thessalonica. Another work connected to this episode is the *Debate with the Chiones*, compiled by the doctor Taronites, who witnessed Gregory's debates with the Muslims.

In addition to theological questions, such as the doctrine of the one God, faith in the divinity of Jesus Christ, and the significance of Muhammad, a number of historiosophical arguments were advanced during the debates. For example, the Muslims saw their military superiority over the Greeks as God's blessing. Gregory responded to this assertion in the following words:

> It is only an impious and criminal people, hateful to God, which boasts that it has prevailed over the Romaeans because of its love for God, not knowing that this world lies in evil (1 Jn 5.19) and that evil people, slaves of the underworld, often rule over it, having conquered their neighbors by

---

[33]The Greek word *olosfyros* literally means "completely round," i.e., closed within himself or one and indivisible.

the power of their weapons. This is why idolaters had dominion over nearly all the inhabited world until the reign of Constantine, who was truly guided by love for God, and why the world was ruled for a long time thereafter by people who differed in no way or in almost no way from them.[34]

The last sentence refers to the heretical emperors of the age of the ecumenical councils.

While Gregory did not mince words concerning Muslims in this letter, he was considerably more restrained and even affable during the debates with them. Military superiority cannot be the criterion of the truth of a religion, in his opinion, and religion should not be forced upon others. Palamas held that Christianity was superior to Islam since it is the religion of freedom, an idea he elucidated during one of the debates:

> After leaving from the east, Muhammad did conquer lands until the west. But he conquered by war, by the sword, by pillage, by enslavement, by the slaughter of people. Of all this nothing could have come from God, who is good. This was rather caused by the will of man and the devil, who from the beginning has been a murderer (Jn 8.44). What shall we say? Did not Alexander leave the west and subjugate the entire east? And many others in different times have undertaken military campaigns and frequently gained dominion over the entire world. However, no people have ever entrusted their souls to them as you have to Muhammad. Still, while using force and promising delights, he has not been able to draw over to his side any single part of the world in its entirety. But although Christ's teaching rejects almost all the pleasures of life, it has spread to all the ends of the earth and reigns among those who wage war with it—without using violence, or better yet, having triumphed over violence, which it encounters constantly. This is an example of the "victory that has overcome the world" (1 Jn 5.4).[35]

This debate ended favorably for the saint, who was able to display the necessary tact at the right moment:

> Meanwhile, seeing that the Turks would become angry any minute, some Christians who happened to be next to me made signs hinting that it was

---

[34]Gregory Palamas *Letter to My Church* 8.
[35]*Letter to my Church* 28.

time to stop speaking. In order to relieve the tension that had mounted,
I said to the Turks with a smile: "If we agreed with each other's words, we
would adhere to the same teaching" . . . One of them said: "The time will
come when we shall arrive at a consensus with each other." And I agreed
with this and expressed my wish that this time would come as soon as
possible.[36]

THE UNION OF FLORENCE AND THE FALL OF BYZANTIUM: ORTHODOXY UNDER THE TURKISH YOKE

The middle of the fifteenth century witnessed two tragedies for the Orthodox Church: the Florentine union and the fall of Constantinople. By this
time all that was left of the Byzantine empire was Constantinople with its
suburbs, a small territory in the south of Greece, and several islands. All the
remaining lands that had formed part of a once powerful empire were now
occupied by the Turks or, in the west, by the Latins. The Byzantine emperor
became a vassal of the Turkish sultan, and the days of the great Christian
empire were numbered.

In an attempt to save the remnants of the empire from inevitable destruction, Emperor John VIII Palaeologos (1425–1448) made a desperate decision:
on November 24, 1437 he left for Italy to meet with Pope Eugene IV
(1431–1447), hoping to obtain military assistance from the Latins against the
Turks. Around six hundred people traveled with the emperor, including the
aged Patriarch Joseph II (1416–1439), twenty-two bishops, and numerous
clergy and laymen. The delegation also included representatives of the patriarchs of Alexandria, Antioch, and Jerusalem. On April 9, 1438, a council
chaired by Pope Eugene was opened in Ferrara, at which the differences
between the Greeks and the Latins were to be discussed. To this end a theological commission was formed. The Greek members included Metropolitan
Mark of Ephesus and Metropolitan Bessarion of Nicaea; the Latin members
consisted of several cardinals. Emperor John Palaeologos, who frequently
took part in the debates, was the official head of the Greek delegation.
Among the Greek delegates was also Isidore, who had been appointed metropolitan of Kiev not long before the council.

[36]*Letter to my Church* 29.

The first question the delegations discussed at the Ferrara council was that of purgatory. According to the Latin teaching, purgatory is a place where those who died in peace with the Church and did not commit mortal sins are posthumously exposed to temporary suffering; at the end of this period of suffering they enter into the kingdom of heaven. At the council the Latins maintained that "there is no need to pray for those who are in heaven since they have no need of this, nor for those who are in hell, since they cannot be freed or cleansed from sins."[37] Thus, they declared that it is possible to pray only for those who are in purgatory. The theology of the eastern Church, however, did not know of the doctrine of purgatory, and St Mark of Ephesus wrote in his answer to the Latins that the Church prays for all the departed, both those in heaven and those tormented in hell, in the hope that its prayers will be heard by God. Consensus between the two parties, however, could not be reached on this first issue.

The second topic of discussion was the Latin doctrine of the *filioque*. During the debates Mark of Ephesus and Bessarion of Nicaea came out against the teaching, which the Latins stubbornly defended. Once again, agreement could not be reached. After the council's sessions were transferred to Florence in February 1439, the decision was made not to discuss the insertion of the *filioque* into the creed and to limit the deliberations to general considerations on the procession of the Holy Spirit. In Florence the Latins declared their belief that the only source of the procession of the Holy Spirit is God the Father, after reading an excerpt from Maximus the Confessor's *Epistle to Marinus*. Still, the Greeks were not satisfied by their explanation, and St Mark of Ephesus presented a treatise entitled *Testimony on the Procession of the Holy Spirit Only from the Hypostasis of the Father*, in order to refute the doctrine of the *filioque*.

After a year and a half of intense theological discussions, the Latins issued an ultimatum, which basically stated that the Greeks had to accept the Latin doctrine. Should they do so, the pope promised military aid to the Byzantine emperor. On July 4, 1439 the Greeks presented a statement to the Latins declaring: "We agree with your teaching and with your addition to the Symbol, made on the basis of the holy fathers. We conclude a union with you and acknowledge that the Holy Spirit proceeds from the Father and the Son

[37]Mark of Ephesus, "The Chapters of the Latins to the Greeks on the Purifying Fire," in Archimandrite Amvrosy (Pogodin), *St Mark of Ephesus and the Union of Florence* (Moscow, 1994), 51.

as from one single source and cause."[38] This statement was signed by all members of the Greek delegation except St Mark of Ephesus, who refused to yield.

After receiving the statement, the pope demanded that they also agree with the Latin understanding of purgatory, the practice of serving the liturgy using unleavened bread, and the Latin teaching on the transubstantiation of bread and wine into Christ's body and blood during the utterance of the words "Take, eat; this is my body" and "Drink of it, all of you: this is my blood" (the Greeks believed that the holy gifts are transformed after the utterance of these words, when the priest says "changing them by your Holy Spirit"). They also required that the Greeks consent to the Latin doctrine on the primacy of the Roman pontiff not only in honor but also in jurisdiction (i.e., the eastern patriarchs should be subject to his jurisdiction), that they call the pope the "vicar of Christ" and "head of the Church," and that they recognize his right to interfere in matters of the Orthodox Church without hindrance. After much hesitation, thirty-three representatives of the Greek delegation finally signed the act of union on the conditions advanced by the Latins. The only official member of the delegation who did not sign the document was St Mark of Ephesus. The act was also not signed by Patriarch Joseph, who had passed away by that time.

After returning to Constantinople, St Mark wrote an encyclical in which he clearly distanced himself from the Council of Ferrara-Florence. As for the Greeks who had signed the act of union with the Latins, he wrote:

> Run from them as one runs from snakes . . . as from those who have sold and bought Christ . . . For we, along with the Damascene and all the fathers, do not say that the Spirit proceeds from the Son; but they, joining the Latins, say that the Spirit proceeds from the Son. And we say together with the divine Dionysius that the Father is the sole source of the supernatural Divinity; but they with the Latins say that the Son is also the source of the Holy Spirit, thereby clearly excepting the Spirit from the Godhead . . . And we say, in accordance with the fathers, that the will and energy of the uncreated and divine nature are uncreated; but they, along with the Latins and Thomas, maintain that the will is identical with the nature, and that the divine energy is created . . . And we say that the saints

[38]Ibid., 229.

do not enter into the kingdom and the unspeakable delights prepared for them, nor are sinners sent to Gehenna, but both await their fate, which will be entered into in the age to come after the resurrection and judgment; but they, along with the Latins, wish that these might receive according to their deeds immediately after death, granting those in between[39] . . . the purifying fire, which is not identical to that of Gehenna . . . And we, in obedience to the apostles who commanded us, shun the Jewish unleavened bread; but they, in the same act of union, proclaim that that which is celebrated by the Latins is the body of Christ. And we say that the addition to the Symbol was made iniquitously and illegally and against the fathers; but they affirm that it is lawful and blessed . . . For us the pope is one of the patriarchs, and only if he is Orthodox; but they declare with great self-importance that he is the vicar of Christ, the father and teacher of all Christians . . . Therefore, brethren, run from them and avoid contact with them.[40]

The Ferrara-Florence council had all the formal signs of an ecumenical council: it was attended by the pope and the emperor, the patriarch of Constantinople and representatives of the other ancient eastern patriarchates, as well as the first hierarch of the Russian Church, which at the time was not yet autocephalous but part of the Constantinople patriarchate. In the Catholic Church this council is recognized as ecumenical. However, in the Orthodox east it was rejected since it required capitulation from the Orthodox Church, a renunciation of its age-old theological tradition. The Russian Church was the first to reject the union.

When Isidore, the metropolitan of Kiev who represented the Russian Church at the Council of Florence, returned to Rus' two years after the council's end, he led a service in the Dormition cathedral of the Moscow Kremlin on July 5, 1441. At the service the Roman pontiff was commemorated and the act of union with Rome was read. At first none of the boyars and bishops present expressed dissent; on the contrary, according to the chronicler, "the boyars and many others were silent, as were the Russian bishops, and dozed and slept." However, three days later, Grand Prince Vasily Vasilievich declared Isidore a heretic and ordered his arrest. It was then that "all the Russ-

---

[39]That is, those in purgatory.

[40]Mark of Ephesus, *To All Orthodox Christians on the Continent and the Islands*, 6–7. Cited in Amvrosy, *St Mark of Ephesus*, 336–38.

ian bishops arose; the princes and boyars and the multitude of Christians then . . . began . . . to call Isidore a heretic."[41] Attempts were made to force Metropolitan Isidore to renounce the union, and he was even threatened with capital punishment. Nevertheless, he remained adamant and finally fled to Rome, where the pope made him a cardinal. Thus, on the initiative of the secular authorities of Rus', the Council of Ferrara-Florence was rejected by the Russian Church.

At a council in Jerusalem in 1442, the patriarchs of Alexandria, Antioch, and Jerusalem refused to recognize the Council of Ferrara-Florence, calling it "dirty, anticanonical, and tyrannical," and severed communion with Patriarch Metrophanes II of Constantinople (1440–1443), who was elected to replace Patriarch Joseph. Eight years later, a council in Constantinople deposed Gregory III Mammas (1443–1450), the Uniate patriarch of Constantinople, and anathematized the Council of Ferrara-Florence in the presence of the patriarchs of Alexandria, Antioch, and Jerusalem.[42] Greek sentiment on the eve of the fall of Byzantium was captured in the following words by the Byzantine naval commander and Grand Duke Lucas Notaras: "I would rather see the Turkish turban reigning in the city than the Latin tiara."

Fourteen years after the conclusion of the Florentine union and three years after its condemnation at the council in Constantinople, the capital of the Byzantine empire ended up in the hands of the Turks, and Lucas Notaras and his fourteen-year-old son were beheaded on the order of the sultan.

As mentioned earlier, the Greeks signed the union in Florence hoping that the Latins would render them military assistance against the Turks. However, their aid was limited to the dispatching of three Genovese galleys with several hundred volunteers on board, who nevertheless fought valiantly alongside the Greeks. Moreover, the cardinal-metropolitan Isidore (the same who had signed the union on behalf of the Russian Church and was thereafter banished from Moscow in disgrace) was sent to Constantinople, where the emperor allowed him to serve in Hagia Sophia. When the Turks began their siege of Constantinople on both land and sea in April 1453, the number of Turkish troops exceeded the Byzantine army by a factor of twenty. Still, Constantinople was defended for the next seven weeks. In the night between May 28 and 29, 1453, the last Christian service was held in Hagia Sophia. In

---

[41]Cited in A.V. Kartashev, *History of the Russian Church* (Paris, 1959), 1.356.
[42]Amvrosy, *St Mark of Ephesus*, 363.

the evening of May 29 the city was taken by the Turks, and the last Byzantine emperor, Constantine XI Palaeologos, died during the defense of the city. On order of Sultan Mehmed II, Hagia Sophia was turned into a mosque.

Sultan Mehmed II and Patriarch Gennadios Scholarios

The taking of Constantinople was accompanied by three days of pillage, during which the Turks, with the permission of the sultan, murdered and robbed anyone they wished.[43] The sultan commanded the execution of several surviving members of the Byzantine aristocracy and clergy, including Cardinal Isidore. Many churches were looted and desecrated. On the initiative of Mehmed II, the learned monk Gennadios Scholarios (†c. 1468), a strong opponent of union, was elevated to the patriarchal throne of Constantinople. The sultan, like the Byzantine emperors before him, personally handed him the patriarchal staff. Gennadios became the head of the *millet*, the Greek community, which was granted the rights of a self-governing ethnic minority. The sultan presented the patriarch with a *firman* (decree) that accorded him the rights of a spiritual and secular head of the Greek population of the Ottoman empire (a mosaic that depicts Mehmed II granting a firman to Gennadios can be seen in the building of the Constantinople patriarchate in Istanbul).

The influence of the patriarchate of Constantinople among the Christian flock of the empire was not only preserved but even consolidated, since the patriarch received from the sultan not only ecclesiastical but also a certain degree of political power. At the foundation of the religious-political structure of the newly created empire lay the principle of combining spiritual and secular power in one person, characteristic of the Islamic world. Being an absolute monarch and religious leader of the empire at the same time, the Turkish sultan delegated part of his powers to the patriarch of Constantinople, who became a mediator between the sultan and the Christian population. The patriarch was forced to play the role of communicator of the sultan's will, giving him certain privileges within the Ottoman empire but also depriving him of the possibility of wielding ecclesiastical power beyond

[43]See Steven Runciman, *The Fall of Constantinople 1453* (Cambridge, 1969), 145.

its borders.[44] For several centuries to come, the fate of the patriarch of Constantinople was intimately linked to that of the Ottoman empire.

Although the Orthodox minority received from the sultan a defined place within the structure of Turkish society, it soon became clear that Christianity was viewed as a second-class religion and Christians second-class citizens. They were heavily taxed and could only wear rough clothing; moreover, the Church was banned from conducting missionary activity, and the conversion of Muslims to Christianity was a crime. In order to take up his office, the patriarch was forced to pay an exorbitant sum to the sultan, and as a rule only those candidates who were able to pay more could become patriarch. Thus, the sultans had a vested interest in changing patriarchs as often as possible.[45] Other reasons for the frequent change of patriarchs were internal strife in the patriarchate and struggles for the patriarchal throne. Furthermore, all manifestations of disloyalty toward the Turkish regime were severely punished. As a result, of the 159 Constantinople patriarchs who occupied the throne between the fifteenth and twentieth centuries, 105 were removed by the Turks, 27 were forced to renounced the throne, 6 were murdered, and only 21 died a natural death. One and the same person could become patriarch and be deposed several times.[46]

After the capture of Constantinople the Turks continued their conquests, subjugating territories that had been Orthodox for ages. In 1459 Mehmed II conquered Serbia. In the first quarter of the sixteenth century, as a result of the military campaigns of Sultan Selim I (1512–1520), the patriarchates of Alexandria, Antioch, and Jerusalem found themselves within the borders of the Ottoman empire. The Serbian Church lost its autocephaly after Serbia was made a province of the Ottoman empire and its church entered the jurisdiction of the patriarchate of Constantinople (earlier, at the end of the fourteenth century, the Bulgarian Church was incorporated into the Constantinopolitan patriarchate after Bulgaria was overrun by the Turks). Although the ancient eastern patriarchates were not abolished, in reality they were dependent on the patriarch of Constantinople, who was recognized by the state as the sole head of the Orthodox Church within the territory of the Ottoman empire.

[44]See *The Local Orthodox Churches* (Moscow, 2004), 14.
[45]Ware, *The Orthodox Church*, 96–100.
[46]B.J. Kidd, *The Churches of Eastern Christendom* (London, 1927), 304.

The Turkish conquest paralyzed the intellectual life of the Greeks to a considerable extent, and Orthodox theology ceased to develop. The primary task of the Church now was to survive and preserve its tradition. This was necessary not only in view of the constant repressions by the Muslims, but also in view of the regular attempts of the Latin west to persuade the Greek Church to subordinate itself to Rome. In their search for allies against the Latins, the Greeks established relations with European Protestants. The last quarter of the sixteenth century witnessed correspondence between Patriarch Jeremias II (1572–1579, 1580–1584, 1587–1595) and theologians of the University of Tübingen. The seventeenth century was marked by a "Protestant disturbance" within the Greek Church, caused by the influence of Calvinist ideas on Patriarch Cyril I Loukaris (†1638).[47] In Geneva, the main center of European Calvinism, a *Confession of Faith* containing many Calvinist ideas was published in 1629 under Loukaris' name. Cyril Loukaris himself, who became patriarch six times and was also deposed six times, ended his life tragically: he was strangled by the Janissaries, who then threw his body into the Bosphorus. Loukaris' ideas were condemned numerous times at church councils between 1638 and 1691.[48]

Turkish domination also led to the gradual weakening of many Athonite monasteries during the sixteenth and seventeenth centuries and to the extinction of the hesychast tradition on Mount Athos. Although the sultans were protectors of Athos, the arbitrary acts of minor Turkish officials, the heavy taxes the monks were forced to pay, and numerous pirate raids combined to impede the flourishing of monastic life. By the seventeenth century many monasteries on the Holy Mountain had fallen into decline.

A certain renewal of Athos' spiritual life can be observed in the middle of the eighteenth century thanks to the *kollyvades* movement, which had penetrated Athonite monasteries and later spread to continental Greece. This movement began from a debate over an insignificant question: the permissibility of commemorating the deceased on Sundays. At the beginning of the nineteenth century the dispute was renewed, the main issue this time being the frequency of receiving holy communion. The *kollyvades* insisted on reviving the ancient practice of frequent communion, whereas their opponents

---

[47]For more on this cf. A.P. Lebedev, *The History of the Greek-Eastern Church under the Turks* (St Petersburg, 2004), 2.202–58.

[48]See Ware, *The Orthodox Church*, 106–7.

held that it should be taken only two or three times per year. The spiritual program of the *kollyvades* was not, however, limited to the commemoration of the deceased and the frequency of communion. Their aim was rather to revive the spiritual tradition connected to St Gregory Palamas and the hesychasts of the fourteenth century, which had almost been completely forgotten by the eighteenth century. A central theme of their program was the revival of the practice of "noetic activity" and the Jesus prayer.

One of the main members of the movement was St Nicodemus the Hagiorite (1748–1809), who wrote a number of original works, including the book *On Frequent Communion*, as well as commentaries on the epistles of St Paul and on liturgical texts. His book *Unseen Warfare*, which was widely read and was translated at the end of the nineteenth century into Russian, is actually a reworking of a treatise written by the Latin Theatine monk Lorenzo Scupoli. Nicodemus' main work is the *Philokalia*, a collection in several volumes of writings by eastern Christian ascetics from the fourth through fifteenth centuries on noetic activity. Thanks to the *Philokalia*, which was printed for the first time in Venice in 1782, many works of ancient church writers, such as Evagrius of Pontus, Mark the Ascetic, Maximus the Confessor, Hesychius of Sinai, and the Byzantine hesychasts Nicephoros the Solitary, Gregory of Sinai, and Gregory Palamas, were revived. In 1793 the *Philokalia* was translated into Slavonic, at the end of the nineteenth century into Russian, and during the twentieth century into several European languages. Today this collection remains one of the most widely read books among monastics and laymen of the Orthodox Church.[49]

---

[49]For more on the *kollyvades* see S. Hovorun, "From the History of the Philokalia," *Tserkov' i Vremya* 1.14 (2001): 262–95; and his "The Kollyvades Movement: Preconditions for the Appearance of the Movement," *Tserkov' i Vremya* 3.16 (2001): 86–106.

7

Orthodoxy in Rus'

ORTHODOXY IN KIEVAN RUS'

I N HIS BOOK *The Historical Road of Eastern Orthodoxy*, Alexander Schmemann wrote: "the Russian chapter in the history of Orthodoxy inevitably takes on a universal significance." According to him, Russia's importance in the historical development of Orthodoxy is singular, and cannot be compared to anything else.[1]

When Byzantium fell, Orthodoxy had already been in Rus' for several centuries. After Rus' was baptized by Prince Vladimir, the metropolia of Kiev was established within the jurisdiction of the patriarchate of Constantinople. The first metropolitans were Greeks sent from the Byzantine capital, and the liturgical services were at first celebrated in Greek. The precise date of the founding of the metropolia, as well as the names of the first metropolitans, are still debated by scholars. The Russian Orthodox Church believes that the first metropolitan of Kiev was Michael (†992); it is thought that the holy prince Vladimir brought him from Cherson. Along with the metropolia in Kiev, episcopal sees were established in Novgorod, Polotsk, and several other cities. Many churches were built throughout Rus', parish schools were opened, and mass baptisms were conducted in all cities and villages. Toward the end of Vladimir's reign there were approximately four hundred churches in Kiev alone.

After Prince Vladimir's death in 1015, a power struggle ensued between his sons. Svyatopolk had declared himself prince of Kiev, and in order to eliminate any possible rivals, he killed his own brothers: Boris, who ruled in Rostov, and Gleb, who was prince of Murom. The veneration of Boris and Gleb began soon after their deaths, and already in 1026 a church was consecrated

---

[1]Schmemann, *Historical Road*, 293.

at the place of their burial by Metropolitan Ioann I of Kiev. Boris and Gleb were the first saints canonized by the Russian Church. Although they were not martyrs for Christ, they were proclaimed "passionbearers": not wishing to raise their hands against their own brother, they instead sacrificed their lives in order to put an end to civil war and establish peace.

The murderer of Boris and Gleb, Svyatopolk the Accursed, was conquered in 1019 by another of St Vladimir's sons, Yaroslav the Wise (†1054), whose long rule was marked by the further spread of Christianity. During his reign were built the Cathedral of the Holy Wisdom in Kiev and cathedrals in Novgorod and many other cities. This time also saw the founding of the first monasteries and the systematic translation of Greek liturgical books into Slavonic, something that is mentioned in the *Tale of Bygone Years*:

> Yaroslav founded a large city, where the Golden Gates now stand. He also built the church of the Holy Wisdom, the metropolia, and then the church of the Holy Mother of God of the Annunciation at the Golden Gates, then the monastery of St George and St Irene. During his time the Christian faith began to bear fruit and spread, the number of monks grew, and monasteries appeared. Yaroslav loved the regulations of the Church, provided extensive support to priests and particularly to monks, and displayed a zeal for books, often reading them day and night. He gathered a multitude of scribes, who translated from Greek into Slavonic. And they wrote many books, from which the faithful learn and delight in the divine teaching. Just as when one person tills the soil, another sows, and a third reaps the harvest and eats the food that never grows scarce, so was it here. For his father, Vladimir, tilled and softened the soil, that is, he enlightened the people through baptism. Yaroslav sowed the words of books into the hearts of the faithful, and we reap the harvest, accepting the teaching of the books . . . Yaroslav . . . loved books, and having copied many of them, placed them in the church of the Holy Wisdom, which he had founded himself. He adorned it with gold, silver, and church vessels, and here the prescribed prayers are sent up to God at the appointed time. And he founded other churches in cities and other places, appointing priests and paying their salaries from his coffers, commanding them to teach the people since this has been entrusted to them by God, and to go to the churches frequently. And the number of presbyters and the baptized

grew, and Yaroslav rejoiced, seeing the multitude of churches and the baptized, while the enemy lamented this, for he had been vanquished.[2]

During Yaroslav's reign the first metropolitan of Russian origin, Hilarion, was elected to the Kiev metropolia by a council of Russian bishops. Before his consecration he was a priest in the princely village of Berestovo, and was well known as a "benevolent man who loved learning and fasting." He had dug out for himself a cave on the banks of the Dniepr and retired to it for prayer and psalmody.[3] However, he occupied the Kievan see for only a short time, since the Greek Ephraim is mentioned in the chronicles as metropolitan of Kiev from 1055 onward. A number of scholars have suggested that after stepping down, Hilarion may have been tonsured a schema-monk with the name Nikon, that he settled in the Kiev Caves Lavra, and that he later became abbot of the monastery.[4] In the Russian Orthodox Church, however, St Hilarion and St Nikon are venerated as two distinct people.

Metropolitan Hilarion went down in the history of the Russian Church as an outstanding enlightener and spiritual writer. One of his writings that was especially popular in Rus' was his *Sermon on Law and Grace*, one of the first original works of Russian church literature. In addition to his unquestionable literary talent, the author of the sermon possessed an outstanding theological gift and was well acquainted with the theological questions of his day. One of the themes of this work is the contrast between Christianity and Judaism, and between grace and the law. At the same time, the work is an attempt at understanding Christianity as the universal faith of salvation, which the Russian people were able to share thanks to the holy prince Vladimir. Metropolitan Hilarion speaks of the fruits of the Christianization of Rus' with great inspiration:

It was meet for grace and the truth to shine over the new people since, according to the words of the Lord, new wine—or grace-filled teaching—is not poured "into old wineskins" that have become decrepit in Judaism . . . The new teaching called instead for new wineskins, new peoples! "And both are preserved." This is exactly what happened, for the grace-filled faith spread throughout the entire world and has reached our Russian

[2] *Tale of Bygone Years*, year 6545 (1037), 302–3.
[3] *Tale of Bygone Years*, year 6559 (1051), 305.
[4] See, e.g., I.K. Smolich, *Russian Monasticism (988–1917)* (Moscow, 1997), 26, 40–41.

people. The lake of the law has dried up but the spring of the gospel, full of water, has covered the entire world and overflowed even unto our lands. And we glorify the Holy Trinity with all the Christians . . . And we are no longer called idolaters but Christians, and we no longer live without hope but with the hope of eternal life. And we no longer build satanic temples but churches of Christ . . . Our most good God has had mercy on all peoples and has not overlooked ours, for he desired to save and has indeed saved us by bringing us to the knowledge of the truth.[5]

Metropolitan Hilarion saw the baptism of Rus' by Prince Vladimir as a turning point in Russian history. He captured the spiritual exultation characteristic of young Russian Christianity as a new faith that had replaced a decrepit paganism:

All at once our entire land began to glorify Christ with the Father and the Holy Spirit. Then the darkness of idolatry began to depart from us and the dawn of the right faith arrived; then the darkness of demonic service disappeared and the word of the gospel shone upon our land. Then the temples were destroyed and churches were built, and the idols were smashed and holy icons appeared; then the demons fled and the cross sanctified the cities. Bishops—pastors of Christ's logical sheep—stood before the holy altar and offered the bloodless sacrifice; and presbyters, deacons, and all the clergy beautified the holy churches and clothed them in glory. The trumpet of the apostles and the thunder of the gospel sounded in all the cities; and the incense offered to God sanctified the air. Monasteries and monks appeared in the mountains. Men and women, the small and the great, and all who filled the churches to overflowing glorified the Lord, crying: "One is holy, one is Lord, Jesus Christ, to the glory of God the Father! Amen. Christ is victorious! Christ has prevailed! Christ reigns! Christ has been glorified! Great art thou, O Lord, and wondrous are thy works! O our God, glory be to thee!"[6]

The sermon ends with an inspired prayer addressed to the holy prince Vladimir, equal of the apostles:

[5]Hilarion, Metropolitan of Kiev, *Sermon on Law and Grace*, trans. Deacon Andrei Yurchenko, in *Literary Monuments of Ancient Rus'* 12.3 (Moscow, 1994), 606–7.
[6]Ibid., 609–10.

Arise from your grave, O honorable leader! Arise, shake off your sleep!
For you have not died but slumber until the universal resurrection. Arise,
for you have not died! You should not have died—you who have believed
in Christ, who is the life granted to the entire world. Shake off your sleep,
look up, and you will see that the Lord, having vouchsafed you such
honor in the heavens, has also left your son not without remembrance on
earth. Arise and behold your child . . . behold your grandchildren and
great-grandchildren: see how they live, how they are protected by the
Lord, how they preserve the right faith given to them by you, how they
zealously attend the holy churches, how they glorify Christ, how they
bow down before his name. And look at the city, glistening in grandeur,
look at the flourishing churches and how Christianity grows; look at the
city, which shines with the icons of the saints and is sanctified by them,
fragrant with incense, filled with divine doxologies, and resounding with
holy hymns. Beholding all these things, rejoice, be glad, and praise the
most good God, who arranges all things.[7]

The chronicles also associate the name of Metropolitan Hilarion with the
founding of the Kiev Caves monastery, which is mentioned in the *Tale of
Bygone Years* and which had become a major center of spiritual life and religious enlightenment by the end of the eleventh century. It all began with the
cave on the banks of the Dniepr where Hilarion prayed before his appointment to the metropolitan see of Kiev.[8] It was in this cave that St Anthony of
the Kiev Caves (†c. 1073) settled, later gathering around himself a community of disciples. Anthony blessed the construction of the Dormition church
and monastic cells, and a wall was erected around the monastery. During the
years when St Theodosius (†1074) was abbot, the monastery's stone cathedral
of the Dormition began construction. According to his *vita*, compiled by St
Nestor the Chronicler (†c. 1114), Theodosius led a very ascetic life, demanded
unquestioning obedience from his monks, and introduced the Stoudios
typikon to the monastery. The veneration of St Theodosius began soon after
his death, and even earlier than the veneration of his teacher, St Anthony.
Both saints entered the history of the Russian Church as the founders of
monasticism in Rus'.

[7] Ibid., 612–13.
[8] *Tale of Bygone Years*, year 6559 (1051), 307.

The Mother of God of the Caves with Ss Theodosius and Anthony (Kiev, 13th c.)

From the last third of the eleventh to the first third of the thirteenth century, the influence of Ss Anthony and Theodosius and the monastery founded by them was immense. Monks from the Kiev Caves monastery were appointed bishops in many Russian cities, and every single cathedral in the dioceses that appeared during this period—Rostov, Vladimir in Volhynia, Turov, Galicia, Ryazan, Vladimir on the Klyazma—were dedicated to the Dormition of the Mother of God, just like the main church of the Kiev Caves Lavra. The Kievan princes frequently turned to the abbots of the monastery for help, and the latter played a significant role not only in the country's religious but also its political life. Finally, the Kiev Caves monastery became an important center of historical records and hagiography.[9]

Twelfth-century Russia was marked by feudal divisions, with domestic policy being defined by conflict between provincial princes. During this time the importance of the metropolitan of Kiev greatly increased, as he was the only person whose jurisdiction extended to all the Russian territories. Beginning in the middle of the twelfth century, the metropolitans bore the title "of Kiev and all Rus'." At the same time, most of the Kiev metropolitans of this period were Greeks, and they could not always orient themselves in the complex vicissitudes of Russian political and ecclesiastical life. In those cases where a Russian did become metropolitan on the initiative of the prince, Constantinople, as a rule, protested vehemently. The troubles caused by the difficult relations with Constantinople, however, did not hinder the subsequent consolidation of Orthodoxy in Rus' and the increase in the number of dioceses, of which there were around fifty by the beginning of the thirteenth century.

Several outstanding rulers, such as the holy prince Andrei Bogolyubsky (c. 1111–1174), contributed to the consolidation of church life. St Andrew entered history as a builder of churches and a pious ruler; during his reign the city of Vladimir on the Klyazma became one of the main political and religious centers of Russia. Andrew even wished to establish a separate metropol-

[9]Nazarenko, "The Russian Church," 43–44.

itan see in the city, but was refused the blessing to do so by Constantinople. During his time were built the Dormition cathedral in Vladimir and the church of the Protection of the Mother of God on the Nerl. Moreover, he is associated with the establishment in Russia of the feast of the Protection of the Mother of God.

The significance of the city of Vladimir grew after armies of the Golden Horde, led by Batu Khan (1208–1255), grandson of Genghis Khan, swept through Rus' in 1237–1240, devastating everything in their path. During this invasion, which marked the beginning of the Mongol-Tatar yoke that lasted for more than two centuries, many large cities of Rus' were seized and destroyed, including Ryazan, Moscow, Vladimir on the Klyazma, Kozelsk, Pereyaslavl, Chernigov, Kiev, Kamenets, Vladimir in Volhynia, Galicia, and Lodyzhin. The Mongols looted and destroyed churches, killing or taking captive clergymen and monks. Joseph, the metropolitan of Kiev (from 1236 onward), went missing, and several bishops perished. All territories of Rus' conquered by the Mongols were forced to pay tribute, and for more than two hundred years thereafter Russian princes and metropolitans had to travel to the horde and obtain a *yarlyk* (permission) from the khan before taking up their offices: without this *yarlyk* no prince or metropolitan could be considered legitimate.

The sack of Kiev by the Tatar-Mongols on December 6, 1240 made it impossible for the metropolitans of Kiev to remain in the city. While formally remaining metropolitan of Kiev, St Kirill II (1242/47–1281) spent most of his time in the northeast of Russia, and his successor, St Maxim (1283–1305), moved to Vladimir on the Klyazma in 1299 after combining Vladimir and Kiev into one metropolitan region.

The importance of Vladimir continued to increase during the reign of the holy prince Alexander Nevsky of Novgorod, Kiev, and Vladimir (1220–1263), who went down in Russian history as a brilliant ruler whose political foresight determined the fate of Rus' for decades to come. St Alexander realized that fighting with the Mongols would be fruitless, and instead focused his efforts on protecting the northwestern borders of Rus'. His rule coincided with the heightened activity of the Catholic knightly orders, which acted on the direct command of the Roman pontiff. On December 9, 1237, Pope Gregory IX (1227–1241) ordered the archbishop of Uppsala to organize a crusade against the Russians and Finns. Obeying the papal edict, the Swedish king sent a large

The holy prince Alexander Nevsky (Moscow Kremlin, 17th c.)

army into Russian territories in 1240, but it was defeated by Alexander's forces. In 1242 the holy prince gained a historic victory over the knights of the Livonian order on the ice of Lake Peipus.

Having lost all hopes of conquering Rus' through the knightly orders, the popes resorted to exhortations and threats. On November 15, 1248, Pope Innocent IV (1243–1254) sent a letter to Alexander Nevsky, in which he wrote that the recognition of the Latin hierarchy would allow him to "attain the gates of heaven very easily and swiftly," since "the keys to these gates were entrusted by the Lord to the blessed Peter and his successors, the popes of Rome, so that they would not admit those who do not recognize the Roman Church as the mother of our faith, as well as those who do not respect the pope as the vicar of Christ."[10] Around 1250 the pope dispatched two cardinals to Alexander who suggested that he become Catholic. St Alexander answered the pope: "We know well the holy fathers from Adam . . . until the First Ecumenical Council . . . and from the First to the Seventh Council . . . [and] that the gospel of Christ was preached by the holy apostles throughout the entire world, and the traditions of the holy fathers of the seven ecumenical councils. We preserve all of this, as is well known, but we reject your teaching and refuse to listen to your words."[11]

In order to achieve peace with the Tatar-Mongols, the holy prince had to travel four times to the Golden Horde. After returning from his fourth trip, he fell ill and, after being tonsured a monk with the name Alexei, passed away. When news about his death reached Vladimir, the metropolitan of Kiev, Kirill, who was in Vladimir at the time, declared to the people: "My dear children! The sun of the Russian land has set." These words reflected the love that surrounded the grand prince during his lifetime. The Church's veneration of Alexander Nevsky began soon after his death, and he was officially canonized in the middle of the sixteenth century.

[10]Cited in Matuzova and Nazarova, *The Crusaders and Rus'*, 268–69.
[11]*The Novgorod Primary Chronicle, Older and Newer Editions* (Moscow-Leningrad, 1950), 305–6.

ORTHODOXY IN MUSCOVITE RUS'

At the beginning of the fourteenth century, Vladimir remained the residence of the metropolitan of Kiev and all Rus'. However, Metropolitan Peter (1308–1326) spent the last years of his life in Moscow and was buried in the Dormition cathedral of the Moscow Kremlin. St Peter's successor, Metropolitan Theognost (1327/28–1353), also settled in Moscow. The transformation of Moscow into the de facto center of the metropolia was connected with the city's rise in importance as the main political center of northeastern Rus' during the reign of Grand Prince Ivan I Kalita (c. 1243–1341). In the second half of the fourteenth century Moscow became the center of the armed struggle against the Mongol-Tatar yoke. Major figures in Russian church life during this period were the Moscow metropolitan Alexei (c. 1304–1378) (who continued to bear the title of metropolitan of Kiev and all Rus') and St Sergius of Radonezh (1314–1392).

Metropolitan Alexei came from a Moscow boyar family, and his godfather was Ivan Kalita. As a young boy he strove for the monastic life, and was tonsured at the age of twenty. During the lifetime of Metropolitan Theognost, Alexei was appointed his deputy and successor. In 1354, Patriarch Philotheos Kokkinos of Constantinople, a disciple of St Gregory Palamas, confirmed Alexei as metropolitan of all Rus', although this was done as an exception: according to the rule only ethnic Greeks were to be appointed to the Russian metropolitan see. During the reign of Prince Ivan II (1326–1359), who ruled in Moscow for five years, and particularly during the nonage of the holy prince Dimitry Donskoy (1350–1389), St Alexei was in charge of Moscow's foreign policy. Among other things, he established diplomatic relations with the Lithuanian prince Olgerd (c. 1296–1377), who had significantly enlarged the Great Principality of Lithuania by annexing Russian territories and had obtained from Constantinople a separate metropolia for Lithuania. St Alexei contributed to the overcoming of divisions in the then splintered Rus' and the creation of an alliance of Russian princedoms in order to oppose the Golden Horde, which had weakened considerably by that time.

St Sergius of Radonezh was a younger contemporary and spiritual friend of St Alexei. He also came from a boyar family and was distinguished from his childhood by his profound piety. After the death of his parents, he retired

St Sergius of Radonezh (Trinity-St Sergius Lavra, 15th c.)

to the forests around Moscow with his older brother Stephen, and built a cell—and later a small church of the Holy Trinity—twelve versts from the village of Radonezh. Unable to endure the severe conditions, Stephen left his brother in isolation and moved to the Theophany monastery in Moscow. After several years of life as a hermit, St Sergius began to accept disciples, and a brotherhood of twelve monks was soon formed, for whom St Sergius built several cells with his own hands. In 1354 he was ordained hieromonk and appointed abbot of the monastery he founded. His fame grew from day to day, and among those who revered him were princes, boyars, bishops, and priests. St Sergius was granted the gift of clairvoyance and miracle-working, as well as numerous visions. One of these is described in the *Life of St Sergius,* written by his disciple, St Epiphanius the Wise:

> Once the blessed father was praying as usual, before an icon of the mother of our Lord Jesus Christ . . . And when he finished the canon and sat down to take a brief rest, he said to his disciple Micah: "Child! Be vigilant and awake, for a marvelous and awesome vision will appear to us at this time." And as he said this, a voice suddenly proclaimed "Lo, the Most Pure One is coming!" Upon hearing this, the saint quickly left his cell for the porch. And a blinding light, shining more brightly than the sun, engulfed the saint; and he saw the Most Pure Mother of God, glistening in unspeakable brilliance, together with the apostles Peter and John. And when the saint saw her, he prostrated himself, not being able to endure this unbearable light. The Most Pure one touched the saint with her hands and said: "Do not be afraid, my chosen one, for I have come to visit you. Your prayers for your disciples have been heard, as well as those for your monastery. Do not be sorrowful any longer, for from now on it will enjoy abundance in everything, and this not only during your lifetime, for I will not abandon your monastery after you depart for the Lord, granting all that is necessary in abundance, providing it with everything, and defending it." Having said this, she disappeared. The saint was over-

come with great trepidation and fear. When he had come to his senses, Sergius saw his disciple prostrate from fear like a dead man, and lifted him up. He fell to the feet of the elder and said: "Tell me, father, for the Lord's sake, what was this marvelous vision? For my spirit nearly separated from my body because of its brilliance." The saint's soul rejoiced so much that his face was radiant with joy, but could not answer anything except: "Have patience, my child, for my spirit is trembling too from the wondrous vision."[12]

Epiphanius relates how once, when St Sergius was celebrating the liturgy, one of his disciples saw a fire that moved around the table of preparation, illuminated the altar area, and surrounded the altar table from all sides. When Sergius prepared to take communion, the divine fire rolled up like a shroud and entered the holy chalice. After the service the disciple said to the saint: "Master! I beheld a wonderful vision of how the grace of the Holy Spirit assists you." The saint replied: "Tell no one about what you have seen until the Lord has taken me from this life."[13]

The lives of the holy prince Dimitry Donskoy, St Alexei, and St Sergius were spent in different circumstances: one ruled the state, the second governed the Church, and the third led an ascetic life in the forests around Moscow. But when the Mongol khan Mamai invaded Rus', the state and the Church were united in their realization of the necessity of resisting the enemy. Before the decisive battle, Prince Dimitry gathered his troops and went to St Sergius for his advice and blessing. St Sergius blessed the prince, foretold victory, and gave him two monks from his monastery—the schema-monks Andrei Oslyabya and Alexander Peresvet. Both monks fought heroically along with the grand prince and his forces against the army of Mamai, and on September 8, 1380 the Russian troops achieved victory in the Battle of Kulikovo. This historical battle marked the beginning of the liberation of Rus' from the Tatar-Mongol yoke.

St Sergius and Dimitry Donskoy (miniature, 17th c.)

---

[12] *The Life of Sergius of Radonezh*, trans. M.F. Antonova and D.M. Bulanina, in *Literary Monuments of Ancient Rus'* 4 (Moscow, 1981), 395–97.
[13] Ibid., 403.

The veneration of St Sergius, whom the faithful called the "abbot of the Russian land," began already during his lifetime and continued after his death. The monastery he founded soon expanded and became a major spiritual center, whose significance for Muscovite Rus' was similar to that of the lavra of Ss Anthony and Theodosius for Kievan Rus'. To this day, the Trinity-St Sergius Lavra remains the most important monastery of the Russian Orthodox Church and is visited by dozens of bishops, hundreds of clergymen, and thousands of laypeople on the feast days of St Sergius (July 5 and September 25).

St Kiprian (Moscow Kremlin, 17th c.)

During these times, the Russian Church continued to be dependent on Constantinople. In 1371 Patriarch Philotheos, on the insistence of the Polish king Casimir III, established a separate metropolia of Galicia and appointed his cell attendant, the Bulgarian Kiprian, to the see (†1406).[14] Succumbing to pressure from the Lithuanian prince Olgerd in 1375, Patriarch Philotheos appointed Kiprian "metropolitan of Kiev, Rus', and Lithuania," extending his jurisdiction to the territories of the Great Principality of Lithuania. He insisted that Kiprian was to succeed St Alexei after the latter's death, and that the Russian metropolia be reunited. However, Grand Prince Dimitry Donskoy, who considered Kiprian a protégé of Lithuania, began to prepare his own candidate for the metropolitan throne: the priest Mityai of Kolomna, who was tonsured a monk with the name Mikhail. When Kiprian arrived in Moscow after the death of St Alexei, he was driven out by the prince, and Mikhail-Mityai set out for Constantinople for episcopal consecration; however, he died while on his way. This story was subsequently described in a colorful literary work entitled *The Tale of Mityai*, which satirically depicts the candidate for the metropolitan see.[15] The unrest in the Russian Church

---

[14]The diocese of Galicia first became a metropolia around 1303. In 1317, during the reign of Grand Prince Gedimin (1316–1341), the Lithuanian metropolia was founded—subsequently to be abolished and reconstituted several times.

[15]See G.M. Prokhorov, *The Tale of Mityai: Rus' and Byzantium in the Age of the Battle of Kulikovo* (Leningrad, 1978).

caused by Dimitry Donskoy's reluctance to accept Kiprian in Moscow continued for ten years and ended with the death of the prince. In early 1390, St Kiprian was greeted in Moscow by Grand Prince Vasily I (1389–1425) and ruled the Church until his death, succeeded by Metropolitan Photius (†1431), a Greek sent from Constantinople.

A new period in the life of the Russian Church began during the rule of Metropolitan Jonah (1431–1451), an ethnic Russian elected to the metropolitan throne after the death of Metropolitan Photius. In accordance with the canonical practice of the time, Jonah intended to travel to Constantinople to be confirmed in his position. The political situation, however, did not allow this, and he governed the Church for several years as designated metropolitan. By autumn 1435, when Jonah finally had the possibility of traveling to Constantinople, the Greek Isidore had already been consecrated as metropolitan of Rus'. After spending five months in Moscow, Isidore set out for the Council of Florence in September 1437. Upon returning from the council, Isidore was, as mentioned earlier, imprisoned and fled to Rome. As the metropolitan appointed by Constantinople had become a Roman cardinal, and as the patriarchal throne in Constantinople was occupied by the Uniate Gregory III Mammas, Grand Prince Vasily II (1415–1462) decided to convene a council to elect a metropolitan without the permission of Constantinople. The Moscow Council of 1448 elected Jonah metropolitan, and the Council of 1459 legitimated his appointment "through the election of the Holy Spirit, and in accordance with the holy canons of the holy apostles and holy fathers, and on the command of our lord the grand prince, the Russian autocrat."[16] The decisions of these councils marked the de facto beginning of the autocephaly of the Russian Church. Subsequently, Russian metropolitans were consecrated without the blessing of Constantinople.

Having lost its authority over Moscow, Constantinople decided to consolidate its position in Kiev, and to this end in 1458 Patriarch Gregory Mammas consecrated a separate metropolitan for Kiev: Gregory the Bulgarian (†1472). In 1467 Patriarch Dionysios I (1466–1471, 1489–1491) attempted to make Gregory metropolitan of Moscow as well, but this encroachment by Constantinople was rejected in Moscow. From the middle of the fifteenth century the single Russian metropolia was in reality divided in two. The divi-

[16]Cited in N.V. Sinitsyna, "The Russian Orthodox Church in the Period of Autocephaly," in *Orthodox Encyclopedia*, 66.

sion continued until 1685, when the Kiev metropolia became part of the Moscow patriarchate.

The period between the mid-fifteenth and the end of the sixteenth century saw the consolidation of the political might of Rus' around Moscow. Ancient princedoms—Yaroslavl (1463), Rostov (1474), Novgorod (1478), Tver (1485), Pskov (1510), and Ryazan (1521)—joined Moscow one after the other. In 1480, following the bloodless victory of Russian troops over the forces of Akhmat Khan, the Tatar-Mongol yoke was overthrown once and for all.

Simultaneously with the gathering around Moscow of territories that had been occupied by Russians for ages, new territories also joined the Russian state. In 1472 Grand Prince Ivan III (1440–1505) married Sophia Palaeologos, niece of the Byzantine emperor, giving him in the eyes of the Russians additional legitimacy as Orthodox autocrat and successor of the Byzantine emperors. In the early sixteenth century the theory of Moscow as the Third Rome was formulated by, among others, elder Philotheos of the Savior-Eleazar monastery in Pskov: "The first Rome fell from impiety, the second [Constantinople] from the force of the Turks, the third is Moscow, and there will be no fourth." The importance of the metropolitan of Moscow naturally grew as the power of the grand prince of Moscow increased.

The beginning of the sixteenth century was marked by debates between the "acquisitors" and the "nonacquisitors," between the proponents and opponents of monastery ownership of land. At this time there were many monasteries in Rus', categorized as either cenobitic or idiorrhythmic. In cenobitic monasteries emphasis was placed on obedience, bodily asceticism, common prayer, and charity work; idiorrhythmic ones stressed "noetic activity" and retirement from the world. The rules of both monasteries prescribed that monks could not acquire possessions. Still, both cenobitic and idiorrhythmic monasteries could possess land, villages, and peasants, as well as receive income, which was distributed among the members of the brotherhood. Moreover, dioceses and parishes also owned land. Monastery and church ownership of land frequently evoked the discontent of state authorities, resulting in periodic attempts to confiscate church lands. One such attempt was undertaken during the reign of Grand Prince Ivan III, who took the initiative in trying to seize lands from metropolitans, bishops, and monasteries and placing the episcopate and monasteries on the payroll of the state treasury. This initiative evoked a heated and generally negative reaction in the

Church. In 1503 a church council was held in Moscow that supported the Church's possession of land, in opposition to the grand prince.

The primary proponent of church land ownership at the beginning of the sixteenth century was St Joseph of Volotsk (1439/40–1515), who held that the possession of land and property guarantees the Church its independence from secular authorities and enables it to conduct charity work. The Voloko-lamsk monastery founded by him was an example of wide-ranging charity work: during years of crop fail-ure the monastery fed up to seven hundred people

St Joseph of Volotsk (fragment of Russian icon, 17th c.)

daily, including fifty orphans. When the monastery ran out of bread, Joseph ordered its purchase; when funds for the purchase of bread were no longer available, he ordered that manuscripts be sold, "so that nobody leaves the monastery without having eaten." The monks complained: "We are being starved; all of them cannot be fed." But the saint called on his monks to endure and be obedient.[17]

Joseph of Volotsk was an outstanding educator who fought against the heresy of the Judaizers, a rationalistic movement that appeared in Novgorod at the end of the fifteenth century. Under the influence of Judaism and, pos-sibly, the religious reform movements that had arisen in Europe, the Judaiz-ers criticized the fundamental dogmas of Christianity: the Holy Trinity, Jesus Christ as God and Savior, and the veneration of icons. The founder of the heresy, according to Joseph, was a Jew named Skharia, who had won over the Novgorod priests Dionysius and Alexei to his side. From Novgorod the heretical movement quickly spread to Moscow, where it counted several high-ranking persons among its adherents, including the diplomats Fedor and Ivan Kuritsyn. The priests Dionysius and Alexei were then transferred from Novgorod and appointed archpriests of the Kremlin cathedrals. Joseph wrote his well-known treatise *The Enlightener* against this heresy, presenting testimony from the writings of the church fathers in defense of Orthodox dogma.

In his struggle against the Judaizers, St Joseph joined forces with St Gen-nady of Novgorod (†1506), another outstanding enlightener who for the first

---

[17]George P. Fedotov, *The Saints of Ancient Rus'* (Paris, 1989), 170.

time collected all the books of holy scripture into one volume and who issued in manuscript form the so-called "Gennady Bible." The collection of testimony from scripture and church tradition was an integral part of the strategy to uproot the heresy.

However, there was another element in this program: namely, the demand for punishment and even capital punishment for apostates from Orthodoxy. In spelling out this demand, Joseph of Volotsk cited Byzantine history:

> Were not the Orthodox emperors and holy fathers at the ecumenical and local councils merciful and clement? But they commanded to all, wrote in the holy canons, and ordered to all future generations that kings, princes, and judges commit heretics, and especially apostates, to terrible punishment and death, along with murderers, robbers, and other criminals . . . This is the punishment that was meted out to the patriarchs, metropolitans, and bishops who adhered to heresy. Do not the current apostates, who are worse than all other heretics and apostates, deserve the same sentence as the heretics just mentioned? And if Orthodox autocrats do not do the same now, it will be totally impossible to eradicate heretics and apostates in any other way. If they are moved to do so and display zeal for Christ, if they imprison heretics and apostates until their very deaths, then peace will be restored to God's Church and the impure Jewish teaching of the impious heretics and apostates will become extinct.[18]

In 1504 a council was held in Moscow in the presence of Grand Prince Ivan III and his son Vasily, which sentenced to death the heretics against whom Gennady of Novgorod and Joseph of Volotsk had struggled. This was followed by executions, the likes of which had never been seen in Rus'. On December 27 of the same year Ivan Kuritsyn and his companions were locked in cages and burned alive; in Novgorod Archimandrite Kassian of Yurev and other heretics were burned at the stake, and many adherents of the heresy were imprisoned or sent to monasteries for penitence.

The ideological antithesis of Joseph of Volotsk was St Nilus of the Sora (1433–1508), who suggested at the council of 1503 that "monasteries not have villages, and that monks live in hermitages and feed themselves by the work

---

[18]Joseph of Volotsk, *Homilies* 16, in *The Enlightener, or the Denunciation of the Heresy of the Judaizers* (Kazan, 1903), 533–39.

of their hands."[19] St Nilus believed that charity work did not suit the monastic way of life. As for his attitude toward heretics, Nilus also differed radically from Joseph and did not share the latter's view that heretics should be physically punished.

St Nilus belonged to the spiritual tradition that was embodied by the Athonite hesychasts of the fourteenth century. He spent some time on Mount Athos in his youth, and after returning to Russia he founded a small skete on the river Sora, where he spent his entire life in ascetic labors and literary activity. The *Tradition of Skete Life*, written by St Nilus, represents a systematic collection of thoughts of the holy fathers on the battle with the passions. Among the most frequently cited authors in it are John of the Ladder, Isaac the Syrian, Symeon the New Theologian, and Gregory of Sinai. Unlike Joseph of Volotsk, whose rule was primarily devoted to the external aspects of monastic life, St Nilus devotes most of his attention to inner activity and noetic prayer, which he—again, unlike Joseph—valued higher than church psalmody.

Church veneration of St Joseph Volokolamsk began soon after his death, and he was solemnly canonized in the sixteenth century. The veneration of St Nilus of the Sora was much less conspicuous, and his name was introduced to the church calendar only in 1903. One of St Nilus' disciples, the monk Vassian (Patrikeev), came out firmly against monastery land possession and capital punishment for heretics. Unlike his teacher, he wrote in a harshly polemic and accusatory tone. Vassian was condemned by a council in 1531.

The fate of another spiritual child of the "nonacquisitors," St Maxim the Greek (c. 1480–1556), was also characteristic of the times. He came from a rich Greek family and traveled to Italy in his youth, where he was educated in leading universities. Here he also became acquainted with leading humanists such as Pico della Mirandola. Under the influence of Savonarola, whose preaching made a powerful impression on him, Maxim entered the Dominican order.[20] However, he

Maxim the Greek (Russian icon, 19th c.)

---

[19] *The Epistles of Joseph of Volotsk* (Moscow-Leningrad, 1959), 299.

[20] See A. Ivanov, "On Maxim the Greek's Time in the Dominican Monastery of St Mark in Florence," *Bogoslovskie Trudy* 1 (1973): 112–19; and Ivanov, "Maxim the Greek and Savonarola," *Bogoslovskie Trudy* 12 (1974): 184–208.

later left Italy and in 1505 became a monk of the Vatopedi monastery on Mount Athos, where he soon became famous for his learning. When Grand Prince Vasily III (1505–1533) asked Constantinople to send a learned Greek to compare existing translations and make new ones, Maxim was chosen for the task. After arriving in Rus' Maxim began to translate the *Commented Psalter*. But since he did not know Russian, he had to translate into Latin, whereupon Russian linguists then rendered his texts into Russian. This manner of translation obviously could not be of very high quality. After translating the psalter, Maxim wished to return to Greece; however, he was entrusted with the translation of the *Commented Epistle Lectionary* and the comparison of Slavonic liturgical books with Greek originals. During the course of this work he discovered a large number of mistakes.

Over time Maxim learned Russian and was drawn into the debate between the acquisitors and the nonacquisitors, in which he decisively took the side of the latter. Moreover, he spoke out against the autocephaly of the Russian Church and protested the second marriage of Grand Prince Vasily III. Maxim's activities evoked the ire of the court, and people began to look for mistakes in his translations and heresy in his statements. All of this culminated in his condemnation at a council in 1525, and again, together with Vassian Patrikeev, at a council in 1531. Maxim asked to be released in order to return to Vatopedi, but was instead excommunicated and exiled at first to the monastery of St Joseph of Volotsk (the main bastion of the acquisitors), and then, after the council of 1531, to the Otroch monastery in Tver, where he was kept under house arrest. Only in 1553 was he permitted to settle in the Trinity-St Sergius Lavra, where he died.

Despite his extremely difficult and tragic fate, Maxim never ceased to translate and to write original works, even while in prison. His numerous writings include the *Debate on the Monastic Life* and *A Homily Highly Beneficial to the Souls of Those Who Attend to It*, in which he demonstrates the impermissibility of monasteries owning land. Some of Maxim's works, such as his *Instructive Chapters to Those Who Rule in the Right Faith* and *A Homily Which Sorrowfully Describes at Length the Confusion and Disorder of the Kings and Authorities of Late*, are devoted to church-state relations. Maxim also wrote polemical works, including a *Homily against the Greek Error*; a *Homily against the Muslim Error*; a *Homily against the Armenian Impiety*; *Against the Latins, on how Nothing Should be Added to or Removed from the Divine Confession of the Christian Faith*; and *Against the Lutherans—A Homily on the Veneration of Holy Icons*.

In *A Horrible and Remarkable Tale,* Maxim writes to Russian readers with admiration about life in Catholic monasteries in France and Italy: the different monastic orders, the election of the abbot by a council of the brethren, and the education and piety of Latin monks. The final section of the tale portrays the life of Girolamo Savonarola (†1498), whom Maxim describes as a person "filled with all wisdom, the understanding of the divinely inspired scriptures, and outer learning," as "a great ascetic," and as "richly adorned with divine zeal." Savonarola's preaching, according to Maxim, made a profound impression on the residents of Florence, many of whom were inspired to repent and renounce their sinful lifestyles. Others, on the contrary, "hated his holy teaching from the very beginning," calling him a "heretic, blasphemer, and flatterer." Savonarola and his two assistants were sentenced by corrupt judges to double punishment: hanging on a tree and burning at the stake. "Thus ended the lives of these three saintly monks," Maxim writes. "I am so far from agreeing with those unjust judges that I would gladly number the victims tortured by them among the ancient defenders of piety, if they had not been of the Latin faith."[21]

In 1542 St Makary (1482–1563) became metropolitan of Moscow. Makary is associated with an entire era of the Russian Church. In 1547 he crowned as tsar the sixteen-year-old Moscow Grand Prince Ivan IV (1530–1584), who would later be called "the Terrible." Church councils were held in Moscow in 1547, 1549, and 1551, in which the tsar and the metropolitan took part. These canonized numerous saints, elaborated a model of church-state relations that imitated the Byzantine ideal of "symphony" as closely as possible, and examined many other pressing questions of ecclesiastical life. The council of 1551 went down in history as the "Council of the Hundred Chapters," since the document produced by it was divided into one hundred sections. Councils of 1553 and 1554 condemned the heresy of Bashkin and Kosoy, whose beliefs were similar to those of the Judaizers. All these councils were convened by the tsar, who actively participated in the discussion of church affairs.

Being an outstanding church educator, Metropolitan Makary undertook the monumental work of collecting all the spiritual literature that was read in Rus'. He began this labor while still archbishop of Novgorod (1526–1542), and continued it in Moscow. His *Great Menaion Reader* is a collection of lives of

[21]St Maxim the Greek, *Works* 3 (Trinity-St Sergius Lavra, 1996), 128–33.

saints, sermons, and theological and historical treatises—both original works and translations from Greek and Latin. Makary is also associated with the dawn of book printing in Russia: the first books—the *Epistle Lectionary* and *Book of Hours*—were printed with the metropolitan's blessing by Ivan Fedorov from 1564 to 1565, although they appeared after Makary's death.

The early years of Ivan the Terrible's rule were marked by a number of major military and political successes: in 1552 Kazan was taken, in 1556 Astrakhan, and in 1563 Polotsk. The people rallied to their tsar, in whom they saw a sincere defender of the Orthodox faith and guarantor of the integrity of the state. However, soon after the death of Metropolitan Makary, a radical change took place in the tsar, caused by, among other things, his heightened suspicion and fear of conspiracy. In late 1564 the tsar left Moscow and settled in Alexandrov, where he created a semblance of a monastery headed by himself, and in early 1565 he established the *oprichnina*, a punitive organization that was accountable only to him and not under the jurisdiction of any public authorities. The nation was divided into the *oprichnina*, which included the tsar's boyars, and the *zemshchina*, comprised of the other boyars and their courts. One of the responsibilities of the *oprichnina*, which was made up of young boyars who had taken an oath of loyalty to the tsar, was to expose all possible political conspiracies and execute the conspirators. Executions began, and many boyars and their families were accused of treason and exiled to different cities. The property of the executed and exiled was transferred to the tsar and the *oprichnina*. The insignia of this group, attached to the saddles of the horses they rode, was a dog's head and a broom, which signified that they bit and swept away traitors to the tsar.

The tyranny and brutality of the "terrible" tsar caused unrest in the Church. Athanasy, the tsar's spiritual father, was elected to the metropolitan see in 1564 after the death of Metropolitan Makary, but for unknown reasons he left the throne two years later and retired to a monastery. St Gury of Kazan, who was elected metropolitan in 1566, was brought inside the metropolitan palace but driven out two days later. Finally, in accordance with the will of the tsar, the abbot of the Solovki monastery, Philip, was chosen metropolitan. Philip was from the boyar family Kolychev, and was elevated to the see in June 1566. St Philip protested—at first in private with the tsar, but later in public—the division of the nation into the *oprichnina* and *zemshchina*, as well as the autocrat's brutality.

In March 1569, during the week of the Veneration of the Cross, when the tsar entered the Dormition cathedral with his *oprichniki*, the metropolitan, standing in his appointed place, refused to bless the tsar and addressed the following accusation to him: "How many Orthodox faithful are suffering! The Tatars and pagans have a law and truth, but we do not; mercy can be found everywhere, but none is shown to the innocent in Rus'." This infuriated the tsar, who proceeded to initiate litigation against the saint. In autumn 1569, when St Philip was serving the liturgy, a group of *oprichniki* entered the Dormition cathedral. The service was stopped, an accusation against him was read aloud, his episcopal vestments were removed, and he was taken out of the Kremlin on a wood sledge. The saint was imprisoned in the Otroch monastery in Tver (which had also been the place of exile for Maxim the Greek), and members of the Kolychev family were tortured and executed. After decapitating the hierarch's nephew, Ivan sent it to the metropolitan with the words: "Here is the head of your relative, whom your charms could not help." In December 1569 St Philip was strangled by Malyuta Skuratov, head of the *oprichnina*, on the personal order of the tsar.

Another victim of Ivan the Terrible, who combined pathological brutality with a dark but sincere religiosity, was St Cornelius of the Pskov Caves (1501–1570). When the tsar visited the monastery, Abbot Cornelius went out to meet him holding a cross in his hands. Angered by slander, Ivan himself cut off the abbot's head in a fit of rage. However, he repented immediately and took his body to the monastery. Since then the path from the monastery gates to the church of the Dormition has been called "the bloody path." In order to expiate his guilt, the tsar generously donated to the Pskov Caves monastery and wrote Cornelius' name into his list for commemoration at prayer.

Ivan the Terrible was replaced by Fedor (1557–1598), who was known for his ill health, meekness, and piety. During his rule a historic event for the Russian Church took place: the establishment of the patriarchate. Unlike autocephaly, which had been proclaimed without the consent of the patriarch of Constantinople, the Moscow patriarchate was founded in adherence to all the necessary canons. In 1586 the patriarch of Antioch, Joachim V (1581–1592), visited Moscow, and in 1588 Patriarch Jeremias II of Constantinople did likewise. Both hierarchs had come to Moscow to collect money, which they received from the generous hands of the tsar. While in Moscow, Jeremias II

was asked to consider the transfer of the patriarchal throne of Constantinople to Vladimir but he declined, justifiably affirming that the patriarchal
throne should be where the royal throne is. The patriarch was then asked to
elevate Metropolitan Job of Moscow (†1607) to the "patriarchate of Vladimir
and Moscow." Patriarch Jeremias initially refused, citing lack of authority, but
later conceded.

Metropolitan Job was enthroned as patriarch with the participation of
Jeremias, and the establishment of the patriarchate was confirmed by a special conciliar decree. In 1590 a church council in Constantinople confirmed
the Russian patriarchate and assigned the patriarch of Moscow the fifth place
in the diptychs after the patriarchs of Constantinople, Alexandria, Antioch,
and Jerusalem. The Constantinople Council of 1593, in which four eastern
patriarchs took part, confirmed the establishment of the patriarchate in
Moscow and sent a decree to Moscow signed by forty-two bishops.

During the patriarchate of St Job, the ruling Rurik dynasty came to an
end: in 1591 the tsarevich Dimitry was killed in Uglich, and in 1598 Tsar Fedor
died. The throne went over to the boyar Boris Godunov, but was taken over
in 1605 by an impostor claiming to be tsarevich Dimitry, who had miracu-
lously survived the attempt on his life. The impostor had the aged Patriarch
Job replaced, and Ignaty, archbishop of Ryazan, was elected patriarch. After
the false Dimitry I was removed in 1606, Ignaty was defrocked and his actions
during the "Time of Troubles" were declared criminal. The boyar Vasily
Shuisky became tsar, and the archbishop of Kazan, Germogen (†1612), was
elected patriarch.

The confusion, however, continued, and another impostor, false Dimitry
II, appeared. In 1609 troops of the Polish king Sigismund III (1566–1632)
invaded Russia; in 1610 Vasily Shuisky was overthrown, and after state power
formally went over to the boyar duma, it soon wound up in the hands of
Vladislav, the son of the Polish king. The patriarch led the opposition against
the Poles and blessed the formation of an armed popular resistance in 1611.
For this the Poles imprisoned him in the Chudov monastery, and Ignaty, who
had been defrocked earlier, took his place. From his imprisonment Patriarch
Germogen continued to send letters calling on the people to defend Orthodoxy. In February 1612 the patriarch starved to death, and in October of the
same year the popular resistance headed by Minin and Pozharsky liberated
Moscow. Ignaty fled to Poland, became a Uniate, and was appointed abbot

of the Holy Trinity monastery in Vilnius. Patriarch Germogen's courage went down in the annals of the Russian Church, and he was canonized in 1913 during the celebration of the three-hundred-year anniversary of the Romanov dynasty.

When Mikhail Romanov was elected tsar in 1613, his father, the boyar Fedor Romanov, became metropolitan of Moscow and the "designated patriarch." The latter had been forcibly tonsured a monk with the name Philaret in 1600, during the rule of Boris Godunov. Being the father and spiritual guide of the tsar, Philaret took an active role in governing the state, was called "Great Sovereign" (earlier, the patriarchs only bore the traditional ecclesiastical title of "Great Lord"), created his own court according to the model of the

Patriarch Philaret (Romanov; miniature, 17th c.)

tsar's, and directly governed the patriarchal territories, which comprised more than forty cities. During Philaret's time the patriarchate became a significant center of power that essentially existed in parallel to tsarist rule—predetermining to a great extent the tensions between the tsar and patriarch in the middle of the seventeenth century and the abolition of the patriarchate at the beginning of the eighteenth century.

Conflict flared up during the times of Tsar Alexei (1629–1676), son of Mikhail Romanov. On the tsar's initiative, the young and energetic Nikon (1605–1681) was elevated to the patriarchal throne. The biography of this hierarch was untypical of the higher church clergy of his time: he came from a peasant's family, was a parish priest, and later became a monk at the Anzer skete of the Solovki monastery. In the mid-1640s he became acquainted with the tsar, who at first made him archimandrite of the Novospassky monastery in Moscow, then metropolitan of Novgorod, and finally patriarch. Like Philaret, Nikon wielded not only spiritual but also secular authority, and from 1654 to 1655, during the tsar's military campaigns against Poland, he governed the nation de facto. Like Philaret, Nikon also bore the title "Great Sovereign."

For more than ten years, Alexei and Nikon were bound in a close friendship. However, Nikon fell into disgrace in 1658, and the tsar ceased to attend services celebrated by him. Instead of attempting to mend relations with the tsar, Nikon, without permission, abandoned the patriarchate in protest and

Patriarch Nikon

retired to the New Jerusalem monastery. A council in 1660 elected a new patriarch to replace Nikon, but the latter refused to acknowledge the decision of the council, calling it a "satanic synagogue" and "demonic mob."

After being deprived of the patriarchal throne, Nikon attempted numerous times to interfere in church and state affairs, wrote letters to the tsar, and in 1662, on the Sunday of Orthodoxy, anathematized Pitirim, the metropolitan of Krutitsk and locum tenens of the patriarchal throne, during a service in his monastery. The "Nikon affair," which lasted for more than eight years, involved the tsar, boyars, many hierarchs, and even the eastern patriarchs. Finally, in 1666, a council was convened in Moscow, attended by Patriarchs Paisius of Alexandria and Macarius of Antioch. At the council the tsar and former patriarch met each other for the first time in eight years, but this time not as friends but enemies. Nikon was asked questions, which he answered evasively and haughtily, contesting the authority of the eastern patriarchs and calling the Greek church canons heretical. After tortuous debates lasting many days, Nikon was—with the participation of the tsar and the eastern patriarchs—deposed, defrocked, and exiled to a monastery for penance.

Patriarch Nikon is associated with one of the most tragic pages in the history of the Russian Church: the schism of the Old Believers. After becoming patriarch, Nikon continued the correction of liturgical texts begun by his predecessor. However, he went considerably further in revising service books and church practice. For example, he demanded that the sign of the cross be made not with two fingers, which had been traditional in Rus', but with three, in accordance with the Greek practice of the time. Archpriests Ioann Neronov and Avvakum, who enjoyed the support of the simple folk, came out against Nikon's reforms.

In 1654 Nikon convened a council that decided to bring Russian liturgical books in line with Greek ones and affirmed making the sign of the cross with three fingers. When Bishop Paul of Kolomna wished to object, Nikon threw him down from his seat and beat him severely; as a result of this he went insane. In 1655, the patriarchs of Antioch and Serbia, whom Nikon wished to gain as allies in his liturgical reform, visited Moscow. After liturgy on the Sunday of Orthodoxy, Nikon began with his own hands, in plain view of a surprised tsar and faithful, to destroy icons painted in the western style, throwing them to the ground. Nikon's actions were viewed by the reform's opponents as blasphemy, and the leaders of the schism saw him as the antichrist. The anathemas against the old rite pronounced by the Moscow council of 1656, in which the patriarchs of Antioch and Moscow took part, did not hinder but on the contrary only fostered the further spread of the Old Believers. The schism did not end after Nikon's departure from the patriarchate or even after his deposal, since the Great Moscow Council of 1667, which followed Nikon's deposal, left the anathemas against the old rite in force and gave its approval to Nikon's reforms.

For some time, one bastion of the old rite was the Solovki monastery. In 1658 its abbot, Archimandrite Elias, held a council in the monastery that rejected the newly printed books. When the monks also refused to recognize the acts of the council of 1666, Tsar Alexei dispatched troops to Solovki in order to quell the uprising. The siege of the monastery lasted eight years and went down in the history of the Old Believers as the "Solovki resistance," a courageous defense of the faith and the old rite. During the siege most of the monks died of hunger and disease, and those who were still alive were killed. In 1676, soon after the victory over the schismatics, Tsar Alexei died, which the Old Believers perceived as divine retribution. From this time onward the Old Believers opposed the state authorities, which subjected them to severe persecution. Archpriest Avvakum, who became a symbol of the opposition to "Nikonianism," along with other leaders of the old rite, were burned at the stake in 1681. The Old Believers answered this execution with acts of mass self-immolation.

In the eighteenth and nineteenth centuries the old rite, despite state repression, spread throughout all of Russia and even beyond its borders. The Old Believers later split into numerous groups or "agreements"; the main ones at the present time are the *popovtsy* and the *bespopovtsy*—the former have a church hierarchy and priesthood while the latter do not. In 1971 a national council of the Russian Orthodox Church lifted the anathemas on the old rite pronounced by the councils of 1656 and 1667, underscoring that "the salvific importance of rites is not contradicted by the diversity of their external manifestations, which was always inherent in the ancient undivided Christian

Church and which did not represent a stumbling block or cause for division."[22] The tragic division, however, continues to this day.

ORTHODOXY IN WESTERN RUS':
THE UNION OF BREST AND ITS CONSEQUENCES

The history of Orthodoxy in Little Russia after the creation of the later Kievan metropolia in the middle of the fifteenth century is characterized by a constant opposition to papal attempts to spread the Unia. The first metropolitan, Gregory, who was consecrated in Rome in 1458, broke with Rome already in the mid-1460s because the Orthodox people of the Great Principality of Lithuania and the Kingdom of Poland refused to recognize the Union of Florence. Subsequent metropolitans of Kiev placed themselves under the jurisdiction of the patriarch of Constantinople, although this submission was purely formal. The rulers of Poland and Lithuania, who were Latin-rite Catholics, assisted the spread of Catholicism in their territories and infringed on the rights of the Orthodox. They also interfered in the inner life of the Orthodox Church, appointing and replacing bishops and even elevating laymen to episcopal sees.

Some hierarchs, striving for more independence from the secular authorities, saw a solution in entering into union with Rome, which would allow them to serve unhindered according to the eastern rite. Still, the majority of bishops opposed this idea, despite the pressure placed on them.

From 1590 to 1596 several councils were held in Brest. Their aim was to regulate church life in the Kiev metropolia and to elaborate a strategy for combating Protestantism and Latin Catholicism. However, at the last of these councils, which took place in 1596, a decision was made to unite with Rome. This was preceded by an exchange of letters with Pope Clement VIII, during which the metropolitan and bishops attempted to secure for themselves equal rights with the Latin bishops should they accept the Unia. Although the bishops received neither the privileges nor the autonomy they had sought, they attended the council in October 1596 intending to enter into union. The oppo-

---

[22]"The Act of the Holy National Council of the Russian Orthodox Church on the Abolishment of the Anathemas against the Old Rite and its Adherents, June 2, 1971," *Journal of the Moscow Patriarchate* 6 (1971).

nents of the union, led by Prince Constantine Ostrozhsky, convened their own council in Brest, to which they invited proponents of the union. The council was attended by two bishops—Gideon of Lvov and Michael of Peremyshl—the abbots of the most important monasteries, as well as Cyril Loukaris, the representative of the patriarch of Alexandria (who later became patriarch of Constantinople). On October 9 a council chaired by Metropolitan Michael Ragoza (†1599) decided to join the Kiev metropolia to Rome. On the same day the Orthodox council deposed the bishops who had accepted the union. On October 10 the Uniate council deposed the opponents of the union and appealed to King Sigismund III to hand over their dioceses, monasteries, and churches to the Uniates. The king supported the union and upheld the deposition of the bishops who remained faithful to Orthodoxy.

Patriarch Meletius I Pigas of Alexandria (1590–1601), who at the time was locum tenens of the patriarchal throne of Constantinople, attempted to counteract the union by dispatching the protosyngelos Nicephoros, exarch of the Constantinople patriarchate, and by appointing three other persons as his exarchs: Bishop Gideon of Lvov, Cyril Loukaris, and Prince Constantine Ostrozhsky. However, King Sigismund staunchly opposed the election of an Orthodox metropolitan. The centers of opposition to the union during this period were the monastic and lay brotherhoods, such as the Brotherhood of the Holy Spirit in Vilnius, which was headed in the 1610s by Leontius (Karpovich), abbot of the monastery of the Holy Spirit. Meletius Smotritsky, a monk of the monastery, authored numerous works in defense of the Orthodox faith against Latin and Uniate Catholicism. One of these, entitled *Thrinos, or the Lamentation of the Eastern Church*, enjoyed great popularity.

In the spring of 1620 Patriarch Theophanes III of Jerusalem (1608–1644) arrived in Kiev while returning from Moscow to the Holy Land. Soon after his arrival he issued a decree "To All Who Shine in Orthodoxy in Little Russia, Particularly the Inhabitants of Kiev." In autumn of the same year, at the request of numerous priests and laypeople, he began to consecrate bishops for Little Russia. The first to be elevated to the episcopacy was Hegumen Isaiah Kopinsky, who was consecrated for the diocese of Peremyshl. After this Hegumen Job Boretsky was made metropolitan of Kiev and Galicia, and finally Meletius Smotritsky was elevated to the rank of archbishop of Polotsk. However Smotritsky, who wrote the *Thrinos* and the well-known *Grammar of the Slavonic Language,* joined the Uniates several years later.

The restoration of the Orthodox hierarchy of the Kiev metropolia provoked new repressions from the Polish government and the Uniate bishops. One of the main zealots of the union at the time was Joasaphat Kuntsevich, the Uniate archbishop of Polotsk. His tragic history is one of the many testimonies to the mutual hatred that existed between the Orthodox and the Uniates. After receiving a decree from the king that placed all the Orthodox monasteries and churches under his jurisdiction, Kuntsevich began to demand that all priests of his diocese join the union. He not only confiscated churches from the Orthodox but also banned the celebration of Orthodox services in private homes and huts. Moreover, he imprisoned priests who refused to obey this order. On November 12, 1623, Kuntsevich was brutally murdered by inhabitants of Vitebsk, and his body was mutilated and thrown into the Dvina.

The king reacted to Kuntsevich's murder by ordering severe punishment: nineteen citizens were decapitated, and around one hundred other residents of Vitebsk who had fled were sentenced to death in absentia. Pope Urban VIII (1623–1644), not knowing that the executions had already taken place, wrote a letter on February 10, 1624 demanding that punishment be meted out to those guilty of Kuntsevich's murder: "The brutality of the murderers must not go unpunished. Where so serious a crime requires the whip of God's vengeance, let those be cursed who keep their sword from spilling blood. And you, sovereign, must not refrain from using the sword and fire; let the heresy feel that there is no mercy for savage criminals."[23] In 1643 Pope Urban VIII beatified Kuntsevich, and in 1867 Pius IX (1846–1878) canonized him, proclaiming him the spiritual patron of Rus' and Poland.

An important role in the history of the Kiev metropolia was played by Metropolitan Peter Mogila (†1646). He was elected to the metropolitan see after the death in 1632 of King Sigismund III, who had ruled Poland for forty-five years and had actively supported the union. In 1633, after obtaining a decree confirming his elevation from the new king Vladislav IV (1595–1648), Mogila arrived in Kiev and began tackling church matters, which had fallen into total disarray during the years of persecution of Orthodoxy. First of all, he restored the Cathedral of the Holy Wisdom and several other ancient churches. He transformed the school of the Kiev brotherhood into a collegium and made it a major center of spiritual education. Instruction in the

[23]Cited in Makary, *History of the Russian Church*, 6.429.

Kiev collegium was conducted in Latin, and the textbooks used were written according to scholastic models. The first rector of the collegium was Isaiah Kozlovsky (†1651), author of the famous *Confession of the Orthodox Faith*, which entered history as the *Catechism* of Peter Mogila and was written to refute the *Confession* of Patriarch Cyril Loukaris of Constantinople. The writings of Metropolitan Peter Mogila aimed at cleansing Orthodox service books, into which Latin and Uniate customs had found their way. This culminated in the publication of the *Book of Needs*, which included not only the texts of Orthodox sacraments and rites but also commentaries on these texts.

In 1654 the Ukraine became part of Russia, and some thirty years later, in 1685, during the reign of Patriarch Joachim of Moscow and all Rus', the metropolia of Kiev joined the Moscow patriarchate. The entry of Kiev into the Moscow patriarchate was recognized in 1686 by Patriarch Dionysios IV of Constantinople (†1694).

8

The Russian Church
during the Synodal Period

THE SYNODAL ERA IN THE HISTORY OF THE RUSSIAN CHURCH

AFTER THE DEATH of Patriarch Adrian in 1700, Tsar Peter I (1682–1725) prevented the election of a new patriarch, and from December 16, 1700 until 1721 the Russian Church was governed by the patriarchal locum tenens, Metropolitan Stephen Yavorsky (1658–1722). In 1721, several months before Russia was proclaimed an empire and Peter received the title of emperor, a decree was issued establishing a "spiritual collegium," headed by a president (abolished after the death of Metropolitan Stephen). However, at the first session of the newly created collegium, it was decided to rename it the Holy Governing Synod. In 1722 the post of "oberprocurator" of the synod was established (the emperor was to appoint to this position "a good person from among the officers"). Among his duties were the controlling and supervision of the synod's activities. Thus, the oberprocurator became the "eye of the tsar." In 1723 the abolition of the Moscow patriarchate was recognized by the patriarchs of Constantinople and Antioch, who called the Russian Holy Synod its "sister in Christ" (in Greek the word *synodos* is feminine in gender).

Stephen Yavorsky

The decision to replace the individual authority of the patriarch with the collegial authority of the synod matured in Peter's mind over many years. The main reason for this move was the emperor's unwillingness to allow the existence of a potential parallel center of authority (as was the case with Patriarchs Philaret and Nikon). Peter decided to head the Church himself and to

Theophan Prokopovich

adapt the system of church governance to the model of church administration in Protestant countries as closely as possible. The ideological basis of this reform was elaborated by a favorite of the emperor, Archbishop Theophan Prokopovich of Pskov (1681–1736), author of the Spiritual Regulation, which speaks of the danger of patriarchal authority for the state: "It is a great merit of conciliar governance that the fatherland need not fear it might cause revolt and confusion, which occur when spiritual authority is concentrated in one person. The simple folk do not know how spiritual authority differs from the authority of the monarch; and if they are governed by the great honor and glory of a supreme pastor, they believe that he is a second emperor, equal to the monarch or greater than him, and that the spiritual order is another and better state."[1] In another work Theophan characterized tsarist authority in the following words: "The emperor, the supreme authority, is the perfect, highest, supreme, and all-powerful supervisor, i.e., he has power, command, supreme judgment, and the authority to punish over all the ranks and authorities under him, both secular and spiritual. And since imperial supervision of the spiritual ranks has been established by God, every lawful emperor is truly the bishop of bishops within his empire."[2]

After the death of Stephen Yavorsky, Theophan Prokopovich became de facto head of the synod (from 1726 he bore the title of first vice president). Theophan was one of the most dismal figures in the history of Russian Orthodoxy. Vindictive and brutal, he dealt mercilessly with his many ideological opponents. During the period of his autocratic rule in the synod, several bishops whom Prokopovich considered his enemies or who protested against Peter's reforms were defrocked and imprisoned in monasteries. Reprisals against rebellious bishops also continued after his death, and by the end of the reign of Empress Anna (1730–1740) practically all resistance to the Petrine reforms among the higher clergy had been subdued.

During the course of Peter's reforms, which aimed at transforming the Church into a socially useful state institution, a devastating blow was dealt to monasticism. In 1722 a supplement to the Spiritual Regulation was published

---

[1]Cited in Georges Florovsky, *Ways of Russian Theology* (Paris, 1933), 86.
[2]Ibid., 87.

that dealt with monasteries and monasticism, and in 1724 Peter signed a special decree on monks and monasteries. The authors of this decree were the emperor himself and his faithful assistant Theophan Prokopovich, who later added to the emperor's text necessary historical and theological information and refined many general recommendations made by the emperor. The decree, which reflects the extremely negative attitude of its authors toward the very idea of monastic life, contains a "project for reforming all aspects of monasticism in Russia."[3] In it, monasticism is viewed as a legalized form of parasitism that should be combated by all possible means. The authors were particularly harsh in their assessment of urban monasteries, which in their opinion appeared after several Byzantine emperors took monastic vows and after "rogues" from the aristocracy appeared among the monastic ranks. "When the Greek emperors began their hypocrisy after leaving the throne, some rogues came to them and started to build monasteries not in the desert, but in the cities themselves and in their environs, demanding money for these sham holy sites. What is worse, they did not work but chose to feed themselves off the labor of others . . . This gangrene was large, and began to spread throughout our land as well under the auspices of the autocrats of the Church."[4] Peter's edict contains a negative assessment of the state of Russian monasticism at the time: "Since the present lifestyle of monks is only a show and a sham, it gives rise to a large number of evils, for the majority of them are sponges, and the root of all this evil is idleness, and everyone knows how many schismatics and troublemakers this has produced." The authors of the decree see absolutely no benefit in the existence of such monks: "And what if people say that they pray? Everyone prays! . . . What benefits does society reap from this? As the old proverb rightly says: neither God nor the people [gain from them]."[5]

During Peter's reign, the founding of new monasteries was forbidden without a special mandate from the synod, small monasteries were annexed to larger ones, and several were simply closed. Moreover, a number of monastic properties were confiscated. The repressions against monasteries begun during Peter's times were continued during the reigns of Catherine I (1725–1727) and Anna. In 1730 monasteries were prohibited from acquiring

[3]P. Znamensky, *Religious Schools in Russia up to the Reform of 1808* (Kazan, 1881), 138.

[4]That is, the patriarchs. The text of the decree is quoted from I. Chistovich, *Theophan Prokopovich and his Times* (St Petersburg, 1868), 709–18.

[5]Ibid., 714.

land, and in 1734 a comprehensive ban on tonsuring new monks, with the exception of widowed clergymen and retired soldiers, was introduced. Monasteries were subjected to "inspections" conducted by the Secret Chancery, which physically punished and exiled monks who were illegally tonsured. From 1724 to 1738 the number of monastics sank by 40 percent.

However, the monastic reforms elaborated by Peter and Theophan Prokopovich were not fully implemented. Although they did deal a powerful blow to traditional Russian monasticism, they were not able to transform all existing monasteries into orphanages or nursing homes, or turn all monks into infirmary workers.[6] In 1740 the synod decided to inform the empress that "monasticism in Russia is on the verge of total extinction. Only elderly monastics, tonsured before the reforms and unfit for any kind of obedience or service, remain in the monasteries, and several monasteries are completely empty."[7] Thereafter, monastic tonsures were allowed once again, thanks to a petition from the synod.

The rules governing monasteries and monasticism were relaxed during the reign of Elizabeth I (1741–1761), when many monasteries were renovated. In 1761 permission was granted to tonsure people from all levels of society. However, during the rule of Peter III (1761–1762) the secularization of monastery lands along with the serfs who lived on them began. This confiscation of church property continued during the time of Catherine II (1762–1796). In 1764 a decree was issued on the secularization of all church lands, including those of the synod, episcopal sees, and monasteries, the earnings from which were now deposited in state coffers. More than one-half of the monasteries of Russia–469 out of 881–were closed. The number of monastics in the provinces was reduced by approximately 50 percent, from 11,000 to 5,450.[8] In the nineteenth century the state of monasticism began to improve once again. Along with the closure of old monasteries (a total of 822 monasteries were closed from 1701 to the mid-nineteenth century), new ones began to appear. During the nineteenth century many monasteries that had been closed earlier were reopened. From 1810 until the end of the century their number rose from 452 to 1025.

---

[6]Florovsky, *Ways of Russian Theology*, 102.
[7]Hegumen Andronik (Trubachev), A.A. Bovkalo, and V.A. Fyodorov, "Monasteries and Monasticsm 1700–1998," in *Orthodox Encyclopedia*, 326.
[8]Ibid., 327–28.

The secularization of church lands during Catherine II's time met with vigorous protest from Metropolitan Arseny Matseevich of Rostov (1697–1772). In 1762 he sent two reports to the synod in which he sharply criticized the decrees of the empress and argued that church property should be inviolable. The empress was incensed by the content of these reports, perceived their rebellious spirit, and ordered the synod to defrock Arseny, who was exiled as a simple monk to a distant monastery. Not satisfied with this act of retribution, in 1767 Catherine ordered that he be stripped of his habit and imprisoned in the fortress of the city of Revel under the name "Andrew the Liar"; here he was kept under inhumane conditions. After Arseny's death the people

Metropolitan Arseny of Rostov

began to venerate him as a saint, culminating in his canonization by a bishops' council in 2000. His fate horrified the church hierarchy of his time, forcing it to observe the confiscation of church property in silence.[9]

The reforms begun by Peter I and continued by his successors significantly weakened the higher church authority and monasticism while at the same time fostering the development of theological education. This was a direct consequence of Peter's views on the necessity of educating the people and on the Church as one of the institutes that should contribute to this aim. Theological schools had been opened in Muscovite Rus' before Peter's time. For example, the Slavic-Greek-Latin Academy, which later became the Moscow Theological Academy, was opened in Moscow in 1685 by the brothers Ioannicius and Sophronius Likhud. However, during the rule of Peter I, and especially after the publication of the Spiritual Regulation, the opening of theological schools became systematic. Between 1721 and 1725 alone seminaries and lower-level theological schools were opened in St Petersburg, Nizhny Novgorod, Kharkov, Tver, Kazan, Vyatka, Kholmogory, Kolomna, Ryazan, Vologda, and Pskov. Theological schools continued to be opened during the entire eighteenth century. By 1808 there were 150 theological schools in Russia, and by 1825, after the educational reforms of Emperor Alexander I (1801–1825), there were 340, including 3 theological academies (in

[9]Smolich, *Russian Monasticism*, 282.

Kiev, Moscow, and St Petersburg), 39 seminaries, 128 lower theological schools, and 170 parish schools.[10]

One characteristic of the theological schools opened during and after the reign of Peter I was that instruction was conducted in Latin, with the program of study copying that of western Jesuit schools of the seventeenth century. This was caused by the influence of the Kiev academy and its graduates who, after coming to Muscovite Rus', became bishops, rectors, and teachers at the theological schools. Lectures were read, papers were written, and examinations were held entirely in Latin. P. Znamensky noted that "with such persistent training in the Latin language, the students attained such an astonishing degree of fluency . . . that it seemed as if they thought in Latin. Or at least when they had to write something in Russian . . . they unwittingly peppered their Russian with Latin phrases. Some experts indeed wrote their compositions in Latin and then translated them into Russian."[11]

Even today the library of the Moscow Theological Academy houses dissertations written in Latin by graduates of the eighteenth century. The bishops of the time, particularly those who came from the Kiev Theological Academy, spoke Latin better than Russian. An eloquent testimony to this is a letter of Metropolitan Stephen Yavorsky addressed to the members of the Holy Synod, in which he recommends the appointment of Theophan Prokopovich to the see of Kiev: "Ex vi officii mei I entreat you, most honorable members of the synod, to exercise care in the election to the see of Kiev, publicum spectando bonum, laying aside all private interests . . . My votum from the bottom of my heart et ex amore publici boni goes to the Right Reverend Theophan, archbishop of Pskov. He is, omnibus spectatis circumstantiis et ejus dotibus, highly suited for the position."[12]

The fate of "learned monasticism" as a special class within the Russian Church was inseparably linked with that of the theological schools. The idea of a "bureaucratic learned monasticism"[13] was supported by the imperial authorities as early as 1724, when Peter I divided the monastics into two classes: those who became monks "in order to satisfy their weak consciences,"

[10]Priest Maxim Kozlov, "Theological Education: Seventeenth-Twentieth Centuries," in *Orthodox Encyclopedia*, 409–12.

[11]Znamensky, *Religious Schools in Russia*, 740.

[12]Cited in Chistovich, *Theophan Prokopovich*, 107–8.

[13]This expression was coined by Archimandrite Cyprian (Kern). See his work *Father Antonin Kapustin: Archimandrite and Head of the Russian Spiritual Mission in Jerusalem (1817–1894)* (Moscow, 1997), 6.

and those who became monks "in order to become bishops and other church teachers." Unlearned monks were directed to work in monastery almshouses, infirmaries, and hospitals, and to care for retired soldiers, the elderly, and the poor. They were "not to have their own cells but store-rooms in hospitals," received no salary, and were not allowed to travel outside the monastery.[14] As for the learned class, "they are to be made monks not for the sake of monasticism, but in order to teach the people and administer the church sacraments. They are to be given the monastic tonsure only if necessary, and if possible, they should be relieved of their vows . . . Since it is impossible for those monks who are made teachers to read their entire monastic rule, it is enough for them to learn their appointed task and teach the people."[15] In order to create a class of learned monks, Peter ordered the establishment of theological seminaries in which future bishops and teachers were to receive the necessary education. Upon graduation the students were to be tonsured monks ("this might seem to contradict righteousness, but since there is no other solution, it is better to choose the lesser of two evils," as Peter wrote himself[16]) and sent to the "Nevsky monastery," i.e., the Alexander Nevsky Lavra, which was a smithy for episcopal candidates.

The idea of learned monasticism formulated by Peter I determined the life of the Russian Church for the next two centuries. Unlike monastics in monasteries, learned monastics in the eighteenth century not only did not suffer persecution but, on the contrary, emerged as a privileged class in whose hands the governance of the Church was concentrated. As a rule, graduates of the theological academies who expressed a desire to become monks were tonsured immediately, ordained, and appointed to a teaching position in a seminary or academy. The most gifted of them later became inspectors and rectors of theological academies and were simultaneously entrusted with governing monasteries. However, in most cases they were abbots only in name, visiting their monasteries for only one or two days at a time or not at all. The last rung of the career ladder was the episcopal consecration. By the second half of the eighteenth century, bishops who were not learned monks had already become a rarity. This situation obtained in the Church over the course of the entire nineteenth century.[17]

[14]Cited in Chistovich, *Theophan Prokopovich*, 714–15.
[15]Ibid., 716–17.
[16]Ibid., 716.
[17]Smolich, *Russian Monasticism*, 308–9.

During the entire first half of the eighteenth century, the majority of learned monks who were elevated to episcopal sees were Little Russians and members of the Kievan intelligentsia. The situation began to change only during the reign of Catherine II, when Great Russians were allowed to be appointed rectors and bishops. In 1758 Gabriel (Petrov) was made rector of the Moscow Theological Academy; he later became metropolitan of St Petersburg. Soon after this Platon (Levshin), later metropolitan of Moscow, was appointed professor. In 1758 Tikhon (Sokolov) was made prefect of the Novgorod seminary; subsequently he became the hierarch of Voronezh and Zadonsk. Toward the end of Catherine's reign, a group of learned Great Russian monks had formed and ousted the dominant Little Russian party.[18] Latin influence among the learned monks and in the theological schools began to weaken with the increase in the number of Great Russian bishops. Despite the strong influence of Latin scholasticism remaining in the nineteenth century, an increasing number of dissertations were written in Russian, and interest in patristic theology steadily increased.

The Petrine reforms also affected the parish clergy, which crystallized into a separate social class in the eighteenth century. The children of clergymen, whether they wanted to or not, were obliged to study at institutions of theological education. It was nearly impossible to escape from the clerical class, just as it was almost impossible (at least until the mid-nineteenth century) for members of other classes to become clergymen. Holy orders were frequently handed down from father to son, or went over from father-in-law to son-in-law. As a result, the freely chosen nature of the parish clergy characteristic of Muscovite Rus' was destroyed during the synodal period. Until the second quarter of the nineteenth century, government policies were marked by their striving to reduce the number of parishes. Members of the clerical class (clergymen and their children) were occasionally "drafted" for state and military service. Despite all the measures taken by the state, the number of parishes and clergy gradually rose; nevertheless, this growth was disproportional to the growth of the population. At the end of the nineteenth and beginning of the twentieth century, there were half the churches and one-sixth the clergymen per capita than two centuries earlier.[19]

[18]Znamensky, *Religious Schools in Russia*, 432–34.

[19]P.S. Stepanovich, "The Parish and Parish Clergy: Eighteenth–Nineteenth Centuries," in *Orthodox Encyclopedia*, 267–68.

While the eighteenth century was, according to Georges Florovsky, a time of "Babylonian captivity" for the Russian Church,[20] the nineteenth century witnessed the gradual weakening of western influence in theological education and a softening of state policies toward the Church. The synodal system continued to function, the oberprocurator was still present in the synod, and the decisions of the synod were still issued with the stamp "By Decree of His Imperial Majesty." However, the synod of the nineteenth century was no longer the powerless and impersonal "spiritual collegium" conceived by Peter I, but an institution endowed with real powers and capable of taking sufficiently effective action. Among its members were many brilliant and outstanding hierarchs who shaped the destiny of the Russian Orthodox Church. It was still possible, moreover, to exert influence on church life without taking part in the meetings of the synod.

This fact is confirmed by the life of one of the most outstanding hierarchs in the entire history of world Orthodoxy—St Philaret (Drozdov), metropolitan of Moscow (1782–1867). His ecclesiastical career was typical of nineteenth-century Russia. The son of a deacon, he graduated from a lower theological school, seminary, and academy, and in 1808, after being tonsured a monk, he was appointed professor of philosophy at the St Petersburg Theological Academy. In 1811 Philaret was elevated to the rank of archimandrite, and in 1812 he was appointed rector of the academy. In 1817 he was consecrated bishop of Revel, and in 1819 he was transferred first to the

St Philaret (Drozdov)

diocese of Tver and then to Yaroslavl. In 1821 he was made bishop of Moscow, and in 1826 he was elevated to metropolitan of Moscow and appointed a member of the Holy Synod. In 1842 he ceased traveling to St Petersburg to attend the meetings of the synod, but until his death he continued to participate in all serious church matters as the most authoritative hierarch of his time. Philaret governed the metropolia of Moscow for forty-six years, a period of time called "the age of Philaret"—not only for the diocese of Moscow, but for the entire Russian Church. Through his authority, Philaret was to a great extent able to fill the canonical vacuum that had formed after the abolish-

[20] *Ways of Russian Theology*, 89.

ment of the patriarchate. It was not by chance that A.N. Muravyev, the ober-procurator at the time, wrote after Philaret's death: "We have lost a great luminary and defender of Orthodoxy, who, while not being a patriarch in rank, was nevertheless like a true patriarch for us, for he resolved all difficult ecclesiastical questions with the wisdom given him from above, and the Russian Church will continue to feel the weight of his opinion for a long time to come."[21]

Philaret's attitude toward the state authorities was respectful and reverent: he saw the tsar as the anointed of God, who "receives all his legitimacy from his anointment by the Church." It follows from this that the tsar is obliged to defend the interests of the Church: "In our fatherland . . . the most pious tsars are the supreme defenders of the right faith and the good order of the Holy Church."[22] Because of this closeness to the throne and unconditional support for the policies of the imperial government, Philaret was harshly criticized by liberals and revolutionaries. In his work *My Past and Thoughts*, Alexander Herzen writes of a service of supplication served by Philaret after the uprising of December 1825:

> In the center of the Kremlin, Metropolitan Philaret thanked God for the killings. The entire imperial family prayed, surrounded by the senate and ministers; around them were the enormous, thick masses of the guard on their knees, without shako, who also prayed. The cannons thundered from the Kremlin heights . . . I was present at this prayer as a boy of around fourteen years, lost in the crowd, and here, before the altar defiled by this bloodstained prayer, I swore to take revenge for the executed and doomed myself to fighting against this throne, this altar, and these cannons.[23]

It goes without saying that Philaret thanked God not for the killings but for the miraculous rescue from death of Emperor Nicholas I, whom the Decembrists had attempted to murder.

While metropolitan of Moscow, for almost half a century Philaret held thanksgiving services on the namedays and anniversaries of the tsar and the members of his family, and participated in all gala events of the tsarist government. During the reign of Emperor Nicholas I (1825–1855), Philaret was fre-

[21]Cited in I.K. Smolich, *History of the Russian Church: 1700–1917*, part 1 (Moscow, 1996), 219–20.
[22]Ibid., 221.
[23]Alexander Herzen, *My Past and Thoughts* (Moscow, 1958), 75.

quently invited to take part in discussions of matters of state importance. To his credit, Philaret also wrote the text of the manifesto of February 19, 1861 on the liberation of serfs—the most important event in the reign of Alexander II the Liberator (1855–1881).

Faithful to the tsar and the homeland, Philaret also fought for more independence of the Church from the state authorities. The synod's oberprocurator at the time was Count A.F. Protasov (1836–1855), an authoritarian and despotic figure. Many members of the synod lost their positions due to disputes with him, and the reason for Philaret's departure from the synod was, unsurprisingly, his dissatisfaction with Protasov's autocratic behavior. Philaret is believed to have said: "Count Protasov's spurs catch on my episcopal *mantia*." Philaret was not a proponent of the restoration of the patriarchate, and considered the synodal structure to be quite appropriate for governing the Church. Still, he thought that the Church should be granted a greater degree of self-governance.[24]

Philaret had a part in many historical events. In 1821, on commission of the synod, he wrote an Orthodox catechism that was approved by the entire Church. In 1858, on his insistence, the first Russian translation of the Bible was published. Philaret himself directly participated in the translation work, which lasted for more than forty years. He also initiated the systematic translation and publication of the writings of the holy fathers in Russian, a labor that was carried out by the combined forces of four theological academies: those of Moscow, St Petersburg, Kiev, and Kazan. The publication of the works of the church fathers contributed to the liberation of Russian theology from the influence of Latin scholasticism, which had dominated throughout the eighteenth century.

Metropolitan Philaret made an enormous contribution to reforming the theological academies and seminaries. He undertook this reform almost singlehandedly: he proposed complex and wide-ranging projects for their reform, organized the study programs for academies and seminaries, wrote textbooks, and reviewed those written by others. Philaret considered theological education an extremely important aspect of the activity of the Christian Church: "In Christianity, nobody is allowed to remain completely unlearned and ignorant. Did not the Lord himself call himself teacher and his followers disciples? Before Christians began to be called Christians, all of them

[24]Smolich, *History of the Russian Church*, 220.

without exception were called disciples. And why did the Lord send the apostles into the world? First and foremost in order to teach all the peoples: 'Go therefore and make disciples of all the nations.' If you do not wish to teach and enlighten yourself in Christianity, you are not a disciple and follower of Christ."[25] The hierarch demanded that students' interest in independent research be nurtured during the course of studies: "A good method of study consists in developing the capabilities and intellectual activity of the students."[26] According to Florovsky, Philaret "was not afraid of stimulating thought, although he was aware of the temptations this could cause. This was because he believed that these temptations could be overcome and vanquished only through creative activity . . . Philaret always underscored the necessity of theologizing as the sole and irreplaceable foundation of an integral spiritual life."[27]

While striving to raise the educational level of the clergy, Metropolitan Philaret also actively participated in the projects of Nicholas I for improving secular education. Philaret contributed to the opening of an entire chain of new educational institutions, helped increase funding for schools, and supported the publication of new textbooks written by Russians. Seeing the lack of education as the cause of all problems, Philaret lamented: "Of course, there is a large gap between theory and practice. Knowledge is not faith but a path to it. Many people, having become bored with learning, abandon it, wrongly hoping to achieve practice without it . . . Learning is light, and ignorance darkness. Judging from the fact that there is little light among us, it is evident that we do not study as we ought. It is obvious that the seed has been sown on untilled and unprepared ground, which is why it does not bear any fruit. Thus, one should not blame learning but oneself."[28]

Philaret also made a significant contribution to the development of monastic life. Already during his first tour through the Moscow diocese in 1821 he noted that a large number of monasteries did not adhere to the cenobitic rule. Subsequently he strove to introduce this rule to the monasteries under his jurisdiction and thereby strengthen discipline. He paid special attention to the Trinity-St Sergius Lavra, which he visited numerous times every year. Many of his sermons were devoted to the feast day of St Sergius;

[25]Metropolitan Philaret of Moscow, *Homilies and Speeches* (Moscow, 1873–1885), 5.250.
[26]Cited in Florovsky, *Ways of Russian Theology*, 145.
[27]Ibid., 172.
[28]N.V. Sushkov, *Notes on the Life and Times of Metropolitan Philaret* (Moscow, 1868), 8.

in them he expounded his views on monasticism and the inner spiritual life. Philaret's authority in the mid-nineteenth century was highly respected not only among the clergy, aristocracy, and the simple folk, but also in monasteries, where he was justifiably viewed as a practitioner of the great tradition of "noetic activity."[29]

Monastic life in Russia began to revive in the last quarter of the eighteenth century and continued to flourish throughout the nineteenth century. The revival was sparked by changes in state policy on monasteries and inner processes that took place among broad sections of monasticism. These processes were linked to the spread of elderhood in Russia, a phenomenon that had been known since the Byzantine period. St Paisy Velichkovsky (1722–1794), a contemporary of the Greek *kollyvades* movement, is considered to be the founder of Russian elderhood. At the age of thirteen, Paisy entered the Kiev Theological Academy but later felt a profound dislike for the spirit of Latin scholasticism that reigned there. After leaving the academy, he visited numerous Ukrainian monasteries before setting off for Mount Athos, where he became abbot of the Russian St Elias skete. Here he introduced the long-forgotten practice of "noetic activity."

St Paisy Velichkovsky

Paisy paid special attention to the study and translation of the works of the church fathers. He saw their works as the primary guide to the spiritual life: "He who reads the books of the holy fathers is guided in faith or right understanding by one, in silence and prayer by another, in obedience, humility and patience by still another, and in self-accusation and in love for God and one's neighbor by yet another. To put it briefly, one is taught the life according to the gospel by the many books of the holy fathers."[30] After spending seventeen years on the holy mountain, Paisy moved to Moldavia, where he became abbot of the Neamt monastery. Here he occupied himself with new translations and the correction of existing Slavonic translations of patristic works. St Paisy's Slavonic rendering of the *Philokalia* was published

---

[29]For more on Metropolitan Philaret as a practitioner of the tradition of "noetic activity" see I. Kontsevich, *The Optina Hermitage and Its Times* (Jordanville, 1970), 131–63.

[30]Archpriest Sergei Chetverikov, *The Moldavian Elder Paisy Velichkovsky: His Life, Teaching, and Influence on Orthodox Monasticism* (Paris, 1976), 89.

in St Petersburg in 1803 through the efforts of Metropolitan Gabriel (Petrov) of St Petersburg. At the Neamt monastery Paisy amassed a large group of disciples, to whom he taught Greek; under his direction they translated and copied patristic books.

Paisy's activities, however, were not limited to books. He was an outstanding spiritual father and instructor of "noetic activity." After the end of the eighteenth century his influence spread to more than a hundred monasteries, thanks to his more than two hundred disciples,[31] who proceeded to settle throughout Russia.

Synaxis of the Optina elders (contemporary Russian icon)

The main center of elderhood in the nineteenth century was the Optina hermitage, one of the monasteries in Kaluga province. A group of Paisy's disciples headed by the elder Leo (1768–1841), the first of the many Optina elders, moved here from the forests of Roslavl. One of his disciples was Makary (1788–1860), who continued St Paisy's educational work and exerted considerable spiritual influence on his contemporaries. The most famous of the Optina elders was St Amvrosy (1812–1891), who was visited by the faithful from all parts of Russia seeking spiritual advice. Although seriously ill, he always found words of consolation and support for everyone, from the simple peasant to the aristocrat, from the clergyman to the member of the intelligentsia. Among those who visited the Optina elders were many outstanding writers and thinkers, including the Slavophile Kireevsky brothers, Nikolai Gogol, Fedor Dostoyevsky, Konstantin Leontiev, Vladimir Soloviev, and Leo Tolstoy. Among their disciples were also several hierarchs, including St Ignaty Brianchaninov (1807–1867), an author of many ascetic writings that contributed to the revival of monastic life.

St Seraphim of Sarov (1754–1833), one of the greatest saints of the Orthodox Church, exerted enormous influence on spiritual life in nineteenth-century Russia. He came from a family of merchants and desired the monastic life from his early years. For eight years he was a novice in the monastery of Sarov, after which he was tonsured a monk and ordained a hierodeacon.

---

[31]Ibid., 6.

Already in his early years St Seraphim was granted numerous charismatic visions. Once, during the liturgy, he saw angels concelebrating with the monastery brethren. Another time, during the liturgy on Great Thursday, when the young hierodeacon was standing by the royal doors and pointing with his orarion toward the faithful in the church, saying "until the ages of ages," a brilliant light suddenly shone on him, and he saw Christ surrounded by angels, approaching him in the air from the western

St Seraphim of Sarov

doors of the church. After reaching the ambo, the Lord blessed those praying and entered his icon. Struck by the vision, Seraphim could not say a word and did not move. He was taken back into the altar, where he stood for another three hours in spiritual ecstasy. At the age of thirty-nine Seraphim was ordained hieromonk and continued to serve in church. After the death of the abbot he retired to the forest and settled in a lonely cell, where he devoted himself to severe ascetic labors. For three years the saint spent every night kneeling on a rock in prayer.

After many years of life as a hermit, St Seraphim opened the doors of his cell to visitors, each of whom he greeted with the words "Christ is risen, my joy!" His fame as a great ascetic rapidly spread throughout Russia, and people from every corner of the country hastened to the elder seeking spiritual solace and succor. St Seraphim accepted visitors until his very death; among them were simple peasants, merchants, aristocrats, and the intelligentsia.

On one winter day, when everything around the saint's cell was covered with snow, a disciple named Motovilov spoke with the holy elder about the aim of the Christian life. St Seraphim responded: "As good as prayer, fasting, vigils, and all other Christian deeds are in themselves, the aim of our Christian life consists not only in doing them, although they are necessary means to attaining it. The true aim of our Christian life lies in the acquisition of the Holy Spirit of God." Motovilov asked him about the meaning of these words, whereupon the elder answered: "The Grace of the Holy Spirit is a light that enlightens the person." Motovilov asked how one can recognize the presence of the grace of the Holy Spirit. "This, your godliness, is very simple," answered Seraphim, taking Motovilov firmly by the shoulder. "My son, both of us are now together in the Spirit of God. Why don't you look at me?" "I cannot look, father, for lightning shines from your eyes. Your face has become brighter than the sun, and looking at you causes my eyes pain." Fr Seraphim said: "Do not be afraid, your godliness, for you yourself have also become as bright as me. Now you are in the fulness of the Spirit of God, otherwise you would not be able to see me like this . . . What do you feel now?" Motovilov answered: "I feel such quietness and peace in my soul that no words can express . . . an extraordinary sweetness . . . an extraordinary joy in all my heart . . . an extraordinary warmth!" "How can you feel warmth, my son? For we are sitting in a forest. It is winter outside, and there is snow beneath our feet and more than an inch of snow on you . . . What warmth can there be?" "Such as there is in a bath-house." "And is the smell the same as in a bath-house?" "No, there is nothing on earth like this fragrance." Then St Seraphim said to Motovilov with a smile: "My son, I know this just as well as you do, but I am only asking you on purpose if you feel this in the same way . . . The snow has not melted either on you or on me, nor has it melted above us. Thus, the warmth is not in the air but in ourselves."[32]

In the history of Russian sanctity, a special place is occupied by the righteous St John of Kronstadt (1829–1908). He is one of the rare members of the married clergy whose name has been included in the Orthodox calendar (among the saints of the Orthodox Church are many bishops, princes, monks, and martyrs, but almost no married priests). This great pastor, however, sacrificed his family life from the very beginning for the sake of service to the Church and charity, abstaining from marital relations with his own wife. For more than half a century St John was dean of St Andrew's cathedral in Kronstadt, where he served the Divine Liturgy every day, seven days a week. During the service he heard confessions, administered communion to those present, and pronounced fiery sermons. St John had the gift of miracle-working and clairvoyance, which attracted large crowds of people to him. An unending line of people came to visit the "father of Kronstadt," and thousands of letters and telegrams asked for his prayers or help. He refused assistance to none—neither Orthodox, nor Lutherans, nor Muslims, nor Jews. His fame was so great that when he traveled to Russian cities (something he did regularly), he was met everywhere by thousands of believers on bended knees as his carriage approached.

[32]"Dialogue of the Elder Seraphim with N.A. Motovilov on the Aim of the Christian Life," in *St Seraphim of Sarov as Remembered by His Contemporaries* (Moscow, 2003), 320–23.

The scale of the charity work conducted by Fr John was immense: in Kronstadt he established a "house of industry," where up to a thousand poor people were fed daily, with its own hospital and school for poor children. The numerous donations that the pastor of Kronstadt received in envelopes every day were distributed for charity purposes on the same day. St John was close to the imperial court: he personally administered the final sacraments to the dying Emperor Alexander III (1881–1894), and was deeply revered by the family of the last Russian emperor, Nicholas II (1894–1917).

In assessing the synodal period as a whole, it should be noted that despite the subjugation of the Church to the state and the lack of a patriarch, this era witnessed the greatest flourishing of the Russian Orthodox Church ever. The steady increase in the population of the Russian empire fostered the numerical growth of the Church. During the synodal period, the number of Orthodox believers grew ten times, and by 1914 had reached almost 100 million. The number of churches grew more than three-fold, the clergy almost two-fold, and monastics almost four-fold.[33]

The expansion of the Russian empire fostered the development of the Church's missionary work both within and beyond the borders of the empire. Inside Russia missionary activity was carried out primarily among the pagan populations of regions that had been joined to the empire, as well as in areas overtaken by the Unia. Although missionary work was also conducted in the pre-Petrine period, it was during the synodal era that it attained a particularly large scale. An outstanding missionary of the eighteenth century who labored for the conversion of pagan peoples was St Innocent of Irkutsk (1680–1731), who contributed significantly to the enlightenment of Siberia.

In the eighteenth century the Belorussian archbishop George Konissky (1717–1795) played an important role in bringing Uniates back to the Orthodox Church. Through his efforts more than 100,000 Uniates returned to Orthodoxy.[34] In 1839, thanks to the labors of Metropolitan Joseph Semashko (1789–1868), the Uniate Church in Belorussia and Lithuania rejoined the Orthodox Church.

[33]Archpriest Vladislav Tsypin, "The Russian Orthodox Church in the Synodal Period: 1700–1917," in *Orthodox Encyclopedia*, 132.

[34]A.S. Pushkin wrote a review of the works of George Konissky: *The Collected Works of George Konissky, Archbishop of Byelorussia, Published by Archpriest Ioann Grigorovich*, in *Complete Works* 7 (Leningrad, 1978), 223–35.

Outside of Russia, large-scale missionary activities were conducted in China, North America, and Japan, as well as in Urmia at the end of the nineteenth and beginning of the twentieth centuries. Among the outstanding missionaries of the synodal period were Innocent Venyaminov (1797–1879) and Nicholas of Japan (1836–1912). St Innocent, who devoted many years to preaching Christianity among the Kaloshes, Koryaks, Chukchi, Tungus, and Aleuts, became the first Orthodox bishop whose jurisdiction covered North America. St Nicholas was the first Orthodox bishop of Japan and the founder of the Japanese Orthodox Church, which preserves its canonical dependence on the Moscow patriarchate to this day.

The main paradox of the synodal period is that, while it witnessed the greatest flowering and expansion of the Orthodox Church ever, it was also a time when the upper classes of Russian society, particularly the aristocracy and intelligentsia, left it en masse. Herzen's words about Philaret of Moscow quoted earlier are but one of the numerous testimonies of the spiritual gulf that had formed between the Church and the world of the liberal intelligentsia, the majority of whom were estranged from the Church in the nineteenth century. The exodus of the educated classes from the Church began already during the reign of Peter I. During the reign of Elizabeth II, the upper classes became enamored of Voltaire (the empress herself, while remaining an Orthodox Christian, was highly interested in Voltaire). In the nineteenth century enlightened deism was replaced by atheism, which by the end of the century had gained a significant number of adherents among the intelligentsia. While Russia at the beginning of the synodal period was an Orthodox nation, in which all aspects of life of all classes of society were permeated by the Church and religiosity, by the end of the synodal period Russia had turned into a secular state whose life was by no means determined only by Orthodox ideals and principles. In the second half of the nineteenth and the early twentieth century, the estrangement from the Church had penetrated the working class and even the peasantry, becoming particularly noticeable in the period between the revolutions of 1905 and 1917.

The synodal period ended almost simultaneously with the fall of the Russian monarchy. Debates on the convening of a national council with the aim of restoring the patriarchate began within the Church as early as the beginning of the twentieth century, and a preconciliar commission, whose aim was to work out the agenda for the upcoming council, was formed in 1906. However, it was only after the February Revolution of 1917 that the council could be convened. In the period before the revolution, nearly the entire Russian Church—which counted many millions of faithful—took part in the preparations for this council, from the Holy Synod to the parish clergy and laymen. The council opened on August 15/28, 1917, on the feast of the Dormition of the Most Holy Mother of God. The Provisional Government was still in power, but its days were numbered. After the Bolsheviks came to power in October 1917, the council continued its work for the following ten-and-a-half months.

The council of 1917–1918 was the largest, longest, and most fruitful council in the entire history of the Russian Church. Almost all bishops of the Russian Church, as well as many clergy, monastics, and laymen, attended the council, and decisions on many key issues of church life were taken. During the three conciliar sessions, a total of 170 plenary sessions were held, at which questions that were previously discussed in the sections were openly debated. The council had 22 sections, 3 consultations, and approximately 10 temporary commissions that met daily, at times of the day when the plenary sessions were not being held.[35] Moreover, certain sections also had their own subsections. The fruits of the council were 170 acts reflecting a broad spectrum of ecclesiastical questions. Its main achievements were the restoration of the patriarchate in Russia and the elevation of Metropolitan Tikhon of Moscow (1865–1925) to the patriarchal throne. With his election, which took place on November 5, 1917, the two-hundred-year synodal period of the Russian Orthodox Church came to an end.

RUSSIAN SPIRITUAL WRITERS OF THE SYNODAL PERIOD

Thanks to the substantial rise in the educational level of the clergy during the eighteenth and nineteenth centuries, to the revival of monastic life in the nineteenth century, and to the quantitative and qualitative growth of the Church as a whole, the synodal period saw a flourishing of Russian Orthodox theology. During this time many original theological, moral, and ascetic works were written. While Orthodox theology at the beginning of the syn-

[35]See the speech of L.K. Artamonov at the closing of the third session of the council, September 7/20, 1918, in *Acts of the Holy Council of the Russian Orthodox Church* (Moscow, 2000), II.239–40.

odal period was in captivity to western scholastic schemes due to the influence of the Kiev school and its graduates, this dependence was overcome to a significant degree during the eighteenth and particularly the nineteenth centuries. Among the most outstanding spiritual writers of the eighteenth century were Dimitry of Rostov and Tikhon of Zadonsk, and of the nineteenth century Philaret of Moscow, Ignaty Brianchaninov, Theophan the Recluse, and the righteous John of Kronstadt.

St Dimitry of Rostov
(Russian icon, 18th c.)

St Dimitry of Rostov (1651–1709) lived at a time when the influence of the Kiev school was at its strongest, and he himself was one of its graduates. His main work is the *Menaion Reader*, which contains lives of saints for each day of the year, compiled primarily on the basis of Latin and Polish sources. He also penned a number of original works, such as *The Bedewed Fleece*, devoted to the miracles of the Chernigov-St Elias icon of the Mother of God; *An Examination of the Schismatic Brynian Sect*, against schismatics; *Reflections on the Image and Likeness of God in Man*, which was written against those who refused to shave on the order of Peter I; and his *Diarium* (diary), written in Ukrainian. St Dimitry's sermons on the church feasts and days of special importance are outstanding examples of the rhetorical tradition of the Kiev academy. Many of his works are of a moral character; among these is the highly popular *Spiritual Alphabet*, which contains homilies on fundamental questions of faith arranged in alphabetical order. St Dimitry also wrote works for the theater and religious poems in syllabic verse.

St Dimitry's times coincided with a period in the history of the Russian Church marked by a "separation between theology and piety, between theological erudition and prayerful meditation on God, between the theological school and church life."[36] Moreover, the gap between the academic and monastic traditions widened: theology became more "scholastic" and separated from religious life, while piety oriented itself ever less toward theology. Despite this St Dimitry absorbed, along with his Kievan erudition, the age-old spirit of monastic piety that had been preserved in Russian monasteries. He wrote much on prayer, on the inner life, and on spiritual experience. The

---

[36]Florovsky, *Ways of Russian Theology*, 502.

theme of his treatise *On the Prayer of a Person Who Has Retired to the Closet of His Heart* is the contrast between the internal and the external—in the person, in how he learns, and in prayer:

> Man is dual in nature: he is external and internal, fleshly and spiritual . . . And there are two kinds of learning—the external and the internal: the external through books, the internal through meditation on God; the external through the love of wisdom, the internal through the love of God; the external in rhetoric, the internal in prayer; the external in wittiness, the internal in the warmth of the spirit . . . Prayer is also two-fold— external and internal: that which is said in front of others and that which is said secretly; that which is conducted in concert with others and that which is read alone; that which must be read and that which is voluntary . . . The former is read out loud with the voice, the latter only by the mind. The former is read standing, the latter not only while standing or walking, but also lying in bed, in other words, at all times whenever one raises his mind to God . . . Interior prayer . . . requires neither a mouth, nor books, nor movements of the tongue, nor the voice in one's throat . . . but only the lifting of the mind to God and meditation, which can be done in any place.[37]

St Tikhon of Zadonsk (1724–1783) belonged to the "learned monasticism" that emerged in the eighteenth century: after systematically holding a number of administrative positions in institutions of theological education, he was consecrated bishop before he was even forty years old. However, his yearning for the ascetic life moved him to submit a petition to retire to the Zadonsk monastery, where he wrote his main works. All of these writings bear witness to the saint's profound roots in the eastern Christian patristic tradition, despite the fact that western influence also bore its mark. The style of his works is plain and edifying, intended for the simple reader. In his book *Spiritual Treasures Collected from the World*, St Tikhon cites various phenomena in the visible world as examples of Christian virtues or vices. His chapters on "Sheep" and "Goats" illustrate this:

> In holy scripture, Christians are called sheep because there are many similarities between them. Just as sheep do not offend any animal, so do

[37]Cited in Hegumen Chariton, ed., *Noetic Activity: On the Jesus Prayer. A Collection of Homilies of the Holy Fathers and Experienced Practitioners* (Sortavala, 1936), 6–8.

Christians offend no one . . . Sheep are known for their meekness and patience, and when they are sheared they are silent. In the same way Christians are humble, meek, and patient . . . Just as sheep are obedient to their shepherds, so do Christians render obedience to their Shepherd and Lord Jesus Christ . . . Do you see, Christian, the characteristics of Christ's sheep, of true Christians? Ask yourself if you belong to this blessed flock . . . Evil people liken themselves unto goats, for there is much in common between them and evil people. Just as goats butt and harm almost all animals with their horns, so do evil people do harm to all persons . . . Just as goats give off a particular stench, so do the evil reek with their evil character and lawless lives.[38]

St Tikhon's main work is *On True Christianity*, an extensive and systematic exposition of Christian morality. The title was taken from a work by the German spiritual writer Johann Arndt, and several chapters (e.g., "On the Veneration of Christ's Passion") reveal the influence of Catholic mysticism. Although the book is lacking in quotations of patristic literature, it is strewn with biblical quotes from beginning to end. St Tikhon assigned particular importance to the reading of the Bible. Thus, the first chapters of the first and second volumes of *On True Christianity* are devoted to the necessity of reading the Bible and the gospel. At a time when there was still no Russian translation of the Bible and when the simple folk heard scripture only at church services, St Tikhon called on the faithful to read the Bible at home every day, which he considered the foundation of a Christian's spiritual life.

A major spiritual writer of the second and third quarters of the nineteenth century was St Philaret of Moscow, whose archpastoral service was examined earlier. Philaret was not only an outstanding hierarch, preacher, churchman, and social figure, he was also a major theologian with extensive knowledge in the areas of biblical studies, patristics, church history, and other disciplines. His first significant work was *Notes for a Thorough Understanding of the Book of Genesis*, in which he reveals his knowledge not only of patristic scriptural exegesis but also biblical criticism. His *Colloquy between a Believer and a Skeptic on the True Doctrine of the Greco-Russian Church* spells out the main differences between Orthodoxy and the western confessions. Philaret's *Longer Catechism of the Orthodox Catholic Eastern Greco-Russian Church* was important as a short,

---

[38]*The Works of Our Father among the Saints Tikhon of Zadonsk* (Moscow, 1889; repr. Pskov Caves Monastery, 1994), 4.36.

official introduction to the teaching of the Orthodox Church, although it is not completely free from the influence of Latin scholasticism, which is reflected not only in its form but also in its content. Another important work is his *Collection of Opinions and Comments*, which contains his resolutions, notes, and reports on various questions of a theological, historical, social, and political nature. St Philaret's extensive correspondence throws light on many aspects of his theological and moral teaching.

The main and most significant part of St Philaret's literary output was his sermons, which were published during his lifetime in Christian journals and collected in five volumes with the general title *Homilies and Speeches*. These speeches reveal the rhetorical talent of the "Russian Chrysostom," the depth and incisiveness of his theological thought, and the profundity of his religious feeling. His sermons can be divided into three categories: those devoted to church feasts and saints' days; those given at the consecration of newly built churches; and those on the occasion of memorable events in the life of the imperial family or greetings to its members. These events, however, were often simply an occasion to expound upon a particular theological teaching. Since he was not able to write theological treatises on particular themes, probably due to a lack of free time, Philaret made use of sermons to express his theological views. Each sermon was carefully prepared and was read from a text written in advance.

St Philaret's sermons on feast days are outstanding examples of church rhetoric. On Great Friday in 1816, remembering the crucifixion and Christ's death on the cross, St Philaret gave a homily on love:

> Is it now that some would speak of love? Is it now, when the fruit of hatred has ripened in the garden of the Beloved, when even the earth shudders from fear and the hearts of rocks are rent apart, and the eye of heaven has grown dark with indignation? Is it now that some might speak of love for the world, when the Son of God, who suffered in the world, was left without consolation and his prayerful cry "My God, my God, why have you forsaken Me?" (Mt 27.46) without a fatherly answer? Yes, Christians! This is indeed a day of hatred and horror, a day of wrath and retribution. But if this is so, what will become of us when the earth shakes beneath us and the heavens above us become turbulent? Whither shall we flee from the quaking ground? Where shall we take refuge from the

ominous heavens? Gaze more fervently at Golgotha, and there, where all misfortunes are concentrated, you shall find refuge. While *the earth shook and trembled; the foundations of the hills also quaked and were shaken, because he was angry* (Ps 18.7), do you not see how firmly the cross stands there? Though the dead do not rest in their graves, do you not see how peacefully he who was crucified reposes on the cross? . . . Christian! Let *darkness cover the land*! Let *darkness fall upon the peoples*! Arise from your fear and doubts! *Shine* with faith and hope! *Your light shines* through the darkness (Is 60.1–2). Walk the path that opens up to you the torn curtain of the mysteries, enter into the inner sanctuary of Jesus' sufferings, leaving behind the outer courtyard, which was given over to the nations to trample upon. What do you find there? Nothing but the holy and blessed love of the Father, Son, and Holy Spirit for the sinful and wretched human race. The love of the Father is a crucifying love; the love of the Son is a crucified one; and the love of the Spirit is one that triumphs through the power of the cross. This is how God has loved the world![39]

In his sermon on Christmas 1826, Philaret returns to the theme of kenosis, of how Jesus Christ, God who became man and conquered death through his death, emptied and humbled himself:

Those who are attached to earthly greatness have often been scandalized by Jesus Christ's humiliation. However, the experience of so many centuries has proven that God exalted him, and that *all tribes in the heavens, on earth, and in the underworld* (Phil 2.9–10) bow down to him. For since the days when he arose and ascended, thousands of witnesses have seen how the heavenly powers obediently fulfil his commands, how the forces of hell were cast into the abyss by his name; moreover, millions of those on earth find bliss in worshiping his name. After all this we can spare ourselves the effort of defending and justifying his humiliation before those who have gathered to bow down before the name of Jesus. There is nothing to hinder us from beholding his humiliation with the same reverence with which we admire his majesty.[40]

---

[39]Philaret (Drozdov), "Homily on Great Friday, 1816," in *Selected Works: Letters, Memoirs* (Moscow, 2003), 124–25.

[40]Philaret of Moscow, "Christmas Homily, 1826," in *Homilies and Speeches*, 3.66.

As metropolitan of Moscow, St Philaret consecrated churches in Moscow and the Moscow region for several decades. At each consecration he gave a sermon, in which he spoke of the church as God's dwelling-place, as a continuation of the heavenly Church, and as a type of the New Jerusalem that will descend from heaven. While preaching after the consecration of the church of the Holy Trinity in Klin near Moscow, he emphasized that:

> God is omnipresent and therefore does not need churches, which are always small for him and cannot contain him. But man is limited, and thus needs a limited revelation of God's presence. God condescended to this need of man and deigned that this church exist, granting it the grace of his particular presence. We know of only one state of man in which he has no need of churches: the eternal life in the New Jerusalem, under a new heaven and on a new earth . . . The seer of mysteries notes a special, distinguishing feature of the New Jerusalem, namely that there is no church there: *and I saw no church there* (Rev 21.22) . . . But we are not yet in the New Jerusalem, which will descend from the heavens, and therefore need a church. Belonging to creation after the fall, our own flesh, rough and unpurified, blocks our entrance into the holy, grace-filled presence of God. This is why it is necessary for his charismatic presence to reveal itself to us in the holy churches. The heavens—where Christ, our light, ascended—have not yet opened up and revealed to us the radiance of his glory. Because of this we need for the time being at least a small heaven on earth, as well as light—even though it may be hidden in mystery. We can find all this in the church, through prayer, the word of God, and the sacraments.[41]

As titular abbot of the Trinity-St Sergius Lavra, St Philaret always visited the monastery on the feast days of its founder, St Sergius, the abbot of Radonezh, and celebrated festal services there. St Philaret spoke of St Sergius as a wonderworker whom God placed over the entire Russian land:

> His lord said to him, "Well done, good and faithful servant; you were faithful over a few things, I will make you ruler over many things" (Mt 25.21) . . . Do you wish to see in real life that which you have heard in a

---

[41]"Homily on the Consecration of the Cathedral of the Most Holy Trinity in the City of Klin, 1836," in *Homilies and Speeches*, 4.2–3.

parable? While still on earth you can observe how the law of the kingdom of heaven works in people whom the heavenly King has specially chosen, tested for faithfulness, and found *faithful in small things*, and have therefore been *placed over many things* as exalted and powerful tools of his kingdom . . . Did our holy father Sergius possess many things when he chose this place for himself, or rather when God chose him in order to bless this place through him? It would be easier to say what he did not have and what he had left behind than what he did have. He left his social standing, his parents' house, his inheritance, and found here an unpopulated and untraversable wilderness, a place with enough water for one person but scarcely enough for many. He built a hut and a small church but had no clergy for it; sometimes he had no bread in his hut or even an ordinary lamp for his nighttime prayers in church. There was one talent given to him early on that could be noticed—his desire to serve God. But only time could reveal if this talent was of pure gold and to what extent it would enrich him who labored. And what did time reveal? Behold *just how many things he who had been faithful in small things was placed over*. How many heavenly things did he have power over while he was still alive on earth? To how many earthly things does his authority extend now, when he is in heaven? . . . What can be more powerful and broader than this authority, which enabled him to transform this wilderness into an age-old monastery and whose positive influence and actions—such as blessing, protection, comfort, healing, help in doing good, and succor against evil—span the centuries and encompass different places and people, so that, thanks to the grace of God, who is wondrous in his saints, it is impossible to discern either an end or a boundary to this? This is a marvelous, obvious experience of how *he who is faithful in small things will be placed over many things* in the kingdom of God.[42]

Services on the namedays of the emperor or members of the imperial family, which Philaret unfailingly celebrated, provided him with the opportunity to give sermons in accordance with the event being celebrated. However, in most cases he went beyond the official theme and offered his listeners an extensive theological treatise on a particular theological question. For

---

[42]"Homily on the Feast of the Finding of the Relics of St Sergius, July 5, 1836," in *Homilies and Speeches*, 4.18–19.

example, in his sermon on the nameday of Emperor Alexander I, St Philaret elaborates on the teaching on names as the "essence or property of a thing" expressed in words, as the "power of a thing contained in words":

> *But rather rejoice because your names are written in heaven* (Lk 10.20) . . . If certain earthly names are considered important, how much more important are heavenly names? . . . The word of God and living words in general—and particularly names, which should be understood as living words—force us in many cases to think carefully and seriously about names . . . Is it necessary to show the wisdom that has come from the hands of a creative person and his authority over all earthly creatures? The word of God tells us that it was he who gave names, and attributes dignity to the names given by him, which is why they should not be changed: *And whatever Adam called each living creature, that was its name* (Gen 2.19). Should we not glorify the supreme wisdom and power of God himself? He is said to have given names to heavenly things: *He counts the number of the stars; He calls them all by name* (Ps 146.4). Is it necessary to promise a reward, the highest honor, and bliss to those who fight and are victorious for Christ? A new name is promised to them: *And I will give him a white stone, and on the stone a new name is written* (Rev 2.17). What exactly is a name, according to the word of God? A name is the essence or property of a thing embodied in a word. A name is, in a certain way, the power of a thing contained in a word: for as the apostles themselves noted, the name of Jesus drove out evil spirits (Mk 9.38), even when it was uttered by those who did not follow him but had received the Holy Spirit. Thus, we can understand just how important a name is that is written in the heavens, that is, a heavenly name, and how joyful it is to receive such a name. For a heavenly name should represent a heavenly characteristic and contain heavenly power. *Rejoice because your names are written in heaven*, if they are indeed written there.[43]

A younger contemporary of Philaret of Moscow was St Ignaty Brianchaninov. He came from an aristocratic family, which was extremely rare for clergymen in the nineteenth century (the overwhelming majority came from clergy families). In his youth he was a disciple of the elder Leo of Optina, then abbot

---

[43]"Homily on the Nameday of His Imperial Majesty, the Right-believing Sovereign Emperor Alexander Pavlovich, August 30, 1825," in *Homilies and Speeches*, 2.401–3.

St Ignaty Brianchaninov

of the St Sergius monastery near St Petersburg, and for some time bishop of Stavropol. He spent the last years of his life in retirement, devoting his time to writing. He wrote a compendium of sermons entitled *Ascetic Sermons*, a collection of theological treatises and reflections entitled *Ascetic Essays*, a collection of letters, the anthropological writings *Homily on Man* and *Homily on Death*, and other theological, spiritual, and moral writings. St Ignaty's main work is *An Offering to Contemporary Monasticism*, which he considered to be his spiritual testament; it contains exhortations on the external appearance of the monk and his inner activity.

St Ignaty possessed an exceptional literary gift, and several of his works are marked by their imagery and poetic style. Like Gregory the Theologian and the author of the Macarian homilies, he examined natural phenomena, in which he saw types of spiritual realities. In one of his essays he describes a winter garden with bare trees covered with snow:

> Everything around me is quiet, and there is a dead and magnificent peace . . . Suddenly the curtain covering the eyes of my soul fell, and the book of nature opened up before them. This book, given to Adam the first-created to read, contains the words of the Spirit, just like holy scripture. What lesson did I read in the garden? A lesson on the resurrection of the dead, a powerful lesson, one that was taught by the depiction of an action similar to resurrection. If we had not become so accustomed to seeing the rejuvenation of nature in the spring, it would seem miraculous and unbelievable to us. But we are not amazed due to habit; although we witness a miracle, it is as if we did not see it! I look at the bare boughs of the trees, and they say to me convincingly in their mystical language: "we will come back to life once again; we will be covered with leaves, become fragrant, and adorn ourselves with flowers and fruits. Will not the dry bones of humans also come back to life when their springtime comes?" . . . Every year nature repeats the lesson of the resurrection of the dead before the eyes of the entire human race, depicting it in its transfiguring, mystical activity.[44]

---

[44]"A Garden in Wintertime," in *The Works of Bishop Ignaty (Brianchaninov)*, vol. 1: *Ascetic Experiences*, 3d ed. (St Petersburg, 1905), 179–80.

St Ignaty advocated a serious attitude toward the tradition of the Orthodox Church, called on the faithful to read the gospel and the works of the holy fathers (which during his time began to be published in Russian), and to "stay away from books containing false teachings." Several of his writings are devoted to the Jesus prayer; in them he speaks of the Jesus prayer as a daily action of monks and laymen. A central place in his works is accorded to warning readers of "spiritual delusion" under the influence of false mystical experiences. Ignaty's attitude toward the Catholic mystics of the middle ages and renaissance, such as Thomas à Kempis, Francis of Assisi, Ignatius of Loyola, and Theresa of Avila, was sharply critical. During his lifetime interest in Catholic mysticism was widespread among the aristocracy, and Thomas à Kempis' *Imitation of Christ* was highly popular. Ignaty contrasted the works of Catholic mystics with those of the ascetic writers of the eastern Church— Symeon the New Theologian, Gregory of Sinai, and others. He also published a compilation of the sayings of the Egyptian desert fathers, translated into Russian, entitled *Book of the Fathers*, which was read widely.

St Ignaty's view of the church reality of his times was extremely pessimistic. He considered it necessary to hold a council to remedy the imperfections in church life that had appeared as a result of the Petrine reforms. The "notes" that he wrote on this question begin with a declaration of the total de-Christianization and de-churching of Russian society: "The spirit of the times is such, and apostasy from the Orthodox faith and immorality are so widespread and deeply rooted, that a return to Christianity seems impossible." Despite this beginning, he later calls on Russian society to effect a "complete renunciation of depravity and a total subjugation of oneself to strict Christian morality." This would mean that Christians are to refrain from "theaters, dances, cards, and other satanic games," as well as from the reading of pagan literature.[45]

Speaking of the situation in the Russian Church, St Ignaty notes that beginning with the end of the seventeenth century, "much filthy dust has been blown by western winds into the heart of the Church and into the heart of the nation, doing harm to our faith, morality, and national character." He also observed that people had begun to look at the Church through the prism

---

[45]"On the Necessity of a Council to Examine the Contemporary State of the Russian Orthodox Church: Notes of Bishop Ignaty Brianchaninov," in L. Sokolov, *St Ignaty: His Life, Personality, and Moral and Ascetic Views*, part 3 (Kiev, 1915; repr. Moscow, 2003), 58.

of "debauchery, Protestantism, and atheism." He believed in the necessity of immediately convening a council with representatives of the eastern patriarchs. The latter would, in Ignaty's view, "inevitably call for a substantial rejection of deviations necessary for the restoration of the spirit of the ecumenical Church in the Russian Church, from which it had deviated primarily through its synod, vainly called holy, and through its institutions of theological education, which almost produce more Protestants and atheists" than believers. In addition to representatives of the eastern patriarchs, the council should be personally attended by all Russian hierarchs, as well as selected deputies from among the monastics, the married clergy, and laymen. The council, according to Ignaty, should bring the canon law of the Russian Church into accordance with the decisions of the eastern churches, abolish the caste nature of the clergy, restore the practice of electing candidates to the clergy and episcopate, adopt measures for raising the level of morality of the clergy and monastics, and reintroduce ancient monastic rules.[46]

Despite the fact that Ignaty personally knew the Optina elders, he gave a highly negative assessment of the state of monastic life in the Russian Church:

> In our Church monasteries have been distorted, everything in them has been distorted, and their very significance has been distorted. The theological schools are so alien to the spirit of the Orthodox faith that those who enter monasteries after graduating from seminary are an extreme rarity, and in the fifty years since the establishment of theological academies in Russia, there has not been a single person who entered a monastery after graduating from an academy . . . Monasteries in our land are in a state of extreme decay; I repeat: they are distorted. Nearly all who enter them come from the masses. They engage only in physical asceticism, almost always bearing no fruits or bearing false fruits, having mistaken the means for the end and essence. But even physical asceticism has now become a rarity: monasteries have now become a haven of debauchery, places of open or hidden hypocrisy, places of exile, places of extortion and various forms of abuse.[47]

In his notes St Ignaty does not call for the restoration of the patriarchate, but does underscore the necessity of "organizing the synod correctly" and

---

[46]Ibid., 59–63.
[47]Ibid., 63–64.

greatly limiting the power of the oberprocurator. He also calls for a reform of institutions of theological education, stressing the necessity of "expunging them of everything that is pagan, everything that might even indirectly lead to free thinking, immorality, irony, jokes, playfulness, everything that is so contrary to the spirit of Christianity and acts so contagiously on corrupt human nature." In seminaries should be taught philosophical subjects, the teaching of the church fathers, as well as the natural sciences, which were invoked by nihilists. Ignaty writes: "Nature proclaims God . . . and the sciences that explain the laws of nature proclaim God all the more powerfully. All great scholars, mathematicians, and natural scientists, such as Newton, Leibniz, and Nekker, were not only deists but also recognized Christianity. Almost all atheists were sophists, who did not know real sciences and spent their time in unrestrained philosophizing and dreaming."[48]

The note just cited could not be published during Ignaty's lifetime—for obvious reasons. However, the harshly critical view of church reality voiced in it was also present in a softer form in his published writings. Ignaty was not alone in his criticism of the synodal system, monasteries, and theological schools. During his time this criticism was voiced within secular society, including by those who had broken with the Church. *Memoirs of a Seminarian*, written by the former seminarian H.G. Pomyalovsky, paints a horrible picture of life at lower-level theological schools and seminaries in the middle of the nineteenth century. Neither one's belonging to the clerical class nor seminary studies could provide a reliable inoculation against atheism and nihilism, as the cases of Dobrolyubov and Chernyshevsky demonstrate: both were sons of priests and seminary graduates, but left the Church and became materialists. Ignaty Brianchaninov, who did not belong to the clerical class by birth, came out against its caste nature because he was aware of the vulnerability of a class-based clergy to the threat of materialism, which was gaining ever more supporters among the aristocracy and intelligentsia. In order to combat this threat, he wrote that the Church must be reformed from the top to the very bottom, from the synod to the seminaries and lower theological schools.

St Theophan the Recluse (1815–1894) differed significantly from Ignaty Brianchaninov both in his theological views and in his overall mindset. Ignaty was characterized by his pessimistic view of the church realities of his times, and his books were full of warnings against spiritual delusion, error, and per-

[48]Ibid., 66.

St Theophan the Recluse

nicious influences. Theophan the Recluse instead accentuated the positive sides of spiritual life, and there is more healthy optimism and spiritual sobriety in his writings. Polemics were waged between the two hierarchs over the physical nature of the soul and angels: in his "Homily on Death," Ignaty affirmed that the human soul and angels have a thin ("ethereal") bodily shell, while Theophan wrote that "the human soul and angels are not bodies, but spirits." Both hierarchs translated from Greek, but their attitudes toward the original text were different: Ignaty strove to reproduce the sources as exactly as possible, while Theophan's approach was marked by a higher degree of freedom, rendering what was necessary and omitting what seemed unnecessary or unprofitable. The majority of St Theophan's translations are more of a paraphrase, an adaptation of the text to the needs of his contemporaries than a translation in the strict sense. This is true, for example, of his translation of the *Philokalia*, in which the original work of Nicodemus of the Holy Mountain was expanded with the addition of a number of writings, while some original texts were shortened. In addition to the *Philokalia*, Theophan translated ancient monastic rules and the works of St Symeon the New Theologian.

St Theophan authored a large number of original works, mainly spiritual, moral, and exegetical. He wrote a *Commentary on the Apostolic Epistles* numbering many volumes; the books *The Path to Salvation* and *The Spiritual Life and How to Be Attuned to It*; *Meditations for Each Day of the Year*; and a collection of letters and sermons. The majority of these works (excluding the sermons) were written during his years as a hermit, which lasted for twenty-eight years after he voluntarily retired from governing the diocese of Vladimir.

The essence of the spiritual and moral teaching of St Theophan is expressed in the following words: "What does it mean to be a Christian? It means to believe rightly and live in holiness, to be sanctified by the sacraments and listen to the guidance offered by our shepherds, to belong to the Orthodox Church of God and strictly fulfil all that is commanded by it. In other words, doing everything that . . . makes up the path to salvation."[49] The

---

[49]Theophan the Recluse, *Letters to Various People on Questions of Faith and Life* (Moscow, 1892), 8.11.

Orthodox Church is, according to him, a spiritual mother who accompanies the person throughout his entire life—from birth to death—and brings him to the saving gates of the kingdom of heaven. The Church possesses everything necessary for salvation and edification:

If you need guidance, go to the Church, listen and look—and all kinds of lessons will flow into your ears and eyes. Listen to the epistles, the gospel, the prophets, and learn. Pay attention to the hymns and be enlightened. Look at the actions of the clergy and be lifted up, reflecting on their significance and meaning. Look at the icons, remember the glorious deeds depicted in them, and strive to emulate them . . . Do you wish to accustom yourself to prayer and receive guidance in it? Ah! The holy Church is above all rich in this. It will provide you with ready prayers and teach you to raise yourself toward God in prayer in your own words. In her everything is prayer, and everyone will find in her prayers of all kinds and for all occasions . . . Do you need to humble the flesh? . . . Let one fast after another be your help and guidance . . . If you have fallen and need to cleanse your conscience, these fasts will also furnish strong motivation for this and a favorable time. Fast, confess, partake of the holy mysteries and, having set foot firmly on the right path once again, walk it with vigilance. Do you have private needs? You will find that the Church can satisfy all of them, regardless of what they might be. Do thoughts bother you, do spirits disturb you, does sorrow weigh you down, or are you planning to travel or begin something at home? For all of this and many other things you will find in the Church prayers of intercession, acts of blessing and consecration, and the necessary guidance . . . We have a neverending list of needs that must be fulfilled throughout our lives, beginning from the moment of our birth until our death. The holy Church encompasses the entire person throughout his entire life: she welcomes him into her embrace immediately after birth, accompanies him during his whole life, and sees him off to the other world . . . Glorify the Lord, who has given us such a rich, powerful, and caring Church, and always be obedient to it with your entire heart and with faith.[50]

In his writings and letters, St Theophan constantly spoke of the didactic quality of Orthodox services and the necessity for all the faithful to partici-

[50]Ibid., 29.

pate in them regularly. At the same time he realized that Church Slavonic, in which the services are held, was not understandable for the majority of believers. As a solution to this dilemma he proposed not the translation of liturgical texts into Russian but the creation of a new, simplified, and understandable Slavonic translation:

> All of our liturgical hymns are edifying, profound, and sublime. They contain all our theological science, and all Christian moral teaching, all consolation and warning. He who pays attention to them can do without all other Christian doctrinal books. But the greater part of these hymns are completely incomprehensible; this deprives our church books of the fruits they might otherwise bear, and hinders them from serving the aims for which they are appointed and exist. In view of this, a new translation of church liturgical books is immediately necessary.[51]

St John of Kronstadt

The necessity of a conscious participation in the divine services was repeatedly affirmed by St John of Kronstadt. He wrote that indifference to church services is caused by two things: "some do not understand them, while others, though they may have studied the science of the divine services, were taught dryly, without examples, and only with the intellect."[52] In order for the services to become understandable, every believer should learn Slavonic: "The reading and singing in church is conducted in a sacred language; all Orthodox Christians should learn it in order to understand the sweet sayings of their mother, who raises her children for heaven, for eternal life."[53] St John writes elsewhere:

> Since our first teacher of prayer is the Church, which was taught to pray so beautifully by the Holy Spirit himself, and since we ourselves do not know what we should pray for as we ought (Rom 8.26), it is the duty of

[51]Theophan the Recluse, letter 289, in *The Works of Our Father among the Saints Theophan the Recluse: Collection of Letters*, part 2 (Moscow, 1994), 143.

[52]St John of Kronstadt, *My Life in Christ* (Moscow, 1999), 441.

[53]*Reflections on the Divine Services of the Orthodox Church: From the Diary of Father John of Kronstadt* (Jordanville, 1954), 27.

every Christian to know the language of his mother, the Church. He who does not know it sufficiently commits a sin; and those who have learned foreign languages but did not and do not wish to learn the tongue of their mother and savior are especially guilty of sin. In other words, everyone should understand and learn Slavonic.[54]

In his diaries, sermons, and letters, the shepherd of Kronstadt returns time and again to the notion of the all-encompassing character of the Orthodox services, their profoundly edifying and saving nature:

> The Church and its services are an embodiment and realization of Christianity in its entirety. Here, in words, persons, and actions are proclaimed the entire economy of our salvation, all of sacred and church history, all the goodness, wisdom, faithfulness, and immutability of God in his deeds and promises, his truth and holiness, his eternal power. Here there is a wonderful harmony in all things and a striking, logical coherence in both the whole and the parts. This is truly divine wisdom, accessible to simple, loving hearts.[55]

St John assigned particular importance to the Divine Liturgy. Finding consolation and a constant source of spiritual energy in the daily celebration of the liturgy, the shepherd of Kronstadt called on the faithful to visit the church, attend the liturgy, and receive the holy mysteries as often as possible. He saw the liturgy not only as the very heart of Christian life, but also as the spiritual focus of the entire universe and a great miracle of God:

> What can be more majestic, touching, and life-giving on earth than the celebration of the liturgy? Here is depicted and accomplished the great mystery of God's love for the human race—God's uniting with mankind through his incarnation, teaching, suffering, death, burial, and resurrection, the sacrament of the renewal and deification of mankind, and the sacrament of people uniting with God by partaking of his flesh and blood. With its grandeur, this sacrament strikes the mind, inspiring reverence, thanksgiving, and the glorification of God by all conscious Christians. God's work accomplished in the liturgy exceeds in its magnificence

---

[54] *My Life in Christ*, 766.

[55] St John of Kronstadt, *Reflections on the Church and the Orthodox Divine Services* (St Petersburg, 1905), 1.185.

all of his works done in the world, and even the creation of the world. This is truly God's heavenly service on earth, at which being reasonable and worthy is bliss, peace, and joy for the soul.[56]

John of Kronstadt was undoubtedly one of the most outstanding spiritual writers of the end of the nineteenth and beginning of the twentieth century. His book *My Life in Christ* and other writings and sermons contain a multitude of precious reflections on faith and the Church, on the services and prayer, on Orthodoxy and heterodoxy, on the present state and future of Russia. In these works St John speaks primarily as a teacher of Christian morality and an exposer of the people's lack of faith. His prophetic voice, which thundered throughout all of Russia, called on people to repent and return to the fold of the Orthodox Church. St John was highly negative in his assessment of the state of Russian society and believed that the unhindered spread of atheism, the decline of Christian morality, and the intelligentsia's abandoning of Orthodoxy would lead the country to spiritual death. The shepherd of Kronstadt spoke out in favor of strict repressive measures against anarchists and nihilists, for which he was branded as an arch-monarchist and "black hundredist." In the years following the Russian revolution of 1905, St John wrote:

Because of the godlessness and impiety of many Russians, the so-called intelligentsia, who have strayed from the path, fallen away from the faith, and revile it in all possible ways, who have trampled upon all the gospel commandments and allow all kinds of debauchery in their lives—because of all this the Russian empire is not the kingdom of the Lord but a broad and depraved kingdom of satan that has penetrated deeply into the hearts and minds of the "learned," the half-educated, and all who give free reign to their passions and live according to the false, delusive understanding of their errant minds, who disdain God's mind and the revelation of the word of God. Because of this, look at what is happening in it at the present time: everywhere there are strikes by students and workers from various institutions; the uproar of parties whose aim is to overthrow the current monarchic system established by God; the ubiquitous spread of impudent, mad proclamations, the lack of respect for the divinely estab-

---

[56]St John of Kronstadt, *My Life in Christ. Part 3: Reflections on the Divine Services of the Orthodox Church* (Moscow, 2001), 167.

lished authorities . . . children and the youth have imagined themselves to be leaders and the masters of their fate; marriage has lost all meaning for many, and divorces on a whim have increased infinitely; many children have been left to fend for themselves by unfaithful spouses; and a certain meaninglessness and arbitrariness reigns. Is this an Orthodox empire, is this a kingdom of the Lord? . . . If things continue the way they do, and the godless and the mad anarchists are not subjected to righteous punishment by the law, and if Russia is not cleansed of its many weeds, it will become deserted, just like the ancient kingdoms and cities that were wiped from the face of the earth by God's justice for their godlessness and lawlessness.[57]

St John considered Tolstoy, who will be discussed in more detail later, to be one of the worst enemies of Orthodoxy. Over the course of many years St John of Kronstadt fought against Tolstoy's teaching, and wrote in his diary before his death: "How long, O Lord, will you endure Leo Tolstoy, the terrible atheist who has brought disturbance to the entire world? How long will you not call him to your judgment? . . . Lord, the earth is weary of enduring his blasphemy."[58] St John criticized the tsar and the government for their inability to counter the influence of Tolstoy's teaching: "The earthly fatherland suffers from the sins of the tsar and people, from the tsar's lack of faith and foresight, from his pandering to the unbelief and blasphemy of Leo Tolstoy and the entire so-called educated world of ministers, bureaucrats, officers, and students." Later on, addressing himself, he wrote: "Pray to God with tears of blood for the overall lack of faith and depravity of Russia."[59]

John of Kronstadt acquired fame throughout all of Russia as a pastor and author of spiritual and moral works. He was also, however, an outstanding theologian. His importance for Russian Orthodox theology, in the words of Georges Florovsky, has not yet been fully realized: "It has even become habitual to view Fr John *only* as a practical pastor, philanthropist, and man of prayer. Seldom is his remarkable diary *My Life in Christ* read as a theological book."[60] Although there is no theological system in his writings, they are

---

[57]Cited in *Stern New Homilies of Father John (of Kronstadt): On the Truly Dread Judgment of God That Is Approaching (1906–1907)* (Moscow, 1993), homily 19.

[58]John of Kronstadt, "Diary, Entry of August 24, 1908," in St John of Kronstadt, *Works: Diary Before his Death (May–November 1908)* (Moscow-St. Petersburg, 2003), 58.

[59]Ibid., 68.

[60]Florovsky, *Ways of Russian Theology*, 400.

strewn with a multitude of profound reflections and insights that call for a separate study, which has yet to be undertaken.

John of Kronstadt expounded, among other things, an original theological teaching on the name of God and the names of saints. He wrote that "the name of God is God himself"; this expression can be found in many places of his diary *My Life in Christ*. The shepherd of Kronstadt underscored that God, being simple and indivisible, is present in his name in all his essence, and not only in part:

> The name of God is God himself . . . Therefore call upon the name of the Lord. If you call upon the Lord, the Savior of the faithful, you will be saved.[61]

> To those who pray: let the name of the Lord, or the Mother of God, or an angel, or a saint, take the place of the Lord, the Mother of God, angel or saint themselves; may the nearness of your word to your heart be the assurance and testimony of the nearness to your heart of the Lord himself, the Most Pure Virgin, an angel or saint. The name of the Lord is the Lord himself, the Spirit who is everywhere present and fills all things; the name of the Mother of God is the Mother of God herself, the name of an angel—the angel, and the name of a saint—the saint.[62]

> When you say or pronounce the name of God, the Lord, the Most Holy Trinity, the Lord Sabaoth, or the Lord Jesus Christ silently in your heart, you have the entire essence of the Lord in this name: in it are his eternal goodness, his boundless wisdom, his unapproachable light, his omnipotence and immutability . . . His name is he himself—the one God in three persons, a simple being which is described and contained in one word, and which at the same time is not contained, that is, not limited by it or by anything that exists.[63]

These statements formed the basis for "name-worshiping," the teaching on the divine nature of the name of God and the name of Jesus. This teaching was formulated for the first time in a book devoted to the Jesus prayer entitled *In the Mountains of the Caucasus*, by schema-monk Hilarion (†1916), a

[61] *My Life in Christ*, 759.
[62] Ibid., 683.
[63] Ibid., 587.

hermit of the Caucasus. After the publication of the book, debates ensued among the Russian monks of Mount Athos, creating two warring parties within Russian monasticism there—the so-called "name-worshipers" (venerators of the name of God) and the "name-fighters" (opponents of the veneration of the name of God). The former, following John of Kronstadt, taught that "the name of God is God himself" and that the entire fulness of the divinity is contained in God's name. They considered the name "Jesus" to be sacred and deserving of worship, insisting that it is higher than the other names of God and coeternal with God himself.

The opponents of the name-worshipers, on the contrary, maintained that the name of God cannot be equated with God; and if this name does have some kind of power, it does so not by itself, but due to the content it is given by those who utter it. Thus, they viewed the name "Jesus" as nothing more than a simple human name. Refuting the teaching of the name-worshipers that a name is inseparably linked with an object, they pointed to the relative nature of all names and underscored that "objects are the causes of names; names are not the causes of objects." The leader of the name-worshipers was the hieromonk Anthony (Bulatovich; †1918), who had earlier been a hussar and a well-known traveler who had settled down on Athos and had become involved in the polemics over the veneration of the name of God. He authored numerous writings in defense of name-worshiping, including the *Apology of the Faith in the Name of God and the Name of Jesus*. This work, like the majority of Bulatovich's other writings, is marked by a lack of objectivity and a polemical tone, which did not help the name-worshiper's cause.

The name-worshiping debates led to bloody clashes and resulted in the exile of approximately one thousand Russian monks from Mount Athos in the summer of 1913. The teaching of the name-worshipers was officially condemned by the Holy Synod in 1913, and the name-worshipers were stripped of their monasticism and wandered throughout the cities and villages of Russia. The debates, however, did not end there, and polemics continued on the pages of religious-philosophical journals and newspapers. The name-worshipers were supported in these polemics by many notable religious philosophers of the early twentieth century, including Pavel Florensky, M.D. Muretov, S.N. Bulgakov, N.A. Berdyaev, and V.F. Ern; the standpoint of their opponents was voiced by S.V. Troitsky. In 1914 Emperor Nicholas II intervened on behalf of the name-worshipers, causing the Holy Synod to relax its position. The national council of the Russian Church of 1917–1918 returned to the name-worshiping debates and created a special Subcommission on Name-Worshiping headed by Archbishop Theophan (Bystrov). However, the council did not make any final decisions on the matter. The debates over the veneration of the name of God continued throughout the twentieth century both in Russia and in the diaspora.[64]

ORTHODOXY IN NINETEENTH-CENTURY RUSSIAN CULTURE

Over the course of many centuries, Orthodoxy decisively influenced the formation of Russian identity and Russian culture. In the pre-Petrine period secular culture in Rus' hardly existed: the entire cultural life of the Russian people was centered on the Church. In the post-Petrine age Russia saw the emergence of a secular culture—poetry, painting, and music—which reached its peak in the nineteenth century. Having detached itself from the Church, however, Russian culture did not lose the powerful spiritual and moral energy given to it by Orthodoxy, and preserved a living connection with church tradition until the 1917 revolution. After the revolution, when access to the treasures of Orthodox spirituality was forbidden, Russians learned about the faith, God, Christ, the gospel, prayer, and the theology and liturgy of the Orthodox Church through the works of Pushkin, Gogol, Dostoyevsky, Tchaikovsky, and other great writers, poets, and composers. During the entire seventy-year period of state atheism, prerevolutionary Russian culture brought the Christian good news to millions of people who had been artificially cut off from their roots, continuing to bear testimony to the spiritual and moral values that the atheistic powers questioned or strove to destroy.

Nineteenth-century Russian literature is justifiably considered to be one of the apogees of world literature. However its main feature, which distinguishes it from western literature of the same period, is its religious character, its profound ties with Orthodox tradition. "All our literature of the nineteenth century is wounded by a Christian theme, all of it seeks salvation, all of it searches for deliverance from evil, suffering, the horrors of human life,

[64]For more on the debates over name-worshiping see Bishop Hilarion (Alfeyev), *The Sacred Mystery of the Church: An Introduction to the History and Problematics of the Name-worshiping Debates*, 2 vols. (St Petersburg, 2002).

the nation, mankind, and the world. In its most important works it is permeated by religious thought," wrote Nicholas Berdyaev.[65]

This also holds true for the great Russian poets Pushkin and Lermontov, and for the writers Gogol, Dostoyevsky, Leskov, and Chekhov, whose names occupy a place of honor not only in the history of world literature but also in the history of the Orthodox Church. They lived at a time when an increasing number of the intelligentsia was turning away from the Orthodox Church. Baptism, marriage, and burials were still conducted in church, but attending the

Alexander Pushkin
(watercolor, P.F. Sokolov, 1830)

church every Sunday was seen as bad form among members of the social elite. When one of Lermontov's acquaintances entered a church and saw the poet praying there, the latter became embarrassed and began to excuse himself by saying that he had come on an errand for his grandmother. And when a visitor entered Leskov's office and found him praying on his knees, the writer pretended that he was looking for a coin that had fallen to the floor. Traditional churchliness was still preserved among the simple people, but was increasingly being lost among the urban intelligentsia. The departure of the intelligentsia from Orthodoxy increased the gap between it and the people. It is therefore all the more surprising that Russian literature did preserve its deep ties with Orthodox tradition, despite the spirit of the times.

Although the great Russian poet Alexander Pushkin (1799–1837) was raised in the Orthodox spirit, he departed from the traditional church-centered lifestyle in his youth. Still, he never completely broke with the Church, and he wrote on religious themes on numerous occasions. Pushkin's spiritual path can be defined as one from pure faith through the unbelief of his youth to the conscious religiosity of his mature period.[66] Pushkin traversed the first part of this path during his years of study at the lyceum of Tsarskoe Selo, and already at the age of seventeen he wrote a poem entitled "Unbelief," which bore witness to his inner loneliness and the loss of his living link with God:

---

[65]Nicholas Berdyaev, "On the Character of Russian Religious Thought of the Nineteenth Century," in *On Russian Philosophy* (Ural University, 1991), 23.

[66]For more see B.A. Vasiliev, *The Spiritual Path of Pushkin* (Moscow, 1994).

Together with the crowd he enters the church of the Most High,
But there he only increases the anguish of his soul.
Seeing the splendid celebration at ancient altars,
Hearing the voice of the pastor and sweet singing of choirs,
He is troubled by the torment of unbelief.
He sees the hidden God nowhere, nowhere,
And stands with his darkened soul before the sacred.
Cold toward everything and a stranger to tender emotion,
He attends to the quiet prayer with irritation.[67]

Four years later Pushkin wrote the blasphemous poem "Gavriiliada," which he later disavowed. However, a turning point came in Pushkin's world view in 1826, reflected in the poem "The Prophet," in which Pushkin speaks of the calling of a national poet using an image evoked in chapter 6 of the book of Isaiah:

Tormented by spiritual thirst,
I dragged myself through a dark desert
When a six-winged Seraphim
Appeared to me at a crossroads.
With fingers light as sleep
He touched my pupils.
The prophetic eyes opened
Like those of a frightened eagle.
He touched my ears
And filled them with sound and ringing.
And I hearkened to the shudder of heaven,
And the lofty flight of the angels,
And the movements of the beasts of the sea,
And the flourishing of the vine below.
And he leaned toward my mouth
And pulled out my sinful tongue,
Full of idle words and cunning,
and with his bloodied right hand
He placed the forked tongue
of a wise snake

---

[67]"Unbelief," in *Complete Works* (Moscow, 1956–1958), 1.252.

into my paralyzed mouth.
And he split my chest open with a sword,
And drew out my palpitating heart,
And a glowing coal ablaze with fire
Did he place in my open chest.
I lay like a corpse in the desert
When the voice of God said to me:
"Arise, O prophet, behold and take heed,
Be filled with my will,
And, traversing the sea and land,
Ignite the hearts of people with your word."[68]

Archpriest Sergius Bulgakov commented on this poem: "If we did not have all of Pushkin's other writings, but only this mountain peak glistening with eternal snows, we could see with total clarity not only the greatness of his poetic gift, but also the entire loftiness of his calling."[69] The acute sense of a divine calling reflected in "The Prophet" contrasts with the emptiness of the worldly life that Pushkin, due to his social standing, was obliged to live. As he grew older he became increasingly weighed down by this life, something he wrote about in his poems numerous times. On his twenty-ninth birthday he wrote:

A gift in vain, a gift by chance,
O Life, why have you been given to me?
And why have you been sentenced to death
By inscrutable fate?

Who has called me forth from nothingness
By his hostile power,
And filled my soul with suffering
And my mind with anguishing doubt? . . .

There is no goal before me:
My heart is empty, my mind lies idle,
And the monotonous din of life
torments me with anguish.[70]

[68]*Complete Works*, 2.338–39.
[69]Sergius Bulgakov, "Pushkin's Destiny," in V. Perelmuter, ed., *Pushkin in the Emigration* (Moscow, 1999), 62.
[70]"It is not in vain or by chance," *Complete Works*, 3.62.

The poet, who at the time was wavering between faith, unbelief, and doubt, received an unexpected answer from Metropolitan Philaret of Moscow:

> Not in vain or by chance
> has life been given to me by God,
> And it is not without God's mysterious will
> that I have been sentenced to punishment.
>
> It is I myself who, by my wayward use of power,
> have brought forth evil from the dark depths,
> It is I myself who have filled my soul with suffering
> and my mind with anguishing doubt.
>
> Remember what you have forgotten!
> Let it shine through the twilight of thoughts—
> And through thee will be created
> a pure heart and a bright mind![71]

Struck by the fact that an Orthodox bishop had answered his poem, Pushkin wrote some "Stanzas" addressed to Philaret:

> In moments of amusement or idle boredom,
> I would entrust my lyre
> with the delicate sounds
> of madness, sloth and passions.
>
> But then I unwittingly interrupted
> The sound of the playful strings
> When your majestic voice
> Suddenly struck me.
>
> I poured forth streams of unexpected tears,
> And the pure oil
> Of your fragrant words was
> Soothing to the wounds of my conscience.
>
> And now, from the spiritual heights
> You stretch forth your hand to me,

[71]Philaret of Moscow, "Not in vain or by chance," quoted in P.O. Morozov, *Works and Letters of A.S. Pushkin* (St. Petersburg, 1903), 2.435–36.

> And with your meek and loving power
> you humble my turbulent dreams.
>
> My soul has been warmed by your fire
> and has rejected the darkness of earthly vanity,
> and the poet attends to the harp of Philaret
> in holy trepidation.[72]

The censors demanded that the final strophe be altered, and in its final variant it read:

> My soul has been burnt by your fire
> and has rejected the darkness of earthly vanity,
> and the poet attends to the harp of the Seraphim
> in holy trepidation.

The poetic correspondence between Pushkin and Philaret was a rare nineteenth-century instance of the meeting of two worlds divided by a spiritual and cultural gap: the world of secular literature and the world of the Church. This correspondence testifies to Pushkin's departure from the unbelief of his youth, his renunciation of the "madness, laziness, and passions" characteristic of his early works. Pushkin's poetry, prose, articles, and dramatic works of the 1830s bear witness to the increasing influence of Christianity, the Bible, and Orthodox church life on him. He re-read the holy scriptures several times, finding it a source of wisdom and inspiration. He had the following to say about the religious and moral significance of the scriptures:

There is a book whose every word has been interpreted, explained and preached in all corners of the world, and applied to every possible circumstance of life and events in the world. There is a book from which it is impossible to repeat a single expression that everyone does not know by heart, that were not already a proverb of nations. This book, which no longer holds anything unknown to us, is called the gospel—and its eternal attractiveness and novelty is such that if we, sated by the world or weighed down by despondency, happen to open it, we are unable to withstand its sweet attraction and immerse our spirits in its divine eloquence.[73]

---

[72]A.S. Pushkin, "In moments of amusement or idle boredom," *Complete Works*, 3.62.
[73]"On the Duties of the Person," *Complete Works*, 7.470.

I believe that we will never be able to give the people anything better than scripture . . . One can understand their taste when one begins to read scripture, since all of human life can be found in it. It is religion that created art and literature, and everything that was great in the depths of antiquity depended on this religious feeling, inherent in the person just like the ideas of beauty and the good . . . The poetry of the Bible is particularly accessible to those with a pure imagination. My children will read the Bible in the original with me . . . The Bible is universal.[74]

Another source of inspiration for Pushkin was the Orthodox services, which had left him indifferent and cold during his youth. One poem, dated to 1836, includes a versification of the prayer of St Ephraim the Syrian: "O Lord and Master of My Life," which is read during Great Lent.[75]

During the 1830s, Pushkin's religious fervor and enlightenment alternated with outbursts of raging passions—something S.L. Frank described as a characteristic of the "broad nature" of the Russians.[76] Dying from a gunshot wound received during a duel, Pushkin confessed and took holy communion. Before his death he received a note from Emperor Nicholas I, whom he had known since his youth: "Dear Friend, Alexander Sergeevich, if it is not fated for us to see each other in this world, take my last advice: try to die a Christian." The great Russian poet died a Christian, and his peaceful end marked the completion of a path that I. Ilyin described as one "from disillusioned unbelief to faith and prayer; from revolutionary rebelliousness to freely willed loyalty and a wise statism; from a dreamy worship of freedom to an organic conservatism; from the love of many things in his youth to the cult of the family hearth."[77] In walking this path, Pushkin earned a place not only in the history of Russian and world literature, but also in the history of Orthodoxy—as a great representative of a cultural tradition that was totally permeated by this spiritual legacy.

Another great Russian poet, Mikhail Lermontov (1814–1841), was also an Orthodox Christian; religious themes repeatedly appear in his poems. An exponent of the "Russian idea" who was aware of his prophetic calling and endowed with a mystical gift, Lermontov strongly influenced Russian litera-

---

[74]Cited in *The Unknown World of Faith* (Moscow, 2002), 211.
[75]"Hermit Fathers and Chaste Women," *Complete Works*, 3.370.
[76]S.L. Frank, "The Religiosity of Pushkin," in *Etudes on Pushkin* (Munich, 1957), 11.
[77]I.A. Ilyin, *Pushkin's Prophetic Calling* (Riga, 1937), 19.

ture and poetry after his death. Like Pushkin, Lermontov knew the holy scriptures well: his poetry is filled with biblical allusions, several of his poems represent a reworking of biblical subjects, and many epigraphs were taken from the Bible. Like the works of Pushkin, Lermontov's are characterized by their religious perception of beauty, especially the beauty of nature, in which he sensed God's presence:

When the yellowing fields sway
And the fresh forest rustles in the wind,
And the crimson plum hides in the garden
Under the shadow of a sweet green leaflet . . .

Mikhail Lermontov

Then the anxiety of my soul is humbled,
Then the wrinkles on my forehead disappear,
And I can attain happiness on earth,
And in the heavens I behold God.[78]

In another of his poems, written not long before his death, a reverent sense of God's presence is intertwined with themes of weariness from earthly life and the thirst for immortality. Lermontov's profound and sincere religiosity is combined with romantic motifs—a characteristic trait of his lyric poetry:

I set out on the road alone;
Through the fog the stony path glitters;
The night is still, the desert attends to God,
And the stars speak with each other.

It is jubilant and marvelous in the heavens!
The earth sleeps in a light blue radiance . . .
Why, then, do I feel such pain, why is everything so difficult
    for me?
Am I waiting for something? Do I regret something?[79]

Lermontov's poetry reflects his experience of prayer, the moments of tender emotion he felt, and his ability to find comfort in spiritual experience.

[78]"When the yellowing fields sway," in *Selected Works* (Moscow, 1957), 90–91.
[79]"I set out on the road alone," ibid., 151–52.

Several of his poems are actually prayers clothed in poetic form; of these, three have the word "prayer" in their titles. The most famous reads:

> In difficult moments of life
> When my heart is filled with sorrow,
> I learn by heart
> One beautiful prayer.
>
> There is a grace-filled power
> In the harmony of living words,
> and an incomprehensible, holy delight
> can be perceived in them.
>
> Like a heavy weight,
> Doubt is dispelled far from my soul—
> I believe and weep,
> and feel lightness, lightness.[80]

This poem became extremely popular both in Russia and abroad. More than forty composers set it to music, including Glinka, Dargomyzhsky, Rubinstein, Moussorgsky, and Liszt (in the German translation of Bodenstedt).

Another poem with the same title is a prayer to the Mother of God:

> I, Mother of God, now send up my prayer
> Before your icon and radiant splendor,
> neither for salvation, nor before battle,
> nor with thanksgiving or repentance,
>
> Nor for my decrepit soul do I pray,
> the soul of a wanderer in a world without kith or kin;
> Instead, I wish to entrust an innocent maiden
> To the fervent intercessor for a cold world.[81]

It would be a mistake to think of Lermontov as an Orthodox poet in the strict sense. In his works, traditional piety frequently contrasts with the passions of youth (e.g., in the poem "The Novice"); and many of Lermontov's characters (including that of Pechorin) personify the spirit of protest and

---

[80]"Prayer," ibid., 105.
[81]"I, Mother of God, now send up my prayer," ibid., 91.

disillusionment, loneliness and disdain for people. Moreover, all of Lermontov's brief literary activity was colored by an unmistakable interest in demonic themes, which found its most perfect expression in the poem "The Demon."

Lermontov borrowed the theme of demons from Pushkin; after Lermontov this theme would establish itself in Russian art of the nineteenth and early twentieth century, culminating in the works of Blok and Vrubel. However, the Russian "demon" is by no means an antireligious or anti-Church character; it instead reflects the shady flipside of religion, which runs through all of Russian literature. The demon is a tempter and deceiver, a proud, passionate, and lonely being overcome by protest against God and the good. In Lermontov's poem, however, the good is victorious, an angel of God finally lifts the soul of a woman tempted by the demon into heaven, and the demon remains once again in his proud loneliness. Lermontov essentially examines the eternal moral problem of the relation between good and evil, God and the devil, and angels and demons. While reading the poem it might seem that the author's sympathies lie with the demon, but in the end the work leaves no doubt that the author believes in the final victory of God's righteousness over the temptations of the devil.

Lermontov died in a duel, not having reached his twenty-seventh birthday. Although he was able to become a great national poet of Russia during the short time allotted to him, it was not enough for him to form a mature religiosity. Nevertheless, his profound spiritual insights and the moral lessons contained in many of his works have allowed his name to be written—along with Pushkin's—not only into the history of Russian literature, but also into the history of the Orthodox Church.

Among the Russian poets of the nineteenth century whose output was marked by a strong influence of religious experience, A.K. Tolstoy (1817–1875), the author of the poem "John of Damascus," should also be mentioned. The poem was inspired by an episode from the life of St John of Damascus: the abbot of the monastery in which the saint lived forbade him from writing poetry, but God appeared to the abbot in a dream and commanded him to lift the ban. Against the backdrop of this simple plot unfolds this multidimensional poem, which contains monologues of the protagonist. In one of these, which was later set to music by Tchaikovsky, the protagonist of the poem praises life, nature, and the beauty of the created world:

I bless you, forests,
valleys, fields, mountains and waters!
I bless freedom
and the blue skies!
I bless my staff
And this humble bag,
And the steppe from beginning to end,
And the light of the sun, and the darkness of night,
And the lonely path
That I walk, pauper that I am,
And every blade of grass in the field,
and every star in the sky!

Oh, if only I could merge all my life,
And fuse my soul with yours!
Oh, if only I could embrace you all—
Enemies, friends and brothers,
And enfold all of nature in my arms![82]

Russian art of the nineteenth century is characterized by its profound interest in Christ, and this poem is but one of the many manifestations of this interest. One of the protagonist's monologues is an ecstatic hymn to Christ:

I behold him before me
With the crowd of poor fishermen;
With quiet, peaceful steps
He walks between the ripened bread;
He pours the joy of his benevolent words
Into simple hearts;
He leads his flock, hungering for righteousness,
to its waters.
Why was I not born at the time
When he was among us in the flesh,
walking life's path
and bearing his agonizing burden! . . .

[82]A.K. Tolstoy, "John of Damascus," chapter 2, in *Complete Works* (St Petersburg, 1907), 1.34.

> O, my Lord, my hope,
> My strength and protection!
> I wish to give you
> All my thoughts,
> the grace of all songs,
> the ruminations of the day and the vigils of night,
> every beat of my heart
> and my entire soul!
> Do not open anymore for anybody else,
> prophetic mouth!
> Thunder only my ecstatic word
> In the name of Christ![83]

Tolstoy's poem includes a lyric paraphrase of stichera by John of Damascus, which are sung at services for the departed. The text of these stichera reads:

What sweetness of life remains unmixed with grief? What glory stands unchanging on earth? All are weaker than shadows. All are more deceitful than dreams. Only a moment and death shall sweep them all away. But in the light of your countenance and in the sweetness of your beauty, give rest to him whom you have chosen, for you are the Lover of mankind.

All human accomplishments are vanity, since none exist after death. Riches do not endure; glory does not come along with us. For when death comes, all these have utterly vanished . . .

Where are this world's pleasures? Where is the dream of glories that pass away? Where are the gold and silver? Where are the throng of servants and their clamor? All are ashes, dust, and shadows . . .

I remembered the prophet who said: I am earth and ashes. And I thought of those in the tombs and saw their bones laid bare. Then I said: "Who is the king or the soldier? Who is the rich man or the beggar? Who is the just man or the sinner?" But give rest to your servant with the saints, O Lord.[84]

---

[83]Ibid., 35–36.
[84]The Burial Service for Laymen, in *The Book of Needs* (Moscow, 2004), 187–90.

And here is the lyric paraphrase of the same text by A.K. Tolstoy:

> What sweetness in this life
> Is not mixed with earthly grief?
> And where is he who is happy among people?
> All is false, all is insignificant:
> What have we acquired through our efforts,
> what glory on earth
> is lasting and immutable?
> All are ashes, illusions, shadows and smoke,
> All will disappear like a dusty whirlwind,
> And we stand before death
> Defenseless and powerless.
> The hand of the mighty is weak,
> The commands of kings are worthless—
> Receive, O Lord,
> Your reposed servant
> Into the mansions of the blessed! . . .
>
> Among the heap of rotting bones
> Who is the king? Who is the slave? The judge or the soldier?
> Who is worthy of the kingdom of God?
> And who is the outcast evildoer?
> O brethren, where is the silver and gold?
> Where is the throng of many servants?
> Among the unknown graves
> Who is the pauper, who is the rich man?
> All are ashes, smoke, dust and earth,
> All are illusions, shadows and phantoms—
> Only with You, O Lord, in the heavens
> Can be found a haven and salvation!
> All that was flesh will disappear,
> And our grandeur will turn into corruption—
> Receive, O Lord,
> Your reposed servant
> Into the mansions of the blessed![85]

[85]Chapter 8, *Complete Works*, 43–44.

Religious themes also occupied an important place in the later works of Nikolai Gogol (1809–1852). After winning fame throughout all of Russia for such satiric works as *The Inspector General* and *Dead Souls*, Gogol significantly altered the course of his creative activity in the 1840s, paying increasing attention to questions related to the Church. The liberal intelligentsia of his day reacted with misunderstanding and dismay to Gogol's *Selected Passages from My Correspondence with Friends*, published in 1847. In it he criticizes his contemporaries—members of the worldly intelligentsia—for their ignorance of the teachings and traditions of the Orthodox Church, and defends the Orthodox clergy from attacks of western critics:

Nikolai Gogol

> Our clergy is not inactive. I know very well that irrefutable writings in defense of our Church are being prepared in the depths of monasteries and the quiet of monastic cells . . . But even these apologies will not fully convince western Catholics. Our Church should be hallowed in ourselves, and not in our words . . . This Church, like a chaste virgin, has alone been preserved from apostolic times in its original, immaculate purity; this Church, which with its profound dogmas and small external rituals has, as it were, been brought down from the heavens to the Russian people, is alone able to undo all the knots of doubt and answer all our questions . . . And yet we do not know about this Church! We have not yet brought this Church, which was created so that we might live, into our lives! Only one kind of propaganda is possible for us—our own lives. We must defend our Church with our lives, for she is life; and we must proclaim her truth by the fragrance of our souls.[86]

Of particular interest are Gogol's *Meditations on the Divine Liturgy*, which are based of the liturgical commentaries of Byzantine authors such as Patriarch Germanos of Constantinople, Nicholas Cabasilas, and St Symeon, as well as a number of Russian church writers. Gogol writes with great reverence of the changing of the holy gifts into the body and blood of Christ at the Divine Liturgy:

---

[86]N.V. Gogol, *Selected Passages from My Correspondence with Friends*, letter 8: "Some Words on our Church and Clergy," in *Short Stories: Correspondence with Friends* (Berlin, 1922), 294–96.

After blessing the priest says: "Changing them by thy Holy Spirit"; the deacon says thrice: "Amen," and the body and blood are on the altar; the transubstantiation has taken place! The Eternal Word has been summoned by a word. The priest, using words instead of a sword, has accomplished the sacrifice. Whoever the priest may be—Peter or Ivan—it is the Eternal High Priest himself who accomplishes this through him, and eternally accomplishes it through his priests, just like he did through his word: "let there be light," and the light shines eternally; like he did through his word: "let the earth bring forth grass," and it sprouts from the earth eternally. On the altar is not an image, not a semblance, but the very body of the Lord—the very body that suffered on earth, endured beatings, was spat on, crucified, buried, arose from the dead, and ascended together with the Lord and sits at the right hand of the Father. It maintains the appearance of bread only because it is food for man, and because the Lord himself said: "I am the bread." The bells in the belfry are rung in order to announce to everyone the great moment, so that the faithful, wherever they may be at this time—walking, traveling, tilling their fields, sitting at home or busy with something else, suffering on their sickbed, or locked up within the walls of prison—in other words, wherever they might be, that they might send up prayers from everywhere during this awesome moment.[87]

In the afterword to this book Gogol writes of the moral significance of the Divine Liturgy for every person who participates in it, as well as for all of Russian society:

The effects of the Divine Liturgy on the soul are great: they are both visible to the entire world and hidden. And if he who prays reverently pays attention to every action, obedient to the call of the deacon, his soul acquires a sublime frame of mind, the commandments of Christ become fulfillable, and the yoke of Christ easy and his burden light. After leaving church, where he was present at the divine table of love, he looks upon all people as his brethren. Whether undertaking his usual tasks at work, or together with his family—wherever he might be . . . he unwittingly preserves in his soul the desire to treat others with love, brought from the heavens by the *theanthropos* . . . All who diligently attend the Divine

[87]N.V. Gogol, *Reflections on the Divine Liturgy* (Jordanville, 1952), 34.

Liturgy leave it meeker, more endearing in their dealings with people, friendlier, and more peaceful in their actions. For this reason, anyone who wishes to progress and become better should attend the Divine Liturgy as frequently as possible and listen attentively, for it builds up the person unbeknownst to the senses. And if society has not yet completely fallen apart, if people do not yet hate each other with irreconcilable animosity, the hidden reason for this is the Divine Liturgy, which reminds man of the holy, heavenly love for one's brethren . . . The effects of the Divine Liturgy could be great and innumerable if those who attend it did so in order to implement what they hear in life. Teaching all in the same way, acting in the same way on all ranks of society—from the tsar to the last pauper—it communicates the same message to all, although not in the same way, it teaches everyone about love, which binds society and is the hidden spring of everything that functions smoothly; it is the food and life of all people.[88]

It should be noted that Gogol writes not so much about partaking of Christ's holy mysteries at the Divine Liturgy as about "hearing" the liturgy and being present at the service. This reflects the practice, widespread in the nineteenth century, of Orthodox Christians communing only once or several times a year, as a rule during the first week of Great Lent or during Holy Week. Moreover, communion was preceded by several days of strict fasting as well as confession. They attended the liturgy on Sundays and feast days only in order to stand through or "listen" to it. The *kollyvades* came out against a similar tendency in Greece, and in Russia St John of Kronstadt called on the faithful to commune as often as possible.

There were two giants among the Russian writers of the nineteenth century—Fedor Dostoyevsky and Leo Tolstoy. The spiritual path of Dostoyevsky (1821–1881) in some respects repeats that of his contemporaries: he was raised in a traditional Orthodox spirit, left the Church in his youth, and returned to it as a mature man. The tragic life path of Dostoyevsky, who was sentenced to death for his participation in a revolutionary plot but pardoned one minute before his planned execution and then spent ten years in hard labor and exile, was reflected in all of his diverse writings, particularly in his eternal novels *Crime and Punishment, The Insulted and Humiliated, The Idiot, The Possessed, The*

[88]Ibid., 46–47.

Fedor Dostoyevsky (engraving by V.A. Favorsky, 1929)

Raw Youth, The Brothers Karamazov, and in his many short stories. In these works, as well as in *A Writer's Diary,* Dostoyevsky developed his religious and philosophical views, based on Christian personalism. At the heart of his writings is always the human person in all its diversity and contradictions, and Dostoyevsky examines the life of the person and the problems of human existence from a religious perspective that assumes faith in a personal God.

The main religious and moral idea uniting all of Dostoyevsky's writings is summarized in the well-known words of Ivan Karamazov: "If there is no God, everything is permitted." Dostoyevsky rejected autonomous morality, based on arbitrary and subjective "humanistic" ideals. The only solid foundation for human morality, according to him, is the idea of God, and the divine commandments in particular—the absolute moral criterion toward which humankind should oriented itself. Atheism and nihilism only lead the person to moral permissiveness and pave the way for crime and spiritual death. The criticism of atheism, nihilism, and revolutionary sentiments, in which Dostoyevsky saw a threat to the spiritual future of Russia, was a leitmotif of many of his works. This is the main theme of *The Possessed* and a significant part of *A Writer's Diary.*

Another characteristic of Dostoyevsky is his profound christocentrism. "Throughout his entire life Dostoyevsky had an exceptional and unique feeling for Christ, a kind of ecstatic love for the person of Christ," wrote Berdyaev. "Dostoyevsky's faith in Christ went through the crucible of all doubts and was tempered by fire."[89] For him God was not an abstract idea: he equated faith in God with faith in Christ as the God-man and the Savior of the world. He saw apostasy from the faith as a renunciation of Christ, and the embracing of faith was above all an embracing of Christ. The quintessence of his christology is contained in the chapter "The Grand Inquisitor" from *The Brothers Karamazov*—a philosophical parable spoken by the atheist Ivan Karamazov. In this parable Christ appears in medieval Seville, where he is met by the cardinal-inquisitor. After arresting Christ, the inquisitor deliv-

---

[89]"Dostoyevsky's World View," in Berdyaev, *Collected Works* (Paris, 1997), 5.221.

ers a monologue on man's dignity and freedom, with Christ remaining silent throughout. In the inquisitor's monologue, the three temptations of Christ in the desert are interpreted as the temptations of miracles, mystery, and authority. Although Christ rejected them, they were not rejected by the Catholic Church, which had acquired earthly power and deprived people of spiritual freedom. In Dostoyevsky's parable medieval Catholicism is a proto-type of atheistic socialism, at the foundations of which lie unbelief in the free-dom of the human spirit, unbelief in God, and ultimately unbelief in man.[90] Without God, without Christ, there cannot be true freedom, as the writer affirms through the words of his protagonist.

Dostoyevsky lived the life of the Church in a profound way. His Chris-tianity was not abstract or cerebral: having been tried and tested throughout his entire life, it was rooted in the tradition and spirituality of the Orthodox Church. One of the main protagonists of *The Brothers Karamazov* is the elder Zosima, whose prototype was St Tikhon of Zadonsk or St Amvrosy of Optina, but who in reality was a collective image embodying the best—in Dostoyevsky's understanding—of Russian monasticism. One of the chapters in the novel, entitled "From the Conversations and Teachings of Elder Zosima," is a moral-theological treatise written in a style close to that of the church fathers. In the words of the elder Zosima Dostoyevsky expounds his teaching on all-encompassing love, reminiscent of the teaching of St Isaac the Syrian on the "merciful heart":

> Brethren, do not fear the sins of people, love the person in his sin, for this is an imitation of the divine love and the summit of love on earth. Love all of God's creation, both the whole and every grain of sand. Love every leaf and every ray of God. Love the animals, plants, and all things. If you love all things, you will understand the mystery of God in things. If you under-stand it once, you will begin to understand it more profoundly every day. Finally, you will come to love the entire world with a total, universal love . . . You will be puzzled by any other thought, especially while seeing human sin, and you will ask yourself: "shall I conquer by force or by hum-ble love?" Always decide: "I will conquer through humble love." If you decide to do so once and for all, you can conquer the entire world. Loving humility is a terrible force, the most powerful of all, which has no equals.[91]

[90] Ibid., 348–49.
[91] *The Brothers Karamazov* (Paris, 1954), 416–17.

Religious themes occupy a significant place in *A Writer's Diary*, a collection of essays. One of the central themes of the diary is the fate of the Russian people and the significance of the Orthodox faith for them:

It is said that the Russian people know the gospel poorly, and do not know the basic rules of faith. Of course this is true, but they do know Christ and have had him in their hearts from time immemorial; there can be no doubt about this. How can there be a true understanding of Christ if one has not been taught the faith? This is another question. But there is indeed a knowledge of Christ in their hearts and a true idea of him, which has been handed over from generation to generation and has merged with the hearts of the people. Perhaps the only love of the Russian people is Christ, and they love his image in their own way, even unto suffering for him. They are proud first and foremost of being called Orthodox, that is, confessing Christ more truly than all others.[92]

The "Russian idea," according to Dostoyevsky, is nothing other than Orthodoxy, which the Russian people can communicate to all mankind. In it Dostoyevsky sees a Russian version of "socialism" that is the antithesis of atheistic communism:

The overwhelming majority of the Russian people are Orthodox and live the idea of Orthodoxy to the fullest, despite the fact that they do not understand this idea logically or scientifically. *In essence* our people have no other "idea" except this one, and everything proceeds from it. Our people desire this from the depths of their hearts and out of profound conviction . . . I am not speaking now about church buildings or the clergy, but about our Russian "socialism" (I use this word, which is the exact opposite of the Church, in order to explain my thinking, strange as it might seem), the aim and result of which is a Church that encompasses the entire nation and the entire world, and that is realized on earth to the extent this is possible. I am speaking about the tireless thirst that the Russian people have always had for a great, universal unity in Christ's name that includes the entire nation and all their brethren. And if this unity has not yet been achieved, if the Church has not yet been united completely, that is, not only in prayer but in reality, the instinct for this Church and

92 *A Writer's Diary*, "1873" (Paris, 1954), 228.

the tireless thirst for it, sometimes almost unconscious, are nevertheless undoubtedly present in the hearts of the many millions of Russians. It is not in communism or in mechanical forms that the socialism of the Russian people consists, for they believe that they will be ultimately saved only by *universal unity in Christ's name* . . . At this point it is possible to say the following: those who do not understand the Orthodoxy of our people and its final aims will never understand our people themselves.[93]

Like Gogol, who defended the Church and clergy in his *Selected Passages*, Dostoyevsky speaks reverently of the work of bishops and priests, contrasting them with visiting Protestant missionaries:

Are our people really Protestant and German? And why should they learn German in order to sing the psalms? Cannot everything they are searching for be found in Orthodoxy? Is it not here, and only here, that the truth and salvation of the Russian people—and all of humanity in the coming centuries—are to be found? Is it not in Orthodoxy alone that Christ's divine countenance has been preserved in all its purity? Perhaps the primary, predestined purpose of the Russian people with regard to the fate of all humankind consists only in preserving this divine image of Christ in total purity, and when the time arrives, in revealing this image to the world, which has gone astray . . . Incidentally, what about our priests? What is being said about them? People say that our priests are also awakening, that our clerical class began to display signs of life long ago. We read with tender emotion the exhortations of bishops to their churches on preaching and the life in piety. Our pastors, according to all accounts, have vigorously begun to write sermons and prepare themselves to deliver them . . . We have many good shepherds, perhaps more than we hoped to have or deserve.[94]

While Gogol and Dostoyevsky arrived at the realization of the truth and the saving importance of the Orthodox Church, Leo Tolstoy (1828–1910) abandoned Orthodoxy and openly opposed the Church. Tolstoy described his spiritual path in *A Confession*: "I was baptized and raised in the Orthodox Christian faith. I was taught this faith from my childhood, and during

[93]Ibid., "1881." Italics are in the original.
[94]Ibid., "1873," 258–59.

Leo Tolstoy

my entire youth and adolescence. But when I left the second year of the university at the age of eighteen, I no longer believed in anything I had been taught."[95] With staggering candor Tolstoy speaks about the thoughtless and immoral way of life he led in his youth, and of the spiritual crisis that befell him when he was fifty and nearly led him to commit suicide. In his search for a way out, Tolstoy immersed himself in the reading of philosophical and religious literature and conversed with official representatives of the Church, monks, and wanderers. This intellectual search led Tolstoy to faith in God and a return to the Church, and after a hiatus of many years, he began to attend church regularly, observe the fasts, confess, and take holy communion. However, communion did not renew him and give him life; on the contrary, it left a heavy weight on the writer's soul:

I will never forget the agonizing feeling I experienced on the day I took communion for the first time after many years. Services, confession, the rule of prayer—all of this was understandable for me and evoked a joyful awareness of the fact that the meaning of life was being opened up to me. I explained communion to myself as an act conducted in remembrance of Christ and signifying cleansing from sin and the complete acceptance of Christ's teaching. If this explanation was artificial, I was not aware of this. It was so joyful to humiliate myself before my father-confessor, a simple, timid priest, to reveal all the filth in my soul and repent of my vices, so joyful to merge my thoughts with the aspirations of the fathers who wrote the prayers in the rule of prayer for communion, so joyful was it to unite myself with all the believers of the past and present, that I did not sense the artificiality of my explanation. But when I approached the royal doors and the priest forced me to repeat that I believe, that that which I will swallow is truly body and blood, I was deeply incensed: this was not just a false note but a harsh demand made of someone who has obviously never known what faith is . . . I humbled myself, swallowed this blood and body without any blasphemous feeling, desiring to believe, but the blow had already been dealt. And, knowing what to expect, I could no longer go there again.[96]

Tolstoy's return to Orthodox Christianity was temporary and superficial. He only accepted the moral aspect of Christianity; its entire mystical life, including the sacraments of the Church, remained foreign to him, as they did not fit into the framework of rational knowledge. Tolstoy's world view was characterized by an extreme rationalism, and it was precisely this that did not allow him to embrace Christianity in all its fulness. After a long and agonizing search, which was not crowned with an encounter with the living, personal God, Tolstoy proceeded to create his own religion, based on faith in an impersonal God who guides human morality. This religion, which combined disparate elements of Christianity, Buddhism, and Islam, was marked by its extreme syncretism and bordered on pantheism. Tolstoy did not recognize Jesus as God incarnate, seeing him only as one of the outstanding teachers of morality alongside Buddha and Muhammad. Tolstoy did not create his own theology, and his numerous religious-philosophical writings that followed the *Confession* were mainly moral and didactic in character. An important element of Tolstoy's teaching was the idea of not resisting evil with violence, something he borrowed from Christianity but took to an extreme that contradicted church teaching.

Tolstoy went down in the history of Russian literature as a great writer, the author of the novels *War and Peace* and *Anna Karenina*, and numerous tales and stories. However, he is remembered by the Orthodox Church as a blasphemer and false teacher who sowed temptation and discord. In his moral and literary works written after the *Confession*, Tolstoy undertook a harsh and malicious attack on the Orthodox Church. His *Study of Dogmatic Theology* is a pamphlet that subjects Orthodox theology (which Tolstoy had studied in an extremely superficial manner—basically through catechisms and seminary textbooks) to disdainful criticism. The novel *Resurrection* contains a caricature of Orthodox services, which are presented as a series of "manipulations" of bread and wine, "senseless babbling," and "blasphemous sorcery" supposedly contrary to Christ's teaching.

---

[96]Ibid.,chapter 16, 150–51.

Not limiting his attacks to the doctrine and services of the Orthodox Church, in the 1880s Tolstoy proceeded to alter the gospel, publishing several works in which the gospel was "purified" of mysticism and miracles. In Tolstoy's version of the gospel there is no account of Jesus' birth from the Virgin Mary and the Holy Spirit, of Christ's resurrection, and many of the Savior's miracles are either absent or presented in a distorted form. His *Union and Translation of the Four Gospels* is an arbitrary, biased, and at times simply illiterate translation of gospel fragments with commentaries that reflect Tolstoy's hostility toward the Orthodox Church. For example, Tolstoy renders the word "pharisee" as "Orthodox," and all of Jesus' accusations of the pharisees become, as it were, denunciations of Orthodoxy. (Tolstoy noted: "I translate the word 'pharisee' with the word 'Orthodox' on the ground that all studies demonstrate that it means the exact same thing that 'Orthodox' means to us."[97]) Tolstoy writes blasphemously on the nativity of Christ: "There was a girl named Maria. This girl became pregnant unknown from whom. The man betrothed to her took pity on her, and in order to hide her shame, took her as his wife. Thus, the boy was born of her and an unknown father. This boy was named Jesus."[98] On the appearance of John the Baptist he had the following to say: "Ioann Kupalo appeared in the steppe and preached bathing as a sign of change in one's life, as a sign of liberation from error."[99] On Jesus' expulsion of the money-changers in the temple: "He came to the temple and threw out all that was necessary for their prayer, just as one might now come to our churches and throw out all the prosphora, wine, relics, crosses, antimensia, and all those things deemed necessary for the liturgy . . . Both the circumstances themselves and the words clearly say: your appeasing of God is a vile lie, you do not know the real God, and the deception of your divine services is harmful and must be destroyed."[100] Tolstoy categorically rejected the resurrection of Christ:

> The lie about the resurrection of Christ was, during the time of the apostles and martyrs of the first centuries, the main proof of the truth of Christ's teaching. This fable about the resurrection was also the main cause of disbelief in this teaching. In all the *vitae* of the first Christian mar-

[97] *Union and Translation of the Four Gospels*, in *Complete Works* (Moscow, 1928–1958), 24.104.
[98] Ibid., 48.
[99] Ibid., 52.
[100] Ibid., 124–25.

tyrs, the pagans describe them as people who believe that their Crucified One rose from the dead, and justifiably mocked them. But the Christians did not see this, just as the priests in Kiev do not see now that their relics stuffed with straw do, on the one hand, encourage faith, but on the other, are the main obstacles to it.[101]

The hostility toward the Church expressed in Tolstoy's literary and journalistic output in the 1880s and 1890s evoked harsh criticism from the Church, which only hardened the writer's resolve. One of his most prominent accusers was St John of Kronstadt. On February 20, 1901, by a resolution of the Holy Synod, Tolstoy was excommunicated from the Church. The synod's decision contained the following formula: "The Church does not consider him its member and cannot do so until he repents and restores his communion with it." Tolstoy's excommunication provoked an enormous outcry from the public: liberal circles accused the Church of cruelty toward the great writer. However, in his "Answer to the Synod," dated April 4, 1901, Tolstoy wrote: "It is fully correct that I renounced the Church that calls itself Orthodox . . . And I am convinced that the teaching of the Church is an insidious and harmful lie, a collection of the crudest superstitions and sorcery that completely hides the entire meaning of Christian doctrine."[102] Tolstoy's excommunication from the Church was thus only a confirmation of a fact that Tolstoy himself did not deny: his conscious and voluntary renunciation of the Church, reflected in many of his writings.

Tolstoy continued to spread his teaching until the end of his life, gaining many followers. Some of them joined together to form sectarian communities, with their own cult that included a "prayer to Christ the sun," "Tolstoy's prayer," the "prayer of Muhammad," and other creations. Numerous admirers gathered around Tolstoy and vigilantly kept watch over him so that he would not alter his teaching. Unexpectedly, Tolstoy secretly left his estate in Yasnaya Polyana several days before his death and set out for the Optina monastery. What exactly in Orthodoxy brought him to the very heart of Russian Orthodox Christianity remains a mystery. Before reaching the monastery, Tolstoy was stricken with a serious case of pneumonia at the Astapovo post station. His wife and several close friends arrived there and found him in grave spiritual and physical condition. Elder Barsanuphius was

---

[101]Ibid., 796.
[102]Cited in Smolich, *History of the Russian Church*, 188.

sent from the Optina monastery to Tolstoy, in case the writer should wish to repent and unite with the Church before his death. But those surrounding Tolstoy did not tell him about this and did not allow the elder to visit him on his deathbed, since they perceived a great risk that Tolstoy would break with his adherents. The writer died without repentance, taking the secret of his spiritual aspirations to the grave.

There were no more contrasting personalities in nineteenth-century Russian literature than Tolstoy and Dostoyevsky. They differed in everything: in their aesthetic views, philosophical anthropology, religious experience, and world views. Dostoyevsky affirmed that "beauty will save the world," while Tolstoy maintained that "the concept of beauty not only does not coincide with the good, but is opposed to it."[103] Dostoyevsky believed in a personal God, in the divinity of Jesus Christ, and in the saving character of the Orthodox Church; Tolstoy believed in the existence of an impersonal divine being, denied Christ's divinity, and rejected the Orthodox Church. Nevertheless, both Dostoyevsky and Tolstoy cannot be understood outside the context of Orthodoxy. "Tolstoy is Russian to the core, and he was able to appear only on the soil of Russian Orthodoxy, although he betrayed it," wrote Berdyaev. "Tolstoy belonged to the higher cultural class, which to a significant extent had fallen away from the Orthodox faith, which permeated the lives of the people . . . He wanted to believe as the simple folk, who were not spoiled by culture. But he was unable to do this even to the smallest degree . . . The simple people believed in an Orthodox way, but with Tolstoy the Orthodox faith clashed irreconcilably with his reason."[104]

Among other Russian writers who devoted considerable attention to religious themes was N.S. Leskov (1831–1895). He was one of the few secular writers who made members of the clerical class the protagonists of his works. His novel *Cathedral Folk* is a chronicle of the life of a provincial archpriest, written with great mastery and knowledge of life in the Church (Leskov himself was the grandson of a priest). The protagonist of his *At the Edge of the World* is an Orthodox bishop sent to Siberia for missionary service. Religious themes are touched upon in many of his other works, such as the stories "The Sealed Angel" and "The Enchanted Wanderer." His well-known work *Trivia from the Life of a Bishop* is a compilation of stories and anecdotes from the lives of

---

[103]"What is Art?," in *Collected Works* (Moscow, 1964), 15.101.
[104]Berdyaev, *On Russian Philosophy*, 38–39.

Russian bishops of the nineteenth century; one of the protagonists of this book is Metropolitan Philaret of Moscow. To the same genre belong *The Judgment of the Master, Episcopal Visits, Diocesan Court, Shadows of Hierarchs, Synodal Persons*, and others. Leskov also penned religious-moral works such as *The Mirror of the Life of a True Disciple of Christ, Prophecies on the Messiah, Guide to the New Testament*, and an *Anthology of Patristic Opinions on the Importance of Holy Scripture*. In the last years of his life Leskov came under Tolstoy's influence, began to show interest in

N.S. Leskov

schisms, sectarianism, and Protestantism, and departed from traditional Orthodoxy. However, in the history of Russian literature his name remained connected primarily with the stories and narratives from the lives of the clergy that had earned him recognition from his readers.

At this point, the influence of Orthodoxy on the works of Anton Chekhov (1860–1904) should also be mentioned. In his stories, Chekhov depicts seminarians, priests, and bishops, as well as prayer and the Orthodox services. Chekhov's stories frequently unfold during Holy Week or on Easter. In "The Student," a twenty-two-year-old student of a theological academy tells two women on Good Friday the story of Peter's renunciation of Christ. In the short story "In Holy Week," a nine-year-old boy describes confession and communion in an Orthodox church. "Easter Night" tells the story of two monks, one of whom dies on the eve of easter. Chekhov's best-known religious story is "The Bishop," which describes the last weeks of the life of a provincial vicar bishop recently returned from abroad. Chekhov's love for the Orthodox church services can be felt in his description of the service of the twelve gospels, held on the eve of Good Friday:

> During all the twelve gospel readings it was necessary to stand in the church motionlessly, and he read the first gospel, which is the longest and most beautiful. A cheerful, healthy mood overcame him. He knew this first reading, beginning with the words "Now the Son of Man has been glorified," by heart. While reading it, he sometimes raised his eyes and saw an entire sea of flames on both sides, and heard the crackle of burning candles, but could see nobody, just as in previous years. It seemed that these were the very same people who had been there during my child-

hood and youth, that the same people would be there every year until God knows when. His father was a deacon, his grandfather a priest, his great-grandfather a deacon, and all his ancestors since perhaps the baptism of Russia had been clergymen. He had a love for church services, the clergy, and the ringing of bells that was innate, profound and ineradicable. When in church he felt alive and joyful, especially when he took part in the services.[105]

This innate and ineradicable churchliness permeates all of Russian literature of the nineteenth century.

The same churchliness is also reflected in the works of the great Russian composers Glinka (1804–1857), Borodin (1833–1887), Moussorgsky (1839–1881), Tchaikovsky (1840–1893), Rimsky-Korsakov (1844–1908), Taneev (1856–1915) and Rachmaninoff (1873–1943). Many stories and characters of Russian operas are linked to church tradition, such as the Fool for Christ's sake, Pimen, Varlaam, and Misael in Moussorgsky's *Boris Godunov*. A number of works, such as Rimsky-Korsakov's "Russian Easter Overture" and Tchaikovsky's "1812 Overture" and Sixth Symphony make use of church melodies. Imitations of church bells can be found in the works of many Russian composers, such as Glinka's opera *A Life for the Tsar*, Borodin's *Prince Igor* and "In a Monastery," Moussorgsky's *Boris Godunov* and "Pictures from an Exhibition," and in several operas and the "Russian Easter Overture."

The element of church bells occupies a special place in the creative opus of Rachmaninoff: church bells (or an imitation of them on musical instruments and in vocal music) can be heard at the beginning of his Piano Concerto no. 2, in the symphonic poem "The Bells," in "Easter" from the Suite no. 1 for Two Pianos, in the Prelude in C-sharp minor (op. 3), and in "Lord, Now lettest Thou Thy Servant Depart in Peace" from the *All-Night Vigil*.

Certain works by Russian composers, such as Taneev's cantata "John of Damascus," set to a text by A.K. Tolstoy, are works of secular music on spiritual themes.

Many of the great Russian composers also wrote church music. Tchaikovsky composed a *Liturgy* and Rachmaninoff a *Liturgy* and an *All-Night Vigil* for liturgical use. Written in 1915 and banned during the entire Soviet period, Rachmaninoff's *All-Night Vigil* is a grand choral epic composed on the basis of ancient Russian church chant.

[105]"The Bishop," in *Collected Works* (Moscow, 1956), 8.469.

All of these are but some examples of the profound influence that Orthodox spirituality exerted on the works of Russian composers.

In Russian academic painting of the nineteenth century, religious themes were taken up by many artists. Russian artists frequently turned to the person of Christ, a fact exemplified by such paintings as "The Appearance of Christ to the People" by A.A. Ivanov (1806–1858), "Christ in the Desert" by I.N. Kramsky (1837–1887), "Christ in the Garden of Gethsemane" by V.G. Perov (1833–1882), and the painting with the same title by A.I. Kuindji (1842–1910). In the 1880s Christian themes were taken up by N.N. Ge (1831–1894), who created numerous paintings on gospel themes, V.V. Vereshchagin (1842–1904), a painter of battle scenes who also created the "Palestine Series," and V.D. Polenov (1844–1927), who painted "Christ and the Sinful Woman." All of these artists depicted Christ in the realistic manner inherited from the age of enlightenment, far from the tradition of ancient Russian iconography.

Interest in traditional iconography is reflected in the works of V.M. Vasnetsov (1848–1926), who created numerous paintings on religious themes, and M.V. Nesterov (1862–1942), whose many religious paintings on themes from Russian church history include "The Vision of the Boy Bartholomew," "The Youth of St Sergius," "The Labors of St Sergius," "St Sergius of Radonezh," and "Holy Russia." Vasnetsov and Nesterov also painted the interiors of churches; for example, they painted the Cathedral of St Vladimir in Kiev together with M.A. Vrubel (1856–1910).

RUSSIAN RELIGIOUS PHILOSOPHY

Russian religious philosophy of the nineteenth and first half of the twentieth century occupies a special place in the history of the Orthodox Church. Although they were not studied theologians or church leaders, the majority of Russian religious philosophers answered the challenges of westernism, liberalism, nihilism, and atheism from an Orthodox standpoint. Russian religious philosophy is a profound treasure of Orthodox thought that dealt with a wide range of theological, philosophical, cultural, historical, and social themes.[106] Some of these themes will be discussed in later volumes. Here we

[106]See the list of themes enumerated in N.A. Poltoratsky, "Russian Religious Philosophy," *Mosty* 4 (1960): 175.

will limit our discussion to a short description of just several of the most prominent religious thinkers of Russia in the nineteenth and first half of the twentieth century who made significant contributions to the development of Orthodox thought.

A notable phenomenon in nineteenth-century Russian society were the debates between the westernizers and Slavophiles. Although these polemics had primarily a cultural and historiosophical character, they did touch upon theological and ecclesiological questions. The westernizers, headed by P.Y. Chaadaev (1794–1856), favored Russia's orientation toward the cultural values and world view of western Europe. In his *Philosophical Letters*, Chaadaev harshly criticized Russian history: "Standing between the two main parts of the world, between the east and west, with one elbow in China and the other in Germany, we should have combined both of the two great spiritual elements—imagination and reason—and fused in our civilization the history of the entire world. But this is not the role that Providence has accorded us." According to Chaadaev, Russia's fate was to be left entirely on its own, so that the universal laws of the world could not work in it. Russia gave nothing to the world and did not foster the progress of the human mind, and everything it received from this progress was distorted by her.[107] Chaadaev criticized Orthodoxy for its social passivity and for the fact that the Orthodox Church had not come out against serfdom.[108] He contrasted the isolationism and statism of Russian Orthodoxy with the universal and supra-state nature of Catholicism, and dreamed of the day when all Christian confessions would unite around the papacy, which in his opinion was an "abiding visible sign" and center of unity of world Christianity.[109] After acquainting himself with one of Chaadaev's works, Emperor Nicholas I called it a "mixture of brazen nonsense worthy of a madman," and Chaadaev was officially declared insane.

The antithesis of the westernizers, the Slavophiles, who included among their ranks A.S. Khomiakov, I.V. Kireevsky, and a number of other thinkers, asserted that Russia has its own path of development different from that of western Europe, and that the uniqueness of this path is determined above all by Orthodoxy, which Russia inherited from Byzantium. Replying to

---

[107]P.Y. Chaadaev, philosophical letter 1, in *Articles and Letters* (Moscow, 1989), 47.
[108]Letter 2, ibid., 61.
[109]Letter 6, ibid., 122–23.

Chaadaev's first philosophical letter, Khomiakov wrote that "as for religion, Russia only needs to respect its own religion, whose holiness and might permeate the centuries so peacefully."[110]

A.S. Khomiakov

Khomiakov (1804–1860) was the first original religious philosopher of nineteenth-century Russia. As leader of the Slavophiles, Khomiakov wrote numerous treatises on ecclesiology. As a free lay theologian, he did not receive the support of the Russian theological censors and could not publish his works in his homeland. He therefore wrote them in French and published them abroad. During his lifetime they were little known in Russia, but after his death they exerted considerable influence on the subsequent development of Russian philosophical and theological thought.

The main theme of Khomiakov's work was the Church, a subject he wrote about in a polemical tone, contrasting Orthodoxy as the true faith with the western confessions—Catholicism and Protestantism. His only nonpolemical theological work is the short treatise *The Church Is One*, in which Khomiakov presents his teaching on the Church as the body of Christ, identifying the one, holy, catholic, and apostolic Church with the Orthodox Church. As was the case with the other Slavophiles, a key role is played in Khomiakov's works by the notion of *sobornost'*, which the Slavophiles understood as inner wholeness, fulness, and the organic unity of the Church's children, gathered together in the bond of love. According to the Slavophiles, *sobornost'* is the fundamental principle of the organization of the Orthodox Church and a basic characteristic of the Russian spirit.

In his "Some Words of an Orthodox Christian on the Western Confessions," Khomiakov polemicizes with writings of western Catholic authors who accused Orthodoxy of tending toward "Protestantism." He demonstrates that Protestantism, understood as resistance to church tradition, had on the contrary been in the Catholic Church from the time it began to introduce dogmatic innovations, the first of which was the *filioque* and the latest the teaching on papal infallibility. Khomiakov considered the Roman

---

[110]A.S. Khomiakov, "Some Words on the Philosophical Letter Published in the Fifteenth Booklet of *Telescope* (letter to Mrs. N.)," *Symbol* 16 (Paris: December 1986): 128.

Church to be one of the local churches that accepted heretical teaching not authorized by the ecumenical councils, thereby placing itself outside the unity with the true Church, which is the Orthodox Church. He rejects the possibility of a rapprochement between Orthodoxy and "Romanism," calling such a union an ecclesiological lie inadmissible from the standpoint of Orthodoxy:

> Is rapprochement between us possible? No other answer can be given to this question than a decisive rejection. The truth does not allow for bargaining. It is evident that papism invented the Greek-Uniate Church . . . Of course, they [the Uniates] do not inspire anything else in the Latins except for pity mingled with contempt; but they are useful as allies against their eastern brethren, whom they betrayed by succumbing to persecution . . . Such unity is unthinkable in the eyes of the Church, but it is wholly compatible with the precepts of Romanism, for which the Church is essentially concentrated in one person, namely, the pope. Underneath him is an aristocracy of his bureaucrats, the highest among whom bear the pompous title of princes of the Church. Underneath them are the masses of the laity, for the majority of whom ignorance is almost obligatory. Still lower are the Greek-Uniate helots, who were spared as a reward for their submissiveness and who are offered absurdity, which is recognized as their right. I repeat: Romanism can allow such unification, but the Church does not know of any bargaining in dogmatic questions and the faith. It demands complete unity—nothing less. In exchange for this it grants total equality, for it knows of brotherhood but not citizenship. Thus, rapprochement is impossible without a complete rejection by the Romans of their error, which has lasted for more than ten centuries.[111]

Speaking of western Protestantism, Khomiakov underscores that it was not a schism within the Church but a schism within a schism, which is why it did not affect Orthodox countries. Khomiakov sees the rationalism of the "Roman confession," which separated itself from unity with the eastern Church, as the source of Protestantism. He harshly characterizes the contemporary state of Protestantism:

---

[111]A.S. Khomiakov, "Some Words of an Orthodox Christian on the Western Confessions," part 1: "On the Brochure of Mr Laurency," in *The Essence of Western Christianity* (Montreal, 1974), 44.

On its negative side, Protestantism has come under the sole rule of manifest rationalism for good, while the positive elements that survived in it have disappeared in a fog of arbitrary mysticism . . . Rejecting lawful tradition, not having any living unity either in the past or in the present, not able to satisfy either the needs of the human soul, which requires undoubting faith, or those of reason, which calls for concrete teaching, the reform continuously changes its foundation, going from one proposition to another. It does not even have the courage to declare the validity and indubitability of any truth, since it knows in advance that tomorrow it will probably have to demote this truth to the rank of a simple symbol, a myth, or an error caused by ignorance. Sometimes it begins to speak about its hopes, but in its voice despair can be heard.[112]

While decisively rejecting Protestantism, Khomiakov was more conciliatory toward the Anglicans, a fact testified to by his copious correspondence with the theologian William Palmer (1811–1879).[113] As a deacon of Magdalen College, Oxford, Palmer visited Russia for the first time in 1840 with the intention of becoming Orthodox, but he found the demand by the synod that he renounce the errors of Anglicanism unacceptable. Palmer then went to Constantinople with the same aim, but the Greeks demanded that he be rebaptized. Russian Orthodoxy repulsed Palmer with its synodal structure subjugated to the tsar, and Palmer's conscience did not allow him to undergo baptism once again. The correspondence between Palmer and Khomiakov was conducted in English and touched upon a broad spectrum of theological and ecclesiological questions. As in his other writings, in his letters Khomiakov asserted to Palmer the truth of the Orthodox Church and criticized Catholicism. The arguments of the Russian philosopher, however, did not convince the Anglican theologian, and after much consideration he joined the Roman Catholic Church.

The problem of relations between the Christian east and west aroused the interest of Russian philosophers throughout the second half of the nineteenth century. It was profoundly treated in the works of the Russian philosopher, literary scholar, and poet Vladimir Soloviev (1853–1900), particularly in his paper "The Russian Idea," read in Paris in 1888 and published soon there-

[112]Ibid., 52–53.
[113]Published in W.J. Birkbeck, *Russia and the English Church during the Last Fifty Years* (London, 1895), 4–175.

Vladimir Soloviev

after in French (it was published in Russian only in 1909). Although the term "Russian Idea" was used for the first time by Dostoyevsky,[114] it was only with Soloviev that it became established in Russian religious philosophy.

In "The Russian Idea," Soloviev speaks of a certain contribution that Russia must make to world civilization. "The Russian people are a Christian people," Soloviev writes, "and therefore, in order to know the true Russian idea, one cannot ask himself the question of what Russia will do through itself and for itself, but what it must do in the name of the Christian principle recognized by it and for the good of the entire Christian world, of which it sees itself as part."[115] Soloviev believed that the fact that the Russian people were Christian did not mean that it had a "monopoly on faith and Christian life." And the Russian Church should not become a "palladium of narrow national particularism." The religion of Russia is Orthodox to the extent that it is manifested in the faith of the people and in church services. And the Russian Church participates in the unity of the ecumenical Church founded by Christ to the extent that it preserves the truth of faith, unbroken apostolic succession, and the validity of sacraments. However, "the official institution, the representatives of which are our church administration and our theological schools," do not constitute a living part of the true ecumenical Church.[116]

Soloviev wrote that in order to restore the ties between Russia and the ecumenical Church, the unity of the three members of social existence must be restored; these are the *Pontifex Maximus* (the Roman pontiff, whom Soloviev called the "infallible head of the priesthood"), the head of state (i.e., the Russian emperor), and the prophet, "the inspired leader of the whole of human society" (by which Soloviev understood himself).[117] In other words, the Russian Church, which was, like Russia itself, headed by the emperor,

[114]Dostoyevsky, "Declaration of Subscription to the Journal for 1861," in *Complete Works* (Leningrad, 1972–1990), 18.37.

[115]Vladimir Soloviev, "The Russian Idea," chapter 5, in *On Christian Unity* (Brussels, 1967), 229.

[116]Ibid., 230.

[117]Ibid., chapter 10, 242.

needed to place itself under the Roman Church. This would bring about the restoration of the ecumenical unity of state, church, and society:

> The Russian idea, the historical duty of Russia, demands that we acknowledge our inseparable bonds with the ecumenical family of Christ and use all the gifts of our nation, all the might of our empire for the final realization of the social trinity, in which each of the three main organic unities—church, state, and society—are absolutely free and sovereign, not in separation from the other two or absorbing or destroying them, but in the affirmation of the absolute inner bond with them. It is the restoration of this faithful image of the divine Trinity on earth that is the Russian idea.[118]

Soloviev's paper contained the quintessence of the ideology that he developed more fully in his "Russia and the Ecumenical Church." In the foreword to this work Soloviev speaks of himself: "As a member of the true and revered Orthodox eastern or Greco-Russian Church, which speaks not through an anticanonical synod and not through bureaucrats of secular authorities, but through the voice of its great fathers and teachers, I acknowledge as the supreme judge in matters of religion . . . the apostle Peter, who lives on in his successors."[119] The first chapter of this work deals with the ecumenical calling of Russia, cites the Slavophile critique of the synodal system, speaks of the contradictions in the relations between the Russian Church and those of Greece, Bulgaria, and Serbia, and on the impossibility of creating a center of Christian unity in the east, either in Constantinople or in Jerusalem. The true Orthodoxy of the Russian people is contrasted with the false Orthodoxy of the "anti-Catholic theologians," by which Soloviev meant the theologians of the "official Church," beginning with Patriarch Photius and ending with the Russian Holy Synod. The second chapter contains a justification of the papacy as the cornerstone of the "church monarchy founded by Jesus Christ." In the third chapter Soloviev develops his idea on Russia's calling to restore the trinitarian unity of state, church, and society that he outlined in "The Russian Idea." He dreamed of a theocratic world state in which the ecclesiastical authority of the Roman pontiff would be united with the state authority of the Russian emperor; this state would become the

---

[118]Ibid., 245.
[119]"Russia and the Ecumenical Church," introduction, in *On Christian Unity*, 279.

third and final empire that would replace the empires of Constantine and Charlemagne.[120]

The ideas outlined above prove that Soloviev cannot be considered a wholly Orthodox thinker, since the idea of ecumenical Christianity he advocated called for the subjugation of the Orthodox Church to Rome, and since his theological thought was under strong Roman Catholic influence.

Another of Soloviev's ideas is even less in harmony with Orthodoxy, namely his concept of Sophia, which exerted enormous influence on the subsequent development of Russian philosophy, literature, and poetry. This idea was founded on three mystical experiences that Soloviev had in different years, which he described in his poetic cycle "Three Meetings." The first of these occurred in 1862, when Soloviev was nine and saw a mysterious feminine being at a Sunday liturgy during the singing of the Cherubic Hymn:

> The altar is open . . . But where is the priest and deacon?
> And where is the crowd of believers praying?
> The torrent of passions has suddenly dried up without a trace,
> And I am surrounded by azure, there is azure in my soul.
>
> Penetrated by a golden azure,
> Holding in my hand a flower from unearthly lands,
> You stood with a radiant smile,
> Nodded your head to me and disappeared in a haze.[121]

The second vision, according to Soloviev, took place in 1875 in the British Museum in London, and the third in 1876, in the Egyptian desert. Soloviev identified the being he saw with the biblical Sophia, the Wisdom of God (Prov 8.1–36; 9.1–12), and returned to this theme constantly in his philosophical works. In Orthodox tradition, however, Sophia, the Wisdom of God, is equated with Christ: the St Sophia cathedrals in Constantinople, Kiev, and other ancient cities were dedicated to Christ, and the angelic feminine being on ancient Russian icons of "Sophia–the Wisdom of God" is a symbolic depiction of Christ. According to Soloviev, however, Sophia is a certain divine principle that is different from Christ and is even contrasted to him. In the *Lectures on Godmanhood*, Soloviev describes Sophia as an "essential ele-

---

[120]Ibid.
[121]"Three Meetings," in *The Poems of Vladimir Soloviev*, 3d ed. (St Petersburg, 1900), 182–83.

ment of the Divinity," as "the body of God, the material of the Divinity permeated by the principle of divine unity." Sophia is contrasted with the Logos: "In Christ's divine organism the active unifying principle, the principle that expresses the unity of that which exists absolutely, is obviously the Word or the *Logos*. The unity of the second kind, a produced unity, is called Sophia in Christian theosophy. If we distinguish in the absolute unity as it is, as that which exists absolutely, from its content, its essence or its idea, we find a direct expression of the former in the Logos, and the second in Sophia, which is therefore the expressed, realized idea."[122] As Soloviev further explains, "Sophia is ideal, perfect humankind, which is eternally contained in the integral divine essence, or in Christ."[123] Sophia is also identified with the "universal soul," which, "perceiving the one divine principle and binding with this unity the entire multitude of beings . . . thereby grants the divine principle complete and actual realization in all things; through it God manifests himself as a living, active power in all creation, or as the Holy Spirit."[124]

The nebulousness and ambiguity of Soloviev's formulations is a direct result of the impossibility of harmonizing his sophiology with traditional Christian teaching on the Holy Trinity. Soloviev's Sophia is not Christ or the Holy Spirit, but a certain "second" unifying element in the divinity separate from the Logos, as well as a link joining the divine and created worlds. In *The Meaning of Love*, this second element is described as passive and feminine, and is called the "eternal femininity." God's eternal femininity "is not only an inactive image in the mind of God, but also a living spiritual being possessing the entire fulness of power and action."[125] Being the sole absolute object of love for all, God, however, can be realized and incarnated "in another, lower being of the same feminine form, but having an earthly nature."[126] Following Plato, Soloviev sees in earthly love the reflection of an ideal love; however, for Soloviev the object of ideal love acquires the characteristics of a "living spiritual being."

Soloviev's teaching on Sophia is intimately linked with his theory of "all-unity" (*vseedinstvo*), indirectly connected to the Slavophile idea of *sobornost'* but with roots in neoplatonism and several other philosophical conceptions.

[122]*Lectures on Godmanhood*, lecture 7, in *Collected Works*, 2d ed. (Brussels, 1966), 3.115.
[123]Ibid., lecture 8, 121.
[124]Ibid., lecture 9, 141.
[125]*The Meaning of Love*, part 4/7, in *Collected Works*, 7.46.
[126]Ibid., 47.

The theory of all-unity was meant to reveal the inner, organic unity of existence, the various elements of which are in a state of mutual permeation and identity while preserving their individual qualities and specificity. "I call true or positive all-unity one in which one exists not at the expense of others or to their detriment, but for the benefit of all," writes Soloviev. "False, negative unity crushes or absorbs the elements that comprise it and thus proves to be *emptiness*; true unity preserves and strengthens its elements, realizing itself in them as the *fulness* of existence."[127] Within the created world, all-unity is accomplished through Sophia as an intermediary link between the unity of God and the multitude of created existence. Soloviev holds that the essence of the historical process lies in the restoration of all-unity as the fulness of existence, a task that has been entrusted to man.

Soloviev's philosophical views were reflected in his poetry, which is marked by its subtle intellectualism and profound religious feeling. Here is one of his most famous poems:

> Dear friend,
> Do you not see that everything we see
> Is only a reflection, only a shadow
> Of that which is invisible to the eyes?
>
> Dear friend,
> Do you not hear
> That the pompous clamor of life
> Is but a distorted echo
> Of jubilant harmonies?
>
> Dear friend,
> Do you not sense
> That the only thing in the entire world
> Is that which one heart says to another
> In a mute greeting?[128]

Soloviev's philosophy, poetry, and theological, cultural, and historiosophical views undoubtedly exerted a profound influence on Russian religious philosophy, literature, and poetry of the first half of the twentieth

---

[127]"The First Step Toward a Positive Aesthetics," in *Collected Works*, 7.74. Italics are the author's.
[128]"Dear Friend, do you not see," in *Poems of Vladimir Soloviev*, 22.

century. The idea of eternal femininity was taken up by poets of the Silver Age and was continued, for example, in the "Verses about the Beautiful Lady" by Blok. The theological concept of Sophia, despite its seemingly obvious incompatibility with Orthodox tradition, was further developed by major Orthodox theologians such as Fr Paul Florensky and Archpriest Sergius Bulgakov. Sophiology and the theory of all-unity were given further philosophical treatment by S.N. and E.N. Trubetskoy, N.O. Lossky, S.L. Frank, A.F. Losev, L.P. Karsavin, and a number of other thinkers.

With Soloviev began a religious-philosophical movement at the turn of the twentieth century that would later be called the "Russian religious renaissance." This movement coincided with an overall revival of social and church life in Russia, with the beginning of the preparations for the national council, a considerable relaxation of censorship, and the creation of conditions for an open dialogue on theological and philosophical questions. This dialogue included both members of the clergy as well as religious philosophers, poets, and public figures. From 1901 to 1903, "Religious-Philosophical Gatherings" were held in St Petersburg, initiated by D.S. Merezhkovsky and Z.N. Gippius and chaired by the rector of the St Petersburg Theological Academy, Bishop Sergius (Stragorodsky), later patriarch of Moscow. The gatherings were succeeded in 1907 by the Religious-Philosophical Society, which was founded–once again–by Merezhkovsky and Gippius and lasted until 1917. From 1905 to 1918 the Religious-Philosophical Society in Memory of Vladimir Soloviev met in Moscow and founded the Free Theological University in 1907. From 1907 onward a Circle of Those Seeking Christian Education also gathered in Moscow.

Around these societies, universities, and circles gathered the major representatives of the Russian religious renaissance: the philosophers S.N. Bulgakov, P.A. Florensky, E.N. Trubetskoy, V.F. Ern, N.A. Berdyaev, L.I. Shestov, V.V. Zenkovsky, V.P. Sventsitsky, P.B. Struve, S.L. Frank, N.S. Arseniev; the writers and literary scholars D.S. Merezhkovsky and V.V. Rozanov; and the poets A. Bely and V.I. Ivanov. All of these very different people were united by their lively interest in religious-philosophical questions and sincere concern over the fate of Russia.

In 1909 a collection of essays entitled *Landmarks* (*Vekhi*) appeared, containing articles by M.O. Gershenzon, Berdyaev, Bulgakov, A.S. Izgoev, B.A. Kistyakovsky, Struve, and Frank. This book was devoted to the religious-philosophical understanding of the processes that had led to the first Russian revolution in 1905. The authors pointed to the tragic gap between the intelligentsia and the simple folk and to the departure of the former from Orthodoxy, warning that any further estrangement would lead to the spiritual death of Russia. Salvation was to be found in a religious renaissance encompassing all walks of life—from the intelligentsia to the simple folk. In an article entitled "Heroism and Selfless Devotion," the future archpriest Bulgakov wrote:

> The nature of the Russian intelligentsia is religious. In his novel *The Possessed*, Dostoyevsky compared Russia and particularly its intelligentsia with the possessed man in the gospel who was healed only by Christ and was able to find health and the restoration of his powers only at the feet of the Savior. This comparison is true even today. A legion of demons has entered the gigantic body of Russia and convulses, torments, and wounds it. Only serious religious efforts, invisible but great, can heal her and liberate her from this legion. The intelligentsia has rejected Christ, turned away from his countenance, and expelled his image from their hearts; it has deprived itself of the inner light of life and is paying for this treason, this religious suicide, along with its homeland.[129]

The Russian religious renaissance of the early twentieth century unfolded against this background of heightening revolutionary sentiments, a constantly widening chasm between the nihilistic intelligentsia and the people, and a deepening gap between the Church and society. In a desperate attempt to save the country from impending catastrophe, the best minds of Russia addressed questions that were raised in the works of Pushkin, Dostoyevsky, the Slavophiles, and Soloviev: the "Russian idea," the religious calling of the Russian people, and the significance of Orthodoxy for history and Russia's future.

A major figure of the Russian religious renaissance and the most outstanding religious philosopher of Russia in the first half of the twentieth century was Nicholas Berdyaev (1874–1948). His philosophical activities began in Russia and ended abroad, after exile in 1922 along with a group of philosophers, theologians, and cultural figures. While in Russia he wrote *The Philosophy of*

---

[129]Sergius Bulgakov, "Heroism and Selfless Devotion," in *Landmarks: A Collection of Articles on the Russian Intelligentsia* (Moscow, 1909), 68–69.

Freedom, *The Meaning of Creative Activity*, and *The Fate of Russia*. In emigration he produced *A New Middle Ages: Reflections on the Fate of Russia and Europe*; *The Destiny of Man*; *On Slavery and the Freedom of Man*; *The Sources and Meaning of Russian Communism*; *The Philosophy of Inequality*; *Philosophy of the Free Spirit*; *An Outline of Eschatological Metaphysics*; *Truth and Revelation*; *Self-Knowledge*; *The Kingdom of the Spirit and the Kingdom of Caesar*; *The Existential Dialectics of the Divine and Human*, and other works. In addition to purely philosophical works, Berdyaev also wrote the exhaustive study *The World View of*

Nicholas Berdyaev

Dostoyevsky, one of the best works on the great Russian writer, as well as works on Tolstoy, Khomiakov, K. Leontiev, L. Shestov, and other Russian writers and thinkers.

Although Berdyaev is sometimes called the founder of Russian existentialism, his existentialism had an unmistakably religious, Christian character. He saw the return to religious sources as the aim of philosophy: "Philosophical thought cannot feed on itself, i.e., it cannot be abstract and self-sufficient. It cannot live on science alone . . . The ancient nourishment of philosophy was religious . . . Without an understanding of religious mystery and without partaking of religious sacraments there can be no nourishment, and knowledge wastes away and becomes abstract, breaking with real existence."[130] Berdyaev contrasted the rationalism and positivism of western philosophy with free philosophy or the philosophy of freedom, which has restored its ties with religious sources and is founded on the dogmas of faith. According to Berdyaev, "Christian dogmas are not intellectual theories, not metaphysical teaching, but facts, visions, and living experience. Dogmas speak of that which has been experienced and seen; dogmas are facts of a mystical nature."[131]

A true philosophy of freedom should be based on Christian experience and rooted in the Church, which is, according to Berdyaev,

> a theanthropic organism and theanthropic process. The free activity of the human will organically enters the body of the Church and is one side

[130]Berdyaev, *The Philosophy of Freedom: The Sources and Meaning of Russian Communism* (Moscow, 1997), 17–18.

[131]Ibid., 22.

of church life. The charismatic gifts of the Holy Spirit do not depend on anything human: they are poured out from above and are an unshakable sacred thing of the Church. But the growth of the person in the divine life is a creative and voluntary process. This process is not human and not divine, but theanthropic, i.e., ecclesiastical. Church life is the mystical unification of the divine and the human, of human activity and freedom on the one hand and God's grace-filled help on the other. God, as it were, awaits from man voluntary and creative initiative. The humiliation and degradation of the Church is a humiliation and degradation of human activity, the aversion of the human will to the will of God, a godless refusal of the person to bear the burden of freedom entrusted to man by God. People are responsible for the abomination of desolation in the Church since they are free in religious life. It is not the Church that is responsible for the fact that nearly the entire intelligentsia has left it, and that almost the entire spiritual hierarchy has come to a state of unprecedented moral decline, but people. It is not the Church that is bad, but us: the Church has unfailingly preserved its holy things, while we have betrayed that which is holy and been constantly unfaithful to it. Only an increase in voluntary human responsibility and creativity can heighten awareness of the unshakable holy things of the Church. Only *the free* are capable of strengthening the Church in spite of all things, of overcoming all temptations. The Church has on numerous occasions experienced difficult moments in its history, and righteous people were always found, thanks to whom her holy things were preserved. In these difficult moments the fate of the Church depends not on external things, not on forced protection, not on state interference, not on political revolutions, not on social reforms, but on the intense mystical experience of the Church among the faithful, and above all on mystical freedom.[132]

The antithesis of Christianity as the religion of freedom is atheistic communism, which demands a "forced unity of thinking." Communism's implacable hostility toward Christianity can be explained by its claim to a monopoly on world views; moreover, communism views itself as a religion that has come to replace Christianity.[133] But since man, according to

[132]Ibid., 193–94. Italics are in the original.
[133]Ibid., 384.

Berdyaev, is a "religious animal," "when he rejects the true, one God, he creates for himself false gods and idols and worships them."[134]

Berdyaev considered Orthodoxy the most perfect expression of Christianity as the religion of freedom. He sometimes spoke of his "revolt against official Orthodoxy, against the historical forms of church life."[135] His opinions on the church fathers, whose writings he knew poorly, on Theophan the Recluse and several other Russian theologians, were often superficial and subjective. At the same time, beginning in the 1900s, Berdyaev was a practicing Orthodox Christian and remained one until his death, and even built a chapel in his home in Clamart, a suburb of Paris. In his philosophical writings and literary criticism, Berdyaev proceeded from an Orthodox understanding of the world, examining everything through the eyes of an Orthodox Christian. His creative output was a powerful testimony to the western world on the beauty and truth of the Orthodox faith.

Berdyaev expounded his understanding of Orthodoxy in his article "The Truth of Orthodoxy," published posthumously.[136] In it, he notes first and foremost that "the Christian world knows little about Orthodoxy. It only knows the external and primarily negative sides of the Orthodox Church, but not its inner, spiritual treasures." He declares that "Orthodoxy is the form of Christianity that has been the least distorted in its essence by human history. In the Orthodox Church there have been moments of historical sin, mainly in connection with its external dependence on the state, but the Church's teaching itself and inner spiritual path were not distorted."

According to Berdyaev, "the Orthodox Church is above all the Church of tradition, unlike the Catholic Church, which is the Church of authority, and the Protestant churches, which are churches of personal faith. The Orthodox Church does not have a single external, authoritarian organization and has remained unchanged through the power of its inner tradition, and not through external authority."[137]

Berdyaev underscores that Orthodoxy "is, above all, orthodoxy of life, and not orthodoxy of doctrine . . . Orthodoxy is above all not doctrine, not an external organization, not an external form of behavior but spiritual life,

[134]Ibid., 386.
[135]*Self-Knowledge* (Moscow, 2004), 185.
[136]"The Truth of Orthodoxy," *Vestnik Russkogo Zapadno-Evropeiskogo Exarkhata* 11 (Paris, 1952): 4–11.
[137]Ibid., 4.

spiritual experience, and the spiritual path. It sees inner, spiritual activity as the essence of Christianity." In Orthodoxy, which is based on the teaching of the eastern church fathers, Christianity has not been rationalized to the extent that it has in the west. "Orthodoxy is foreign to rationalism and juridicism, as well as to all kinds of normatism. The Orthodox Church cannot be defined in rational concepts: it is understandable only for those who live in her, for those who partake of her spiritual experience."

Berdyaev writes that Orthodoxy understands itself as the religion of the Trinity: it is not an abstract monotheism but a concrete trinitarianism. The life of the Holy Trinity is reflected in the spiritual and liturgical experience of Orthodoxy, in which spiritual life is determined not by the ascent of man to God but by the descent of the Trinity to man. Orthodoxy is pneumatological in its very nature, for in it the Holy Spirit is revealed more than in Catholicism. For this reason the Orthodox Church "did not accept the *filioque* because it views it as subordinationism in the teaching on the Holy Spirit. Although the nature of the Holy Spirit is revealed the least through dogmas and doctrines, the Holy Spirit is through his actions the closest of all [the Trinity] to us, the most immanent with regard to the world."[138]

Orthodoxy, according to Berdyaev, is first and foremost liturgical in nature. It "instructs the people and fosters their growth not so much through sermons and the teaching of norms and laws of behavior as through liturgical actions, which foreshadow the transfiguration of life." Orthodoxy "also instructs the people through the examples of the saints and inspires the cult of holiness. But the examples of the saints are not normative: they instead reflect grace-filled enlightenment and the transfiguration of creation by the Holy Spirit. This non-normative nature of Orthodoxy makes it more difficult to apply to human history, human organization, and cultural activity."[139]

Unlike Catholicism, Orthodoxy is the religion of freedom, underscores Berdyaev. But Orthodoxy understands freedom differently from Protestantism: "In Protestantism, as in all western thought, freedom is understood individualistically, as the right of the individual who protects himself from encroachment by other individuals and determines himself and his actions autonomously. Individualism is foreign to Orthodoxy, which is characterized by a distinctive form of collectivism."[140] In the Orthodox Church the reli-

[138]Ibid., 6.
[139]Ibid., 7.
[140]Ibid., 7–8.

gious person finds himself within a collective religious body that is not an external authority:

> The Church is found not outside religious persons, who might be opposed to it; it is rather within them and they are within it. The Church is therefore not an authority, but the grace-filled unity of love and freedom. Orthodoxy does not know of authoritarianism because the latter separates the collective religious body and the religious person, the Church and its members. Without freedom of conscience, without freedom of the spirit there is no spiritual life, and there is even no notion of the Church since the Church does not tolerate having slaves within itself, and since God needs only the free. True freedom of religious conscience, or freedom of the spirit, is revealed not in isolated, autonomous persons who assert themselves in individualism, but in persons who are conscious of themselves as being in a supra-personal spiritual unity, in the unity of a spiritual organism, in the body of Christ, i.e., in the Church . . . In Orthodoxy freedom is organically combined with *sobornost'*, that is, with the action of the Holy Spirit on the collective religious body.[141]

The cosmic nature of the Church as the body of Christ was not articulated either in Catholicism or in Protestantism. In Orthodoxy, however, the Church is the "Christicized cosmos": in it "the entire created world is subjected to the action of the grace of the Holy Spirit." The cosmic nature of Orthodoxy is explained in its teaching on redemption:

> Christ's appearance has a cosmic, cosmogonic significance; it signifies, as it were, a new creation, a new day of the creation of the world. Orthodoxy is above all foreign to the juridical understanding of redemption as the settlement of a court case between God and man. Instead, an ontological and cosmic understanding is inherent in it—a manifestation of the new creation and the new humanity. The central and true idea of eastern patristics is that of theosis—the deification of man and all creation. Salvation is deification, something that the entire created world, the entire cosmos can undergo. Salvation is the transfiguration and enlightenment of creation, and not judicial acquittal. Orthodoxy is oriented toward the mystery of resurrection as the culmination and the final aim of Christian-

[141]Ibid., 8.

ity. This is why the main feast in the life of the Orthodox Church is that of Pascha, the radiant resurrection of Christ. The brilliant rays of the resurrection permeate the Orthodox world.[142]

In Orthodoxy salvation is understood "not only individually, but in *sobornost'*, together with the entire world," which is why "the striving for universal salvation has appeared on the spiritual soil of Orthodoxy." Berdyaev writes that Thomas Aquinas' view that the righteous will delight in the torments of sinners in hell could not arise from the depths of Orthodoxy. The Calvinist and Augustinian teaching on predestination is also profoundly alien to Orthodoxy. Orthodox thought "was not stifled by the idea of divine justice and never forgot the idea of divine love. What is most important is that it never defined the person from the standpoint of divine justice but from that of the transfiguration and deification of man and the cosmos."[143] Thus, writes Berdyaev, "the majority of eastern church teachers, from Clement of Alexandria to Maximus the Confessor, supported the idea of the *apokatastasis*, of universal salvation and resurrection" (this affirmation bears witness to Berdyaev's insufficient knowledge of eastern patristics).[144]

The final main characteristic of Orthodoxy, according to Berdyaev, is its eschatological nature: Orthodoxy is "the most traditional, the most conservative form of Christianity, for it has preserved the ancient truth. Nevertheless, it has the greatest potential for religious novelty, not the novelty of human thought and culture that is so great in the west, but a novelty of the religious transfiguration of life." Orthodoxy "looks toward the kingdom of God, which will come not as a result of historical evolution but of the mystical transfiguration of the world."[145]

Berdyaev concludes his article with a call to openness, dialogue, and Christian unity, addressed to both Orthodox and western Christians:

> Orthodoxy cannot be known through the existing theological treatises. It is known in the life of the Church and all the faithful, and is expressed least of all in concepts. But Orthodoxy must emerge from its isolation and mobilize its hidden spiritual riches. Only then will it acquire world-

[142]Ibid., 9.
[143]Ibid.
[144]Ibid.
[145]Ibid., 10.

wide significance. The recognition of the exceptional spiritual significance of Orthodoxy as the purest form of Christianity should not cause
complacency among its faithful or lead to a rejection of the importance
of western Christianity. On the contrary, we must acquaint ourselves with
western Christianity and learn much from it. We must strive for Christian unity, for Orthodoxy favors Christian unity. Since Orthodox Christianity has undergone secularization the least, it can contribute infinitely
to the Christianization of the world. The Christianization of the world
should not entail a secularization of Christianity. Christianity cannot be
isolated from the world, and continues to live within it; it does not separate itself from the world but remains in it; it should triumph over the
world and not be vanquished by it.[146]

[146]Ibid.

9

Orthodoxy in the Twentieth Century

The Persecution of the Faith in Russia

T HE RUSSIAN REVOLUTION was no accident of history, but the result of more than two hundred years of political and spiritual developments in Russia. The reforms of Peter I, which shook the foundations of the centuries-old lifestyle of the Russians and deprived the Church of a canonical leadership, marked the starting point of this path. The next landmark on the way to revolution was the rule of the enlightened empresses of the eighteenth century, who systematically and consistently did harm to the Church, who borrowed standards based on the western world view, as well as Voltairism and freethinking, and inculcated them in the population. The gradual departure of the intelligentsia from the Church in the nineteenth century, the interest of the educated classes in nihilism and atheism under the influence of German materialism and its Russian adherents—Belinsky, Chernyshevsky, Dobrolyubov, and Herzen—as well as Leo Tolstoy's efforts to undermine traditional Orthodoxy all led Russia inexorably to the brink of disaster. By the beginning of the twentieth century the powers of the "restrainer," which traditional Orthodoxy had been for Russia over the centuries, had weakened. After this the monarchy collapsed.

The revolution and fall of the monarchy were predicted by many of Russia's greatest minds. In 1830 Lermontov foretold with horrifying accuracy the events that would transpire ninety years later, during the years of revolutionary terror:

> The year will come, that black year for Russia,
> When the crown of the tsars will fall;
> The masses will forget their erstwhile love for him,
> And death and blood will be the food of many;
> When children and innocent women

Will no longer be protected by the law, trampled upon and rejected;
When the plague from rancid corpses
Begins to wander through dismal villages,
Enticing the people out of their huts,
And famine will begin to ravage this poor land;
And a glow will color the waves of the rivers:
On that day a powerful man will appear,
And you will recognize him—and understand
Why he wields a steel knife in his hand;
And woe to you! Your weeping, your groans
Will then seem ridiculous to him;
And everything about him will be terrible and gloomy,
Like his cloak with his raised forehead.[1]

The revolution was foretold by Dostoyevsky, who in his novels and articles demonstrated the perniciousness of atheism and nihilism and denounced the Russian "demons"—the revolutionaries and those who rejected moral norms. The revolution was also predicted by John of Kronstadt, who in his sermons and writings called the people to repentance and to return to the faith of their fathers. The prominent figures of the Russian religious renaissance were the last who strove to prevent the inevitable from happening, but their voices were not heeded. The ideological ferment among the intelligentsia and the masses, caused by the political incompetence of the imperial government and a number of military failures, first led to the bourgeois February Revolution and then to the proletarian October Revolution of 1917.

When the Bolsheviks came to power on October 25, 1917, the Russian Orthodox Church was at the peak of its glory and power. Ten days after the October Revolution the Russian Orthodox Church restored the patriarchate. However, in his very first pastoral epistle the newly chosen Patriarch Tikhon characterized the times as "full of sorrows and difficulties," as a time when "the Christian principles of state and society have become obscured in the conscience of the people, when faith itself has become weak and when the godless spirit of this world rages."[2]

[1] "Prophecy," in *Selected Works*, 19–20.
[2] M.E. Gubonin, ed., *The Acts of His Holiness Tikhon, Patriarch of Moscow and All Russia: Later Documents and Correspondence on the Canonical Succession of the Higher Church Authority, 1917–1943* (Moscow, 1994), 70.

The struggle against religion was a part of the ideological program of the new Bolshevik government. A pathological hatred of religion characterized all Bolsheviks, particularly the two main leaders of the revolution—Vladimir Lenin and Leon Trotsky. During the first Russian revolution in December 1905, Lenin published an article entitled "Socialism and Religion," in which he wrote: "Religion is one of the forms of the spiritual yoke that weighs down on the masses everywhere, oppressed by eternal work for others, want, and loneliness . . . Religion is the opium of the people. Religion is a kind of spiritual moonshine in which the slaves of capital drown their human image and their demands for a life worthy of a man in at least some way."[3] In the same article Lenin called for the total separation of the Church from the state and school system, and for making religion a private matter.

During the October Revolution, the ideas of the leader of the world proletariat were implemented. On the very first day after coming to power—October 26, 1917—the Bolsheviks issued a "Decree on Land," which declared the nationalization of all church and monastery lands "with all their living and dead inventory." From December 16 to 18 decrees were issued that stripped church marriages of legal force. On January 23, 1918 the Soviet People's Commissariat issued a decree "On the Separation of the Church from the State and the Schools from the Church," which deprived religious organizations of the right to own property and the right to be a legal entity, and banned religious education in schools.

The victory of the October Revolution was immediately followed by the fierce persecution of the Church, with arrests and murder of clergymen. The first victim of the revolutionary terror was the St Petersburg archpriest John Kochurov, who was killed on October 31, 1917. His death headed the tragic list of the new martyrs and confessors of Russia, which contains the names of tens of thousands of clergymen and monastics and hundreds of thousands of laymen. On January 19/February 1, Patriarch Tikhon wrote a letter in which he anathematized all who had spilled innocent blood—first and foremost the Bolsheviks. On January 25/February 7 in Kiev, Metropolitan Vladimir (Bogoyavlensky) was murdered. Members of the national council, which had been convened in Moscow, honored his memory with a requiem service.

The shootings and arrests of clergy soon acquired mass proportions. In 1918 several bishops, several hundred clergymen, and many laymen were

[3]Lenin, *Complete Works*, 5th ed. (Moscow, 1979), 12.143.

Holy Martyr Vladimir,
Metropolitan of Kiev

killed. On July 17 in Ekaterinburg, Emperor Nicholas II, who had abdicated the throne, along with his family—Empress Alexandra, their son Alexei, and their daughters Olga, Tatiana, Maria, and Anastasia—were murdered. On the next day Grand Duchess Elizabeth Fedorovna, founder of the Ss Martha and Mary Convent of Mercy, was buried alive not far from Alapaevsk. Patriarch Tikhon responded to the death of the imperial family in a sermon given in the church of the Kazan Icon in Moscow:

Several days ago a horrible crime was committed—the shooting of the former Emperor Nicholas Alexandrovich. Our government and the executive committee gave their approval for this and recognized its legality . . . But our Christian conscience, guided by God's Word, cannot agree with this verdict. In accordance with the teaching of God's Word we must condemn this act, otherwise the blood of him who was shot will be on us, and not only on those who committed the act. Let them call us counterrevolutionaries for doing this, let them send us to prison, let them shoot us. We are ready to endure everything.[4]

Clergymen were murdered with particular brutality: they were buried alive, had cold water poured over them in subzero temperatures until they froze, were placed in boiling water, crucified, whipped to death, and chopped with axes. Many clergymen were tortured before their death or murdered along with their families or in the presence of their wives and children. Churches and monasteries were demolished and plundered, and icons were desecrated and burned. A fierce campaign against religion was unleashed in the press. In a letter to the Council of People's Commissars of October 26, 1918, on the anniversary of the Bolshevik's seizure of power, Patriarch Tikhon spoke of the sorrows that had befallen the country, the people, and the Church:

You have divided the people into hostile camps and plunged them into fratricide of unprecedented brutality. You have openly replaced the love

[4]Cited in Archpriest Mikhail Polsky, *The New Martyrs of Russia* (Jordanville, 1957), 1.282–83.

for Christ with hatred, and instead of peace you have intentionally aroused enmity between the classes. And there is no end in sight for the war you have caused, since you aim at achieving the victory of the phantom of the world revolution through the hands of Russian workers and peasants . . . Nobody feels safe: all live under the constant fear of being searched, plundered, evicted, arrested, or shot. Hundreds of helpless people are seized, left to rot away in prisons for months on end, and are executed—often without any trial . . . Bishops, priests, monks, and nuns are murdered who have committed no crime, simply on a vague accusation of some undefined form of counterrevolutionary activity. These inhumane executions are made

Patriarch Tikhon

even more unbearable for the Orthodox because they are deprived of their last consolation before death—the holy mysteries—and the bodies of the murdered are not handed over to relatives for a Christian burial . . . There is not a single day when your press does not publish some monstrous slander against the Church of Christ and its servants, or malicious blasphemy. You mock the servants of the altar . . . You have laid your hands on the property of the Church, which has been gathered by generations of believers, and have not hesitated to violate their last will. You have closed a number of monasteries and churches without any reason . . . By throwing out the holy images from schools and forbidding the teaching of the faith in them, you are depriving children of the spiritual nourishment essential for an Orthodox upbringing . . . It is to you, who use your power to persecute your neighbors and exterminate the innocent, that we address our word of admonition: celebrate the anniversary of your rule by freeing those in prisons, ending the bloodshed, violence, destruction, and persecution of the faith. Devote your efforts not to destruction, but to maintaining order and legitimacy; give the people the rest from the civil war that they desire and deserve. Otherwise you will have to answer for all the righteous blood shed by you (Lk 11.50)—and you, who have taken the sword, shall perish by the sword (Mt 26.52).[5]

[5] *Acts of His Holiness Tikhon*, 149–51.

Soon after writing this letter Patriarch Tikhon was placed under house arrest, and persecutions continued with renewed force. On February 14, 1919 the People's Commissariat of Justice issued a decree on the organized opening of relics. To this end special commissions were established that publicly desecrated the relics of saints in the presence of clergymen and laypeople. The aim of the campaign was to discredit the Church and unveil its "tricks and charlatanism." By July 1920 around sixty such acts of desecration had been carried out, including those involving the relics of Ss Metrophanes of Voronezh, Pitirim of Tambov, John of Novgorod, Makary of Kalyazin, Nilus of Stolobensk, and Euthymius of Suzdal. On April 11, 1919 the relics of St Sergius of Radonezh were opened. The evening before, a crowd of pilgrims gathered before the gates of the Trinity-St Sergius Lavra, and prayer services to the saint were served all night long. On July 29, 1920 the Soviet People's Commissariat issued a decree on the liquidation of relics, and on August 23 the People's Commissariat of Justice ruled that relics should be handed over to museums. However, not all relics were destroyed: many were subsequently transferred to the Leningrad Museum of Atheism and Religion, which was located on the premises of the Cathedral of Our Lady of Kazan.[6]

Economic failure resulting from the revolution, civil war, and the drought of summer 1921 caused famine in the Volga region and several other provinces in Russia. By May 1922 around twenty million people had been struck by famine, and approximately one million had perished. Entire villages were emptied of life, children were orphaned, and many who had left the famine-struck regions in search of sustenance died on their way. At first the Bolshevik government turned to Patriarch Tikhon for help, sending the writer A.M. Gorky to the patriarch to hold negotiations. These led to the creation of the All-Russian Committee for Aid to the Starving, chaired by the patriarch. Collections were made to aid the hungry, and Patriarch Tikhon turned to the eastern patriarchs, the Roman pontiff, the archbishop of Canterbury, and the bishop of York for assistance. However, this activity aroused the discontent of the government; the committee was disbanded, and the funds collected were confiscated. In its stead the Central Commission for Aid to the Starving was established under the aegis of the All-Russian Central Executive Committee, which in December 1921 called on the patriarch to donate church valuables. The patriarch blessed the donation of all church decorations not

[6]Archpriest Vladislav Tsypin, *History of the Russian Church: 1917–1997* (Moscow 1997), 67–68.

used in liturgical services for the benefit of the hungry. However, a new campaign against the Church was unleashed in the press, this time accusing the Church of concealing precious objects and of indifference toward the sufferings of the people. On February 23, 1922, the All-Russian Central Executive Committee issued a decree on the forced confiscation of church valuables, including liturgical vessels. The Church regarded this as sacrilege, since the use of liturgical vessels for nonliturgical purposes is forbidden by the canons.

The forced confiscation of these objects began immediately after the decree was issued, and in some cases led to mass disorder. During the confiscation of precious objects from the cathedral in the city of Shuya, crowds gathered to protect their holy things and were shot by the Red Army. On March 19, 1922, Lenin wrote a secret letter to the members of the Politburo, in which he suggested using the famine as an occasion for the total destruction of the church organization in Russia:

> All arguments point to the fact that we will not be able to accomplish this later, since nothing except for a desperate famine can create a frame of mind among the broad peasant masses that might guarantee us their sympathy, or at least the neutralization of these masses, so that victory in this struggle for the confiscation of valuables will be undoubtedly and totally on our side . . . Therefore I draw the certain conclusion that we must now wage the most resolute and merciless war against the Black Hundred clergymen and crush their resistance with such brutality that they will not forget about it for several decades.[7]

At a meeting on March 30 the politburo adopted a plan to rout the Church. It included the arrest of the synod and the patriarch, the launch of a new antireligious campaign in the press, and the confiscation of church valuables throughout the entire country. Patriarch Tikhon was called to the State Political Directorate and interrogated. Trials of clergymen and laypeople, in which they were accused of resisting the confiscation of church valuables, began to be held everywhere. On April 26 one such court case opened in Moscow, with twenty priests and thirty-four laypersons placed on trial. In late May Metropolitan Venyamin (Kazansky) of Petrograd was arrested; he and eighty-five others were accused of inciting believers to oppose the authorities.

[7]Cited in *Archives of the Kremlin in Two Volumes* 1: *The Politburo and the Church: 1922–1925* (Moscow/Novosibirsk, 1997), 141–42.

The defendants on trial for resisting the confiscation of church valuables.

The process was public, lasted around one month, and was followed closely by thousands of the faithful. On July 4 Metropolitan Venyamin gave his last speech, in which he said: "I do not know what sentence you will hand down, whether it will be life or death, but whatever your decision may be I will, with the same reverence, raise my eyes to the heavens, make the sign of the cross [while saying this he made a large sign of the cross], and say: 'Glory to Thee, O Lord our God, for everything.'" The metropolitan and several others were sentenced to death by firing squad, and most of those accused with him were given prison terms of various length. On the night of August 12–13, Metropolitan Venyamin, Archimandrite Sergius (Shevich), Y. Novitsky, and I. Kovsharov were shot. Not long before this happened Metropolitan Venyamin sent a letter to one of the deans of the Petrograd diocese, in which he wrote:

> In my youth and childhood I immersed myself in reading the lives of the saints and admired their heroism and holy fervor. From the depths of my soul I regretted that I did not live in their times and could not experience what they experienced. The times have changed, and new opportunities to suffer for Christ's sake at the hands of one's own people and strangers have appeared. It is difficult and painful to suffer, but the more we suffer the more we receive consolation from God in abundance . . . Now it seems that we must endure almost everything: imprisonment, trials, mockery from society, demands for one's death, ingratitude, mercenari-

ness, inconstancy and similar things, anxiety over and responsibility for the fate of others and even for the Church itself. My sufferings have reached their peak, but my consolation has increased as well. I am joyful and serene, as always. Christ is our life, our light, and our peace. With him one feels fine always and everywhere. I do not fear for the future of the Church. We pastors must have more faith and forget our self-sufficiency, reason, erudition, and powers, and let God's grace act.[8]

In 1918, when the execution of bishops began and several bishops went abroad, the Church started implementing the decision of the national council to increase the number of episcopal sees. In 1918 four new bishops were consecrated, in 1919 fourteen, in 1920 thirty, and in 1921 thirty-nine. The episcopate was thus replenished. However, in 1922 approximately one-half of the episcopate was sent into exile.

In addition to persecution by the atheist government, the Church also suffered from inner tumult and schisms. By 1922 the "renovationist schism" had emerged, initially headed by Bishop Antonin (Granovsky), the Petrograd priests Alexander Vvedensky and Vladimir Krasnitsky, and several Moscow priests. They were called "renovationists" because they fought for a comprehensive renewal of church life, the abolition of centuries-old traditions, the introduction of a married episcopate, and an entire array of other novelties. The main item on their agenda, however, was to overthrow the lawful church hierarchy, headed by Patriarch Tikhon. To this end they entered into an alliance with the State Political Directorate. After obtaining the support of the government, on May 12, 1922 the renovationists demanded that Patriarch Tikhon abdicate the patriarchal throne. The patriarch agreed and sent a letter to the chairman of the All-Russian Central Executive Committee declaring the transfer of his powers to Metropolitan Agathangel (Preobrazhensky) of Yaroslavl. However, the government prevented Metropolitan Agathangel from coming to Moscow, and the patriarch was dismissed from handling church affairs. The NKVD evicted him from the patriarchal residence and placed him under house arrest; his residence was then occupied on the same day by the renovationist Higher Church Administration headed by Bishop Antonin. On May 29 the constitutive assembly of the "Living Church" took place in Moscow, which decreed the introduction of a married episcopate, allowed men in second marriages to be ordained to the clergy, and rescinded

[8]Polsky, *New Martyrs of Russia*, 2.294–95.

the excommunication of Leo Tolstoy. In June the renovationist administration was recognized by Archbishops Sergius (Stragorodsky) of Vladimir, Evdokim (Meshchersky) of Nizhny Novgorod, and Seraphim (Meshcheryakov) of Kostroma. By July 1922 the majority of the seventy-three ruling bishops of the Russian Orthodox Church had submitted to the Higher Church Administration. Only thirty-six diocesan bishops remained loyal to the patriarch.[9]

Between summer 1922 and summer 1923, church authority was de facto in the hands of the renovationists. On May 2, the renovationists held a pseudo-council in the Cathedral of Christ the Savior attended by 476 delegates, including 62 bishops. The pseudo-council decided to defrock Patriarch Tikhon, strip him of the monastic habit, and revoke the restoration of the patriarchate. Vvedensky was proclaimed "archbishop of Krutitsa," Krasnitsky "protopresbyter of the Russian Church," and Antonin "metropolitan of Moscow and All Russia." However, soon after the council ended, Krasnitsky and Antonin left the renovationist Higher Church Council.

Patriarch Tikhon did not recognize the decisions of the pseudo-council. In the second half of 1922 he was under house arrest, and in early 1923 he was transferred to the prison of the State Political Directorate on Lyubyanka Street, where he was regularly interrogated. On July 16 he addressed a declaration to the supreme court in which he repented of his anti-Soviet activities and asked to be released.[10] On July 25 the patriarch was released, and three days later he wrote a letter to his flock stating: "I, of course, did not declare myself an admirer of the Soviet authorities, as the renovationists do . . . But I am also by no means an enemy of the government, as some maintain . . . I firmly condemn all threats against the Soviet government, wherever they may come from. Let all foreign and domestic monarchists and the White Guard understand that I am not an enemy of the Soviet government."[11] The patriarch sent out two more letters in which he recognized his "guilt before the people and the Soviet government" and condemned the renovationist schism.[12]

This radical change in the patriarch's stance on the Soviet government, which he had anathematized in 1918, can be explained both by pressure from the State Political Directorate and by an awareness of the necessity of restor-

[9]Tsypin, *History of the Russian Church*, 92.
[10]*Acts of His Holiness Tikhon*, 280–81.
[11]Ibid., 283.
[12]Ibid., 286–91.

ing the canonical church hierarchy and ending the renovationist schism. Soon after he resumed his ecclesiastical duties, hierarchs who had lapsed into schism began to return to the canonical patriarchal Church. On August 27, 1923, Metropolitan Sergius (Stragorodsky) offered his repentance to the patriarch in the presence of the faithful. Before the beginning of the Divine Liturgy, wearing only a cassock, without a klobuk or bishop's panagia, Sergius pronounced his words of repentance in a muted, trembling voice and prostrated himself at the feet of the patriarch. The patriarch handed him a panagia, a white klobuk, and a bishop's mantle; then Metropolitan Sergius concelebrated with the patriarch at the liturgy. A number of other hierarchs followed Sergius' example.

In 1924 the renovationists attempted to deal yet another blow to the Church. Having secured the support of the eastern patriarchs, they suggested that an "ecumenical council" be convened in Jerusalem, and in order to prepare for this they organized a "preconciliar conference." Not long before it opened Patriarch Tikhon received a letter from the representative of the patriarchate of Constantinople in Moscow, Archimandrite Basil (Dimopoulos), which expressed the wish of Gregory VII, patriarch of Constantinople, that Patriarch Tikhon "sacrifice himself and immediately remove himself from the government of the Church . . . and also that the patriarchate be abolished, at least temporarily." Patriarch Tikhon categorically refused to follow the suggestions of Constantinople, after which Patriarch Gregory VII broke communion with him. The renovationist "preconciliar conference" opened in Moscow on July 23, chaired in absentia by Gregory VII, who was represented by Archimandrite Basil. Around four hundred delegates took part in the conference, including eighty-three pseudo-bishops (of whom forty had been Orthodox hierarchs and forty-three had been "consecrated" by the renovationists). The conference declared the "All-Russian Higher Church Administration" to be the supreme ecclesiastical authority, and Patriarch Tikhon was once again deposed. The patriarch in his turn did not recognize the decisions of this renovationist pseudo-council.

Besides the renovationist schism, the patriarch was also concerned with the divisions that had arisen among the clergy abroad. After the 1917 revolution, some of the hierarchs of the Russian Orthodox Church found themselves beyond the borders of their homeland. In 1920, a group of bishops who had been evacuated along with military and civil persons from Russia convened a council in Constantinople and established the Higher Church Administration Abroad. Metropolitan Antony (Khrapovitsky) was elected head of the new organization. In 1921 the administration was transferred to Sremskie Karlovtsy, Yugoslavia, where the First All-Diaspora Council was convened. The Soviet government placed pressure on Patriarch Tikhon, demanding that he condemn the actions of the diaspora bishops. In 1922 the patriarch issued a decree on the closure of the Higher Church Administration Abroad, and in August 1922 the administration was dissolved. However, the temporary Synod of Bishops of the Russian Church Abroad was established in its place. The efforts of the diaspora bishops to defend the Russian Church only worsened its already terrible situation in the homeland.

On December 9, 1924 an attempt was made on the patriarch's life, resulting in the death of his cell attendant Y. Polozov, who had placed himself between

Metropolitan Kirill (Smirnov) of Kazan

the patriarch and the gunmen. After this the patriarch's health began to deteriorate. In his will he wrote that should he die, the leadership of the Church should be transferred to Metropolitan Kirill (Smirnov) of Kazan; should the latter be unable to fulfil his duties, it should go to Metropolitan Agathangel (Preobrazhensky) of Yaroslavl. Should he too be prevented from doing so, Metropolitan Peter (Polyansky) of Krutitsa should head the Church. In early April, E. Tuchkov, the staff member of the State Political Directorate responsible for contacts with the Church, demanded that the patriarch issue a letter expressing his loyalty to the Soviet government and condemning

the diaspora clergy. The letter had already been drawn up, but the patriarch refused to sign it. On April 7 he died, without having signed the letter. The next day the letter, supposedly signed by the patriarch, was published in *Izvestiya*. Of those who had been close to the patriarch nobody, including Metropolitan Peter of Krutitsa, dared to reveal the fact that it had been forged.[13]

---

[13]The question of the authenticity of this letter has been discussed over many years in the church press. This question can now be considered resolved after a recent comparison of different versions of the letter kept in state archives, to which the patriarch himself made corrections. A copy of the text published in *Izvestiya* is preserved which was crossed out by the patriarch. See D.V. Safonov, "On the Question of the Authenticity of the 'Testament' of St Tikhon the Patriarch," *Bogoslovskii Vestnik* 4 (2004): 256–311.

On April 12, 1925, the day of Patriarch Tikhon's burial, a conference of fifty-eight bishops took place in Moscow. Due to the absence of Metropolitans Kirill and Agathangel, who had been exiled, it elected Metropolitan Peter the locum tenens of the patriarchal throne. During the short period in which he occupied this position before his arrest, Metropolitan Peter continued Patriarch Tikhon's policy of loyalty toward the Soviet government and taking firm measures against the schism. The persecution of the Church, however, only worsened. In 1925 the Union of the Godless, headed by E. Yaroslavsky, was founded (in 1929 it was renamed the Union of the Militant Godless). Just one year later this organ-

Metropolitan Peter (Polyansky) of Krutitsa

ization counted 87,000 members. In December 1925, sensing impending arrest, Metropolitan Peter wrote two letters. In one he transferred the duties of the locum tenens, in the following sequence, to: Metropolitans Kirill, Agathangel, Arseny of Novgorod, and Sergius of Nizhny Novgorod. In the second he transferred his powers to Metropolitan Sergius. On December 10 Metropolitan Peter was arrested, and on December 14 Metropolitan Sergius (Stragorodsky) became deputy of the patriarchal locum tenens.

The canonical chaos that ensued after the death of Patriarch Tikhon and the arrest of Metropolitan Peter, as well as the actions of the State Political Directorate, aimed at further dividing the Church, created a situation in which several claimants to the office of locum tenens appeared. Metropolitan Sergius rejected their pretensions, began corresponding with the imprisoned Metropolitan Peter, and received his backing. However, in late 1926 he too was arrested and removed from governing the Church. At that time many bishops were languishing in concentration camps and prisons throughout Russia. More than twenty hierarchs were interned in the former Solovki monastery, which had been turned into the "Solovki Special Purpose Camp."

On March 30, 1927 Metropolitan Sergius was released from prison. On May 7 he appealed to the NKVD for the legalization of the church administration. In exchange for the Church's legalization, the authorities demanded that Sergius issue a declaration stating his support for the Soviet government and condemning counterrevolutionary activities and the diaspora clergy. On

Metropolitan Sergius (Stragorodsky)

July 29 Metropolitan Sergius and the Provisional Patriarchal Synod founded by him issued a "Declaration" expressing gratitude to the Soviet government for its "attention to the spiritual needs of the Orthodox population," calling on the people to prove their loyalty to the Soviet authorities "not in words but in deeds," and condemning the "anti-Soviet statements" of certain diaspora bishops. "We wish to be Orthodox and at the same time recognize the Soviet Union as our civil homeland, whose joys and successes are our joys and successes, and whose failures are our failures."[14]

The publication of this document caused an uproar within the Church, and a large part of the episcopate refused to accept it. A party of "noncommemorators" was formed, consisting of bishops and clergymen who refused to commemorate Metropolitan Sergius at the church services. The synod of the Russian Church Abroad expressed its disapproval of the declaration and decreed: "The part of the Russian Orthodox Church in the diaspora should sever administrative relations with the Moscow church authorities, in view of the impossibility of having normal relations with it and due to its subjugation to the godless Soviet authorities." In May 1928 Metropolitan Sergius and the provisional synod issued a decree that dissolved the synod of the Church Abroad and its council, and revoked all of its actions. In 1934 the synod of the Church Abroad, headed by Metropolitan Antony, was condemned for a second time, and all of its clergy were forbidden from serving until the ruling of a spiritual court or until they repented. The Church Abroad, however, continued to exist and develop despite the sanctions imposed by Metropolitan Sergius and his synod.

The publication of the declaration did not stop the persecution of the Church. On the contrary, from 1928 to 1931 it even intensified. As of January 1, 1928 there were 28,560 parishes of the Russian Orthodox Church on the territory of the RSFSR; if one took into account the parishes of the renovationists and other schismatics the number was close to 39,000 (i.e., two-thirds of the number before the revolution). In 1928, 354 churches were closed, and in 1929 this number reached 1,119, of which 322 had been demolished. In Moscow, of the 500 churches that had existed, only 224 remained by January

[14]For the full text of the declaration see *Acts of His Holiness Tikhon*, 509–13.

1930, and two years later only 87. In 1931 the Cathedral of Christ the Savior was blown up. A nationwide campaign was launched against the ringing of church bells, and bells were taken down and smashed to pieces. The desecration of icons and other sacred objects continued.

The arrests and shootings of clergymen did not stop. The first blow was dealt to the opponents of Metropolitan Sergius' declaration, and then to the rest of the bishops. Metropolitan Sergius' struggle to legalize the Church and ease the fate of the arrested bishops was only partially successful. On his petition, several bishops returned from imprisonment and exile in 1931, although other archpastors continued to languish in prisons and exile. An increasing number of arrests took place before the eyes of the deputy of the patriarchal locum tenens, who was absolutely powerless in this situation. The locum tenens himself, Metropolitan Peter, was exiled in 1926 to the Tobolsk region, and then to the far north, to the winter camp Khe. He refused numerous suggestions to renounce his office, causing his sentence to be extended even further.

In 1932 the Union of the Militant Godless drew up a five-year plan for their campaign against religion. According to it, churches of all confessions were to be closed and clergymen sent abroad, and "by May 1, 1937 the name of God should be forgotten throughout the entire territory of the USSR." Of course,

Union of the Militant Godless, Moscow region, 1929

the clergy were not sent abroad: instead they continued to be imprisoned and shot. Unlike during Lenin's times, when well-publicized court proceedings took place, now only a sentence handed down by a three-person committee ("troika") was needed to sentence someone to death by firing squad. In the 1930s, when the juggernaut of Stalinist terror wreaked havoc on all sections of society, all clergymen—including the renovationists—were indiscriminately arrested or shot. By the mid-1930s the renovationist schism had basically ceased to exist, and in 1935 the renovationist synod liquidated itself.

In autumn 1936 the Moscow patriarchate was informed of the death of Metropolitan Peter. The patriarchate issued a decree on the transfer of the rights and duties of the locum tenens of the patriarchal throne to Metropolitan Sergius, who in 1934 was granted the title "His Beatitude, the Metropolitan of Moscow and Kolomna." In reality Metropolitan Peter was still alive, though seriously ill. He was shot to death on October 10, 1937, after being sentenced by a NKVD "troika" of the Chelyabinsk region.

In 1937, during the height of the Stalinist repressions, a census of the population was conducted that counted 162 million people in the nation. In 1934 there were 168 million people in the country, and it was thought that by 1937 this number would grow to 170–172 million. The difference of 10 million between the expected and actual results was a direct result of collectivization, the dispossession of the *kulaks*, the abandoning of villages by the peasants, the famine of 1933, as well as the mass repressions that had led to the death of millions and caused a demographic catastrophe. After seeing the results of the census, Stalin accused its organizers of miscalculation and subjected them to repression. The results of the census were made secret. In 1939 a new census was conducted that produced the desired result: 170 million people. The dissatisfaction of the communist authorities with the 1937 census was caused not only by its "miscalculation," but also by the fact that in the section on religion 55.3 million people—56.7 percent of those aged sixteen or older—declared themselves believers (persons under the age of sixteen did not fill in this column[15]). Thus, despite the mass persecution of the clergy and

[15]The instructions for filling out the column on religion in the census form read: "This should only be answered by those sixteen years old or older. It does not concern the confession to which the respondent or his parents officially belonged in the past. If the respondent considers himself a nonbeliever, he should write 'nonbeliever.' If the respondent considers himself a believer, he should write 'believer'; believers who adhere to a particular doctrine should write the name of their religion (e.g., Orthodox, Lutheran, Baptist, Molokan, Muslim, or Buddhist)."

faithful, the closure and destruction of churches and monasteries, and despite the danger of being shot or repressed that threatened everyone—including their families—who openly confessed their faith in God, more than one-half of the adult population proclaimed their religiosity in 1937.[16]

As a result of the unprecedented, massive persecution of the 1930s, the Church in the USSR was almost totally routed. By 1939 there were only one hundred active churches in the entire country, no monasteries, no institutions of theological education, and only four diocesan bishops: Metropolitan Sergius of Moscow, Metropolitan Alexei (Simansky) of Leningrad, Archbishop Nicholas (Yarushevich) of Peterhof, who also administered the dioceses of Novgorod and Pskov, and Archbishop Sergius (Voskresensky) of Dmitrov. Several more bishops served as parish deans. In the Ukraine only 3 percent of the churches active before the revolution were still open.

The situation of the Church started to change after the beginning of World War II. In 1939, as a result of the Molotov-Ribbentrop pact, the western Ukraine and western Belorussia were annexed by the USSR, and in 1940, Bessarabia, northern Bukovina, and the Baltic states. As a result the number of parishes of the Russian Orthodox Church grew dramatically. By the beginning of the Great Patriotic War it counted 3,021 churches and 88 monasteries.

When Hitler's troops attacked the Soviet Union on June 22, 1941, Metropolitan Sergius addressed the people of the USSR:

> The fascist marauders have attacked our homeland. Trampling upon all treaties and promises, they have unexpectedly attacked us, and the blood of peaceful citizens already soaks our soil. The times of Baty, the Teutonic knights, Karl of Sweden, and Napoleon are repeating themselves . . . This is not the first time that the Russian people have had to endure such trials. With God's help they will once again annihilate the fascist enemy . . . The fatherland is being defended by its weapons and the sacrifices of the entire people, by the willingness of all to serve their fatherland with everything they have at this difficult moment . . . Let us remember the holy leaders of the Russian people, such as Alexander Nevsky and Dimitry Donskoy, who gave their lives for the people and the homeland . . . Our Orthodox Church has always shared the fate of the people. Together with

---

[16]The column "religion" was not included in the census form of 1939. For more on the census of 1937 see A.G. Volkov, "The Population Census of 1937: Myths and the Truth," in *The Census of the Population of the USSR of 1937: History and Materials* (Moscow 1990), 6–63.

them it endured trials and took consolation from their successes. And it will not abandon its people now. It calls down the blessing of heaven upon the upcoming sacrifices that will be made by the entire nation.[17]

The patriotic stance of the Church did not go unnoticed, and already in 1942 the persecution of the Church was considerably relaxed. On the petition of Metropolitan Sergius, several bishops were returned from exile and appointed to dioceses, and new bishops were consecrated. But the real turning point in the Church's fate came at a meeting between Joseph Stalin and Sergius, Alexei, and Archbishop Nicholas, which took place on September 4, 1943. During the meeting a number of issues were discussed: the necessity of convening a bishops council to elect a patriarch and synod, the opening of institutions of theological education, the publication of a church magazine, and the release of imprisoned and exiled bishops (this last question was raised by Metropolitan Alexei). Stalin reacted positively to all these questions, and the Moscow patriarchate was given the large house on Chisty Street where it is still housed today.

Four days after this historic meeting, on September 8, a council attended by nineteen hierarchs was held in Moscow. The council elected Metropolitan Sergius patriarch, and established a Holy Synod consisting of three standing and three temporary members. The enthronement of the newly elected patriarch took place in the Theophany cathedral on September 12. On October 8 a Committee for the Affairs of the Russian Orthodox Church, chaired by G.G. Karpov, was established within the Council of People's Commissars of the USSR. The Soviet government charged this organ with communicating with and controlling the Church.

For the Russian Orthodox Church, the period from September 1943 until the beginning of the Khrushchev persecutions at the end of the 1950s saw the partial restoration of what had been destroyed during the years of Stalinist terror. The state preserved its atheist character and the Church remained excluded from public life to a significant extent. Still, the open persecution was temporary halted. Many Orthodox parishes had renewed their activities on the lands occupied by the Germans, and after the Red Army reclaimed the territory these parishes remained open.

On May 4, 1944 Patriarch Sergius died, and Metropolitan Alexei became locum tenens of the patriarchal throne. In autumn 1944 there were approxi-

---

[17] *The Russian Orthodox Church and the Great Patriotic War: Collection of Documents* (Moscow 1943), 3–5.

mately fifty bishops administering dioceses. On November 21–23, a council attended by fifty bishops was held in the patriarchal headquarters on Chisty Street, and on January 31 a national council opened at the church of the Resurrection of Christ in Sokol- niki, Moscow. It was attended by fifty-six bishops, eighty-seven clergymen, and thirty-eight laypersons. The council elected Metropolitan Alexei patriarch and adopted the Statutes on the Government of the Russian Orthodox Church. The council was at- tended by Patriarchs Christopher of Alexandria, Alexander III of Antioch, and Kallistrat of Georgia, as well as representatives of the churches of Constan-

Patriarch Alexei I

tinople, Jerusalem, Romania, and Serbia. The enthronement of Patriarch Alexei took place in the Theophany cathedral in Moscow on February 4, 1945.

In 1946 the Russian Orthodox Church expanded after the reunification of Ukrainian Greek Catholics with the Orthodox Church. The decision to reunite was made on March 8–9, 1946 at the Council of Lvov, in which 204 Greek Catholic priests and 12 laypersons took part. As a result of this decision more than 3,000 Uniate churches became Orthodox. Thus the tragic effects of the Union of Brest, which had weighed over the Ukraine for four-and-a- half centuries, came to an end. This process of unification, however, took place with the active support of the state authorities, which revoked the reg- istration of Greek Catholic parishes that refused to join the Russian Ortho- dox Church and subjected the Uniate clergy to fierce persecution. The Russian Orthodox Church was not responsible for these repressions, since it itself had just begun to rise from the ashes. According to one researcher, "hav- ing been subjected to incomparably more terrible persecution during the 1920s and 1930s, the Russian Orthodox Church did not petition for any kind of assistance from the NKVD in the holy matter of joining the Uniates to the Mother Church. The fact that this unification coincided with considerations of state politics could not and should not have hindered the Orthodox Church from admitting those returning to its saving walls."[18]

---

[18]Archpriest Vladislav Tsypin, "The Russian Orthodox Church in Recent Times: 1917–1999," in *Orthodox Encyclopedia*, 153.

The postwar years witnessed the continuing growth of the Russian Orthodox Church: on January 1, 1949 there were 73 bishops, 14,477 active churches,
75 monasteries, 2 theological academies, and 8 seminaries. However, in 1948
churches began to be closed and clergymen arrested once again.

After Stalin's death on March 5, 1953 many prisoners of conscience,
including clergymen, were released from prison. However, a new campaign
against the Church was launched in 1958 by Nikita Khrushchev, who promised to create a communist state within twenty years and show the "last
remaining priest" on television in 1980. In accordance with the new policy of
uprooting religion, churches and monasteries were closed en masse, and
antireligious propaganda was intensified. From 1961 to 1964, 1,234 people were
condemned by courts for religious reasons and sentenced to imprisonment
or exile. By early 1966 the Russian Orthodox Church had only 7,523 churches,
16 monasteries, 2 theological academies, and 3 seminaries.[19] The number of
clergymen dropped by one-half in comparison to 1948. Churches were spread
unevenly throughout the country: in regions that had not been part of the
USSR before 1939, there were considerably more of them than in other areas.
Some cities with populations of several hundred thousands of people might
have only one or two open churches.

The Khrushchev-era persecution was characterized not so much by an
open repression of the clergy as by the powerful ideological pressure exerted
by the government, which attempted to undermine the Church's potential,
destroy it from the inside, and discredit it in the eyes of the people. To this
end the state security organs began to suggest to priests that they renounce
God and engage in the propaganda of "scientific atheism." For this ignoble
mission the authorities sought out, as a rule, clergymen who had been
banned from serving or had committed canonical violations, or who were at
the mercy of the authorities and feared repression.

On December 5, 1959, an article was published in *Pravda* in which Alexander Osipov, a former archpriest and professor of the Leningrad Theological
Academy, renounced God and the Church. Because he had contracted a second marriage he was forbidden from serving, but not from teaching. In the
morning of the day on which the text of his renunciation was submitted to
Pravda, he still gave lectures in the academy. Although his renunciation may

---

[19]Hieromonk Damaskin (Orlovsky), "The Persecution of the Russian Orthodox Church during
the Soviet Period," in *Orthodox Encyclopedia*, 188.

have seemed sudden and unexpected, Osipov in reality had been an inform-ant for many years and wrote reports to the KGB against his fellow clergy-men, as recent research proves.[20] His renunciation of God was carefully prepared by state security agents over a long period of time. After becoming an atheist, Osipov used his gift for preaching to denounce "religious preju-dices." Thus, from 1960 to 1967 he gave up to 1,000 lectures in 42 regions and republics of the USSR, appeared on radio more than 300 times, published 35 books and brochures, and wrote more than 300 articles and essays.[21] His death was painful and protracted, but even on his death bed he did not cease to declare his atheism: "I do not plan to ask for mercy from the gods."[22] The renunciation of God by Osipov and several other priests dealt a heavy blow to the Church, which nevertheless was not afraid to defrock and excommu-nicate these renegades.

During the Khrushchev years, when the Soviet government pursued a policy of the bloodless destruction of the Church through the forces of athe-ism, which was no longer "militant" as in the 1930s but "scientific," under-pinned by the testimony of renegades and apostates, an important historical role in preserving the Church was played by Metropolitan Nikodim of Leningrad and Novgorod (1929–1978).[23] At the age of eighteen he became a monk, and at thirty-three he headed the diocese of Leningrad, one of the largest in the Russian Church. Being a standing member of the Holy Synod and chairman of the Department of External Church Relations, Metro-politan Nikodim determined the internal and exter-nal policy of the Church to a great extent during the patriarchate of the aged Alexei I. In the early 1960s a change of generations had taken place within the episcopate. Many bishops consecrated before the

Metropolitan Nikodim (Rotov) of Leningrad and Novgorod

---

[20]Cf. S.L. Firsov, *Apostasy: The "Atheist Alexander Osipov" and the Age of the Khrushchev Persecution of the Russian Orthodox Church* (St Petersburg, 2004).

[21]Ibid., 197.

[22]Ibid., 231.

[23]For more on Metropolitan Nikodim, see Juvenaly, Metropolitan of Krutitsa and Kolomna, ed., *A Man of the Church: Dedicated to the Twenty-year Anniversary of the Death and Seventy-year Anniversary of the Birth of His Eminence, the Metropolitan of Leningrad and Novgorod Nikodim (Rotov), Patriarchal Exarch of Western Europe (1929–1978)* (Moscow, 1998).

revolution had passed away, creating a need to find successors. The communist authorities, however, prevented the consecration of young, educated clergymen. Metropolitan Nikodim was able to find a solution to this situation and received permission from the government to consecrate young bishops, justifying this by their necessity for the international peacemaking and ecumenical activities of the Church. In order to forestall the closure of the Leningrad Theological Academy, he created in it a faculty for foreign students, and in order to prevent the mockery of the clergy during Easter processions (which was a common event), Nikodim began to invite foreign delegations to the Easter services. Metropolitan Nikodim saw the expansion of international and ecumenical contacts as one means of protecting the Church from harassment by the godless authorities. In his words he was extremely loyal to them, and in his numerous interviews with the foreign media he denied that the Church was being persecuted. This was the price that had to be paid for the possibility of achieving a gradual rejuvenation of the clergy. Metropolitan Nikodim advocated rapprochement with the Catholic Church, something for which he was criticized by many people. Nevertheless, his outstanding contribution to protecting the Orthodox Church from encroachment by the government was recognized even by his critics.

After Khrushchev resigned and Leonid Brezhnev came to power in 1967, the situation of the Church changed little. Over the next twenty years, the statistics of the Russian Orthodox Church changed only insignificantly: in 1988 the Church had 6,893 parishes, 22 monasteries, 2 theological academies, and 3 seminaries (this was 630 parishes less and 6 monasteries more than in 1966). Although the persecution of the Church was relaxed to a certain extent, the Church remained a social pariah until the end of the 1980s; during this time it was impossible to openly confess one's Christian faith and occupy a position of even relative importance in society. The number of churches, clergymen, seminarians, and monks was strictly controlled, and missionary, educational, and charity work was prohibited. All of the Church's activities were subjected to the extremely rigid control of the Soviet government, which implemented this through the plenipotentiaries of the Council on Religious Affairs, as well as through the highly developed network of the KGB. Clergymen, especially those belonging to the higher ranks, were invited to collaborate with the KGB; in the overwhelming majority of cases this cooperation was forced and purely formal (for example, bishops were obliged to inform the "organs"—either directly or through the local plenipotentiary—about the current affairs of their diocese and receive permission to ordain candidates to the clergy). These were the conditions under which the Church was able to legally exist in the Soviet Union, and clergymen collaborated with the atheist authorities in order to preserve the Church.

THE RUSSIAN DIASPORA IN THE TWENTIETH CENTURY

When speaking of the recent history of the Russian Orthodox Church, it is necessary to mention the part of it that found itself beyond the borders of the homeland after the 1917 revolution. During the 1920s and 1930s, the Russian emigration was divided into three ecclesiastical jurisdictions. The largest group consisted of bishops who had joined the synod headed by Metropolitan Antony (Khrapovitsky). This group broke canonical communion with the Moscow patriarchate during the lifetime of Patriarch Tikhon and was called the Russian Orthodox Church Outside of Russia, or simply the Church Abroad. It was also called the "Karlovtsy schism" by its ideological enemies since its synod was located in the city of Sremskie Karlovtsy in Serbia. Another group was headed by Metropolitan Evlogy (Georgievsky), who separated from the Karlovtsy synod and entered the jurisdiction of the patriarchate of Constantinople. The third group consisted of bishops and clergymen who preserved their loyalty to the Moscow patriarchate. Although the last group was at first the smallest in number, it began to grow after World War II. Relations between these three jurisdictions were marked by fierce antagonism. The most irreconcilable position toward the Moscow patriarchate was taken by

Metropolitan Antony (Khrapovitsky) of Kiev and Galicia

the Church Abroad, which harshly criticized the patriarchate for its collaboration with the godless regime. The Russian exarchate of the patriarchate of Constantinople, although enjoying canonical status, was not in eucharistic communion with the Moscow patriarchate. Dialogue between the Moscow patriarchate and the Russian exarchate began only in the mid-1990s, and with the Church Abroad only at the beginning of the twenty-first century.

During the second and third quarters of the twentieth century, theological thought actively developed in the diaspora—something that was impossible at the time in Russia due to the closure of all institutions of theological education. The St Sergius Institute in Paris, where leading theologians of the Russian diaspora taught, became a major theological center. A group of scholars gathered at and around the institute that would later be called the Paris School of Russian theology. Living outside their homeland, the members of this school continued the traditions of Russian theology under new conditions. Their encounter with the west proved to be fruitful since it encouraged them to reflect upon their own spiritual tradition, which they not only had to defend but also present to the west in a language understandable to it. To a great extent the western world learned about Orthodoxy, which it had known until then only by hearsay, through the works of Russian émigré theologians.

The representatives of the Paris School were able once and for all to overcome the "Babylonian captivity" of Russian theology, which had begun in the seventeenth century through the influence of the Kiev Theological Academy and which had stifled Russian theological thought for more than two centuries by infusing it with the spirit of Latin scholasticism. Although the liberation from this and the return to patristic sources of theology began in Russia in the second half of the nineteenth century, they were completed only in the twentieth century in the works of the Paris School.

Four main groups can be distinguished in this school's theology, each of which is characterized by its particular area of interest and its theological, philosophical, historical, and cultural assumptions.

The first group, which is associated with Archpriest Georges Florovsky (1893–1979), Archbishop Basil (Krivocheine, 1900–1985), Vladimir Lossky (1903–1958), Archimandrite Cyprian (Kern, 1909–1960), and Protopresbyter John Meyendorff (1926–1992), was geared toward the "patristic revival." Guided by the motto "forward to the fathers," they devoted themselves to the study of the legacy of the eastern fathers and revealed to the world the treasures of the Byzantine spiritual and theological tradition, particularly the works of St Symeon the New Theologian and St Gregory Palamas. Florovsky's monumental works *The Eastern Fathers of the Fourth Century* and

The Byzantine Fathers of the Fifth-Eighth Centuries, despite a number of shortcomings (e.g., the lack of a critical apparatus, some superficial assessments, and the insufficient examination of certain themes), still retain their significance as a systematic introduction to the theology of the church fathers. Florovsky's *Ways of Russian Theology* remains the classic introduction to "Russian patristics" and Russian religious thought. Lossky's *The Mystical Theology of the Eastern Church*, *Dogmatic Theology*, and *The Vision of God*, which were written in French, are systematic studies of the main themes of the theology of the eastern church fathers. A number of significant patristic studies were authored by Archbishop Basil, among them *The Ascetic and Theological Teach-*

Georges Florovsky

ing of St Gregory Palamas and *St Symeon the New Theologian*. A broad spectrum of questions is examined in the works of Archimandrite Cyprian, who wrote *The Anthropology of St Gregory Palamas*, *The Eucharist*, and *Orthodox Pastoral Service*. The scholarly legacy of Archpriest John Meyendorff includes monographs in French and English, such as the *Introduction to the Study of St Gregory Palamas*, *Introduction to Patristic Theology*, and *Byzantine Hesychasm*.

The second group laid the groundwork for the "liturgical revival" in the Orthodox Church. This group is associated with the names of such outstanding liturgical scholars as Protopresbyters Nicholas Afanasiev (1893–1966) and Alexander Schmemann (1921–1983). Afanasiev's main work is *The Church of the Holy Spirit*, in which he laid the foundations for the "eucharistic ecclesiology" that would be further developed by Schmemann and the Greek theologian Metropolitan John Zizioulas. The essence of this ecclesiology is its emphasis on the central role of the eucharist in the Church's structure: each eucharistic community, headed by the bishop, is viewed not only as a part of the ecumenical Church but as a local Church, which possesses the fulness of the Church and is united with other local churches through the eucharist. In his books *The Eucharist*, *Great Lent*, *For the Life of the World*, and *Of Water and the Spirit*, as well as in his numerous articles and sermons, Schmemann developed his eucharistic ecclesiology and revealed the treasures of the liturgical tradition of the Orthodox Church.

The third group was characterized by its interest in understanding Russian history, literature, culture, and spirituality. Among its representatives were Archpriest Sergei Chetverikov (1867–1947), Anton Kartashev (1875–1960), George Fedotov (1886–1951), Konstantin Mochulsky (1892–1948), I.M. Kontsevich (1893–1965) and Nicholas Zernov (1898–1980). Archpriest Sergei Chetverikov (from 1942 hieroschemamonk Sergius of the New Valaam Monastery) authored many works on Russian sanctity and contemporary church life such as *The Optina Hermitage*, *The Moldavian Elder Paisy Velichkovsky*, and *The Spiritual Countenance of Father John of Kronstadt and His Pastoral Testament*. While in the diaspora Kartashev, who had been the last oberprocurator of the synod and Minister of Confessions of the Provisional Government, focused his energies on the study of church history. He wrote *The Road to the Ecumenical Council*, *Biblical Criticism of the Old Testament*, *The Rebuilding of Holy Russia*, *Essays on the History of the Russian Church* in two volumes, and *The Ecumenical Councils*. Fedotov, who had been a Marxist earlier and later became a specialist in the western middle ages, focused primarily on Russian church history. He wrote *St Philip: Metropolitan of Moscow*, *Saints of Ancient Rus'*, *Spiritual Poems*, and *The Russian Religious Consciousness: Christianity in Kievan Rus'*. Mochulsky was a philosopher and literary scholar, and wrote studies of Gogol, Dostoyevsky, Soloviev, and the poets of the Silver Age. Kontsevich wrote *The Acquisition of the Holy Spirit in Ancient Rus'* (on Russian sanctity), *Hieroschemamonk Nektary: The Last Optina Elder*, *The Roots of the Spiritual Tragedy of L.N. Tolstoy*, *The Optina Hermitage and its Times*, and *The Northern Thebaid* (on Russian monasticism, in English). Zernov authored numerous works on the history of Orthodoxy, the Russian Church, and the Russian emigration, most of which were written in English. Among these are *Moscow: The Third Rome*, *The Church of the Eastern Christians*, *The Russians and their Church*, *The Ecumenical Church and Russian Orthodoxy*, *Eastern Christendom: A Study of the Origin and Development of the Eastern Orthodox Church*, *At the Turning Point*, *Sunset Years: A Russian Pilgrim in the West*, *Russian Writers of the Emigration*, and *The Russian Religious Renaissance of the Twentieth Century*.

The fourth and final group continued the traditions of Russian religious-philosophical thought. This group included Nicholas Berdyaev (who was examined earlier in connection with the Russian religious renaissance), Nicholas Lossky (1870–1965), B.P. Vysheslavtsev (1877–1954), L.P. Karsavin (1882–1952), I.A. Ilyin (1882–1954), and Archpriest Vasily Zenkovsky (1881–1962).

Nicholas Lossky was a personalist philosopher and the founder of philosophical intuitism; he came out against positivism in philosophy and science and authored *A Substantiation of Intuitivism*, *The World as an Organic Whole*, *The Main Questions of Epistemology*, *Free Will*, *The Conditions for Absolute Good*, and *The World as a Realization of Beauty*. Vysheslavtsev, who wrote *Ethics of a Transformed Eros*, *The Crisis of Industrial Culture*, and *The Eternal in Russian Philosophy*, examined the question of the irrational and the problems of sexual ethics, and criticized the theories of Freud and Jung from the standpoint of Christian ethics. Karsavin, a major philosopher and scholar of culture and medieval history, wrote *The Philosophy of History*; *On First Principles*; *The East, the West, and the Russian Idea*; *On Personality*, and a number of religious and philosophical essays in Russian and Lithuanian. He also developed answers to philosophical questions based on Christian personalism and the theory of all-unity. Ilyin, a prominent philosopher and legal scholar, wrote *The Religious Meaning of Philosophy*, *On Resisting Evil by Force* (against Tolstoy's teaching on pacifism), *The Path of Spiritual Renewal*, and *On the Essence of the Legal Consciousness*. Following the example of Russian writers and thinkers of the nineteenth century, Ilyin examined the phenomena of patriotism and nationalism and wrote on the fate of Russia and the significance of Orthodoxy in its history. The interests of Zenkovsky lay in various aspects of philosophy and psychology (including child and youth psychology). He wrote *The Psychology of Childhood*, *Russian Thinkers and Europe*, *On the Threshold of Maturity*, *Problems of Upbringing in the Light of Christian Anthropology*, *Apologetics*, *N.V. Gogol*, and *The Foundations of Christian Philosophy*. His most significant work, however, was his monumental *History of Russian Philosophy*, in which the Russian philosophical tradition is reflected upon from the standpoint of traditional Orthodoxy.

Other representatives of this current of the Paris School were L.I. Shestov (1866–1938) and S.L. Frank (1907–1950). Although Shestov, who authored *The Apotheosis of Groundlessness* (*An Essay on Adogmatic Thinking*) and numerous works on Chekhov, Dostoyevsky, Tolstoy, Nietzsche, and Berdyaev, was not a Christian, the spectrum of questions examined in his works coincided with those reflected on by representatives of the Russian religious renaissance. Frank wrote *The Object of Knowledge*, *The Human Soul*, *Living Knowledge*, *The Fall of the Idols*, *The Meaning of Life*, *The Spiritual Foundations of Society*, and *The Inscrutable*, as well as articles on Pushkin, Dostoyevsky, and Nietzsche. Frank elaborated on philosophical questions through a Christian prism, although

Sergius Bulgakov

his understanding of God was close to pantheism.

A major figure of Russian Paris was Archpriest Sergius Bulgakov (1871–1944), who belonged simultaneously to several of the currents just mentioned. His works encompass a broad spectrum of questions in the areas of theology, philosophy, and church history. Along with Berdyaev, Bulgakov—the son of a priest and a Marxist in his youth—was one of the leading figures of the Russian religious renaissance at the beginning of the twentieth century. In the diaspora he occupied the chair of dogmatic theology at the St Sergius Orthodox Theological Institute in Paris. In his works the influence of eastern patristics are intertwined with elements of German idealism and the religious views of Vladimir Soloviev and Fr Pavel Florensky. Bulgakov was one of the most brilliant and original theologians of the twentieth century, and authored many monographs on Orthodox theology. Among these are *Unwaning Light*, *The Burning Bush*, *Jacob's Ladder*, *The Lamb of God*, *The Comforter*, *The Bride of the Lamb*, *Philosophy of the Name*, and *Orthodoxy: Essays on the Teaching of the Orthodox Church*.

In his book *Orthodoxy*, Bulgakov attempts to systematize church teaching. This work includes essays on the Church, tradition, the hierarchy, doctrine, the sacraments, the veneration of the Mother of God and the saints, the liturgical services, icon painting, mysticism, ethics, the relationship between Orthodoxy and the state, Orthodoxy and the economy, the apocalypse and eschatology, and Orthodoxy and heterodoxy. Bulgakov stresses that the principle of "Orthodoxy" should not be understood abstractly, outside the context of the historical reality of the Church: "Christianity is a historical religion not only in the sense that it occupies a particular place in the history of humankind, having emerged and developed within this history and being connected to it both externally and internally. It is also a historical religion in the more general sense that the incarnation of God, his indwelling with people, can only occur in the life of this world, by his entering into its temporal context and thus into history . . . Being supra-historical, Christianity is not outside of history but has its own history."[24] It is within the historical

[24]Archpriest Sergius Bulgakov, *Orthodoxy: Essays on the Teaching of the Orthodox Church*, 3d ed. (Paris 1989), 45–46.

context that the meaning of church tradition as the unbroken succession of faith, doctrine, the liturgical services, and church organization has been revealed from apostolic times to the present:

> The fulness of the right faith and right teaching cannot be grasped by the consciousness of an individual member: it is instead preserved by the entire Church and is handed down from generation to generation as the tradition of the Church. This holy tradition is the common form by which the Church preserves the various means of its teaching. Tradition is the living memory of the Church, which preserves the true teaching as it is revealed in its history. It is not an archeological museum or a scientific catalogue, and it is not a dead "deposit" of faith. It is rather a living power inherent in a living organism. During the course of its life it carries its entire past in all of its parts and at all times. The entire past is included in the present and is the present. The unity and continuity of church tradition is established by the self-identity of the Church at all times . . . However different the age of the first Christians may be from ours, we must concede that this is one and the same self-identical Church, which carries all the centuries of its history in the single flow of its tradition and joins together, through its unity of life and community, both the apostle Paul and the local churches that exist today . . . The general principle of tradition holds that every member of the Church, in his life and consciousness . . . should strive for the all-unity of church tradition and examine himself in accordance with it, and in general be a bearer of living tradition, a link that is inseparably joined to the entire chain of history.[25]

A central place in Bulgakov's world view is occupied by his concept of Sophia as a hypostatic principle that serves as an intermediary between the world and God. With regard to God, Sophia is his image, idea, and name; with regard to the world it is the eternal foundation of the world, the world of ideas comprehended by the mind. Bulgakov's sophiology, which represented a further development of the ideas of Soloviev and Florensky, was condemned in 1935 by Metropolitan Sergius and his synod (it was also condemned several years before by the Karlovtsy synod). This was the final verdict against sophiology, with which Vladimir Soloviev had infected Russian theological and philosophical thought for several decades. Moreover, Bul-

[25]Ibid., 47–48.

gakov's teaching was mercilessly criticized by Vladimir Lossky[26] and a number of other theologians of the Russian diaspora, who in their works declared Bulgakov's sophiology foreign to the Orthodox Church.

During the 1950s some members of the Paris school emigrated one after another from France to America. These were Archpriests Georges Florovsky, Alexander Schmemann, and John Meyendorff. All three successively held the office of dean of St Vladimir's Orthodox Theological Seminary in New York, which under their leadership became a leading center of Orthodox theology in North America.

Archimandrite Sophrony (Sakharov)

One theologian who was close to the Paris school—although he went considerably beyond it—was Archimandrite Sophrony (Sakharov; 1896–1993), author of the book *Starets Silouan*, devoted to St Silouan of Mount Athos (†1937), an outstanding ascetic of the twentieth century. Archimandrite Sophrony lived on Mount Athos for many years, serving as a disciple and cell attendant of St Silouan, before moving to Paris and then to England in the 1960s, where he founded the monastery of St John the Baptist. The main theme of Archimandrite Sophrony's theology is God as a personal being and communion with God as an encounter between the personal God and the human personality. In Christ, God is revealed to man as a personal being. Only God himself is personal in the full sense of the word, while man is a person only inasmuch as he is the image and likeness of the personal God. By fulfilling the commandments of Christ and through prayer for the world and love for one's enemies, man can realize his personal potential and even become like God:

> God is love, and the human person is gifted with the ability to receive the flame of this love from God. God is Light, in which there is no darkness, and we are called on to become light in the divine eternity. Everything is completely open to God, and He knows everything without exception.

[26]See his article "The Debate on Sophia," in V.N. Lossky, *Theology and the Vision of God: Collected Articles* (Moscow, 2000), 390–484.

And the human hypostasis, included in the Act of Divine Existence, becomes a bearer of omniscience through God and in God . . . The person is a created hypostasis, although in his inner essence as the image of the Absolute God he is a kind of universal centre, great and marvelous in its final completion through the Son, who is co-unoriginate with the Father.[27]

The works of Archimandrite Sophrony reflect a tradition that goes back to the spiritual experience of St Symeon the New Theologian and the hesychasts of the fourteenth century. One of the elements of this experience is the contemplation of the divine light. In his book *On Prayer*, Fr Sophrony relates his personal experience of contemplation: "I was vouchsafed to contemplate the Divine Light more than once. Enveloped tenderly by it, I was filled with unearthly love. In some instances the world lost its material nature and became invisible."[28] Following Gregory Palamas, Archimandrite Sophrony maintained that the divine light contemplated by ascetics is God himself, in his revelation to the human spirit:

The Heavenly Light defies sensual control. Being different and elusive in its nature, it comes in a manner that is undefinable for us . . . Originating from the One Essence, this Light leads to the single knowledge of the God of Love . . . It is not without fear that the soul decides to speak of the Light which visits those who thirst to see the Face of the Unoriginate One. Its nature is mystical; in what images can one describe it? Ineffable and invisible, it is sometimes visible to these bodily eyes. Quiet and tender, it attracts to itself both the heart and the mind, so that one forgets the earth when one is taken up into the other world. This occurs in both broad daylight and during the darkness of night. Although meek, he is mightier than all that surrounds us. He envelops the person in a strange manner from without: one sees him but one's attention penetrates deep into the innermost self, into the heart warmed by love . . . Sometimes one does not feel matter: neither one's own, nor the reality surrounding us, and one sees oneself as if one were light . . . This holy light, which manifests its power, brings with it humble love, banishes all doubt and fear, and leaves all earthly cares far behind . . . It gives our spirit knowledge of

[27]Archimandrite Sophrony (Sakharov), *We Shall See Him As He Is* (Essex, 1985), 204.
[28]Archimandrite Sophrony (Sakharov), *On Prayer* (Paris, 1991), 54–55.

another Existence that defies description; the mind stands still, having transcended thought by entering into a new form of life . . . Our spirit triumphs: this Light is God, almighty and at the same time ineffably meek. Oh, with what care does he treat the person! He heals hearts crushed by despair; he inspires souls marred by sin with hopes of victory.[29]

Metropolitan Anthony (Bloom) of Sourozh

A special place among the Russian émigré theologians of the twentieth century is occupied by Metropolitan Anthony of Sourozh (Bloom; 1914–2003), who was widely revered for his sermons, talks, and radio programs devoted primarily to questions of Christian morality. One hallmark of Metropolitan Anthony's activities was that he almost never wrote anything: the majority of his publications are actually edited transcripts of talks that he held over the course of more than fifty years in the Russian Orthodox cathedral in London. His *Discussions on Faith and the Church*, *On the Encounter*, *God and Man*, *School of Prayer*, and *Works* are also collections of talks he gave on various topics relating to the spiritual life. From the 1960s to the 1980s Metropolitan Anthony was perhaps the only "free" theologian whose voice—through programs of BBC Radio and many *samizdat* editions—reached Russia, which was still in the clutches of state atheism at the time.

THE REBIRTH OF THE RUSSIAN ORTHODOX CHURCH

Significant changes in the Russian Orthodox Church took place beginning in 1985, when Mikhail Gorbachev came to power in the USSR and began the policies of *glasnost* and *perestroika*. For the first time in many decades the Church began to emerge from its forced isolation, and its leaders started to appear in public forums. The celebration of the millennium of the baptism of Russia in 1988, which was originally conceived as only a church event, turned into a national festival that bore witness to the vitality of the Ortho-

---

[29] *We Shall See Him As He Is*, 154–59.

The 1990 national council of the Russian Orthodox Church

dox Church, undaunted by persecution, and to the high degree of authority it enjoyed in the eyes of the people. The second mass baptism of Russia, which continues to this day, began with this jubilee celebration. In the late 1980s and early 1990s, millions of people throughout the entire Soviet Union embraced the Orthodox faith. In large urban churches dozens and even hundreds of people were baptized daily, and one priest might baptize several thousand people over the course of a year.

The year 1990 was an important milestone in the life of the Russian Orthodox Church. On May 3 of that year His Holiness Patriarch Pimen, who had headed the Church for eighteen years, passed away. In June a national council of the Russian Orthodox Church was held in the Trinity-St Sergius Lavra with the participation of 317 delegates, including 90 bishops, 92 clergymen, and 88 laypersons. After three rounds of voting Metropolitan Alexei (Ridiger) of Leningrad and Novgorod, one of the most experienced and authoritative hierarchs, who had served as administrator of the Moscow patriarchate for many years, was elected to the patriarchal throne. With his election began a new chapter in the life of the Church.

The years of his service as patriarch witnessed the rapid growth of the Church, which had begun in the late 1980s. While the Russian Orthodox Church counted approximately 7,000 parishes in 1988, by the end of 1989 there were around 11,000, by the end of 1994 around 16,000, by late 1997 about 18,000, by the end of 2000 approximately 19,500, and by late 2006 more than

27,000. In comparison with 1988, by 2007 the number of dioceses of the Russian Orthodox Church had doubled, the number of parishes and parish clergy more than quadrupled, and the number of monasteries increased by a factor of thirty-five. Patriarch Alexei's report to a meeting of the clergy of the diocese of Moscow in December 2006 mentioned 136 dioceses and 171 bishops, of whom 131 were diocesan and 40 vicar bishops, not including 13 retired hierarchs. There were 713 active monasteries, of which 208 mens and 235 womens monasteries were in Russia and 89 mens and 84 womens monasteries were in the Ukraine. The CIS and Baltic states counted 38 mens and 54 womens monasteries, and there were 2 mens and 3 womens monasteries abroad. The total number of parishes of the Russian Orthodox Church in Russia, the CIS, and the Baltic states reached 27,393, and the total number of clergy 29,450.[30]

According to statistics, approximately 70 percent of Russia's population considered themselves members of the Russian Orthodox Church. The majority of believers in the Ukraine, Belarus, and Moldova belong to the Moscow patriarchate, and in the Baltic states (Estonia, Latvia, and Lithuania) and Central Asia (Kazakhstan, Uzbekistan, Kyrgyzstan, Tajikistan, and Turkmenistan) the majority of Orthodox believers belong to the Russian Orthodox Church. According to certain statistics, the total number of members of the Russian Church in Russia, in the aforementioned countries, as well as outside them, is approximately 160 million—more than those of all other local Orthodox churches combined.

The unprecedented quantitative growth of the Russian Orthodox Church in the late twentieth and early twenty-first century was also accompanied by radical changes in its sociopolitical status in Russia and in the other states of the former USSR. For the first time in more than seventy years the Church once again became an integral part of society, a recognized spiritual and moral force wielding considerable authority. For the first time in many centuries the Church acquired the right to determine its place in society and its relations with the state without interference from the secular authorities. For the first time the Church was granted a broad spectrum of possibilities for educational, missionary, social, charity, and publishing activities.

This change of status required from the Church and its servants great efforts to overcome the "ghetto mentality" that had been formed during the

---

[30]"Report of His Holiness Alexei, Patriarch of Moscow and All Russia, at the Diocesan Meeting of the City of Moscow," December 5, 2006.

long years of its forced isolation. While in former times the servants of the Church had to deal only with their parishioners, who thought in the same categories that they did, they now faced the challenge of coming to terms with an enormous number of people who had no experience of the Church and only rudimentary or absolutely no knowledge of religion. While in former times priests did not preach beyond the walls of their church, they now had a multitude of opportunities to appear on television, radio, and in the printed media. While for decades society and the Church had lived their separate lives, the Church now found itself drawn into society's discussions of fundamental problems of the times.

Beginning in the late 1980s the state began to return church buildings to the Church, which had to restore them at its own cost or through the voluntary donations of the faithful, as it received no regular subsidies from the state. A significant event in the life of the Church was the restoration of the Cathedral of Christ the Savior from 1995 to 2000. This cathedral was originally built in the nineteenth century in honor of the soldiers who had died in the War of 1812. Erected through donations from the people over the course of forty-six years, it became an outstanding architectural monument of its age. After the cathedral was blown up by the Bolsheviks, plans were made to construct a gigantic "Palace of Soviets" in its place, topped by a statue of Lenin. The foundation pit for the building was dug but the building was never constructed. Finally the pit was filled with water, and in place of the Cathedral of Christ the Savior was built the Moscow swimming pool. At the end of the 1980s debates began over the cathedral's restoration, and a bishops council of 1994 took the decision to rebuild the cathedral. In January 1995 the foundation was laid, and five years later, in the jubilee year 2000, the cathedral was consecrated.

Between 1988 and 2004 more than six hundred monasteries were reopened, including all the major historic centers of Russian monasticism: the Kiev Caves Lavra, the Donskoy and Novodevichy monasteries in Moscow, the Alexander Nevsky Lavra in St Petersburg, the Optina hermitage, and the Valaam, Solovetsky, Kirillo-Belozersky, and Diveevo monasteries. The majority of them were raised from ruins, and many were completely rebuilt. Several monasteries, including the Trinity-St Sergius Lavra and the Moscow Sretensky monastery, conduct wide-ranging educational activities and have major publishing houses. Some of them conduct charity and missionary work. The majority of monks and nuns are middle aged or younger, and there is a lack of elderly monks and experienced spiritual guides. The tradition of eldership (*starchestvo*) in the Russian Church never ceased completely, even during the years of persecution; however, there are only a small handful of spiritually experienced *startsy* today. Among the most respected elders in the Russian Orthodox Church are Archimandrite Kirill (Pavlov), spiritual father of the Trinity-St Sergius Lavra, Archimandrite Ioann (Krestiankin) of the Pskov Caves monastery, and schema-hegumen Eli, spiritual father of the Optina hermitage.

In the 1990s, theological seminaries and schools were opened in many dioceses. By December 2006 the Russian Orthodox Church had five theological academies (Moscow, St Petersburg, Kiev, Minsk, and Moldova), two Orthodox universities, two theological institutes, thirty-seven seminaries, thirty-eight lower-level theological schools, and in one diocese pastoral courses.[31] Moscow hosts the St Tikhon Orthodox Humanities University and the Russian Orthodox University of St John the Theologian. Moreover, there are chairs of theology in twenty-one Russian institutions of higher education, which implement the state educational standards for theology adopted in 2001.

One of the problems of the newly opened theological schools is the lack of highly qualified instructors who can help raise the academic level of these institutions. Teachers of theological schools are often graduates of the very same institution—a situation that does not encourage the qualitative improvement of the educational level since a graduate cannot teach students anything essentially new if he has not studied elsewhere. However, over the past years the number of students educated at foreign theological institutions and at theological faculties of secular universities has grown. Study abroad is helping the Church to overcome the gap that exists between Russian and foreign theological scholarship, which emerged as a result of the forced isolation of Russian theology during the seventy years of communist rule.

The expansion of the Russian Orthodox Church not only affected the states of the former Soviet Union but also nations in other parts of the world, where the number of parishes grew many times from 1988 to 2006. Due to the influx of Russian-speaking immigrants from the former Soviet Union, new parishes were opened in Germany, France, Italy, Great Britain, the Scandina-

[31]Ibid.

vian countries, Latin America, Australia, and southeast Asia. In 2004 the first Orthodox church was built in the Antarctic. As of September 1, 2004, there were 277 institutions of the Moscow patriarchate in 42 countries, including 8 dioceses, 1 mission, patriarchal parishes in the United States, Canada, and Finland, 16 monasteries, 1 skete, 10 chapels, and 46 stavropegial parishes.[32] Since 1989 the external affairs of the Church have been managed by Metropolitan Kirill of Smolensk and Kaliningrad, who is also responsible for the foreign parishes of the Moscow patriarchate.

A highly important task of the patriarch and the Holy Synod in this period has been the preservation of church unity in the face of schisms and other challenges. In the late 1980s the situation of the Church worsened considerably in the western Ukraine, where the Uniate Church banned by Stalin in 1946 began to reemerge. By itself the rebirth of the Uniate Church was a sign that the religious freedom necessary for the normal coexistence of all Christian confessions had reappeared—something that might have helped restore historical justice. Instead, however, efforts were made to compensate for one historical injustice by another, since the revival of Uniate structures in the western Ukraine was accompanied by violence on the part of the Greek Catholics, who unilaterally left the negotiating table and began to seize churches en masse. Due to the actions of Greek Catholics three Orthodox dioceses—those of Lvov, Ivano-Frankovsk, and Ternopol—were reduced to a fraction of their original size.

In autumn 1989 a schism within the Orthodox Church in the Ukraine emerged when the UAOC (Ukrainian Autocephalous Orthodox Church) was formed, headed by "metropolitan" and later "patriarch" Mstislav (Skrypnik). This group is frequently referred to as the "autocephalists." In 1992 the Orthodox Church in the Ukraine was again shaken by another schism that appeared as a result of the actions of Metropolitan Philaret (Denisenko) of Kiev and Galicia. Until then he had occupied the Kievan see of the Moscow patriarchate. Under pressure from Ukrainian hierarchs at the bishops council held in Moscow in April 1992, he swore an oath to resign. After returning to the Ukraine, however, Philaret reneged on his oath and proceeded to create a schismatic structure that he called the UOC-KP ("Ukrainian Orthodox Church—Kiev Patriarchate"). In the "Kiev patriarchate" Philaret at first occu-

[32]"Report of Metropolitan Kirill of Smolensk and Kaliningrad, Chairman of the DECR," at the bishops council of 2004.

pied the post of "patriarchal deputy," but in 1995, after the mysterious death of "patriarch" Vladimir (Romanyuk), Philaret assumed the title of "patriarch of Kiev and all Russia-Ukraine." The Moscow patriarchate at first forbade him from serving, then defrocked him, and finally excommunicated him. Philaret's "patriarchate" is quantitatively the largest schism in the Ukraine: it counts more than 3,000 parishes (compared to the 10,000 parishes of the Ukrainian Orthodox Church of the Moscow patriarchate and the 1,000 parishes of the "autocephalists").

Local schisms also appeared on the territory of Russia. In 1990 the Russian Orthodox Church Abroad began to open parishes in the former Soviet Union. In many instances, former clergymen of the Moscow patriarchate who had been forbidden to serve due to canonical violations or certain vices were appointed to these parishes. Some of these clergymen later left the Church Abroad and founded their own ecclesiastical groups. One example is the ROAC ("Russian Orthodox Autonomous Church") headed by "metropolitan" Valentin (Rusantsov). Several other schisms remain highly marginal phenomena and do not represent any significant threat to church unity, and some have already ceased to exist.

During the 1990s several bishops councils were held in Moscow to deal with various aspects of the revival of church life in the former Soviet Union, to heal schisms, and to resolve current problems.

A milestone in the history of the Russian Orthodox Church was the Jubilee Bishops Council of 2000, whose significance was comparable to that of the national council of 1917–1918. The main highlight of the council was the canonization of all the new martyrs and confessors of Russia—all who were repressed by the Soviet authorities and sacrificed their lives for the faith in the twentieth century. Of the many canonized, more than a thousand were mentioned by name: these were people whose lives had been researched by the Commission for the Canonization of Saints and whose martyrdom had been documented. In canonizing these martyrs, the Church pronounced its assessment of the most tragic period in Russian history. A special place among these new martyrs was occupied by the last Russian emperor, Nicholas II, and his family. For the Church, the canonization of the last emperor and his family was not politically motivated; they were canonized because they had shared the fate of their people and met their deaths with humility, as true Christians and righteous people.

Another important event at the Jubilee Bishops Council was the adoption of the "Basic Principles of the Attitude of the Russian Orthodox Church to the Non-Orthodox." This document reflects the experience of the Orthodox Church's cooperation with other Christian confessions in the twentieth century and outlines the path for its further development. It formulates the principles, aims, and duties of the Russian Orthodox Church in its relations with non-Orthodox Christians and provides criteria for its membership in international Christian organizations.

The council also adopted a detailed document entitled "The Bases of the Social Conception of the Russian Orthodox Church." This document is unique because it deals with almost all the problems the Orthodox Church faces in our times. It is the first of its kind not only in the history of the Russian Orthodox Church but also in the annals of world Orthodoxy. The "Bases" examines a broad spectrum of issues, such as the Church and the nation, the Church and the state, Christian ethics and secular law, the Church and politics, labor and its fruits, property, war and peace, crime and punishment, personal and social morality, bioethics, ecology, secular culture, science, education, the Church and the mass media, international relations, globalization, and secularism. The "Bases" were designed to offer spiritual and moral guidance for both the clergy and laity of the Russian Church, and its moral demands are obligatory not only for clergymen but also for laypersons of the Church.

In 2004 a bishops council was held to deal with the question of relations with the Russian Church Abroad. The council approved the policy of rapprochement with this Church that had been pursued since the beginning of the twenty-first century. Earlier, over the course of many decades, the leadership of the Russian Church Abroad took an irreconcilable stance toward the Moscow patriarchate, which it accused of collaboration with the Soviet authorities and considered to be without grace. The situation did not change even after the fall of the communist regime and the breakup of the USSR. Only after the first hierarch of the Russian Church Abroad, Metropolitan Vitaly (Ustinov), retired in 2001 did official contacts with the Moscow patriarchate begin. Under its new first hierarch, Metropolitan Laurus (Shkurla), the Church Abroad adopted a policy of rapprochement with the Moscow patriarchate. This led Metropolitan Vitaly to establish a new church structure—the so-called "Russian Orthodox Church in Exile."

Some time later, in October 2003, Russian President Vladimir Putin delivered an invitation from Patriarch Alexei of Moscow to Metropolitan Laurus.
From November 18 to 19 of the same year an official delegation of the Church
Abroad arrived in Moscow and met with the patriarch and other leading hierarchs of the Moscow patriarchate, and in 2004 Metropolitan Laurus visited
Moscow. Negotiations began thereafter with the aim of eliminating obstacles
to the restoration of eucharistic communion. These efforts were approved at
the All-Diaspora Council in May 2006.

In November 2006, special commissions of the Moscow patriarchate and
the Church Abroad approved the text of the "Act of Canonical Communion," which entered into force after it was signed by the patriarch of Moscow
and the first hierarch of the Church Abroad. According to the act, the Russian Orthodox Church Abroad would become an "indissoluble, self-governing part of the Local Russian Orthodox Church," preserving its
independence in "pastoral, educational, administrative, economic, property,
and civil matters." The supreme spiritual, legal, administrative, judicial, and
controlling authority in the Russian Orthodox Church Outside of Russia is
its own synod. The first hierarch of this Church is elected by its synod; this
election, however, is subject to confirmation by the patriarch of Moscow and
the Holy Synod of the Russian Orthodox Church. The bishops of the Russian Orthodox Church Outside of Russia are members of the national and
bishops councils of the Russian Orthodox Church. The supreme ecclesiastical authorities of the Russian Church Abroad are the national and bishops
councils of the Russian Orthodox Church.

The Act of Canonical Communion was signed on May 17, 2007 by Patriarch Alexei and Metropolitan Laurus. On the same day the first concelebra-
tion at the Divine Liturgy by hierarchs of the Moscow patriarchate and the
Church Abroad took place in the Cathedral of Christ the Savior. This marked
the end of a schism that had lasted for approximately eighty years.

Despite the fact that many problems facing the Church at the end of the
twentieth and beginning of the twenty-first century have been successfully
resolved, an entire array of challenges remain. The Orthodox Church now
enjoys the right to conduct charity activities unhindered. Nevertheless, the
scale of church charity work is incommensurate with that of the social misfortunes requiring its attention. To a great extent this is due to the fact that the
Church still lacks a stable financial foundation that would allow it to conduct

The signing of the Act of Canonical Communion at the Cathedral of Christ the Savior

a broad spectrum of charitable activities. Before 1917 the Church was a major landowner and possessed a colossal amount of real estate, but all this property was nationalized after the revolution and its restitution has not yet taken place. The state has returned many church buildings, but only for the Church to use, not possess. In practice, this usually means that the Church must restore at its own cost buildings that deteriorated into ruins during Soviet times, but that these buildings remain state property even after restoration.

Unlike countries where church property was not nationalized (e.g., Austria) or where it was restored to the Church (e.g., Lithuania), the Church possesses no real estate—neither in Russia, nor in the Ukraine, nor in the majority of the post-Soviet states—that it might use to derive income. Unlike other countries where a church tax is collected (such as Germany), the Church in Russia is itself heavily taxed. The Church's main source of income is still voluntary donations by the faithful. However, these donations are not enough to allow it to conduct a wide range of charity and social work; only individual projects funded by private sponsors are possible.

Other problems concern the educational activities of the Russian Orthodox Church, which have not reached the scale that they otherwise might have. The debate in Russia at the beginning of the twenty-first century over the teaching of the "Foundations of Orthodox Culture" in state schools has demonstrated that a certain part of society is not morally ready for the Church to become a full-fledged partner of the state in the public school system. Fears have been voiced that the teaching of religious subjects in schools would violate the secular character of the state educational system and cause religious tensions. However, there is complete mutual understanding on this question among representatives of traditional religions: the leaders of the main non-Christian confessions in Russia have spoken out in favor of teaching the foundations of Orthodoxy in those regions where it is the religion of the majority. Discontent with the Church's desire to teach religion to children can be observed only among nonreligious people, who according to various statistics constitute around 20 percent of Russian society.

After long and heated debate, the state finally recognized the right of schools to teach the "Foundations of Orthodox Culture" as an elective. Moreover, standards were elaborated for accrediting theology degrees offered by institutions of higher education. All of this has opened up new possibilities for the Church's educational efforts. This, however, raised another question: does the Church have the necessary strength and will to take advantage of these new possibilities? So far it has not—a fact that Patriarch Alexei spoke about critically in his address to the Moscow clergy in March 2003:

> The missionary and catechetical activities in the parishes are, like in Soviet times, still limited almost exclusively to churches and parish schools. This is still the case despite the fact that there are many other possibilities to convincingly bear witness to the Orthodox faith and Orthodox culture. In addition to the places where catechetical and educational activities are currently being conducted, there are also secular educational institutions of all levels where we can and must organize Orthodox Christian electives, lecture cycles, and pastoral talks with the permission of the administration of these institutions. It is also possible to organize these outside the framework of the main academic process. But because of our inertia and laziness we do not fulfil the commandment of the Lord: "Go therefore and make disciples of all the nations . . . teaching them to observe all things that I have commanded you" (Mt 28.19–20). As we know, a holy place is never left empty, and the vacuum that has appeared due to our indecisiveness is being filled by sectarians and members of other confessions, who can be seen everywhere, from orphanages to elderly care facilities, from schools to universities and academies.[33]

[33]"Report of His Holiness Alexei, Patriarch of Moscow and All Russia, at the Diocesan Gathering of the City of Moscow," December 23, 2003.

Sects and the so-called "new religious movements" present a challenge to the Orthodox Church and other traditional religions, tearing away their potential flock. According to some statistics, there are more than 5,000 sects active in Russia, the largest being the Jehovah's Witnesses, who count 150,000 members. Other large groups are the Church of Scientology, the Neo-Pentecostals, and Sun Myung Moon's Unification Church. Many sects are destructive in character and damage the psyches of their followers. The number of satanic sects, which encourage their members to commit monstrous crimes, is also on the rise. The Russian Orthodox Church has established centers to rehabilitate victims of destructive sects and fight against sectarianism.

THE ANCIENT EASTERN PATRIARCHATES TODAY

The twentieth century witnessed colossal political upheavals and a massive migration of peoples that changed the ethnic and religious makeup of all five continents. The revolutionary events that took place in the 1910s in a number of European states, as well as World War I and the breakup of the Russian, German, Ottoman, and Austro-Hungarian empires, all led to major geopolitical changes that significantly altered the structure of world Orthodoxy.

In the twentieth century the territory of the patriarchate of Constantinople, which had been limited for several centuries to the Ottoman empire, changed considerably. A mighty blow was dealt to this patriarchate by the Asia Minor Catastrophe of 1922, when Greek troops suffered defeat against Turkey and the Turks slaughtered a part of the then two-million-strong Greek population of Asia Minor. In accordance with the Treaty of Lausanne of 1923, the Greeks of Asia Minor were repatriated to Greece; many of them, however, died on the way. The Greek population that remained in Istanbul was subjected to violence and repression. In 1955 a pogrom took place, during which three-fourths of the Orthodox churches in Istanbul were desecrated and looted. In the following years Greeks continued to flee from Turkey, and by the early 1990s the Greek population of Istanbul numbered no more than three thousand. The buildings of the patriarchate in the Phanar were subject to constant attack by Turkish nationalists, who contested the international status of the patriarchate of Constantinople and its "ecumenical" title by invoking the Treaty of Lausanne, which only viewed the patriarch as the

leader of the Greek Orthodox minority in Turkey. Some of the refugees from
Asia Minor settled in Greece, while others emigrated to various countries in
Europe, as well as to the United States and Australia. Thus a large Greek diaspora emerged, which recognized the patriarch of Constantinople as its spiritual leader.

Although the patriarch of Constantinople had been the primate of the
Orthodox Church of the Byzantine empire for an entire millennium and
then the spiritual leader of the Greek population of the Ottoman empire for
more than five hundred years, the patriarchate had to redefine its new role
in the Orthodox world after the fall of the Ottoman empire in 1922. This task
was accomplished by Patriarch Meletios IV (Metaxakis), who occupied the
patriarchal throne from 1921 to 1923. He was the first to formulate the teaching on the jurisdictional rights of the Constantinople patriarch over the
entire Orthodox diaspora, that is, over all countries not within the territory
of a local Orthodox church. In March 1922 the synod of the Church of Constantinople decided to bring under its obligatory and exclusive jurisdiction
all Orthodox parishes and dioceses located outside countries with local
Orthodox churches. This idea, which has not been accepted by the majority
of other local churches, now defines the foreign policy of the Constantinople patriarchate.

In accord with ancient tradition, the jurisdiction of the patriarchate of
Constantinople encompasses all monasteries on Mount Athos, including the
Russian, Serbian, and Bulgarian houses. The twentieth century was a time of
severe trials for Athos. At the beginning of the century several thousand
monks lived on the Holy Mountain, of whom more than one-half were Russians. The monastery of St Panteleimon alone housed around 1,500 monks,
and the same number, if not more, lived in the Russian sketes. In 1913, due to
the banishment of the name-worshipers, the number of Russian monks was
reduced to less than 1,000. After the outbreak of World War I the influx of
Russians to Athos basically came to a halt. By the early 1960s the Russian
monastic houses on Athos were practically empty, and only 14 monks
remained in the St Panteleimon monastery. Until the early 1970s the number
of monastics in the Greek monasteries also decreased. In 1971 there were 1,145
Athonite monks in total, the majority of whom were weak and elderly. However, beginning in 1972 the average age of the Athonite monks gradually
dropped and their number steadily increased. In the Greek monasteries of the

African children being baptized in a river.

Holy Mountain this process was connected to the activity of several abbots who fostered the spiritual renewal there. In the Russian monastery the influx of monks was renewed in the 1960s thanks to the efforts of Metropolitan Nikodim of Leningrad and Novgorod, who obtained permission from the Greek authorities and the patriarchate of Constantinople to increase the quota of Russian monastics on the Holy Mountain.

By the early twentieth century the ancient patriarchate of Alexandria, which had lived for nine centuries under Arab rule (640–1517) and almost three centuries under the Ottomans (1517–1798), counted approximately 100,000 faithful of Greek, Arab, and Syrian extraction. After Meletios (Metaxakis), the former Constantinople patriarch, became patriarch of Alexandria in 1926, the patriarchate began to conduct wide-ranging missionary work among the local African population. Thanks to these efforts, which continue even today, the number of faithful of the patriarchate of Alexandria at the end of the twentieth century exceeded one million, and continues to grow. In Egypt the Alexandrian patriarchate coexists alongside the quantitatively much larger Coptic Church. The patriarchate's flock encompasses many nationalities: alongside Greeks, Arabs, and Syrians, it includes the local populations of African nations.

At the beginning of the twentieth century, the patriarchate of Antioch, which had existed under Arab, Seljuk Turk, and Mameluk rule and whose territory had also been part of the Ottoman empire for four centuries (1516–1918), counted around 350,000 faithful in Syria and Lebanon. After the Treaty of Lausanne, part of the territories of the patriarchate of Antioch found themselves within Turkey, and Orthodox Arabs were deported from these lands together with their Greek coreligionists. Due to mass immigration to Europe, the United States, and Australia, a large Arab Orthodox diaspora emerged and placed itself canonically under the patriarchate of Antioch. By the end of the twentieth century the patriarchate of Antioch had around 500,000 faithful in Syria and approximately 300,000 in Lebanon. This, however, is only about one-half of the patriarchate's total flock, which is scattered throughout the world.

During the twentieth century, the size of the flock of the Jerusalem patriarchate did not change significantly. At present it counts approximately 150,000 faithful. The majority of its flock are Orthodox Arabs living in Israel, Palestine, and Jordan; the patriarchate's administration, however, is dominated by Greeks. The archdiocese of Sinai, which encompasses the brotherhood of the monastery of St Catherine on Mount Sinai, Egypt, is an autonomous church within the patriarchate of Jerusalem. The right of the patriarch of Jerusalem to take up his office is confirmed by the secular authorities of Israel, Palestine, and Jordan. Relations between the Jerusalem patriarchate and the Israeli authorities are tense because of the Israeli state's attempts to interfere in the affairs of the Church.

Also within the territory of Israel are the Russian Ecclesiastical Mission and the Mount of Olives Convent, which are under the direct jurisdiction of the patriarch of Moscow. The emigration of Jews from the Soviet Union and the post-Soviet states from the 1970s to 1990s led to a significant growth of the Moscow patriarchate's flock in Israel, since many of the ethnic Jews who emigrated were Orthodox Christians. Pastoral care for them is conducted by the Russian Ecclesiastical Mission and the church institutions under its jurisdiction, with the permission of the patriarchate of Jerusalem.

ORTHODOXY IN EUROPE

The fate of the Orthodox churches in Europe has differed, depending on political developments in the countries in which they found themselves. During the twentieth century the communist and atheist regimes that held sway in eastern Europe until the 1990s wrought terrible havoc on Orthodoxy.

The Georgian Orthodox Church is one of the most ancient Orthodox churches. In the fourth century it was under the canonical jurisdiction of the see of Antioch, but in the fifth century it became autocephalous.[34] In the fifth century the first hierarch of the Georgian Church began to be called catholicos, and in the eleventh century catholicos-patriarch. In 1811 the Georgian Church became an exarchate within the Russian Orthodox Church. The Georgian Church joined the Russian Orthodox Church as a direct result of Georgia's incorporation into the Russian empire. Although the autocephaly of the Georgian Church was restored in 1917, the Russian Orthodox Church did not recognize the declaration of autocephaly and the election of the new catholicos. Because of this, canonical communion between the churches of Georgia and Russia was broken. In 1943 the Russian Church recognized the Georgian Church's autocephaly; Constantinople accepted it only in 1990.

After Georgia joined the USSR in 1921, the Georgian Church found itself in the same situation as the Russian Church. The Church of Georgia also suffered from the Bolshevik repression of religion, the Stalinist terror, and the persecution of the Khrushchev era. During the 1920s and 1930s many bishops, clergymen, and monks underwent repression or were shot. Monastic life almost died out, and many ancient monasteries and churches were reduced to ruins. The number of churches decreased during the Soviet period. While there were 2,455 churches in Georgia in 1917, there were less than 100 in the 1980s.

Church life was renewed to a certain extent after the election in 1977 of Patriarch Elias II, who gathered around himself the Orthodox intelligentsia and youth. Still, the full-fledged revival of church life began only after the breakup of the Soviet Union and Georgia's independence. The number of dioceses grew significantly and more than fifty monasteries, as well as theological schools, were reopened. At the end of the twentieth century the Geor-

---

[34]The exact date of the autocephaly of the Georgian Church has caused difficulties for scholars. See K. Skurat, *History of the Local Orthodox Churches* (Moscow, 1994), 1.38–42.

Elias II, Catholicos of Georgia

gian Orthodox Church counted more than five hundred parishes and thirty dioceses. The total number of faithful is estimated at three million.

The Georgian Church acquired the status of state church after the nation gained independence. The special position of the Church is reflected in the Constitutional Agreement signed by the patriarch and the president in 2002. According to this document Orthodoxy is the state religion of Georgia, the Georgian Constitution recognizes the special status of the Georgian Church, the catholicos-patriarch enjoys political immunity, and major church feast days are proclaimed national holidays. The state supports the inviolability of the seal of confession and of the secrets of the Church, recognizes church marriages, and exempts the clergy from military service. The state recognizes as church property all monasteries, churches, ruins, and plots of land on which they are located, as well as all church valuables, including those displayed in museums.[35] This document is the only "concordat" that has been concluded between the authorities of an independent state and an Orthodox Church.

The Serbian Orthodox Church has enjoyed autocephaly since 1219 and the status of a patriarchate since 1346. After the Turks conquered Serbia in the fifteenth century the Serbian patriarchate, located in Pech, was abolished, and the Serbian Church was placed under the jurisdiction of the archdiocese of Ochrid. In the mid-sixteenth century the patriarchate of Pech was restored, only to be abolished once again in 1766 on decree of the sultan, and the Serbian Church in the Ottoman empire was placed under the patriarch of Constantinople. All ethnic Serb bishops were forced to relinquish their sees, which were then occupied by Greeks. The Serbs living within the Austro-Hungarian empire joined the autocephalous metropolia of Karlovtsy in 1695, which was canonically independent from Constantinople.

After the end of World War I, when the Kingdom of Serbs, Croats, and Slovenes was founded, the autocephaly of the Serbian Orthodox Church was restored. This took place at a council in 1919 that was attended by Serbian bishops belonging to various jurisdictions. In 1920 the first hierarch of the

[35]For the full text of the agreement see ibid., 221–26.

Serbian Church was elevated to the rank of patriarch.

The Serbian Orthodox Church underwent
severe trials during World War I. The situation was
particularly difficult in Croatia, where the fascist
regime of the Ustasha leader A. Pavelich conducted
genocide—with the connivance of the local Catholic
Church—against more than one-half of the Orthodox population. In Montenegro the Orthodox population was almost completely exterminated during
the war years. From the beginning of the war until
May 9, 1945 the Serbian Church lost 9 bishops and
544 priests. Many bishops were interned by the
occupation forces.[36] After the end of World War II
and the establishment of the communist dictator-
ship in Yugoslavia, persecution of the Church continued. Church property was nationalized, many
churches were closed or destroyed, and the clergy
was repressed.

*The Church of St John the
Forerunner in Grmov,
destroyed by Albanian
extremists in July 1999*

The Serbian Orthodox Church experienced new
tribulations after the breakup of Yugoslavia and the
wars in Croatia and Bosnia-Herzegovina in the 1990s. Just as during the
Ustasha terror, the Serbian population was persecuted, and Orthodox monasteries, cemeteries, and churches were desecrated and destroyed. In Kosovo
and Metohija, a systematic destruction of ancient Orthodox churches began
in 1999, and most of the Serbian population was forced to leave this territory.

At the same time, the 1990s witnessed a religious revival and renewal of
church life in Serbia. One symbol of this renewal was the building of one of
the largest Orthodox churches in Europe—the St Savva cathedral in Belgrade.
At present the Serbian Orthodox Church counts more than 3,500 parishes,
more than 200 monasteries, 2 theological faculties and 6 seminaries, and
approximately 8 million faithful. The Serbian Orthodox Church has dioceses and parishes outside the former Yugoslavia—in the countries of western
Europe, the United States, and Australia.

[36]Ibid., 65–66.

The Romanian Orthodox Church encompasses the Orthodox faithful of several territories—Moldavia, Wallachia, Transylvania, Bukovina, and Bessarabia. Over the centuries these lands were targets of the political interests of the Ottoman, Russian, and Austro-Hungarian empires. After World War I, Transylvania, Bukovina, Bessarabia, and a part of Moldavia were united to form the new Romanian state, while the other part of Moldavia was annexed to the Soviet Union. Earlier, in 1877 to 1878, the synod of the Romanian Orthodox Church petitioned Constantinople for autocephaly. Constantinople recognized the autocephaly of the Romanian Church in 1885, and in 1925 the first hierarch of the Romanian Church was elevated to patriarchal dignity.

During the second half of the twentieth century, the Romanian Church—unlike the other Orthodox Churches in eastern Europe—was not subjected to mass repression by the communist regime. From 1948 until the late 1980s, when Romania was under communist rule, the Church could own property, conduct charity and publishing activities, and received state subsidies. Moreover, the number of faithful, clergy, and church institutions grew steadily. From 1948 to 1986, 454 new churches were built in Romania.

After the fall of Nicolae Ceausescu in 1989, Patriarch Theoctist of Romania was accused of collaborating with the toppled regime and resigned in January 1990. However, the synod of the Romanian Church asked him to return to the patriarchal throne. Under the new government the Romanian Church continued to grow and consolidate itself. At the beginning of the twenty-first century the Romanian Church is the second largest Orthodox Church after the Russian Church: it counts approximately 20 million faithful, more than 13,000 parishes, monasteries, and sketes, more than 500 monastic communities, more than 11,000 clergymen, more than 7,000 monastics, 2 theological faculties, and 7 seminaries. The Church is divided into 30 dioceses, of which 5 are located outside Romania—in western Europe, the United States, and Australia.

The Bulgarian Orthodox Church has existed since the ninth century, when an archdiocese of the patriarchate of Constantinople was established in Bulgaria due to the efforts of Byzantine missionaries. At a council in Preslav in 919, the archdiocese proclaimed itself an autocephalous patriarchate with its administrative center in Dorostol. The patriarchate was later transferred to Triaditsa (today's Sophia), then to Prespa, and finally to Ochrid. After Byzantine Emperor Basil the Bulgar-Slayer conquered Bulgaria in 1018–1019, the

Church of Ochrid lost its autocephaly and patriarchal status. From 1235 to 1393 the so-called Second Bulgarian Patriarchate was centered in Tarnovo, but after the fall of the Second Bulgarian Kingdom the Church was placed under the jurisdiction of the patriarch of Constantinople. In 1872, after the Ottoman empire had been weakened considerably, the Bulgarian Church achieved de facto independence from the sultan and proclaimed autocephaly. However, the patriarchate of Constantinople refused to recognize this status and declared that the Bulgarian Church was in schism. The schism was healed only in 1945, on the request of the Russian Orthodox Church.

During the years of communist rule the Bulgarian Church underwent repression: many churches were closed and monasteries were emptied. In 1957 the Bulgarian Church was raised to the rank of patriarchate. At first the patriarchate of Constantinople refused to recognize the legitimacy of the patriarchate in Bulgaria, and only in 1961, after persistent requests by the Russian Orthodox Church, did it recognize the patriarchal dignity of the Bulgarian Church.

After the fall of the communist regime, problems arose in the Bulgarian Church, caused by the blatant interference of the new authorities in the affairs of the Church and their deposition of Patriarch Maxim in 1992. Several bishops supported this decision, while others remained faithful to the patriarch. An alternative synod was formed, headed by Metropolitan Pimen of Nevrokop. The government recognized this synod as the legitimate church authority. In 1996 Pimen was elected "patriarch" at a schismatic ecclesiastical-popular council. In 1997 the government revoked the registration of Patriarch Maxim and the synod headed by him. Nevertheless, the other local Orthodox churches continued to regard Maxim as lawful patriarch. The canonical ecclesiastical-popular council, held July 2–4, 1997, confirmed Patriarch Maxim's legitimacy. From September 30 to October 1, 1998 an inter-Orthodox council was held in Sophia, chaired by Patriarch Bartholomew of Constantinople, at which schismatic Bulgarian bishops offered their repentance. However, several days later they disavowed their signing of the letter of repentance. The majority of schismatics finally returned to the Church after former Bulgarian King Simeon II became prime minister and his government supported the canonical Church.

At the beginning of the twenty-first century, the Bulgarian Church had 14 metropolias, approximately 3,800 churches, more than 1,300 clergymen, more than 160 monasteries, 2 theological faculties, 1 chair of theology, and 2 seminaries. There are also dioceses and parishes of the Bulgarian Church outside Bulgaria.[37]

The Orthodox Church of Cyprus has enjoyed autocephaly since the fifth century, when its independence was confirmed by canon 8 of the Third Ecumenical Council (431) and canon 39 of the Quinisext Council (691). For almost four centuries (1191–1571) Cyprus was ruled by the crusaders, then by the Turks for three hundred years (1571–1878), after which it was annexed by Great Britain. Cyprus' struggle for independence in the mid-twentieth century was led by Archbishop Makarios III (†1977), who became the first president of the Republic of Cyprus after it declared independence. In 1975 the Turks seized territory in the northern part of the island. They proceeded to expel the majority of the Orthodox population, and desecrated and closed churches and monasteries. The Turkish occupation of Cyprus continues to this day.

The Orthodox Church of Greece was formed in 1833, when Greece was liberated from Turkish rule. At first the patriarchate of Constantinople did not recognize the self-proclaimed autocephaly, but in 1850 it issued a tomos stating that it would recognize its autocephaly on certain conditions. The governance of the newly formed Church of Greece was organized according to the Protestant model, which resembled that of the Russian Church during the synodal period. The king was proclaimed head of the Church and governed it through a standing synod in which his representative took part. In 1912–1913 the "northern territories," including Thessaloniki, were annexed to Greece. The dioceses within these territories, which until then had been part of the patriarchate of Constantinople, were administered by the Church of Greece beginning in 1928, although they still preserved their canonical dependence on Constantinople. After the monarchy was overthrown in 1974, the Church was granted a greater degree of independence from the state, although Orthodoxy preserved its status as state religion.

In the twentieth century the Church of Greece was one of the most dynamically growing Orthodox churches. In 1992 it had 80 dioceses, 7,742 parishes, 8,670 clergymen, and more than 3,000 monastics. The main centers of theological education are the theological faculties of the Universities of

[37]V.I. Kosik, Ch. Temelski, and A.A. Turilov, "The Bulgarian Orthodox Church," in *Orthodox Encyclopedia* 5.615.

Athens and Thessaloniki, and there are also 28 theological schools of various levels. Greece's Orthodox population numbers around 10 million faithful. The Church of Greece does not have dioceses or parishes outside Greece since it recognizes the jurisdiction of the Constantinople patriarchate over the Greek diaspora.

The Albanian Orthodox Church originated in the dioceses on the territory of today's Albania that entered the jurisdiction of the archdiocese of Ochrid in the eleventh century. In 1912 Albania became an independent state, and in 1922 the autocephaly of the Albanian Church was proclaimed. In 1929 all ethnic Greek hierarchs were expelled from Albania and replaced by Albanian bishops. Constantinople at first voiced harsh protest but later, in 1937, it issued a tomos granting legitimate autocephaly to the Albanian Church. In the prewar years the Albanian Church counted 250,000 faithful, 354 churches and 300 chapels, 370 parish clergymen, 28 monasteries and 2 seminaries.

In January 1946 the communist party headed by E. Hoxha (1908–1985) came to power in Albania. Thereafter began the systematic persecution of the faithful, which took on mass proportions. In 1967 Albania became the first nation in the world to officially ban all religious services. After this all clergy were executed, imprisoned, or exiled, and hundreds of churches and most monasteries were destroyed. The Orthodox Church in Albania ceased to legally exist and its governing structure was annihilated. In 1973 Archbishop Damian of Tirana and All Albania died in prison.

The revival of the Albanian Church began in 1991, after the fall of the communist regime. Since no single Albanian bishop remained alive at this time, a bishop of the Church of Greece, Archbishop Anastasios (Yannoulatos), was elected first hierarch of the Church. From 1992 to 2002 several bishops were consecrated, including ethnic Albanians, as well as 114 priests. Moreover, 74 new churches were built, 65 churches and 5 monasteries were rebuilt from ruins, and 130 churches were restored.

The liturgical culture of the renewed Albanian Church was shaped under the influence of two traditions: the Greek and the Russian. During services at the cathedral in Tirana, melodies of Russian

Archbishop Anastasios (Yannoulatos) with Albanian children

church composers set to Albanian texts are mostly sung. The choir is accompanied by an organ. Church architecture, however, is dominated by Greek influence.

The Polish Orthodox Church received its autocephaly from the patriarchate of Constantinople in 1924. The majority of the Orthodox population of Poland lives in the northeastern part of the country, in regions bordering Belarus. In the nineteenth century these lands formed part of the Russian empire, and in 1840 an Orthodox diocese was established in Warsaw. In 1905 the diocese of Holm was founded. The autocephaly of the Polish Church, which was proclaimed in 1922 and later recognized by Constantinople, was at first not confirmed by its mother church, the Moscow patriarchate; Moscow recognized this status only in 1948.

From 1925 to 1939 the Orthodox Church in Poland underwent persecution by the Catholic Church, which was supported by the government of Marshal Pilsudski. On September 8, 1925 a concordat was signed by the Vatican and Poland that recognized Roman Catholicism as the dominant religion. In 1930 Catholics demanded that approximately 700 church buildings be handed over to them; of these around 500 were actually given to the Catholic Church. In Warsaw the Alexander Nevsky cathedral, built in the late nineteenth and early twentieth century, was destroyed. From 1938 to 1939 more than 120 Orthodox churches were destroyed in the Holm region and Podlachia, and thousands of Orthodox believers were converted to Catholicism. During World War II, clergymen who remained faithful to the Orthodox Church sealed their lives with a martyr's death.

In 1939 the Orthodox Church in Poland counted more than 4 million faithful, 2,500 churches and chapels, around 3,000 clergymen, 17 monasteries and sketes, and several institutions of theological education. However, after World War II the size of Poland's territory shrunk when some of its lands were joined to Lithuania and the Ukraine. Because of this the number of faithful of the Polish Church dropped significantly, and this trend continued after the war. At the end of the twentieth century the Polish Orthodox Church counted 7 dioceses, approximately 250 parishes, 410 churches, 6 monasteries, around 250 clergymen, 2 seminaries, and 1 theological faculty. According to various statistics, there are an estimated 600,000–1 million Orthodox faithful in Poland. In 1990 dioceses in Portugal and Brazil entered the jurisdiction of the Polish Orthodox Church.

The Orthodox Church of the Czech Lands and Slovakia proclaimed auto-cephaly in 1920. The history of Orthodoxy in the Czech Republic and Slova-kia can be traced back to the ninth century, when the saintly brothers Cyril and Methodius founded the archdiocese of Moravia and Pannonia. Later on, Catholicism became the dominant religion in these lands, and up to the eigh-teenth century the population was systematically converted to Catholicism. But while Orthodoxy was replaced by Catholicism in western Slovakia and Great Moravia, it was preserved in eastern Slovakia, which was inhabited by a large number of Ukrainians.[38] After the creation of the Czechoslovak Republic in 1918, a National Czechoslovak Church was established that declared itself autocephalous in 1920. Neither the Russian Church nor Con-stantinople recognized this self-proclaimed autocephaly. In 1923 Constan-tinople established an archdiocese of Prague, and in 1924 some of the Orthodox faithful, led by Bishop Gorazd, united to form a diocese of the Ser-bian Church. Moreover, parishes of the Russian Church Abroad existed in Czechoslovakia until the end of World War II. In 1946 all Orthodox parishes in Czechoslovakia were joined together into an exarchate of the Moscow patriarchate, and in 1951 the exarchate was reorganized as the autocephalous Czechoslovak Orthodox Church. For almost half a century, the autocephaly granted to it by the Russian Church was not recognized by the patriarchate of Constantinople, which finally issued a tomos recognizing this status for the Orthodox Church of the Czech Lands and Slovakia in 1998.

This Church received its current name in connection with the division of Czechoslovakia on January 1, 1993 into two states. At present the Church of the Czech Lands and Slovakia counts 4 dioceses, 166 parishes, 184 churches, and 2 theological faculties. Nearly two-thirds of its flock of 74,000 live in Slovakia.

Although the Autonomous Orthodox Church of Finland was granted autonomy from the patriarchate of Constantinople in 1923, the Orthodox parishes of Finland were originally under the jurisdiction of the Russian Orthodox Church. The Church of Finland counts around 50,000 faithful—approximately 1 percent of the country's total population. Despite its small size the Orthodox Church of Finland, like the Lutheran Church, is a state church.

In the twentieth century a large Orthodox diaspora emerged in western Europe as a result of several waves of immigration from Russia, Turkey,

[38]Skurat, *History of the Local Orthodox Churches*, 2.216, 220.

Cyprus, and the middle eastern countries. Although there are no precise statistics on the number of Orthodox faithful in western Europe, their total size is estimated to be no less than two million. Approximately one million of these live in Germany, and several hundred thousand in Great Britain, France, and Italy. One feature of the canonical organization of Orthodox churches in western Europe (with the exception of Greece and Cyprus) is that several parallel Orthodox jurisdictions, each of which is headed by a bishop of a local Orthodox Church, can exist in the same country. For example, in France there are dioceses of the patriarchates of Constantinople, Antioch, Moscow, Serbia, Romania, and Bulgaria.

ORTHODOXY IN AMERICA, AUSTRALIA, AND ASIA

Orthodoxy in America is divided into several jurisdictions, of which the three largest in terms of numbers are the Greek Orthodox Archdiocese of North America (under the patriarchate of Constantinople), the autocephalous Orthodox Church in America, and the American archdiocese of the patriarchate of Antioch.

Orthodoxy was brought to America in the eighteenth century, when Alaska was part of the Russian empire. The first Orthodox episcopal see in America was established by the Holy Synod of the Russian Orthodox Church in 1840, although the ruling bishop of the diocese, St Innocent (Venyaminov), resided in Novoarkhangelsk. In 1872, five years after Alaska was sold to America, the see of the Russian bishop was transferred to San Francisco. From 1898 to 1907 the diocese was governed by St Tikhon, the future patriarch of Russia. During this time the see was transferred once again, to New York. St Tikhon prepared the All-American Council of 1907, which renamed the diocese the Russian Orthodox Greek Catholic Church in North America. This laid the foundation for the future autocephalous Orthodox Church in America.

During St Tikhon's years in America a large number of Antiochian Christians arrived in the New World, for whom a vicar bishop from Syria, Raphael, was consecrated in 1903. This marked the beginning of a new and unique ecclesiological model, which foresaw that bishops of different nationalities could serve within one local church and in which dioceses were created not for a particular territory but for a certain ethnic group. This model did not correspond to the ecclesiology of the ancient Church, but it did suit the new realities that faced the Church as a result of immigration. If the Church in America had continued to develop according to the plan elaborated by St Tikhon, a single local Orthodox Church in America might have emerged as early as the 1920s, headed by one metropolitan with bishops of different nationalities under his authority. Each of them would be responsible for the pastoral care of people of his nationality, be they Russians, Ukrainians, Greeks, Antiochians, or Romanians.

However, after Patriarch Meletios IV (Metaxakis) of Constantinople laid claims to ecclesiastical jurisdiction over the entire Orthodox diaspora in 1922, an archdiocese of the patriarchate of Constantinople was established in America. Antiochian Christians, who were formerly under the jurisdiction of the metropolia, organized a North American archdiocese of the Antiochian patriarchate. As for the Russian metropolia, it declared temporary autonomy in 1924 and left the jurisdiction of the Moscow patriarchate without placing itself under the authority of another local church. The break between the Russian metropolia of North America and the mother church lasted for almost half a century. Thus, there appeared three parallel jurisdictions in the United States, to which were later added dioceses of the Serbian, Romanian, and Bulgarian Orthodox churches. After World War II the American jurisdiction of the Russian Church Abroad, which was not in communion with any of the canonical church jurisdictions, grew significantly.

Negotiations for the restoration of canonical communion between the Russian metropolia and the Moscow patriarchate were renewed in 1969, and in 1970 the Moscow patriarchate granted autocephaly to its former metropolia. It was assumed that the Orthodox faithful of other jurisdictions would join the newly created autocephalous Church, which was called the Orthodox Church in America. However, this did not occur, and Orthodoxy in the United States remains divided into several jurisdictions to this day. The churches of Constantinople, Alexandria, Antioch, Jerusalem, and Greece do not recognize the autocephaly of the Orthodox Church in America.

At present a gradual process of consolidating the Orthodox faithful on the American continent is underway. The Standing Conference of Canonical Orthodox Bishops in the Americas functions successfully and a rapprochement between the Orthodox Church in America and the Antiochian

Orthodox Archdiocese is taking place. Students from different jurisdictions study at St Vladimir's Orthodox Theological Seminary, which inherited the theological traditions of the St Sergius Theological Institute in Paris. All of these processes may ultimately lead to the creation of a single local Orthodox Church in North America. At present the most vocal opponent of this development is the patriarchate of Constantinople, which is interested in preserving its ecclesiastical jurisdiction in America.

The Cathedral of the Resurrection in Tokyo

Orthodoxy was brought to Japan by missionaries from Russia. In 1861 hieromonk Nicholas (Kasatkin) arrived in Japan to serve as dean of the Russian embassy church. His efforts resulted in the founding of the Japanese mission of the Russian Orthodox Church. In 1880 he was consecrated bishop and became the first Orthodox hierarch in Japan, and in 1891 the Holy Resurrection cathedral (known by the Japanese as "Nikolai-Do," according to the name of its founder) in Tokyo was completed. During the Russian-Japanese War of 1904, Archbishop Nicholas remained in Tokyo along with his flock and was responsible for the pastoral care of some 70,000 Russian prisoners of war. The missionary and educational activities of St Nicholas of Japan lasted for half a century. When he died in 1912, the Japanese Church counted 31,984 faithful, 265 churches, 41 priests, 15 choir directors, and 121 catechists.

St Nicholas' successor, Metropolitan Sergius (Tikhomirov), remained faithful to the Moscow patriarchate until his very death in 1945. However, tense relations and military antagonism between Russia and Japan weakened the Japanese Church. After the war communion between the Moscow patriarchate and the Japanese Church was broken; it was restored in only 1970, when the Japanese Church joined the Moscow patriarchate as an autonomous Church. The Japanese Autonomous Orthodox Church currently has 3 dioceses, around 150 parishes, and some 30,000 faithful, the majority of whom are direct descendants of those Japanese who were converted to Orthodoxy through the efforts of St Nicholas of Japan.

Orthodoxy in China has a history that goes back more than three centuries. Orthodox missionaries from Russia visited China as early as the seventeenth century, and in 1717 the Russian Ecclesiastical Mission in Peking was established. From 1896 to 1931 the mission was headed by Archimandrite (later

Metropolitan) Innocent (Figurovsky). In 1905, during the Boxer Rebellion, the mission was pillaged, several Orthodox churches were destroyed, and 222 Orthodox Chinese were tortured to death. Nevertheless, in 1918 there were approximately 10,000 Chinese Orthodox faithful. After the October Revolution in 1917 several waves of Russian immigrants reached China, where they formed a Russian diaspora that numbered half a million persons and built more than a hundred churches. However, a mass exodus of Russians from China began after the outbreak of the 1949 revolution: many left for Australia, others for North or South America. In 1957 the Chinese Orthodox Church received autonomous status from the Russian Church. However, during the Cultural Revolution in the 1960s the Orthodox Church of China was crippled, churches were destroyed, cemeteries were desecrated, and icons were smashed. Many Orthodox Chinese became martyrs for Christ. Despite the requests of believers, there is still not a single Orthodox priest who is regularly active in China.

The situation of the Orthodox Church in Latin America, Australia, and New Zealand in many respects resembles that in North America and western Europe. In these regions of the globe there are dioceses and parishes of various jurisdictions, including the patriarchates of Constantinople, Antioch, Moscow, and Serbia, as well as the Russian Church Abroad.

During the last few decades Orthodox parishes have appeared in southeast Asia, including Hong Kong, the Philippines, Indonesia, Singapore, Thailand, South Korea, Mongolia, and Vietnam.

10

The Orthodox Church on the Threshold of the Third Millennium

THE MAIN FRUIT of the more than two-thousand-years of the Orthodox Church is the fact that, despite severe persecution, it has not lost its faith or its liturgical tradition, which are reflected in its architecture, iconography, singing, and all aspects of the services. The Orthodox Church underwent persecution and repression over many centuries—from the Arabs, crusaders, Mongols, Turks, and the Bolsheviks in the Soviet Union. But the Church survived and preserved its faith and unity, paying the price with the blood of a host of confessors and martyrs.

At the beginning of the twenty-first century the Orthodox Church is one of the most dynamically growing religious confessions in the world. The number of Orthodox faithful is rising in Russia, Ukraine, Belarus, Moldova, Romania, Serbia, Albania, and other countries where atheism once dominated. Churches are being restored and new ones built, and new monasteries and theological schools are being opened. Unlike most Christian communities in the west, the Orthodox Church is not experiencing a crisis of vocations: thousands of young persons are being ordained and beginning their service to the Church. Orthodox churches are replete with people of all ages, including children and the youth.

Today a large number of churches are being built and restored—a fact that testifies to the unwaning relevance of Orthodoxy and people's thirst for it, to its vitality and spiritual power. Churches in Russia and other Orthodox countries are filled with people, and Orthodox faithful who are forced to leave their homeland establish church communities abroad.

The Orthodox Church carefully preserves the "apostolic faith, the patristic faith, the Orthodox faith" preached by the fathers and teachers of the Church. Today few people in the western, "post-Christian" world know the names or read the writings of Basil the Great, Gregory the Theologian, John

Chrysostom, Maximus the Confessor, Isaac the Syrian, and Gregory Palamas. At best these names are known to a handful of scholars and professors who study the works of the holy fathers as monuments of the past, as displays in a museum. For Orthodox believers, however, these works are testimony to a faith that renews and rejuvenates the hearts of people today, just as they did ten or fifteen centuries earlier.

Today only a few people in the west read the writings of the ascetic and spiritual writers of the ancient Church. The Orthodox, on the contrary—be they monastics or laypersons—read these books as guides for the spiritual life. Once a professor of a western theological faculty visited St Silouan, who lived in the first half of the twentieth century on Mount Athos, and asked him, "What do your monks read?" Silouan answered, "Macarius of Egypt, Isaac the Syrian, Symeon the New Theologian, and the *Philokalia*." The professor answered in surprise, "Where I come from these books are read only by learned theologians." Whereupon Silouan said, "Our monks not only read these books, but can also write new ones no worse than these, if they should be lost."[1] This is because the experience reflected in these books is still preserved in Orthodox monasticism.

In the monasteries of the Holy Mountain of Athos and in many other monasteries throughout the world, monks who have devoted their entire lives to God continue to practice asceticism. Among them are many young persons who have "sought out the life of fasting" and left the world to focus on prayer and ascetic labors. Today in many majestic monasteries in the west, where five hundred or even a thousand monks once lived, only ten to fifteen remain, and some monasteries have been completely emptied. This is because the youth do not wish to join monasteries, and because the idea of a solitary life in God has ceased to inspire them. Orthodox monasteries, on the contrary, are filled with monks and nuns. In the Russian Orthodox Church alone there are around seven hundred monasteries, although there were only eighteen of them just decades ago. The reason for the mass influx of young monks is that the Orthodox faith continues to inspire them, just as it inspired their ancestors over the centuries.

Many churches in the west complain of a lack of priests and the gradual decrease in the number of their parishioners. The Orthodox Church, however, is one of the few Christian confessions whose numbers are constantly

---

[1]Archimandrite Sophrony (Sakharov), *St Silouan of Mount Athos* (Paris, 1952), 32.

growing and in which the number of priests is on the rise. In the Russian Church alone the number of priests over the past fifteen years has grown several times and has reached 27,000, and several thousand young people are currently studying in seminaries and other theological schools. A similar spiritual revival can be observed in Romania, Serbia, Georgia, and other countries where Orthodoxy was persecuted only recently.

In the countries of western Europe, the presence of the Orthodox Church has a missionary dimension. The Orthodox Church does not engage in proselytism to the detriment of other Christian confessions and has no strategy for the mass conversion of western Christians to Orthodoxy. The mission of Orthodoxy is not to convert others, but first and foremost to bear witness to God, the truth, and the tradition of the ancient undivided Church, which is preserved in Orthodoxy in all its fulness. While attending Orthodox services, many non-Orthodox Christians have been struck by their beauty, grandeur, depth, and length. The external appearance and interior of Orthodox churches fulfil a mission of testifying to the heavenly realm: the crosses and golden cupolas, icons, and frescoes all remind today's people of the west of the spiritual dimension that has been forgotten by many.

It is this witness that justifies the participation of the Orthodox in the ecumenical movement. Orthodox bishops, priests, and theologians travel to inter-Christian conferences not in order to make doctrinal compromises but in order to bear witness to the Orthodox faith before non-Orthodox Christians, to remind them that the tradition of the ancient undivided Church is not dead but is still preserved and continues to develop in Orthodoxy. Participation in inter-Christian contacts is based on the understanding that the Orthodox Church should not isolate itself, hide from the non-Orthodox world, or avoid fulfilling the mission of witness entrusted to it by the Lord himself.

At the beginning of the twenty-first century, Orthodox theological scholarship continues its active development. One of the most renowned contemporary theologians in the west is the Englishman Bishop Kallistos (Ware), a brilliant popularizer and specialist of the patristic legacy, a systematizer of the main ideas of eastern patristics, and an outstanding scholar of the Byzantine tradition. He has translated many works of the holy fathers and liturgical books into English. Under his guidance and with his direct participation were translated *The Festal Menaion* and *The Lenten Triodion*, as well as five volumes

Kallistos (Ware),
Metropolitan of Diokleia

of the *Philokalia*. Bishop Kallistos is also the author of several monographs, including *The Orthodox Church* and *The Orthodox Way*, which have become classic introductions to the history and spirituality of the Orthodox Church. He has also written more than two hundred articles on various topics connected to the teaching of the Orthodox Church or eastern patristics.

Another major theologian whose writings are well-known in the west is Metropolitan John (Zizioulas), author of several important works on the history of the early Church. In his monographs and articles, Metropolitan John further develops the tradition of the Paris school of Russian theology, particularly the eucharistic ecclesiology of Nicholas Afanasiev and Alexander Schmemann. Although the conclusions that Zizioulas draws are sometimes questionable, his influence on the contemporary theological thought of the west is unmistakable. Zizioulas devotes considerable attention to the Orthodox role in inter-Christian activities and is one of the most active participants in the ecumenical movement.

Among western Orthodox patristics scholars, Jean-Claude Larchet and Fr John Behr, professor of St Vladimir's Orthodox Theological Seminary in New York, should be mentioned. Larchet has written several monographs on the eastern church fathers, including Maximus the Confessor. Fr John Behr

Jean-Claude Larchet

can be described as the rising star of Orthodox theological scholarship. At present he is working on a monumental study in several volumes on the history of patristic theological thought (the first two volumes have already been published, and one has been translated into Russian).

In Serbia the works of Metropolitan Amfilohije (Radovich), Bishop Atanasije (Jevtich), and other students of the outstanding Christian thinker Archimandrite Justin (Popovich), who passed away in 1979 and was recently canonized by the Serbian Orthodox Church, are widely read. In Romania the theological tradition that emerged under the influence of Archpriest Dumitru Staniloae (†1993), a major Romanian theologian of the twentieth century, continues to develop. Metropolitan Anastasios (Yannoulatos), primate of the Albanian Orthodox Church, has also made significant contributions to the development of Orthodox theology.

Metropolitan Amfilohije (Radovich)

In Russia, the Ukraine, and other countries that emerged from the Soviet Union, theological scholarship during the last fifteen years has awoken from the stagnation in which it found itself as a result of persecution. Major centers of theological scholarship have been founded, such as the St Tikhon Orthodox Humanities University and the Orthodox Encyclopedia Center, which attract considerable theological talent. New translations of the works of the church fathers from Greek, Latin, Syriac, and other ancient languages have been published. Original theological works are being written, the works of nineteenth- and twentieth-century Russian theologians are being reprinted, and archive material that was formerly inaccessible is being published, casting new light on the recent history of the Church.

The twentieth century also witnessed a renewal of the ancient traditions of iconography and church architecture. The work of iconographers is in high demand due to the rebuilding and construction of hundreds and thousands of churches in countries where the Orthodox faith is experiencing a revival. In Russia and other countries, schools of iconography have been opened where many students can learn this art under the guidance of experienced masters. One major iconographer at the beginning of the twenty-first century is Archimandrite Zinon (Teodor), who has painted several churches in Russia and abroad, created one-tier and multi-tiered iconostases, and painted hundreds of icons. Today he continues the work of Theophan the Greek, Andrei Rublev, Daniel the Black, and other great iconographers of the past.

The tradition of Orthodox church singing is also being further developed: new choral ensembles are formed and new musical compositions for church choirs are being written. One characteristic of contemporary Russian composers who write church music is their interest in ancient singing traditions, particularly in *Znamenny* chant.

Arvo Pärt

Orthodox spirituality exerts profound influence not only on church music but also on the secular compositions of modern composers who are members of the Orthodox Church. The most prominent among them is Arvo Pärt, an Estonian who resides in Germany and England and who is the spiritual son of Archimandrite Sophrony (Sakharov). Pärt has written a number of compositions set to Orthodox texts, most of which are for a capella choir, such as the *Kanon Pokajanen*, set to words of St Andrew of Crete, *I am the True Vine*, and the *Triodion*, set to words from the Lenten Triodion. Pärt's instrumental works, such as *Silouan's Song* for string orchestra, are also marked by the profound influence of Orthodoxy.

On the threshold of the twenty-first century, Orthodoxy remains a living spiritual tradition that shows no signs of weakening, aging, or dying out. The Orthodox Church continues to live its spiritual life in all its fulness, helping millions of people throughout the entire world find the meaning of life, saving them from hopelessness and anguish, and opening to them the gates of eternal life and the path to the heavenly kingdom.

PART THREE

THE CANONICAL STRUCTURE OF WORLD ORTHODOXY

11

The Formation of the Canonical Structure of the Orthodox Church: The Principle of Canonical Territory

T HE CANONICAL STRUCTURE of the Orthodox Church was shaped over the course of nearly two millennia. The peculiarities of the Church's structure today are rooted in the historical vicissitudes of the times of its development, in the first centuries, in the Byzantine, and in the post-Byzantine periods.

The mother of all Christian churches—both eastern and western—is the Church of Jerusalem: the community of the Savior's disciples in Jerusalem. However, already in the first century Christian communities outside Jerusalem were founded through the missionary efforts of the apostles—for example, in Antioch, Alexandria, Rome, Carthage, and other cities of the Roman empire. Each community was headed by a bishop or presbyter.

In the Acts of the Apostles and the epistles of St Paul, the words "bishop" (*episkopos*) and "presbyter" are often used synonymously (Acts 20.17–18 and 20.28; Titus 1.5–7). The account of the apostolic council in Jerusalem makes no mention of bishops, employing instead the expression "apostles and presbyters" (Acts 15.2, 4, 6). It was the "apostles and presbyters" who made up the *collegium* that, along with the entire Church (Acts 15.22), made the decisions. Elsewhere, St Paul speaks of "bishops and deacons" (Phil 1.1) and is silent about presbyters. From this we can conclude that during the early stages of the Church's development the ministry of the bishop did not differ from that of the presbyter.

In an epistle of Clement of Rome to the Corinthians, there is also no clear distinction between the service of the bishop and the presbyter: "It would not be a small sin if we deprived of the episcopate those who offer gifts blamelessly and in holiness. Blessed are the presbyters who have preceded us, who were released from the body after a highly fruitful and perfect life; they have no reason to fear that somebody might depose them from the place they occupy."[1] Here again the terms "bishop" and "presbyter" are used synonymously. In the same epistle Clement speaks of how the apostles ordained "bishops and deacons,"[2] not mentioning presbyters. This bears witness to how, in his eyes, these two functions were essentially identical.

At the same time, in the epistles of St Paul the ministry of the bishop is connected to the ordination of presbyters. Paul writes to Titus: "For this reason I left you in Crete, so that you should set in order the things that are lacking, and appoint presbyters in every city" (Titus 1.5). The right to ordain presbyters became the prerogative through which the bishop's function differed from that of the presbyter. The presbyter cannot ordain another presbyter since this can only be done by a bishop.

While the differences between the bishop's and presbyter's functions were unclear in the first century, in the second century there did appear a clear differentiation between the two. The bishop was now the head of the local Christian community and the priests became his delegates, who assist him in governing the Church. Ignatius of Antioch testifies to this, and in his writings the principle of the so-called "monarchic episcopate" serves as the basis for the governance of the Church.

In his epistles, Ignatius untiringly stresses the supreme role of the bishop as the leader of the eucharistic gathering, affirming that "the bishop is to be seen as the Lord himself."[3] Everything in the Church should be done with the knowledge of the bishop: "Nobody should do anything that concerns the Church without the bishop. Only that eucharist should be considered true which is celebrated by the bishop or by those whom he has appointed . . . It is inadmissible to baptize or celebrate the feast of love without the bishop; and what he approves of is pleasant to God."[4] This ecclesiology was summarized in the classic formula: "Wherever the bishop is, let the people also be there, just as wherever Christ is, there is the catholic Church."[5]

Thus, already in the second century the hierarchical structure of the Church that still exists today took shape. Its foundation is the notion of the local Church—the ecclesiastical community of a particular locality (city, region) headed by the bishop. Such a community, called a "diocese," is com-

---

[1] Clement of Rome *First Epistle to the Corinthians* 44.
[2] Ibid., 42.
[3] Ignatius of Antioch *Epistle to the Ephesians* 6.
[4] Ignatius of Antioch *Epistle to the Smyrneans* 8.
[5] Ibid.

prised of smaller ecclesiastical units—parishes—which are headed by presbyters. In the main church of a city the eucharist is celebrated by the bishop, and this church is called a "cathedral" since the episcopal see (*cathedra*) is located there. In all other churches or houses of prayer the eucharist is celebrated by "him whom the bishop has appointed," in other words, by a presbyter ordained to serve in a particular community. The presbyter is a delegate of the bishop, his authorized representative. He may not conduct services or dispense the sacraments without the blessing of the bishop.

According to the early fathers, the preeminent role accorded to the bishop is due to the fact that he occupies the place of Christ in the eucharistic gathering. This understanding explains why the principle of the monarchic episcopate—that is, that there should be only one bishop in each eucharistic community or church—became the norm in the ancient Church.[6] Being the head of a church in a particular place, the bishop nevertheless governs the church not singlehandedly but together with the presbyters and deacons. The bishop does not possess ecclesiastical power or authority by himself, by virtue of his rank. He is a clergyman within the local church community, which entrusted him with his service. Outside this church community the ministry of the bishop loses its meaning and efficacy. Moreover, the bishop governs the Church in accord with other bishops. This guarantees the catholicity or *sobornost'* of the Church, which is an important concept in Orthodox ecclesiology.

From the very beginning, the principle of the monarchic episcopate has been intimately linked to the principle of canonical territory, which holds that each bishop is responsible for a particular ecclesiastical region. Although the term "canonical territory" emerged recently, the ecclesiological model it represents goes back to apostolic times. This model foresees that each ecclesiastical region is assigned to a concrete bishop, in accordance with the formula: "one city—one bishop—one Church." Regarding the historical conditions leading to the appearance of this model, Bishop Nikodim (Milas) wrote the following in his commentaries on the Apostolic Canons:

As soon as small, separate ecclesiastical regions started to be organized thanks to the missionary efforts of the apostles, the notion of a constant

---

[6]Cited by John Meyendorff, "What is an Ecumenical Council?" in *Orthodoxy in the Modern World* (Klin, 2002), 98.

priesthood immediately began to establish itself in these areas . . . Each of these regions was founded either directly or indirectly by one of the apostles . . . so that the ecclesiastical regions, which were continuously being formed, comprised separate families in which the bishop was the father and the other clergymen were his assistants.[7]

Based on this principle, the Apostolic Canons[8] and other decisions of the ancient Church state that it is inadmissible for bishops and clergymen to violate the boundaries of ecclesiastical regions. The Apostolic Canons prescribe that bishops may not transfer to other dioceses without permission (canon 14); that bishops may not conduct ordinations outside their dioceses (canon 35); that an excommunicated clergyman or layman may not be accepted into communion by another bishop after he has gone to a different city (canon 12); that a clergyman who transfers to another diocese without the blessing of his bishop is deprived of the right to serve (canon 15); and that a suspension or excommunication imposed on a clergyman by one bishop may not be lifted by another bishop (canons 16 and 32).[9]

In determining the borders of ecclesiastical regions, the fathers of the ancient Church took into account the boundaries of civil territories established by the secular authorities. In the second and third centuries, it was usual for the bishop to head an ecclesiastical region and serve in a city, while the presbyters appointed by him attended to the pastoral care of church communities in nearby settlements. But by the beginning of the fourth century, after Emperor Diocletian united the provinces of the Roman empire into "dioceses," there arose the need for a corresponding consolidation of ecclesiastical regions (dioceses) into larger units; these were subsequently called metropolias. The first bishop of a metropolia (the metropolitan) was the bishop of the capital of the "diocese," who had the other bishops under his administrative jurisdiction.

Nevertheless, within the limits of their dioceses bishops maintained complete ecclesiastical authority, consulting the metropolitan only in matters

[7] Canons of the Orthodox Church, 74–75.

[8] Although it is difficult to date this work exactly, it is evident that some of the canons it contains could not have appeared earlier than the fourth century.

[9] In the Greek text of the Apostolic Canons the word paroikia is used, which today means "parish." However, the context of the canons demonstrates that what was meant was an ecclesiastical region headed by a bishop, i.e., the ecclesiastical unit that would subsequently be called an eparchia (diocese).

that exceeded their competence. Apostolic Canon 34 states the following on the relations between the metropolitan and the bishops: "The bishops of all peoples should know the first among them and recognize him as the head, and do nothing that exceeds their authority without his judgment. Each should do only that which concerns his own diocese and places that belong to it. But the first among them should do nothing without the judgment of all." Canon 4 of the First Ecumenical Council requires that bishops be consecrated by all, or at least three, bishops of a region; moreover, the consecration should be confirmed by the metropolitan.

Although the idea that church regions should correspond to civil ones was a guiding principle of the ancient Church, it was never absolute or thought of as exclusive. Evidence of this can be found in the dispute between St Basil the Great and Bishop Anthimus of Tiana, which has been well documented in various sources, including the writings of Gregory the Theologian.[10] When Basil took over the governance of the Church of Cappadocia in the summer of 370, Cappadocia was a unified province with its center in Caesarea. However, in winter 371–372 Emperor Valens divided the province into two regions: Cappadocia I with its capital in Caesarea, and Cappadocia II with its capital in Tiana. In accordance with the new civil division, Bishop Anthimus of Tiana began to act as metropolitan of Cappadocia II, not recognizing Basil's jurisdiction over himself. However, the latter continued to consider himself metropolitan of all Cappadocia, in accordance with the previous territorial organization. In order to consolidate his authority, in spring 372 Basil consecrated bishops for cities that had de facto entered the "canonical territory" of Anthimus: in Sasima he appointed his friend Gregory the Theologian, and in Nyssa his brother Gregory. In 374 Amphilochius, cousin of Gregory the Theologian and loyal disciple of Basil, was appointed bishop of Iconium. Anthimus saw these actions as uncanonical and hindered the activities of the bishops consecrated by Basil in every way possible. Subsequently, after Basil's death in 379, the bishops of Cappadocia II recognized Anthimus as metropolitan of this ecclesiastical territory.

In the age of the First Ecumenical Council there were several ecclesiastical regions that possessed the rights of a metropolia. In particular, the sixth canon of this council mentions the bishops of Alexandria and Antioch as

---

[10]See particularly his *Orations* 43, dedicated to the memory of Basil the Great, as well as his letters. The correspondence of St Basil also sheds light on this conflict.

having—along with the bishop of Rome—authority over the bishops of their regions, and the seventh canon grants the same power to the bishop of Jerusalem. (At this time there were also other metropolias, such as those of Ephesus, Caesarea in Cappadocia, Heraclea, Milan, and Carthage;[11] however, their importance subsequently waned.)

After Constantinople was proclaimed capital of the eastern empire and granted the status of "New Rome" at the beginning of the fourth century, the bishop of Constantinople was accorded the rights of a metropolitan. By the 380s the bishop of this city had become second in importance after that of Rome. This status was secured by the third canon of the Second Ecumenical Council, which states: "The bishop of Constantinople shall have the prerogative of honor after the Roman bishop, because Constantinople is New Rome." The Fourth Ecumenical Council provided the following explanation for this decision: "For the fathers rightly granted privileges to the throne of old Rome because it was the royal city. For the same reason, the 150 God-loving bishops granted equal privileges to the most holy see of New Rome, rightly judging that the city which has received the honor of being the city of the emperor and the senate, and enjoys equal privileges with the old Rome, should in ecclesiastical matters also be magnified as she is, and rank second after her." Thus, the primacy of the Roman bishop was viewed by the eastern fathers not as being due to the succession from St Peter, but based on the political importance of Rome as the capital of the empire. In the same manner, the privileges enjoyed by the see of Constantinople resulted not from its antiquity (those of Jerusalem, Alexandria, and Antioch were more ancient) or other ecclesiastical considerations, but exclusively from the political significance of Constantinople as "the city of the emperor and the senate."

In the sixth century, the primates of the most ancient Christian churches, including that of Constantinople, began to be called patriarchs. The same period also witnessed the development in Byzantine theology of the idea of the "pentarchy," according to which the ecumenical Church is headed by five patriarchs: those of Rome, Constantinople, Alexandria, Antioch, and Jerusalem. Although this idea was reflected in the laws adopted by Emperor Justinian in the east, its legitimacy was never acknowledged in the west.

During the entire first millennium, ecclesiology developed differently in the east and west. From the times of Ignatius of Antioch and Hippolytus of

[11]Cf. *Canons of the Orthodox Church*, 204.

Rome, in the east each bishop was seen as occupying the place of Christ in the eucharistic gathering. According to Ignatius, "the bishop presides in the place of God, the presbyters occupy the place of the assembly of the apostles, and the deacons have been entrusted with the ministry of Jesus Christ."[12]

However, in the west Cyprian of Carthage already began to develop the idea of the episcopal throne not as the "place of God" but as the see of St Peter.[13] In Cyprian's writings, "the eschatological image of the apostolic college surrounding Christ—an image which was applied to the structure of the local Church by Ignatius and Hippolytus (the bishop surrounded by the presbyterium)—is changed to become an image of the apostolic college surrounding its head, *St Peter* . . . The significance of this alteration is that we can now talk of *unus episcopatus* dispersed over the earth with Peter at its head."[14] This universalist ecclesiology triumphed in the Roman Church toward the end of the first millennium, and contributed to its deepening alienation from the eastern churches.

In the seventh century the outermost regions of the Byzantine empire suffered from the devastating raids of the Arabs. In 638 Jerusalem and Antioch fell, and in 642 Alexandria. This led to a weakening of the three ancient eastern patriarchates, whose first hierarchs frequently had to seek refuge in Constantinople. From the middle of the seventh century, excepting the years when Constantinople was seized by the crusaders (1204–1261), the Constantinople patriarchate remained the main center of ecclesiastical authority in the entire Christian east. After the sundering of eucharistic communion between Rome and Constantinople, the primacy of honor among the primates of the eastern churches automatically went over to the patriarch of Constantinople. The pentarchy had now become a tetrarchy, and the diptychs of the Orthodox churches now included four patriarchates: those of Constantinople, Alexandria, Antioch, and Jerusalem.

The Orthodox eastern patriarchates enjoyed autocephalous status—that is, they managed their ecclesiastical and administrative affairs independently of one another.[15] In addition to these patriarchates, other autocephalous Chris-

---

[12]*Magnesians* 6

[13]Cyprian of Carthage *Epistles* 69(66).5; *Epistles* 43(40).5; *On the Unity of the Church* 4.

[14]John Zizioulas, *Being As Communion* (Crestwood, NY: SVS Press, 1993), 200.

[15]The term "autocephaly," as applied to independent local Orthodox churches, came into use only in modern times. In Byzantine canonical texts the adjective "autocephalous" frequently denoted certain archdioceses that were independent of the regional metropolitan and his synod and were created by either the patriarch or the emperor. See John Meyendorff, "The Catholicity of the Church," in *Orthodoxy in the Modern World*, 159.

tian churches appeared, disappeared, and reappeared in the Orthodox east between the fourth and fifteenth centuries, particularly in the Balkans. In the middle of the fifteenth century the Church of Muscovite Rus', which had been canonically dependent on Constantinople, gained its independence.

After the fall of Constantinople in 1453, when the Byzantine empire ceased to exist, the patriarchs of Constantinople were appointed by the Turkish sultan. The spiritual and political alliance between the sultan and the patriarch resulted in the abolition of church autocephaly in those lands annexed to the Ottoman empire through conquest. The decline of the Ottoman empire in the nineteenth century and the emergence of new states in the territories liberated from Turkish dominion led to the creation of new autocephalous churches and to the restoration of the autocephaly of those churches that had lost it for one reason or another.

The emergence of autocephalous Orthodox churches was never an easy or painless process. There has never existed a unified procedure for granting or obtaining autocephaly that has been approved by all of world Orthodoxy—neither in Byzantine times nor after the empire's downfall. Autocephaly was almost always obtained in the context of the growing political might of a particular state or its acquisition of independence. Conversely, the abolition of autocephaly was usually the direct consequence of the loss of independence by a state on whose territory a local church found itself.

Furthermore, the acquisition of autocephaly by a church has never occurred on the initiative of the mother church. Autocephaly was often not granted but proclaimed without permission, after which the mother church did not recognize the independence of its daughter for a certain period of time. For example, the patriarchate of Constantinople did not recognize the autocephaly of the Church of Greece for seventeen years, that of the Church of Czechoslovakia for forty-seven years, and that of the Bulgarian and Georgian churches for more than seventy years. The Moscow patriarchate did not recognize the autocephaly of the Georgian and Polish Orthodox churches for twenty-six years. In most cases the recognition of self-proclaimed autocephaly was the result of political changes and a complex negotiation process in which, in addition to the mother and daughter churches, representatives of other churches acting as mediators also participated.

12

The Contemporary Canonical Structure
of the Orthodox Church

As MENTIONED EARLIER, the cornerstone of the Orthodox Church's canonical structure is the monarchic episcopate, which acts at the level of the "local Church," that is, that church unit today called the "diocese" (a Church of one region, country, or territory headed by one bishop). In contemporary Orthodox parlance the concept "local Church," however, is used to designate larger ecclesiastical formations, such as groups of dioceses united into patriarchates, metropolias, or archdioceses. At this level the principle of the monarchic episcopate gives way to collegial forms of governance. In practice this means that the first hierarch of a local Church is the "first among equals" among the bishops of his Church. He does not interfere in the internal affairs of dioceses and does not have direct jurisdiction over them, although he is accorded certain coordinating functions in matters that exceed the competence of individual diocesan bishops.

Although the rights and responsibilities of the primate differ in the various local churches, there is not a single local Church in which he enjoys supreme power: in every Church this power is vested only with the council. Thus, for instance, in the Russian Orthodox Church the highest dogmatic authority is the national council, in which not only bishops but also clergy, monastics, and laymen participate; and the highest form of hierarchical government is the bishops' council. As for the patriarch of Moscow and all Russia, he governs the Church between councils together with the Holy Synod, and his name is commemorated in all dioceses before the name of the ruling bishop. In the Church of Greece there is no national council with the participation of laymen: instead the highest authority belongs to the synod of bishops chaired by the archbishop of Athens and all Greece. At services, however, the synod and not the archbishop is commemorated.

At present there are fifteen local Orthodox churches, each of which has its own first hierarch with the rank of patriarch, metropolitan, or archbishop.

Church	Official Number of Believers	Canonical Territory
Patriarchate of Constantinople	7,000,000	Turkey, Crete, Dodecanese islands, the diaspora
Patriarchate of Alexandria	1,000,000	Egypt and all Africa
Patriarchate of Antioch	1,500,000	Syria, Lebanon, Iraq, the diaspora
Patriarchate of Jerusalem	156,000	Palestine, Israel, Jordan
Patriarchate of Moscow	160,000,000	Russia, Belarus, Ukraine, Moldova, the Baltic and Central Asian states, the diaspora
Georgian Orthodox Church	3,000,000	Georgia
Serbian Orthodox Church	8,000,000	Serbia, Montenegro, Slovenia, Croatia
Romanian Orthodox Church	20,000,000	Romania, the diaspora
Bulgarian Orthodox Church	8,000,000	Bulgaria, the diaspora
Orthodox Church of Cyprus	500,000	Cyprus
Orthodox Church of Greece	10,000,000	Greece
Polish Orthodox Church	1,000,000	Poland
Albanian Orthodox Church	700,000	Albania
Orthodox Church of the Czech Lands and Slovakia	74,000	Czech Republic, Slovakia
Orthodox Church in America	1,000,000	USA, Canada, Mexico

The total number of members of these churches taken together is approximately 227 million.[1] Three of them (those of Alexandria, Jerusalem, and

---

[1]These statistics have been taken from Andrea Pacini, ed., *L'Ortodossia nella nuova Europa. Dinamiche storiche e prospettive* (Rome: Fondazione Giovanni Agnelli, 2003). Some changes have been made to the numbers, such as those on the patriarchate of Alexandria.

America) are not represented in Europe; however, they comprise only 6 percent of the overall number of Orthodox in the world. The other 94 percent—209 million—live in Europe. The majority of believers in the following European countries belong to the Orthodox tradition: Russia, Ukraine, Belarus, Moldova, Romania, Bulgaria, Serbia, Montenegro, Greece, Cyprus, Macedonia,[2] and Georgia. In many other European nations, such as Poland, Lithuania, Latvia, Estonia, and Albania, Orthodox faithful make up a significant minority. The largest number of Orthodox faithful live in eastern Europe. Of the western European countries two are Orthodox: Greece and Cyprus.

The primates of the local Orthodox churches bear the title "His Holiness" (the patriarchs of Constantinople, Moscow, Serbia, and Bulgaria), "His Holiness and Beatitude" (the Georgian patriarch), or "His Beatitude" (in the remaining cases).[3] The full title of the first hierarchs of some ancient churches contains traces of the former glory of these churches—which, however, do not always correspond to modern reality. For instance, the full title of the patriarch of Constantinople is "Archbishop of Constantinople, New Rome, and Ecumenical Patriarch"; of Alexandria, "Pope and Patriarch of the Great City of Alexandria, Libya, Pentapolis, Ethiopia, all Egypt and Africa, Father of Fathers, Pastor of Pastors, Hierarch of Hierarchs, the Thirteenth Apostle and Judge of the Universe."

In addition to the autocephalous churches there are several autonomous churches, which govern themselves independently but preserve spiritual and jurisdictional bonds with the more ancient and larger autocephalous churches. Within the jurisdiction of Constantinople is the Finnish Orthodox Church, within the Jerusalem patriarchate the autonomous Church of Sinai, and within the jurisdiction of the Moscow patriarchate the Japanese Orthodox Church.[4] Several other churches within the Moscow patriarchate enjoy wide-ranging autonomy.

---

[2] Concerning the Macedonian Orthodox Church see the chapter 14, "Schisms and Divisions."

[3] In the practice of the Greek Church the patriarch of Constantinople bears the title "His Divine All-Holiness," while the primates of all the other Orthodox churches, including those of Moscow and Serbia, are called "His Beatitude."

[4] The patriarchate of Constantinople does not recognize the autonomy of the Japanese Orthodox Church. The patriarchate of Moscow, in its turn, does not recognize the autonomy of the so-called "Estonian Autonomous Apostolic Church," which was established by Constantinople in 1996.

The canonical dependence of an autonomous church on its mother church is expressed above all in the fact that the election of the former's first hierarch by its council (synod) is confirmed by the primate and synod of the mother church. Moreover, autonomous churches obtain their holy chrism from the primate of an autocephalous church. However, in all other aspects of its life and activity, the autonomous church is independent, guided by its own statutes and governed by its own organs of higher ecclesiastical authority.

Some regard the structure of the Orthodox Church as an eastern counterpart of that of the Roman Catholic Church. Accordingly, the patriarch of Constantinople is viewed, by analogy with the Roman pontiff, as an "eastern pope." The Orthodox Church, however, has never had a single primate. It has always consisted of autocephalous local churches that are independent in their administration while in canonical communion with each other. The patriarch of Constantinople, who from Byzantine times has borne the title "ecumenical," is recognized as the "first among equals" of the primates of the local Orthodox churches. But neither this title nor the primacy of honor accorded to him give the patriarch of Constantinople any jurisdictional rights beyond the boundaries of his own patriarchate.

There are both historical and theological reasons for the absence of a single administrative center in the Orthodox Church. Historically, this is due to the fact that no single primate of the local Orthodox churches—neither in Byzantine nor in post-Byzantine times—has ever enjoyed the same rights as those of the pope in the west. Theologically, the absence of a single head of the Church is explained by the principle of conciliarity, which operates at all levels in the Orthodox Church. Among other things, this principle assumes that each bishop governs his diocese not independently but in agreement with the clergy and laity. In accordance with the same principle the primate of a local Church, who as a rule also chairs the bishops' synod, governs the Church not individually but in conjunction with the synod.

At the level of the ecumenical Church this structure of government gives rise to a number of inconveniences, one of which is the absence of a supreme judge in cases where differences or conflict arise between two or more local churches on questions of ecclesiastical policy. The patriarchate of Constantinople could possibly become such an arbiter, should the other local churches agree to entrust it with this function. However, the great majority of current intra-Orthodox conflicts involve precisely the patriarchate of Constantinople, which rules out its ability to play this role. In the absence of a mechanism that would ensure the settlement of differences between two or more Orthodox churches, problems are resolved differently in each specific case. Sometimes inter-Orthodox conferences are convened; their decisions, however, have only an advisory character and are not binding on the local churches. In other cases two churches in a state of conflict search for solutions through bilateral negotiations, or engage a third church as mediator.

Thus, in the Orthodox Church at the international level there is no external mechanism for guaranteeing catholicity, and there is no external authority—neither one person nor a collegial organ—that might guarantee church unity in questions of inter-Church relations. This does not, however, mean that catholicity in the Orthodox Church exists only in theory and not in practice. In practice, catholicity at the inter-Orthodox level is expressed, first of all, in the fact that all local Orthodox churches are in complete eucharistic communion with each other. Secondly, Orthodox churches take care to maintain unity in their teaching, for which inter-Orthodox conferences are convened whenever necessary. Third, the primates or official representatives of the churches meet with each other occasionally in order to discuss pressing questions or exchange letters. Thus, even in the absence of a pan-Orthodox council, the Orthodox Church at the international level preserves its unity and its conciliar, catholic nature.

13

The Practical Application of the Principle of Canonical Territory

I N THE ORTHODOX WORLD, the principle of canonical territory, which envisions the presence of only one ecclesiastical jurisdiction in a country or region, was observed until the beginning of the First World War. Although a local Church may or may not have autocephalous status, it did possess exclusive jurisdiction in its respective territory. There were practically no "parallel jurisdictions" at that time.

During the First World War and the years after it, a substantial number of Orthodox believers were forced to leave their homeland. This mass exodus led to jurisdictional chaos, as hierarchs, pastors, and the flock of one local church frequently found themselves on the territory of another. The situation worsened beginning in the 1920s, when the patriarchate of Constantinople began to establish new metropolias and archdioceses in Europe and beyond. This occurred after it had declared that the entire church "diaspora"—that is, all countries whose territories were not part of a historical Orthodox Church—was under its jurisdiction. According to this point of view, nearly all of western Europe, North and South America, Australia, and Oceania were encompassed by the notion of "diaspora." However, there already existed an Orthodox Church in America, which was headed by a Russian bishop. The creation there of a jurisdiction under Constantinople caused divisions within American Orthodoxy, which were only aggravated after the appearance of jurisdictions of the Antiochian, Romanian, and Serbian patriarchates.

An equally complicated situation emerged in western Europe during the 1920s. In France, Germany, and other west European countries, as well as outside Europe, there were a significant number of Russian Orthodox believers who began to create their own church structures. Metropolias and archdioceses of the Constantinople and Antiochian patriarchates were founded in parallel. After World War II the Serbian, Romanian, and Bulgarian diasporas in western Europe grew considerably, and new ecclesiastical structures were also created for them.

Despite the fact that there are parallel Orthodox jurisdictions in many parts of the world, it cannot be said that the principle of canonical territory is totally ignored by the Orthodox churches. As before, this principle remains a highly important element of Orthodox ecclesiology and is still applied in practice, though not always and not everywhere. Let us look at some examples of how this principle is applied in practice in inter-Orthodox relations.

Each local Orthodox church has its own canonical territory, whose integrity is acknowledged in principle by the other churches. Other churches do not have the right to establish parishes within this canonical territory. The canonical territory of the patriarchate of Constantinople includes Turkey, northern Greece, and several islands in the Mediterranean; that of the Church of Alexandria all Africa; the Antiochian patriarchate Syria, Lebanon, and some other countries of the near east and the Persian Gulf; the Church of Jerusalem Israel, Palestine, and Jordan. The canonical territory of the Russian Orthodox Church encompasses the Orthodox believers of Russia, Ukraine, Belarus, Moldova, Azerbaijan, Kazakhstan, Uzbekistan, Turkmenistan, Kyrgyzstan, Tajikistan, Estonia, Latvia, and Lithuania. That of the Serbian Church includes Serbia and a number of other countries formerly part of the Socialist Federal Republic of Yugoslavia. The territory of the Georgian, Romanian, Bulgarian, Cypriot, Albanian, and Polish churches, as well as that of the Church of the Czech Lands and Slovakia, encompasses the Orthodox faithful in the respective countries. The canonical territory of the Church of Greece encompasses the country of Greece, with the exception of several islands that are under the jurisdiction of Constantinople.[1] Some churches, namely those of Constantinople, Antioch, Moscow, Georgia, Serbia, Romania, and Bulgaria, have dioceses and parishes outside of their canonical territory, in the so-called "diaspora"; others (e.g., those of Cyprus, Greece and Albania) do not.

In many instances the boundaries of churches coincide with those of states. However, changes in national borders do not necessarily entail the

---

[1] As for northern Greece, the dioceses of the so-called "northern territories," which are part of the Constantinople patriarchate, are also administered by the Church of Greece—an obvious example of double jurisdiction.

breakup of churches. For example, after the collapse of the USSR, the Moscow patriarchate preserved its territorial integrity despite the fact that a number of schismatic structures appeared within its canonical territory (particularly in the Ukraine). After the division of Czechoslovakia into two independent states, the Czechoslovak Orthodox Church was renamed the Orthodox Church of the Czech Lands and Slovakia, and retained its unity without being split into two separate local churches. The Serbian Orthodox Church also maintained its unity after the disintegration of Yugoslavia.

Orthodox tradition recognizes the notion of traditionally Orthodox countries. These are states where the Orthodox Church is the church of the majority of the population. In many of these countries (with the exception of Greece and Cyprus), the Church is separated from the state; still, it enjoys the respect of the state and is an important public force. The Orthodox churches of such countries have a tendency to view the entire population of their nation, with the exception of those belonging to another confession or religion, as their actual or potential flock. In such cases the concept of "cultural canonical territory" can be applied. This principle assumes that the entire population of a state, which by its cultural roots belongs to the Orthodox tradition but which has lost its connection with the faith of its ancestors due to historical circumstances, is the potential flock of the local Orthodox church. Thus, in Russia the absolute majority of Russian people belong—according to their roots—to the Orthodox tradition, and therefore Russia cannot be considered a free missionary territory. This principle does not mean that the Russian Church positions itself as a religious confession that does not permit any alternatives or rejects the right of each person to choose his faith, or that non-Orthodox church communities may not be established in Russia. It signifies instead that non-Orthodox churches that decide to establish their ecclesiastical structures on the canonical territory of the Russian Church should respect the latter as the "Church of the majority." As for the other local Orthodox churches, they may not establish their structures within the canonical territory of the Russian Church.

The observance of the foregoing points can help guarantee the successful development of inter-Orthodox relations. Conversely, failure to apply them in these relations leads to the creation of parallel jurisdictions and conflict situations. This is exactly what happened in 1996 after the patriarchate of Constantinople entered Estonia, which is the canonical territory of the Moscow patriarchate, and founded a parallel jurisdiction there. Similar tensions arose in Moldova, where the Romanian patriarchate created the so-called Bessarabian metropolia in 1992, as a parallel jurisdiction separate from the Moldavian Orthodox Church of the Moscow patriarchate. Both in Estonia and Moldavia the absolute majority of Orthodox believers has remained under the jurisdiction of the Church of Russia, and the newly created parallel structures have proven to be small and marginal ecclesiastical groups. Nevertheless, their presence within the canonical territory of the Moscow patriarchate still complicates inter-Orthodox relations.

14

Schisms

ALONG WITH THE canonical Orthodox Church there are some alternative structures that also call themselves "Orthodox." As a whole they could be termed "shadow Orthodox"—in ecclesiastical language they would be called "schismatics." Among their numbers belong the late-twentieth-century Ukrainian schisms of Philaret (Denisenko) and the Ukrainian Autocephalous Orthodox Church, discussed earlier, as well as the Old Calendarists of Greece and the church schism in Macedonia.

The Old Calendarist schism in Greece arose after the patriarchate of Constantinople and the Church of Greece introduced the use of the so-called "revised Julian" calendar—in other words, the Gregorian calendar. At first it was lay groups and brotherhoods that took up defense of the old calendar, but in 1935 three bishops rebelled against the Greek Church, declaring the calendar change an unlawful and schismatic act. In 1940 the Old Calendarist hierarchy split in two: the "Matthewites" (after their chief bishop Metropolitan Matthew) and the "Florinans" (after their leader Metropolitan Chrysostom of Florina). Subsequently each of these groups split into smaller and smaller groups, ultimately leading to the formation of some ten "synods" each with its own "first hierarch" and little else in common. Most referred to themselves as the "true Orthodox Church."

The church schism in Macedonia began in 1967 when the autonomous Macedonian Orthodox Church, which was centered in Ochrid and was under the jurisdiction of the Serbian Orthodox Church, declared its autocephaly. This was recognized neither by the Serbian nor any other local Orthodox Church, leaving the Macedonian Church isolated. Negotiations with the leadership of the Serbian Church were begun in 1968, were broken off, and were renewed again, without success. In 2005 the Serbian Church declared an end to the negotiations and appointed its own metropolitan for Macedonia, adding the problem of a parallel jurisdiction to the situation. The metropolitan, however, was placed on trial by the Macedonian authorities and subjected to imprisonment. The Macedonian Church numbers more than a million members and is the majority church in the Republic of Macedonia.

We should note that the notion of "schism" is absent from the contemporary political lexicon, as is the idea of "canonical" or "uncanonical" as applied to one church or another. Secular governments (i.e., all the governments of Europe) in the majority of cases make no distinction between canonical and uncanonical churches, giving both the equal right to exist and leaving each to resolve its inner problems.

At the same time, in the recent history of Europe the secular authorities have from time to time directly backed the schismatics. Thus, for example, the Philaret schism in the Ukraine was supported by President Leonid Kravchuk, who allowed the schism to gather considerable momentum. Bulgarian schismatics at the beginning of the 1990s likewise were supported by the authorities in power at the time in Bulgaria. In this and other cases support for schisms by secular authority had most pernicious consequences for the development of the religious situation. In the Ukraine the situation continues to remain extremely tense. In Bulgaria, on the other hand, the schism was practically overcome thanks to the ending of support from the secular authorities in 2001.

Select Bibliography

"The Act of the Holy National Council of the Russian Orthodox Church on the Abolishment of the Anathemas against the Old Rite and its Adherents, June 2, 1971." *Journal of the Moscow Patriarchate* 6 (1971).

Acts of the Holy Council of the Russian Orthodox Church. Moscow, 2000.

Adrianova-Perets, V.P., ed. *Tales of Bygone Years*, trans. D.S. Likhachev and B.A. Romanov. Moscow and Leningrad, 1950.

Amvrosy (Pogodin). *St Mark of Ephesus and the Union of Florence.* Moscow, 1994.

Andronik (Trubachev), A.A. Bovkalo, and V.A. Fyodorov, "Monasteries and Monasticsm 1700–1998," in *Orthodox Encyclopedia* (Moscow, 1997): 325–45.

Archives of the Kremlin in Two Volumes, vol 1: *The Politburo and the Church: 1922–1925.* Moscow/Novosibirsk, 1997.

Athanasius of Alexandria. *On the Incarnation*, trans. A Religious of C.S.M.V. Crestwood, NY: SVS Press, 1953.

———. *The Works of Our Father among the Saints Athanasius, Archbishop of Alexandria*, 4 vols. Sergiev Posad, 1902–1903.

Berdyaev, Nicholas. *Collected Works.* Paris, 1997.

———. *On Russian Philosophy.* Ural University, 1991.

———. *The Philosophy of Freedom: The Sources and Meaning of Russian Communism.* Moscow, 1997.

———. *Self-Knowledge.* Moscow, 2004.

———. "The Truth of Orthodoxy." *Vestnik Russkogo Zapadno-Evropeiskogo Exarkhata* 11 (Paris, 1952): 4–11.

Birkbeck, W.J. *Russia and the English Church during the Last Fifty Years,.* London, 1895.

Bulgakov, Sergius. *Orthodoxy: Essays on the Teaching of the Orthodox Church*, 3d ed. Paris, 1989.

———. "Pushkin's Destiny." In *Pushkin in the Emigration*, ed. V. Perelmuter. Moscow, 1999.

Busygin, M.A. "The Dogmatic Content of the Polemics over Unleavened Bread," in *Patrology, Philosophy, Hermeneutics: Works of the Higher School of Religion and Philosophy*, vol. 1. St Petersburg, 1992.

The Canons of the Orthodox Church with Commentaries by Nikodim, Bishop of Dalmatia and Istria, 2 vols. Moscow, 2001.

Chaadaev, P.Y. *Articles and Letters.* Moscow, 1989.

Chariton, Hegumen, ed. *Noetic Activity: On the Jesus Prayer. A Collection of Homilies of the Holy Fathers and Experienced Practitioners.* Sortavala, 1936.

Chekhov, Anton. *Collected Works,* 12 vols. Moscow, 1956.

Chetverikov, Sergei. *The Moldavian Elder Paisy Velichkovsky: His Life, Teaching, and Influence on Orthodox Monasticism.* Paris, 1976.

Chistovich, I. *Theophan Prokopovich and his Times.* St Petersburg, 1868.

Cyprian (Kern). *Father Antonin Kapustin: Archimandrite and Head of the Russian Spiritual Mission in Jerusalem (1817–1894).* Moscow, 1997.

Cyprian of Carthage. *On the Church: Select Treatises,* trans. Allen Brent. Crestwood, NY: SVS Press, 2006.

Damaskin (Orlovsky). "The Persecution of the Russian Orthodox Church during the Soviet Period." In *Orthodox Encyclopedia* (Moscow, 1997): 179–89.

Dostoyevsky, Fedor. *The Brothers Karamazov.* Paris, 1954.

_____Dostoyevsky, Fedor. *Complete Works,* 30 vols. Leningrad, 1972–1990.

_____. *A Writer's Diary.* Paris, 1954.

Fedotov, George P. *The Saints of Ancient Rus'.* Paris, 1989.

Firsov, S.L. *Apostasy: The "Atheist Alexander Osipov" and the Age of the Khrushchev Persecution of the Russian Orthodox Church.* St Petersburg, 2004.

Florovsky, Georges. *Selected Theological Articles.* Moscow, 2000.

_____. *Ways of Russian Theology.* Paris, 1933.

Frank, S.L. "The Religiosity of Pushkin." In *Etudes on Pushkin.* Munich, 1957.

Gilbert, Peter, trans. *On God and Man: The Theological Poetry of St Gregory of Nazianzus.* Crestwood, NY: SVS Press, 2001.

Gogol, Nikolai. *Reflections on the Divine Liturgy.* Jordanville, 1952.

_____. *Short Stories: Correspondence with Friends.* Berlin, 1922.

Gregory Palamas. *Triads in Defense of the Holy Hesychasts,* trans. V. Venyaminov. Moscow, 1995.

Griggs, Daniel K., trans. *Divine Eros: Hymns of St Symeon the New Theologian.* Yonkers, NY: SVS Press, 2010.

Gubonin, M.E., ed. *The Acts of His Holiness Tikhon, Patriarch of Moscow and All Russia: Later Documents and Correspondence on the Canonical Succession of the Higher Church Authority, 1917–1943.* Moscow, 1994.

Herzen, Alexander. *My Past and Thoughts.* Moscow, 1958.

Hilarion, Metropolitan of Kiev. *Sermon on Law and Grace,* trans. Deacon Andrei Yurchenko. In *Literary Monuments of Ancient Rus',* vol. 12.3. Moscow, 1994.

Hilarion (Alfeyev), ed. *Eastern Fathers of the Fifth Century.* Moscow, 2000.

————, ed. *The Eastern Fathers and Teachers of the Church of the Fourth Century*, 2 vols. Moscow, 1996.

————. *The Sacred Mystery of the Church: An Introduction to the History and Problematics of the Name-worshiping Debates*, 2 vols. St Petersburg, 2002.

————. *St Symeon the New Theologian and Orthodox Tradition*, 2d ed. St Petersburg, 2001.

————. *The Spiritual World of St Isaac the Syrian*, 2d ed. St Petersburg, 2002.

Hilarion (Troitsky). *Works*, 3 vols. Moscow, 2004.

Hovorun, S. "From the History of the Philokalia." *Tserkov' i Vremya* 1.14 (2001): 262–95.

————. "The Kollyvades Movement: Preconditions for the Appearance of the Movement." *Tserkov' i Vremya* 3.16 (2001): 86–106.

Ignaty (Brianchaninov). *The Works of Bishop Ignaty (Brianchaninov)*, vol. 1: *Ascetic Experiences*, 3d ed. St Petersburg, 1905.

Ilyin, I.A. *Pushkin's Prophetic Calling*. Riga, 1937.

Isaac the Syrian. *Ascetical Homilies*. Sergiev Posad, 1911.

Ivanov, A. "Maxim the Greek and Savonarola." *Bogoslovskie Trudy* 12 (1974): 184–208.

————. "On Maxim the Greek's Time in the Dominican Monastery of St Mark in Florence." *Bogoslovskie Trudy* 1 (1973): 112–19.

John of Damascus. *Three Treatises on the Divine Images*, trans. Andrew Louth. Crestwood, NY: SVS Press, 2003.

John of Kronstadt. *My Life in Christ*. Moscow, 1999.

————. *My Life in Christ. Part 3: Reflections on the Divine Services of the Orthodox Church*. Moscow, 2001.

————. *Reflections on the Church and the Orthodox Divine Services*, vol. 1. St Petersburg, 1905.

————. *Reflections on the Divine Services of the Orthodox Church: From the Diary of Father John of Kronstadt*. Jordanville, 1954.

————. *Stern New Homilies of Father John (of Kronstadt): On the Truly Dread Judgment of God That Is Approaching (1906–1907)*. Moscow, 1993.

————. *Works: Diary Before his Death (May–November 1908)*. Moscow-St. Petersburg, 2003.

Joseph of Volotsk. *The Enlightener, or the Denunciation of the Heresy of the Judaizers*. Kazan, 1903.

————. *The Epistles of Joseph of Volotsk*. Moscow-Leningrad, 1959.

Juvenaly, Metropolitan of Krutitsa and Kolomna, ed. *A Man of the Church: Dedicated to the Twenty-year Anniversary of the Death and Seventy-year Anniversary of the Birth of His Eminence, the Metropolitan of Leningrad and Novgorod Nikodim (Rotov), Patriarchal Exarch of Western Europe (1929–1978)*. Moscow, 1998.

Kartashev, A.V. *History of the Russian Church*, 2 vols. Paris, 1959.

Khomiakov, A.S. "Some Words on the Philosophical Letter Published in the Fifteenth Booklet of *Telescope* (letter to Mrs. N.)." *Symbol* 16 (Paris: December 1986).

Kidd, B.J. *The Churches of Eastern Christendom*. London, 1927.

Kontsevich, I. *The Optina Hermitage and Its Times*. Jordanville, 1970.

Kosik, V.I., Ch. Temelski, and A.A. Turilov, "The Bulgarian Orthodox Church." In *Orthodox Encyclopedia*, vol. 5 (Moscow, 2002): 615–43.

Kozlov, Maxim. "Theological Education: Seventeenth-Twentieth Centuries." In *Orthodox Encyclopedia* (Moscow, 1997): 407–26.

Landmarks: A Collection of Articles on the Russian Intelligentsia. Moscow, 1909.

Larchet, Jean-Claude. *St Maximus the Confessor: Mediator between the East and West*. Moscow, 2004.

Lebedev, A.P. *The History of the Greek-Eastern Church under the Turks*, 2 vols. St Petersburg, 2004.

Lenin, Vladimir. *Complete Works*, 5th ed. Moscow, 1979.

Lermontov, Mikhail. *Selected Works*. Moscow, 1957.

The Life of Sergius of Radonezh, trans. M.F. Antonova and D.M. Bulanina. In *Literary Monuments of Ancient Rus'*, vol. 4. Moscow, 1981.

The Local Orthodox Churches. Moscow, 2004.

Lossky, Vladimir. *Dogmatic Theology*. Moscow, 1991.

_____. *Theology and the Vision of God: Collected Articles*. Moscow, 2000.

Makary (Bulgakov). *History of the Russian Church*, 6 vols. Moscow, 1994–1996.

Matuzova, V.I., and E.L. Nazarova. *The Crusaders and Rus'*. Moscow, 2002.

Maxim the Greek. *Works*, vol. 3. Trinity-St Sergius Lavra, 1996.

Meyendorff, John. *An Introduction to Patristic Theology*. Klin, 2001.

_____. "What is an Ecumenical Council?" In *Orthodoxy in the Modern World*. Klin, 2002.

Morozov, P.O. *Works and Letters of A.S. Pushkin*, 8 vols. St. Petersburg, 1903.

Nazarenko, A.V. "The Russian Church from the Tenth to the First Third of the Fifteenth Century." In *Orthodox Encyclopedia* (Moscow, 1997): 38–60.

Nicetas Choniates. *History, Beginning with the Reign of John Comnenos*, 2 vols. St Petersburg, 1860–1862.

Noret, J. "Grégoire de Nazianze, l'auteur le plus cité, après la Bible, dans la littérature ecclesiastique byzantine." In *II Symposium Nazianzenum*, ed. Justin Mossay. Paderborn-München-Wien-Zürich, 1983.

The Novgorod Primary Chronicle, Older and Newer Editions. Moscow-Leningrad, 1950.

Ouspensky, Leonid. *The Theology of the Icon in the Orthodox Church.* Paris, 1989.

Pacini, Andrea, ed. *L'Ortodossia nella nuova Europa. Dinamiche storiche e prospettive.* Rome: Fondazione Giovanni Agnelli, 2003.

Philaret (Drozdov). *Homilies and Speeches,* 5 vols. Moscow, 1873–1885.

———. *Selected Works: Letters, Memoirs.* Moscow, 2003.

Polsky, Mikhail. *The New Martyrs of Russia,* 2 vols. Jordanville, 1957.

Poltoratsky, N.A. "Russian Religious Philosophy." *Mosty* 4 (1960).

Posnov, M.E. *History of the Christian Church (up to the Separation of the Churches – 1055).* Brussels, 1964.

Prokhorov, G.M. *The Tale of Mityai: Rus' and Byzantium in the Age of the Battle of Kulikovo.* Leningrad, 1978.

Pushkin, Alexander. *Complete Works,* 10 vols. Moscow, 1956–1958.

Runciman, Steven. *The Fall of Constantinople 1453.* Cambridge, 1969.

The Russian Orthodox Church and the Great Patriotic War: Collection of Documents. Moscow 1943.

Safonov, D.V. "On the Question of the Authenticity of the 'Testament' of St Tikhon the Patriarch." *Bogoslovskii Vestnik* 4 (2004): 256–311.

Schmemann, Alexander. *The Historical Road of Eastern Orthodoxy.* Crestwood, NY: SVS Press, 1977.

Sinitsyna, N.V. "The Russian Orthodox Church in the Period of Autocephaly." In *Orthodox Encyclopedia* (Moscow, 1997): 61–80.

Skurat, K. *History of the Local Orthodox Churches,* 2 vols. Moscow, 1994.

Smolich, I.K. *History of the Russian Church: 1700–1917,* part 1. Moscow, 1996.

———. *Russian Monasticism (988–1917).* Moscow, 1997.

Sokolov, L. *St Ignaty: His Life, Personality, and Moral and Ascetic Views,* part 3. Kiev, 1915; repr. Moscow, 2003.

Soloviev, Vladimir. *Collected Works,* 2d ed., 10 vols. Brussels, 1966–1968.

———. *On Christian Unity.* Brussels, 1967.

———. *The Poems of Vladimir Soloviev,* 3d ed. St Petersburg, 1900.

Sophrony (Sakharov). *On Prayer.* Paris, 1991.

———. *We Shall See Him As He Is.* Essex, 1985.

Stepanovich, P.S. "The Parish and Parish Clergy: Eighteenth–Nineteenth Centuries." In *Orthodox Encyclopedia* (Moscow, 1997): 259–75.

Sushkov, N.V. *Notes on the Life and Times of Metropolitan Philaret.* Moscow, 1868.

Theophan the Recluse. *Letters to Various People on Questions of Faith and Life.* Moscow, 1892.

_____. *The Works of Our Father among the Saints Theophan the Recluse: Collection of Letters*, part 2. Moscow, 1994.

Tikhon of Zadonsk. *The Works of our Father among the Saints Tikhon of Zadonsk*. Moscow, 1889; repr. Pskov Caves Monastery, 1994.

Tolstoy, A.K. *Complete Works*, 8 vols. St Petersburg, 1907.

Tolstoy, Leo. *Collected Works*, 20 vols. Moscow, 1964.

_____. *Complete Works*, 90 vols. Moscow, 1928–1958.

Tsypin, Vladislav. *History of the Russian Church: 1917–1997*. Moscow, 1997.

_____. "The Russian Orthodox Church in Recent Times: 1917–1999." In *Orthodox Encyclopedia* (Moscow, 1997): 134–78.

_____. "The Russian Orthodox Church in the Synodal Period: 1700–1917." In *Orthodox Encyclopedia* (Moscow, 1997): 109–33.

The Unknown World of Faith. Moscow, 2002.

Vasiliev, B.A. *The Spiritual Path of Pushkin*. Moscow, 1994.

Volkov, A.G. "The Population Census of 1937: Myths and the Truth." In *The Census of the Population of the USSR of 1937: History and Materials*. Moscow, 1990.

Ware, Kallistos, and Mother Mary, trans. *The Lenten Triodion*. London: Faber and Faber, 1977.

Ware, Timothy (Kallistos). *The Orthodox Church*. Harmondsworth, 1967.

_____. "The Spiritual Father in Saint John Climacus and Saint Symeon the New Theologian." In Irénée Hausherr, *Spiritual Direction in the Early Christian East*, trans. Anthony P. Gythiel. Kalamazoo: Cistercian Publishers, 1990.

Yannaras, Christos. "The Church in Post-Communist Europe." *Tserkov' i Vremya* 3.28 (2004).

Zizioulas, John. *Being As Communion*. Crestwood, NY: SVS Press, 1993.

Znamensky, P. *Religious Schools in Russia up to the Reform of 1808*. Kazan, 1881.